WHY NARRATIVE?

WHY NARRATIVE?

Readings in Narrative Theology

Edited by

STANLEY HAUERWAS

and

L. GREGORY JONES

GRAND RAPIDS, MICHIGAN
WILLIAM B. EERDMANS PUBLISHINGCOMPANY

Copyright © 1989 by Wm. B. Eerdmans Publishing Co.
255 Jefferson Ave. S.E., Grand Rapids, Mich. 49503

Printed in the United States of America

Library of Congress Cataloging-in-Publication Data

Why narrative? / edited by Stanley Hauerwas and L. Gregory Jones.
    p.   cm.
   ISBN 0-8028-3668-2 — ISBN 0-8028-0439-X (pbk.)
  1. Storytelling—Religious aspects—Christianity. 2. Narration (Rhetoric).
  3. Narration in the Bible. I. Hauerwas, Stanley, 1940–
  II. Jones, L. Gregory.
  BT83.78.W59   1989
  230'.01—dc20   89-35972
                                             CIP

Contents

Stanley Hauerwas and L. Gregory Jones

III: NARRATIVE'S THEOLOGICAL SIGNIFICANCE

Preface

This book began in a class and we hope that it will be useful for classes. The originating class was a graduate seminar on practical reason and personal identity offered in 1986. The intuitive idea behind the course is that these issues involve a narrative display. During that seminar we became convinced that there was something to this intuition, but that most of the literature about narrative was insufficiently critical. Therefore, we began to plan an anthology that would include the best essays in narrative and theology we could find.

Over the next year we planned such a volume. We can assure you that it took many different shapes and that many diverse essays were considered. The seminar was offered again in 1988 and we asked the students in that seminar to read our proposed anthology. That was an invaluable experience since their critical comments helped us to see which essays worked best as well as how they should be arranged. We are particularly grateful to Andrew Adam, Steve Long, and Jeff Powell for the perceptiveness of their comments. We hope classes that use this book will sense the liveliness of the debate that has gone into the selection and organization of the essays, for our chief concern is that the book generate the kind of critical discussion that we found so lively in these seminars.

This book is also the result of extended conversations between the editors. Our relationship began as student and teacher, but over time those distinctions have become increasingly relativized as a friendship between colleagues has emerged. We have learned much from each other, not only because of our shared commitments and interests but also because our disagreements about issues such as the sig-

Stanley Hauerwas and L. Gregory Jones

nificance of narrative for theology and ethics have forced each of us to think more clearly and deeply. We hope the essays in this book will also stimulate such thinking through the disagreements among the authors.

Most of all we have to thank Gay Trotter for doing most of the typing on this book. Her patience with us is a testimony to her Christian commitment just as her work is a testimony to her extraordinary administrative gifts. We are also in debt to Sarah Freedman, Virginia Parrish, Gail Chappell, and Marjorie Lobsiger of the Duke Divinity School typing pool who aided Mrs. Trotter in the preparation of this manuscript. Finally we would like to thank Jon Pott and all those at Eerdmans Publishing for supporting us in this venture. They are a remarkable publishing house that makes it possible for serious theological scholarship to continue to be made available in a world that is not all that interested.

STANLEY HAUERWAS
L. GREGORY JONES

Introduction: Why Narrative?

Stanley Hauerwas
L. Gregory Jones

I

In recent years appeals to "narrative" and to "story" have been increasingly prominent in scholarly circles, to the delight of some, the consternation of others, and the bewilderment of many. Such appeals have caused delight in that narrative and story appear to provide a cure, if not a panacea, to a variety of Enlightenment illnesses: rationalism, monism, decisionism, objectivism, and other "isms." Or so some defenders of narrative claim. The appeals have caused consternation in that the focus on narrative and story often appear to bear all the markings of an intellectual fad: something short-lived, about which many articles are written, but which quickly meets its demise as people return to more substantive matters. Or so some critics of narrative claim. The appeals have caused bewilderment to those who are outside of the battle between proponents and opponents, a bewilderment increased by the fear that nobody is quite sure precisely what is being proposed or opposed.

It is in such a context that we thought it might be useful to put together this book. While we are convinced that "narrative" raises many important issues and is central to theological and ethical reflection, we are equally convinced that too often it has been put to uncritical "faddish" uses and/or has been the focus of confusion caused by a lack of conceptual clarity. Hence the title *Why Narrative?* has a double mean-

1

ing: on the one hand, the essays have been chosen because of the ways in which we are convinced they illumine the significance of narrative for theology and ethics (thus providing an answer to the question "why narrative?"); and on the other hand, the tensions and divergences among the essays reveal the continuing importance of asking whether appeals to "narrative" are so diverse that the notion has outlived its usefulness (thus the skeptic continuing to ask "why narrative?").

After all, it is not readily obvious what, if anything, the varieties of appeals to narrative have in common. The category of narrative has been used, among other purposes, to explain human action, to articulate the structures of human consciousness, to depict the identity of agents (whether human or divine), to explain strategies of reading (whether specifically for biblical texts or as a more general hermeneutic), to justify a view of the importance of "story-telling" (often in religious studies through the language of "fables" and "myths"), to account for the historical development of traditions, to provide an alternative to foundationalist and/or other scientific epistemologies, and to develop a means for imposing order on what is otherwise chaos.

Proponents of one or more of these uses of narrative are not necessarily proponents of all of them. Indeed some of the uses conflict with each other, as for example the views that the structures of human consciousness are narrative in form and that narrative is a means for imposing order on what is otherwise chaos. Moreover, proponents of a version of one or more of the uses of narrative may not accept a different version of that use, as for example has been the case in Hans Frei's attempt to distance himself from Paul Ricoeur's narrative hermeneutics.

Even so, summaries of views about narrative often oversimplify the wide variety of ways in which the category of narrative has been and can be used. In so doing, a misleading and distorted picture can emerge of what is at stake in appeals to narrative. For example, in a recent lecture on "Varieties of Moral Discourse," James Gustafson identifies narrative as one of four kinds of moral discourse (the others are prophetic, ethical, and policy). He proposes that the central thesis of narrative theology and narrative ethics can be stated fairly, if too simply, in the following terms:

> Narratives function to sustain the particular moral identity of a religious (or secular) community by rehearsing its history and traditional meanings, as these are portrayed in Scripture and other sources. Narratives shape and sustain the ethos of the community. Through our participation in such a community, the narratives also function to give shape to our moral characters, which in turn deeply affect the way we interpret or construe the world

and events and thus affect what we determine to be appropriate action as members of the community. Narratives function to sustain and confirm the religious and moral identity of the Christian community, and evoke and sustain the faithfulness of its members to Jesus Christ.[1]

Gustafson intends this description to reflect his appreciation for the role narrative plays in theological and ethical discourse. But, it needs to be noted, it is a limited role. As Gustafson concludes his discussion, he notes that narratives can be prophetic, but even so:

> Narrative ethics is not sufficient. Symbolic prophetic indictments need to be checked against facts and figures and political analysis. Perceptive intuitions informed by parables need to be checked against more rational analysis. And we all belong to several communities. To live by the story of only one might impede our capacities to communicate with those with whom we share moral responsibilities who are informed by different stories and different communities. And our individual moral integrity is shaped in relation to more than the story of the Christian community; it is shaped by our social backgrounds, our roles in society, and other things. And, just as there is often a gap between prophetic discourses and particular choices made in the midst of medical, political, economic, and other situations, so narrative also leaves that gap.[2]

Gustafson's description is not *prima facie* wrong. People have made appeals to narrative within theology and ethics that are similar to, though not identical with, the kind of description that Gustafson provides.

But Gustafson's description does oversimplify, and thereby distort, the debates about the place or places of narrative in theology and ethics. While very few people, if any, would claim against Gustafson that narrative is sufficient in and of itself, Gustafson's assumptions about what else is needed are closely tied to his understanding of narrative. It is an understanding that is derived in part from H. Richard Niebuhr's important chapter "The Story of Our Life" in *The Meaning of Revelation*, and it is an understanding probably shared by many of those who write about "stories" and their relation to theology and ethics.

But it is an understanding which does not consider the uses of narrative centered on epistemological issues. According to some propo-

1. James M. Gustafson, "Varieties of Moral Discourse: Prophetic, Narrative, Ethical, and Policy," Calvin College, The Stob Lectures, 1988, pp. 19-20.
2. Ibid., pp. 26-27. The concern for some kind of "universal" ethic that transcends narrative is evident also in Paul Nelson's *Narrative and Morality: A Theological Inquiry* (University Park, PA: Penn State University Press, 1987). We think Nelson's proposal is problematic as we know of no unproblematic "universality," but he usefully sketches some of the options and issues involved in appeals to narrative.

Stanley Hauerwas and L. Gregory Jones

nents of narrative in theology and ethics, the crucial appeal to narrative is not because of the significance of "stories," though that may be part of it; rather what is significant is the recognition that rationality, methods of argument, and historical explanation have, at least to some extent, a fundamentally narrative form. This is an issue to which we will return below, but it is important to note that *if* there is a close connection between epistemology and narrative, then the issues Gustafson raises about the status of narrative in relation to other types of discourse (e.g., prophetic, ethical, and policy) and the problems of belonging to multiple communities take on very different shapes from those Gustafson suggests.

Moreover, Gustafson's understanding does not adequately cover issues surrounding personal identity. If personal identity is fundamentally narrative in form, as some of narrative's proponents contend, then the issues are framed somewhat differently than the assumption that moral integrity is something shaped by the story of a community, be it Christian or non-Christian. Such a view, if correct, alters Gustafson's claim that "individual moral integrity is shaped in relation to more than the story of the Christian community" by showing how narrative is crucial both in articulating the narrative of a community and/or tradition *and* in depicting the problems of what it means to have personal identity. But in this view, rather than showing the limitations of narrative, the claim reveals the importance of attending to the diverse ways in which narrative is crucial for understanding human life.

We suspect that Gustafson is concerned with how appeals to narrative, especially in a theological context, can be used to provide an uncritical apologetic for "the Christian story." There is no question that appeals to narrative have had this unhappy result by failing to note the complexities of "the Christian story" or by trying to avoid the epistemological issues of how it might be possible to ask how we might know if such a story is true and/or truthful.[3] It is our belief, however, that attention to the narrative display of Christian convictions can and should help to avoid these uncritical apologetic moves that ultimately result in a vulgar relativism.

We have identified Gustafson's argument in part because the questions and issues he raises are significant, but more importantly be-

3. James W. McClendon's work, both *Ethics: Systematic Theology*, vol. I (Nashville: Abingdon Press, 1986) and his earlier book (coauthored with James M. Smith) *Understanding Religious Convictions* (Notre Dame: University of Notre Dame Press, 1975), represent important attempts to confront these issues. We were interested in including a selection from McClendon as his work over the years has been quite important to the development of narrative, particularly his emphasis on the place of biography and autobiography, but no one selection stood out as a clear choice.

cause his discussion reveals the dangers of oversimplifying what appeals to narrative involve. Too much of the contemporary discussion about narrative, particularly within theology and ethics, has been beset by a poor understanding of what is at stake; proponents and opponents talk past each other, with those on the sidelines perplexed and bemused by these intellectual exercises.

We are convinced that there is a great deal at stake in the discussions about narrative, and the essays we have collected are ones which we think are important in discerning where the issues lie. There are, to be sure, debates about narrative that we have not covered here. For example, we have not included discussions of the important and relevant debates on such matters as narrative and historical explanation, narrative and literary theory, or narrative and biblical scholarship. To be sure these debates have an impact on the issues discussed and arguments advanced by the authors of the essays in this book, but to attempt to include materials from these other areas would have required a much different, and much larger, book than we have provided.

We are concerned with suggesting that narrative is neither just an account of genre criticism nor a faddish appeal to the importance of telling stories; rather it is a crucial conceptual category for such matters as understanding issues of epistemology and methods of argument, depicting personal identity, and displaying the content of Christian convictions. Toward that end, we have brought together several essays that address these topics. The essays do not form any single coherent perspective, nor do the authors all share similar religious convictions. The essays do provide a glimpse into the debates about narrative's significance that we hope will help to clarify what is at stake and hence elevate the debates about narrative to a higher level.

II

The essays have been grouped together into three sections. In the first section, we include four selections that have been influential in the rediscovery of narrative's significance for contemporary theology and ethics. H. Richard Niebuhr's "The Story of Our Life" represents one of the key focal points for this rediscovery of narrative.[4] Niebuhr's influence has justifiably been cast widely across the field. Even so, his argu-

---

4. Of course Karl Barth's *Church Dogmatics* would also have to be included in any account of the rediscovery of narrative for theology and ethics; cf., for example, David Ford, *Barth and God's Story: Biblical Narrative and the Theological Method of Karl Barth in the "Church Dogmatics"* (Frankfurt: Verlag Peter Lang, 1985). Because Barth emphasized the

ments have also too often been assumed to set the context for the debates about narrative's significance in theology and ethics; for example, Gustafson's argument is at least partially predicated on, and involves explicit appeals to, Niebuhr, and Gary Comstock has written an essay in which he uses Niebuhr's problematic distinction between "internal" and "external" history to identify "American narrative theology" after Niebuhr.[5] Thus while Niebuhr was the teacher (or the teacher of the teachers) of many who are now to one degree or another proponents of narrative, and while Niebuhr's essay is important for understanding some of the origins of the rediscovery of narrative, it should not be assumed that his proposals establish the parameters for debate.

The diversity of the appeals can be seen in two other important figures in the rediscovery of narrative, Hans Frei and Stephen Crites. Both Frei and Crites have been influenced by Niebuhr, but their proposals move in quite different directions. Frei, for example, has focused his energies on the recovery of narrative for biblical hermeneutics; his *The Eclipse of Biblical Narrative,* from which the selection in this book is drawn, is an important study of the ways in which eighteenth- and nineteenth-century biblical scholarship eclipsed narrative as crucial to the interpretation of the Bible.[6] But he is not principally concerned with the kinds of distinctions made by Niebuhr; narrative has a quite different focus in Frei's work insofar as he is concerned with developing a strategy for reading Scripture.

Frei has contrasted his hermeneutical proposal with Paul Ricoeur's, Frei claiming that he is not advancing, as Ricoeur does, a general argument for narrative hermeneutics.[7] Frei contends that all he is arguing for is a "regional" hermeneutic seen to be adequate for the interpretation of Scripture.[8] In some circles this contrast has been developed into a "Frei-Ricoeur" debate, a debate over the proper understanding of narrative's

---

display of theological convictions rather than methodological argument, the significance of narrative in Barth's theology cannot be easily summarized or anthologized; hence the absence of a selection from his work in this book.

5. Cf. Gary Comstock, "Telling the Whole Story? American Narrative Theology After H. Richard Niebuhr," in Peter Freese, ed., *Religion and Philosophy in the United States of America* (Essen: Verlag Die Blaue Eule, 1987), pp. 125-152.

6. Frei's work has been discussed in a book of essays dedicated to him. Cf. Garrett Green, ed., *Scriptural Authority and Narrative Interpretation* (Philadelphia: Fortress Press, 1987).

7. Ricoeur's proposal is developed in a wide variety of his works. For the application of his arguments to the task of biblical interpretation, cf. his *Essays on Biblical Interpretation,* ed. Lewis M. Mudge (Philadelphia: Fortress Press, 1980).

8. Cf. Hans Frei, "The 'Literal Reading' of Biblical Narrative in the Christian Tradition: Does It Stretch or Will It Break?" in Frank McConnell, ed., *The Bible and Narrative Tradition* (New York: Oxford University Press, 1986), pp. 36-77.

significance in Christian theology and ethics. But there has not really been a debate between the two thinkers. Rather, there have been attempts to locate the significance of narrative within the context of Frei's and Ricoeur's proposals.[9] Frei's and Ricoeur's proposals are different, and the differences between them need to be recognized and the conflicting claims adjudicated;[10] but it is a mistake either to see Frei's work as set in the context of Niebuhr's or to assume that Frei and Ricoeur represent the two fundamental options.[11]

It is a mistake to see Frei's work in the context of Niebuhr's because of the difference in their theological agendas. Niebuhr's agenda and his views about religious language were marked by a concern for theological translation, whereas Frei is less concerned with translation than with conceptual redescription. Put in the terms of George Lindbeck's influential typology, Niebuhr represents more the "experiential-expressivist" and Frei the "cultural-linguistic" position.[12]

But the reason why it is a mistake to assume that Frei and Ricoeur represent the two fundamental options in discussions of narrative also reveals our discomfort with Lindbeck's categories. While there are important differences in understandings of religious language and theological method between Niebuhr and Frei or between Frei and Ricoeur, Lindbeck's typology makes it appear that these are the two fundamental options when in fact there are many. As this collection of essays shows, the ways of understanding narrative's relation to theology and ethics are multiple; many of the insights and the unresolved issues in narrative are obscured when Frei and Ricoeur are seen as representing an either/or choice about narrative. Even so, it is important to note that in Frei's view the viability of his proposal can and should be assessed independently of the status of broader claims about narrative made by people such as Ricoeur.

Stephen Crites's essay "The Narrative Quality of Experience" moves in a direction strikingly different than Frei and is closer to

9. Cf., for example, Gary Comstock, "Truth and Meaning: Ricoeur Versus Frei on Biblical Narrative," *Journal of Religion* 66 (1986): 117-140; and Ronald Thiemann, *Revelation and Theology: The Gospel as Narrated Promise* (Notre Dame: University of Notre Dame Press, 1985), esp. pp. 82ff. and note 19 on pp. 175-176.

10. William Placher has attempted to do so in an interesting essay where he ultimately sides with Frei and Frei's colleague George Lindbeck against Ricoeur. Cf. "Paul Ricoeur and Postliberal Theology: A Conflict of Interpretations?" *Modern Theology* 4 (1987): 35-52.

11. We were interested in including a piece of Ricoeur's in this anthology to indicate some of Ricoeur's important reflections on narrative and to show the character of the differences between Frei and Ricoeur, but no one essay seemed appropriate in this context.

12. Those distinctions are developed in Lindbeck's *The Nature of Doctrine: Religion and Theology in a Postliberal Age* (Philadelphia: The Westminster Press, 1984).

. Crites turns to the tradition of phenomenology to argue that existence and human experience are fundamentally narrative in form. His argument is closer to Niebuhr's emphasis on the story of our life and he seems to share Niebuhr's views about the place of religious language, but Crites carries Niebuhr's argument further into a general anthropological claim. Crites's basic argument has been developed more fully in the work of such people as Ricoeur and David Carr;[13] but because Crites's essay, originally published in 1971, has had such a wide influence among theologians and ethicists and summarizes that orientation toward narrative so well, it is included here.

The selection from Alasdair MacIntyre's *After Virtue* is both different from and similar to the other essays in this section. It is different in that MacIntyre's contribution to the rediscovery of narrative is more recent (1981) than the other essays, and he works as a philosopher rather than as a theologian or religionist. But the issues with which he is concerned are similar to those raised by Niebuhr, Frei, and Crites. MacIntyre's focus is on rehabilitating the tradition of the virtues for ethics, and he contends that narrative is crucial to such a task. Indeed, more so than any of the other three thinkers, MacIntyre recognizes several diverse uses of narrative. He argues that: (1) intelligible human action is narrative in form, (2) human life has a fundamentally narrative shape, (3) humans are story-telling animals, (4) people place their lives and arguments in narrative histories, (5) communities and (6) traditions receive their continuities through narrative histories, and (7) epistemological progress is marked by the construction and reconstruction of more adequate narratives and forms of narrative.[14]

While MacIntyre appeals to the diversity of uses of narrative more than the other thinkers, it is important to attempt to explicate how those uses are related in his argument. Such questions emerge as: Are his various uses of narrative congruent with each other? Does the significance of narrative stand or fall with any one use? Are each of the uses equally tenable?

MacIntyre's argument is rich and the distinctions he makes are subtle, and it is important to set his proposals about narrative in relation to other arguments. It is useful to contrast Niebuhr, Crites, and MacIntyre on questions about the depiction of personal identity and the relations between personal identity and the narratives of communities and/or traditions. MacIntyre puts the issues at a different level, for by making impor-

13. Cf. Paul Ricoeur, *Time and Narrative,* 3 vols., trans. by Kathleen McLaughlin and David Pellauer (Chicago: University of Chicago Press, 1984-88), and David Carr, *Time, Narrative, and History* (Bloomington, IN: Indiana University Press, 1986).

14. These uses of narrative are discussed somewhat more fully in L. Gregory Jones, "Alasdair MacIntyre on Narrative, Community, and the Moral Life," *Modern Theology* 4 (1987): 53-69.

tant distinctions between "action" and "intelligible action" he shows how claims about narrative and personal identity are bound up with conceptions of practical rationality. MacIntyre's argument about rationality is indebted to Aristotle's claim in his *Nicomachean Ethics* that practical rationality is about "ultimate particulars" which require that persons be virtuously shaped if they are to deliberate well. In MacIntyre's construal, the virtues necessary for practical rationality require initiation into communities and traditions and their attending narratives. Hence MacIntyre argues that practical rationality is inextricably tied to the moral transformation of personal identity occasioned by participation in communities and traditions; ultimately, therefore, MacIntyre contends that practical rationality requires a narrative construal marked by the diverse uses to which he appeals. MacIntyre's claims, and their relation to claims made in the other three essays in this section, will recur in later essays in ways both similar to and different from these ways of framing the issues.

What we have in this section, then, are four essays that have played significant roles in the rediscovery of narrative for theology and ethics. The complexities of the arguments provided by these four thinkers reveal the variety of issues involved in discussions about narrative. While there are similarities of emphasis and overlapping concerns, the four proposals are neither always attempting to make the same point, nor are they ultimately compatible. Frei's case may still be defensible even if the others fall; parts of MacIntyre's case may still be defensible even if Crites's anthropological claim is shown to be mistaken. These essays reveal that even in the days of rediscovering narrative, there have been tensions and a diversity of uses which defy easy categorization about who is arguing for what.

III

Matters become even more complex when we turn to the five essays grouped in the second section, "Narrative as a Critical Tool." The essays in this section explore the significance of narrative for particular topics. In each case, the author takes up a topic or set of topics, and argues that a conception of narrative is methodologically crucial.

Nicholas Lash's "Ideology, Metaphor, and Analogy" explores the relationship between narrative and metaphysics, between metaphor and analogy. In Lash's view Christian theology is poised between the poles of narrative and metaphysics, and both are required for an adequate theological method. He appeals to narrative in the sense of autobiography, claiming that the paradigmatic forms of Christian discourse are self-involving and, as self-involving, they locate the speaker (or the group of which the speaker is a spokesperson) in a particular cultural, historical tradition. In this sense, the Christian is "the teller of a tale, the narrator of a story which he tells as *his* story, as a story in which he acknowledges himself to be a participant" (p. 120).

Thus Lash's conception of narrative is similar to Niebuhr's and at least some of MacIntyre's uses. But Lash goes beyond Niebuhr and MacIntyre in arguing for the countervailing importance of (a specific conception of) metaphysics.[15] Lash believes that narratives are "made," that narratives have to be constructed; hence the circumstances of the "production" of the narrative will always be subject to ideological distortion. What is needed, therefore, is an account of metaphysics which will exercise critical control over narrative, unravelling confusions and inconsistencies that arise from it, and checking the narrative with *praxis* to offset its stereotypical drift. It is particularly worth noting that in Lash's view the question of the truth of theological assertions must finally be answered by another narrative, the lived-out display of the assertions of Christian discourse "in patterns of action and suffering, praise and endurance" (p. 135).

Lash's claim that narratives are "made" and "produced" is not the same as the view that narratives are imposed by the teller upon events which otherwise have no narrative order. On that point it would seem that Lash would side with MacIntyre against Sartre on the relationship of narrative to human life (cf. p. 100). Lash's point rather seems to be that in narrating that which is already "narratable" (and hence not fundamentally a Sartrean absurdity), humans are "making" and "producing" the narratives which are subject to ideological distortion. Indeed it would seem that Lash's theological position is so concerned with ideological distortion precisely because the narratives make claims to being true.

Although they are quite different in focus, there are important similarities between Lash's argument and that offered by Alasdair MacIntyre in his essay "Epistemological Crises, Dramatic Narrative, and the Philosophy of Science." Like Lash, MacIntyre thinks there are important connections between narrative and autobiography and also between narrative and particular cultural, historical traditions. But whereas Lash's focus is theological method and Christian discourse, MacIntyre's focus is philosophical argument and rational progress achieved through the resolution of epistemological crises.[16]

15. Lash's distinctions are derived from Brian Wicker's *The Story-Shaped World* (Notre Dame: University of Notre Dame Press, 1976).

16. For an argument concerned with similar issues of the relationship among narrative, science, and epistemology, cf. Jean-Francois Lyotard, *The Post-Modern Condition: A Report on Knowledge,* trans. by Geoff Bennington and Brian Massumi (Minneapolis: University of Minnesota Press, 1984).

At the heart of MacIntyre's argument is the claim that the notions of narrative and tradition are inextricably interrelated, and in particular that a tradition "not only embodies the narrative of an argument, but it is only to be recovered by an argumentative retelling of that narrative which will itself be in conflict with other argumentative retellings" (p. 146). Because traditions are the bearers of reason, and because traditions are beset from time to time with epistemological crises, MacIntyre argues that such crises can be resolved—and rational progress advanced —only if the writing of a true dramatic narrative (i.e., history understood in a certain way) can be a rational activity.

He has more recently specified three requirements of the activity of narrative in resolving epistemological crises in his *Whose Justice? Which Rationality?*:

> The solution to a genuine epistemological crisis requires the invention or discovery of new concepts and the framing of some new type or types of theory which meet three highly exacting requirements. First, this in some ways radically new and conceptually enriched scheme, if it is to put an end to epistemological crisis, must furnish a solution to the problems which had previously proved intractable in a systematic and coherent way. Second, it must also provide an explanation of just what it was which rendered the tradition, before it had acquired these new resources, sterile or incoherent or both. And third, these first two tasks must be carried out in a way which exhibits some fundamental continuity of the new conceptual and theoretical structures with the shared beliefs in terms of which the tradition of enquiry had been defined up to this point.[17]

MacIntyre's use of narrative in this context is significant for its strong epistemological focus. Whereas Lash thinks that a kind of discourse other than narrative is necessary to counter the tendencies toward ideology, MacIntyre locates both within a broader account of narrative and rational inquiry. MacIntyre's argument represents a challenge both to those critics who think narrative is *just* about telling stories and hence does not entail truth-claims and to those who fear that appeals to narrative, particularly when tied to traditions, inevitably produce either a vicious relativism or an unwillingness to recognize the multiplicity of communities and/or traditions.

In their essay "From System to Story: An Alternative Pattern for Rationality in Ethics," Stanley Hauerwas and David Burrell are also concerned with the methodological significance of narrative for epistemo-

17. Alasdair MacIntyre, *Whose Justice? Which Rationality?* (Notre Dame: University of Notre Dame Press, 1988), p. 362.

logical questions. Hauerwas's and Burrell's focus is on the relationship between narrative and rationality in ethics.[18] In particular, they argue that the intentional nature of human action evokes a narrative account, that a narrative account is concerned with how those intentional actions are woven into the depiction of personal identity and character, and that because the language and moral notions people use to describe their character and their behavior are tied to the narratives of particular traditions, the notion of rationality itself is narrative-dependent.

Hence Hauerwas's and Burrell's argument involves appeals to several different uses of narrative. Their argument is structurally similar to MacIntyre's essay, the primary difference being that Hauerwas and Burrell focus on narrative and rationality in people's lives whereas MacIntyre deals with the philosophy of science. One interesting contrast between the two essays would involve comparing Hauerwas's and Burrell's four criteria for testing the truthfulness of a narrative with MacIntyre's account of truth-claims in the construction and reconstruction of dramatic narratives. Both positions provide criteria for narrative's relation to truth-claims which are tradition-dependent, and they reveal the structure of their argument that the only way to make the case for the connection between narratives, traditions, and rationalities is to display that connection.

David Ford's "System, Story, Performance: A Proposal about the Role of Narrative in Christian Systematic Theology" appears to represent a challenge to Hauerwas's and Burrell's repudiation of the notion of system in theology and ethics. But on closer inspection there exists a great deal of similarity between their proposals, as Ford's conception of systematic theology is quite different from the notion of system from which Hauerwas and Burrell want to move away.[19]

According to Ford, narrative is crucial to systematic theology because of the centrality in Christianity of testimony to Jesus Christ in realistic narrative form. Ford proposes a "middle distance realism" that mediates between one person's agenda and too broad an overview, depending on the ordinary social world of people in interaction. Ford's argument picks up themes of narrative and temporality (similar to Niebuhr, Crites, and MacIntyre), the realistic character of biblical narrative (as argued by Frei), and links between narrative and performance and the narrative structure of worship and praise (structurally similar to Lash and, as will become apparent below, Metz). Moreover, Ford draws on arguments from literary theory in developing his epistemologi-

---

18. For another discussion of this issue that is sympathetic to Hauerwas's and Burrell's argument, cf. Terrence Tilley, *Story Theology* (Wilmington, DE: Michael Glazier, 1985).

19. Cf. also Ford's book on Barth, cited in note 4.

cal proposals. Ford's position shares similarities with both Niebuhr and Frei on the importance of narrative for theological method, but Ford differs from Niebuhr (and hence is closer to Frei) in his view that theological language needs not translation but explication. Hence Ford argues that Christian systematic theology need not be the kind of rigidly rational enterprise that Hauerwas and Burrell (as well as Metz) deplore.

The final essay in this section, Martha Nussbaum's "Narrative Emotions: Beckett's Genealogy of Love," is provocative and important for several reasons. Her argument is important in part because she takes up the question of narrative and human life—discussed in other ways by Niebuhr, Crites, MacIntyre, and Hauerwas and Burrell—in a new way with her argument that the emotions are narratively constructed. It is a move that involves a significant claim not only about narrative but also about the emotions. People have tended (in what Hauerwas and Burrell call "the standard account") to see the emotions as feelings that well up in us in a natural and rather untutored, and perhaps uncontrollable, way. In contrast, Nussbaum argues that emotions are social constructs, that we learn how to feel in and through the narratives of particular societies. Her argument thus stands in continuity with the Aristotelian claim about practical rationality, for the ultimate particulars can only be rightly discerned by a person virtuously trained to think and feel in appropriate ways.[20]

Moreover, she shows how important narrative fiction can be in displaying understandings of, and possibilities for, human life. At the heart of her argument is the idea that if human life in general, and the emotions in particular, are indeed narrative in form, then ethics needs to be concerned with those texts that have the appropriate form. Put in her terms, "literary form and human content are inseparable" (p. 221).

Perhaps what is most provocative about the essay, however, is the connection Nussbaum makes between the construction of Samuel Beckett's narrative and its social significance. Nussbaum argues that Beckett's trilogy *Molloy, Molone Dies, The Unnamable* is a narrative designed to counter a Christian account of the emotions by providing an alternative account. Nussbaum accepts the view that human beings are fundamentally tellers of stories, and she further argues that "since one of the child's most pervasive and powerful ways of learning its society's values and structures is through the stories it hears and learns to tell, stories will be a major source of any culture's emotional life" (p. 225). Hence a criticism of a culture's repertoire of emotions must be, in this view, advanced through an "unwriting of stories."

Nussbaum thereby makes a strong case for the social significance

---

20. James W. McClendon argues a similar case in his stress on the importance of the "bodily strand" in ethics. Cf. his *Ethics: Systematic Theology,* vol. I, cited in note 3.

Stanley Hauerwas and L. Gregory Jones

of narrative, both in its role as transmitter of a culture's beliefs, attitudes, and emotions, and in its capacity of criticizing the dominant culture through the "unwriting" of the dominant narratives and the writing of an alternative account. Her argument thus shows the artificiality of distinctions between "prophetic" and "narrative" discourse; Nussbaum's account shows how Beckett used narrative to provide a prophetic critique of a society's dominant self-understanding.

Nussbaum's argument moves the issue of narrative and ethics into two other interrelated arenas: literary criticism and social analysis. Indeed, while Nussbaum's analysis shows Beckett's criticism of a Christian account of the emotions, other arguments have been advanced that such narrative forms are increasingly unavailable to us because of central features of our political economy and collective psychology.[21] Such issues are important for attempting to discern what significance narrative has, or possibly can have, for contemporary theology and ethics.

In this section we have five essays concerned with the methodological significance of narrative as a critical tool. They are concerned with theological and ethical method; with connections between narrative and rationality, and narrative and truth-claims; with the social significance of narrative in relation to ideologies, other cultures, and dominant forms within a culture; and with the relationship between narrative and understandings of, and possibilities for, human life. Once again, what unites these essays is not so much a common argument as a recognition that narrative has a crucial methodological significance for theology and ethics. What that significance is, however, is a complex matter made even more complex when these essays are seen in relation to those from the first section.

IV

The final essays in this book comprise the third section, "Narrative's Theological Significance." These essays pick up on themes developed in essays in the first two sections as well as offering distinctive theological conceptions of the significance of narrative.

The first essay, "A Short Apology of Narrative," is by the German theologian Johann Baptist Metz. It is significant in part because his argument for the significance of narrative appears to be logically independent of the discussions within Anglo-American philosophy and theology

21. Cf., for example, Richard Harvey Brown, *Society as Text* (Chicago: University of Chicago Press, 1987), esp. pp. 153-171; and Walter Benjamin, "The Storyteller," in his *Illuminations* (New York: Schocken Books, 1969).

14

(which represent most of the essays in this book). Even so, Metz's appeals to several distinct uses of narrative include notions already familiar from other essays in this volume: narrative's relation to experience, its practical and performative aspect, and its role as the structure of critical reason. Metz contends that stressing the place of narrative in practical and performative contexts does not mean relinquishing a place in the debates about truth and reason, thus challenging the unwarranted assertion that appeals to narrative are inevitably "private" rather than "public."

In addition, Metz emphasizes several conceptions of narrative that are distinctive to his argument: narrative's pastoral and social aspect, and its place as the medium of salvation and history. On this last use in particular, Metz's argument is both provocative and significant: he argues that in the face of the history of suffering and the perceived non-identity of history, only a narrative conception of theology will be able adequately to account for history as the history of salvation and hence the identity of history in Jesus Christ. Here Metz, like Nussbaum (though in quite different ways and for quite different purposes), stresses the social significance of appeals to narrative.

Michael Root's essay "The Narrative Structure of Soteriology" is not just another foray into the methodological significance of narrative, but rather is the kind of performance that Lash suggests is needed. Root actually uses narrative to explicate how Christian convictions entail the belief that the work of Jesus Christ has moved humanity from a state of deprivation (i.e., sin) to a release from that deprivation (i.e., liberation, salvation). He argues that it is in and through narrative redescriptions of the story of Jesus that the soteriological task is carried out. The narrative description is designed to explain how the narrative of Jesus Christ is the narrative of redemption. Root argues that there are a variety of ways in which this redescription takes place, ranging from Anselm's focus on Christ's repayment of an infinite debt owed to God's honor, to Schleiermacher's conception of Christ evoking perfect God-consciousness, to liberation theology's focus on Christ's liberation of the captives and oppressed. He easily could have added to the list Metz's account of how narrative renders the history of suffering and the perceived non-identity of history into the history of salvation and the identity of history in Jesus Christ. He also could have added Paul to the list, for as Richard Hays and Stephen Fowl have argued, Paul presupposes the narrative of Jesus Christ in explicating the salvation Christ brings to humanity.[22] Root does not

---

22. Cf. Richard B. Hays, *The Faith of Jesus Christ: An Investigation of the Narrative Substructure of Galatians 3:1–4:11* (Chico, CA: Scholars Press, 1983); Stephen Fowl, "Some Uses of Story in Moral Discourse: Reflections on Paul's Moral Discourse and Our Own," *Modern Theology*, 4, 4 (July 1988): 293-308.

argue that narrative is linked to any specific conception of soteriology in this essay; rather he contends that the logical structure and explanatory power of the Christian account of salvation, whatever the particular conception of the relationship between sin and the release from sin, is a function of its narrative form.

Root thus argues that christology and soteriology cannot be separated, for the person and work of Jesus Christ are conceptually interrelated and are depicted in and through narrative. Such a view entails the important claim that interpretations of the narrative structure of christology and soteriology are tied to social and political contexts.

Root draws on Hans Frei's proposal for reading the Bible as narrative, and his argument is also related to MacIntyre's account of the relationship between narrative, tradition, and historical argument. Moreover, Root's proposal hinges in part on the view that narrative is central for the depiction of personal identity, and in particular (for an account of soteriology) the depiction of the identity of Jesus Christ.[23] So the significance of Root's essay is not so much a distinctive conception of narrative as a distinctive application of narrative to the explication of a theological topic.

The next set of essays presents interesting exchanges about narrative between Julian Hartt, Stephen Crites, and Stanley Hauerwas. Hartt has been an influential figure in discussions about narrative, and in particular about the relationship between narrative and metaphysics in Christian theology. Hartt has been influenced by Niebuhr, and he has been a teacher of both Crites and Hauerwas; he raises some important issues in this essay in a sharp and focused way.

Hartt is concerned with the relationship between narrative and historical facts and between narrative and metaphysical/ontological truth-claims.[24] His argument is important not only for the similarities to and differences from Crites and Hauerwas but also because of the ways in which his understanding of the relationship between narrative and questions of history, truth, and metaphysics are related to the proposals of such other contributors as Niebuhr, Frei, MacIntyre, Lash, Ford, and Metz.

We have included these exchanges in part because of the significance of Hartt's position and the issues he raises, but we have also included them because they reveal both how illuminating the disagreements about narrative can be and why the significance of narrative is

23. Here he follows the lead of Hans Frei's book, *The Identity of Jesus Christ* (Philadelphia: Fortress Press, 1975).

24. Hartt discusses these issues more fully in "Story as the Art of Historical Truth," a lengthy chapter in his *Theological Method and Imagination* (New York: Seabury Press, 1977).

still an open question. These dimensions are also highlighted in the final two essays in the book, for they constitute a quite different display of disagreements about the place of narrative in theology and ethics.

The first of these is taken from Ronald Thiemann's book *Revelation and Theology: The Gospel as Narrated Promise,* and the purpose of the chapter is to show how the God of Jesus Christ is identified in and through and beyond the biblical narrative. The selection is part of Thiemann's attempt to provide a nonfoundational account of revelation through the use of narrative. Thiemann's entire book is an important exercise in displaying a proposal about narrative, and in some ways the selection unfairly isolates a brief treatment of Scripture from its place in Thiemann's larger argument.

Even so, it is included here for two reasons. The first is that it provides an interesting and significant example of a Christian theologian actually displaying a Christian appropriation of Scripture along the lines suggested by Hans Frei's proposal about narrative. The second is that Thiemann's argument, and in particular his reading of Matthew which is included here, has been subjected to vigorous Jewish critique by Michael Goldberg in "God, Action, and Narrative: *Which* Narrative? *Which* Action? *Which* God?"

According to Goldberg, Thiemann is able to provide an account for the unity of biblical narrative and the identifiability of God only through a misunderstanding of the Jewish account of God in Hebrew Scripture.[25] Hence Goldberg's essay represents an exercise in Jewish polemics, challenging Thiemann's use of Hebrew Scripture for the depiction of the God of Jesus Christ. The juxtaposition of Thiemann's and Goldberg's arguments has the effect of a claim that the reading of texts is inextricably tied to the narratives of the communities and traditions that provide the contexts in and through which those texts are read.

Thiemann has responses to Goldberg's critique available to him, but it is not insignificant that *Why Narrative?* ends on the inconclusive note of Goldberg's challenge to Thiemann. Goldberg's challenge represents a fitting reflection of the current state of thinking about the significance of narrative for theology and ethics: the category of narrative is significant enough to be taken seriously, and there are crucial issues in epistemology, personal identity, and theological and ethical method at stake in the debates. Moreover, for all of the crude appeals to narrative by some, the essays in this book reveal the importance of narrative

---

25. Cf. also Goldberg's *Jews and Christians, Getting Our Stories Straight: The Exodus and the Passion-Resurrection* (Nashville: Abingdon Press, 1985). His earlier book, *Theology and Narrative: A Critical Introduction* (Nashville: Abingdon Press, 1982), provides a useful overview of some of the uses of narrative in theology and ethics.

for theology while also displaying the rich results of disagreements about that importance.

We hope the essays in this book will elevate the debates about narrative to a higher level, showing both the significance of narrative and the continuing issues and debates which are raised thereby. Thus the question "Why Narrative?" remains important, as do such related questions as "If Narrative, Which Narrative? Whose Narrative?." The questions are too important, and the results of reflecting on them are potentially too rewarding, to be ignored.

I: NARRATIVE REDISCOVERED

The Story of Our Life

H. Richard Niebuhr

I. The Historical Method of Christian Faith

Our self-consciously historical time accepts the limitations of the historical point of view with a sense of constraint and an air of resignation. In this situation, however, we do well to remind ourselves that the Christian community has usually—and particularly in times of its greatest vigor—used an historical method. Apparently it felt that to speak in confessional terms about the events that had happened to it in its history was not a burdensome necessity but rather an advantage and that the acceptance of an historical point of view was not confining but liberating. The preaching of the early Christian church was not an argument for the existence of God nor an admonition to follow the dictates of some common human conscience, unhistorical and super-social in character. It was primarily a simple recital of the great events connected with the historical appearance of Jesus Christ and a confession of what had happened to the community of disciples. Whatever it was that the church meant to say, whatever was revealed or manifested to it, could be indicated only in connection with an historical person and events in the life of his community. The confession referred to history and was consciously made in history.

H. Richard Niebuhr, "The Story of Our Life," from his *The Meaning of Revelation* (New York, MacMillan Publishing Company, 1941), pp. 43-81.

It is true that when Paul succumbed to his unconquerable tendency to commend himself, he spoke of revelation in private visions; when he attempted to defend himself against the assumption of superiority by Corinthian spiritualists he referred to mysteries and hidden wisdom. But when he went about his proper work of demonstrating to his hearers and readers what he really meant, he did so in the following fashion:

> I declare unto you the gospel which I preached unto you, which also ye have received and wherein ye stand; by which also ye are saved, if ye keep in memory what I preached unto you, unless ye have believed in vain. For I delivered unto you first of all that which I also received, how that Christ died for our sins according to the scriptures; and that he was buried, and that he rose again the third day according to the scriptures; and that he was seen of Cephas and then of the twelve: after that he was seen of above five hundred brethren at once; of whom the greater part remain unto this present, but some are fallen asleep. After that he was seen of James; then of all the apostles. And last of all he was seen of me also, as of one born out of due time.

The great anonymous theologian of the second century spoke in parables of Hellenic wisdom about the gospel of divine grace; but he could indicate what he meant by the Logos, the Light, and the Life only by telling again, in his own way, the story of Jesus Christ. The sermons of Peter and Stephen as reported or reconstructed in the book of Acts were recitals of the great events in Christian and Israelite history. Christian evangelism in general, as indicated by the preservation of its material in the synoptic Gospels, began directly with Jesus and told in more or less narrative fashion about those things "which are most surely believed among us of all that Jesus began both to do and to teach." We may remind ourselves also of the fact that despite many efforts to set forth Christian faith in metaphysical and ethical terms of great generality the only creed which has been able to maintain itself in the church with any approach to universality consists for the most part of statements about events.

We can imagine that early preachers were often asked to explain what they meant with their talk about God, salvation, and revelation, and when they were hard pressed, when all their parables or references to the unknown God and to the Logos had succeeded only in confusing their hearers, they turned at last to the story of their life, saying, "What we mean is this event which happened among us and to us." They followed in this respect the prophets who had spoken of God before them and the Jewish community which had also talked of revelation. These, too, always spoke of history, of what had happened to

Abraham, Isaac, and Jacob, of a deliverance from Egypt, of the covenant of Sinai, of mighty acts of God. Even their private visions were dated, as "in the year that King Uzziah died," even the moral law was anchored to an historical event, and even God was defined less by his metaphysical and moral character than by his historical relations, as the God of Abraham, Isaac, and Jacob.

Interpretation of our meaning with the aid of a story is a well-known pedagogical device. So Lincoln told his homely tales and conveyed to others in trenchant fashion the ideas in his mind; so Plato employed myths to illustrate philosophy and to communicate visions of truth that ordinary language could not describe; so Jesus himself through parable tried to indicate what he meant by the phrase "kingdom of God." Yet what prompted Christians in the past to confess their faith by telling the story of their life was more than a need for vivid illustration or for analogical reasoning. Their story was not a parable which could be replaced by another; it was irreplaceable and untranslatable. An internal compulsion rather than free choice led them to speak of what they knew by telling about Jesus Christ and their relation to God through him.

Today we think and speak under the same compulsion. We find that we must travel the road which has been taken by our predecessors in the Christian community, though our recognition of the fact is first of all only a consequence of the obstruction of all other ways. We must do what has been done because we have discovered with Professor Whitehead that "religions commit suicide when they find their inspiration in dogmas. The inspiration of religion lies in the history of religion." Whether this be true of other faiths than Christianity we may not be sure, but it seems very true of our faith. Metaphysical systems have not been able to maintain the intellectual life of our community and abstract systems of morality have not conveyed devotion and the power of obedience with their ideals and imperatives. Idealistic and realistic metaphysics, perfectionist and hedonistic ethics have been poor substitutes for the New Testament, and churches which feed on such nourishment seem subject to spiritual rickets. Yet it is not the necessity of staying alive which forces our community to speak in historical terms. It is not a self-evident truth that the church ought to live; neither the historical nor the confessional standpoint can accept self-preservation as the first law of life, since in history we know that death is the law of even the best life and in faith we understand that to seek life is to lose it. The church's compulsion arises out of its need—since it is a living church—to say truly what it stands for, and out of its inability to do so otherwise than by telling the story of its life.

The preachers and theologians of the modern church must do

what New Testament evangelists did because their situation permits no other method. From the point of view of historical beings, we can speak only about that which is also in our time and which is seen through the medium of our history. We are in history as the fish is in water and what we mean by the revelation of God can be indicated only as we point through the medium in which we live. When we try other methods we find ourselves still in the old predicament. Since all men are in nature, though their histories vary, we think we may be able to direct them to the God we mean in preaching and worship by pointing as Jesus did to the rain, the sun, the sparrows, and the lilies of the field, or to those subtler wonders which microscope and telescope and even more refined instruments of intelligence discover in the common world. As natural rather than historical theologians we try to divorce nature from history and ask men to listen to its praise of the Creator. But such theology is implicitly historical. Being in Christian history, it looks on nature with the mind of Christ, as even Jesus himself, pointing out God's care of beasts and flowers, did so as one whose eyes had been instructed by Moses and the prophets. We cannot point in space to spatial things or in a general time to generally temporal things, saying that what we mean by "word of God" and by "revelation" can be known if men will but look together at stars and trees and flowers. It is with Kant in his time-space that we must regard the starry heavens, and with Jeremiah see the blossoming almond, and with Jesus behold the lilies of the field before we can read words of God in nature's book. Nature regarded through our history is indeed a symbol of what we mean, a pointer to God; but nature uninterpreted through our history and faith, or torn out of this context and placed in another, does not indicate what we mean. It means various things according to the point of view from which it is regarded and the context in which it stands—utter indifference to man and all his works in the context of despair, a blessing upon brutality from the point of view of confidence in military might, and a dominant interest in mathematics in the context of faith in mathematical thought as the only road to truth.

If nature uninterpreted through our history affords us no symbol of what revelation means, Scripture, nature's rival in theology, is in the same position. It may be said that though we are historical beings we can still contemplate from this moving point that we occupy a super-historical word of God. So many early Protestants seemed to think, in so far as they equated Scriptures with revelation. Yet the Reformers knew—though less vividly it may be than their successors—that the Scriptures as a collection of tales and observations about religion and life, of laws and precepts, as a book containing moral, political, astronomical and anthropological ideas, reveals nothing save the state of culture of the men who wrote its parts or of the groups who related the legends recorded in later time. We cannot point to Scripture saying that what we mean can be known if men will but read what is written there. We must read the law with the mind of the prophets and the prophets with the eyes of Jesus; we must immerse ourselves with Paul in the story of the crucifixion, and read Paul with the aid of the spirit in the church if we would find revelation in the Scriptures. A history that was recorded forward, as it were, must be read backward through our history if it is to be understood as revelation. Doubtless we are confronted here by an ancient problem of the church which appears in all discussions about law and the Gospel and about spirit and letter. Yet it is evident that when the church speaks of revelation it never means simply the Scriptures, but only Scripture read from the point of view and in the context of church history. The Scriptures point to God and through Scripture God points to men when they are read by those who share the same background with the community which produced the letter possessed, or by those who participate in the common life of which the Scriptures contain the record. Doubtless the Bible differs from nature, being the external form in which our history is preserved and so being indispensable to a community whose history is nowhere recorded in nature, as the history of purely natural communities is. But like nature the Bible can be read in many different contexts and will mean different things accordingly. Translated and read in the nationalistic community, it does not point to the Father of Jesus Christ but to blood and soil and tribal deity; read by those whose minds are filled with the history and memories of democratic society, it does not point to the intrinsically good God but to the intrinsically valuable individual, and the word that comes through it is a word about liberty from political and economic bondage rather than about liberty from slavery to self and sin. In Protestantism we have long attempted to say what we mean by revelation by pointing to the Scriptures, but we have found that we cannot do so save as we interpret them in a community in which men listen for the word of God in the reading of the Scriptures, or in which men participate in the same spiritual history out of which the record came. The latest movement in New Testament criticism, Form Criticism, underlines this fact for us—that the book arose out of the life of the church and that we cannot know an historical Jesus save as we look through the history and with the history of the community that loved and worshipped him. A Jesus of history apart from the particular history in which he appears is as unknown and as unknowable as any sense-object apart from the sense-qualities in which it appears to us.

When we have found these ways of circumventing our historical situation and of abandoning our obstructed historical point of view, we may be tempted, with the individualists of all time, to seek a direct path to what we mean through inner religious experience. Can we not say that when we speak of God and revelation we mean events which occur in the privacy of our personal, inner life or what we feel to be basic in our moral consciousness? Yet once more we discover that visions, numinous feelings, senses of reality, knowledge of duty and worth may be interpreted in many ways. We cannot speak of inner light at all, save in ejaculations signifying nothing to other men, unless we define its character in social terms, that is in terms which come out of our history. The "true" seed within, the "right" spirit, can be distinguished from false seeds and evil spirits only by the use of criteria which are not purely individual and biographical. We discriminate between the light within and spiritual will-o'-the-wisps by reference to a "Christ" within. But the word "Christ" comes out of social history and has a meaning not derived from individual experience. Religious experience and moral sense are to be found in many different settings and can be interpreted from many different points of view. The sense of the numinous accompanies many strange acts of worship; it may have been far stronger when human sacrifice was offered to pagan deities than it has ever been in Christianity. High moral devotion and a keen sense of duty point many men today to domestic and tribal gods. What the unconquerable movements of the human heart toward worship and devotion really mean, how their errors may be distinguished from their truths and how they are to be checked, cannot be known save as they are experienced and disciplined in a community with a history. Obedience to moral imperatives, worship, and prayer are indispensable and inescapable in the Christian church; they are inseparable from the listening for God's word. But what they mean, what their content must be, and to what ends they ought to be directed we cannot understand save as we bring to bear upon them our remembrance of an obedience unto death, of the imperatives which have come to us through history, of the Lord's prayers in the garden and on the mount, and of a worship in a temple whose inner sanctuary was empty. Religious and moral experience are always in some history and in some social setting that derives from the past. They also offer us no way of avoiding the use of our history in saying what we mean.

This necessity is a source of scandal in the Christian church, which is a mystery to itself at this point. To live and think in this way seems to mean that we navigate the oceans and skies of our world by dead reckoning, computing our position from a latitude and longitude determined nineteen hundred years ago, using a log that is in part indecipherable and a compass of conscience notoriously subject to deviation. Objections arise in the crew not only because other vessels claim to possess more scientific apparatus for determining where they are and whither they are going, but because revelation, if it be revelation of God, must offer men something more immovable than the pole star and something more precise than our measurements of the winds and currents of history can afford.

Revelation cannot mean history, we must say to ourselves in the church, if it also means God. What we see from the historical point of view and what we believe in as we occupy that standpoint must be two different things. For surely what is seen in history is not a universal, absolute, independent source and goal of existence, not impartial justice nor infinite mercy, but particularity, finiteness, opinions that pass, caprice, arbitrariness, accident, brutality, wrong on the throne and right on the scaffold. The claims of evangelists of historical revelation seem wholly inconsistent with their faith. When they speak of a just God they point to a process so unequal that only those born in a special time and space receive faith in him while all who lived before or in cultures with a different history are condemned to ignorance of what they ought to know for the sake of their soul's health and life.

Moreover revelation cannot mean both history and God any more than it can mean both nature and God. The events of history to which Christian revelation refers may be regarded from the scientific, objective, non-committed point of view as well as nature can be. So regarded, they have no greater value than other events. They can be studied in their cause-effect relationship, in their cultural, geographic, economic, and political contexts; when this is done it is apparent that the scientist has as little need for the hypothesis of divine action as Laplace had in his astronomy. The birth of Jesus and the legends about it, the Sermon on the Mount, the miracles and parables, the crucifixion and resurrection stories, the institution of the sacraments — all these may be explained by noting their place in a series of other events in Jewish and Hellenistic history or in the development of religious, philosophical, political, and economic movements. At best such historic description will make use of the category of individuality, pointing out the uniqueness of each event and the particular way in which general principles are made concrete in it. But such uniqueness is a characteristic of all events in time and the unique Jesus does not differ in this respect from the unique Socrates and the unique Hitler. Objective history cannot, without denying its method and its point of view, require a consideration for the life of Jesus differing from that which it brings to bear on other individual events. It can only record another unique fact—that the church and Western culture have attached great religious significance to Jesus. It may seek further to account for this new individual event by reference to some general tendencies in human na-

27

ture and to their unique manifestations in the first and later centuries of the Christian era.

So it appears that if revelation means history it cannot also mean the object of faith, save in this purely factual and wholly opaque sense in which certain people have attached transcendent value to certain events.

The problem presents itself to the Christian church in a third way. If revelation means history, is not faith in revelation identical with belief in the occurrence of certain past, divine events and is not such an identification an actual denial of faith in a living God? Concentration on history in the church has led to repeated revolts by men of piety and good will for whom God was not a "then and there" but a "here and now" and for whom faith was not belief in the actuality of historical events but confidence in an abiding, ruling will of love. Trusting in God now, seeking to obey his present commandments, struggling with contemporary evil, such men have rebelled against the equation of historical belief with Christian faith and against the identification of present moral commandments with precepts given to Jews or to Pauline churches in ancient times. They have refused to make the forgiveness of sin a juridical act of the past rather than a contemporary experience; they have insisted on the present reality of the Holy Spirit as more important to Christians than a Pentecostal miracle in the early church. Such vital faith, seeking contact with a present Lord and Giver of Life, must always revolt against historical antiquarianism even as it must reject a futurism for which God, forgiveness, and moral obedience are only future possibilities without a present validity.

Revelation in history involves other difficulties. Questions about predestination and freedom, eternity and time, progress and decline, and many others of like sort assail the mind of the Christian in his dilemma of historic faith. Though he concedes the fact that he must speak as an historic being and also that the church has always thought in historical terms, he is puzzled by the revelation of faith and history. History seems always to lead to doubt rather than to faith.

In the bewilderment which assails him in this situation the modern Christian, like many a predecessor in the church, is tempted again and again to drop the history and to hold fast to the faith, to give up the Jesus of history while affirming afresh his loyalty to the Christ of faith. But faith is a strange thing; it is not sufficient to itself and will not work alone. It is like the eye which cannot perceive depth and distance and solidity of things save as it has a partner. Or it is like Adam who seeks a helpmeet among all the creatures and cannot be fruitful in loins or mind until an Eve is given him for conversation. And Christian faith, having tried many other partners, has found that these can speak with it of its God only if they have been schooled in Christian history. Nor are there any among them that speak a universal language; if they do not speak in Galilean accents, some other province not less small in the infinite world has shaped their voices and minds in its own way. Philosophy, as historical in all its forms as religion, can indeed share and strengthen the life of faith, but only when it speaks out of a mind that has been filled with Jewish and Christian memories. The church is not ill at ease with Descartes, Spinoza, Locke, Berkeley, and Kant; but then the God of whom these philosophers write is always something more than their conceptual systems have defined. As Professors Gilson and A. E. Taylor have again reminded us recently, the God of modern philosophers is more than the God of their philosophies; he could not mean so much in their thought if he did not mean more than their thought about him expresses. He is always the God of history, of Abraham, Isaac, and Jacob, or the Father of Jesus Christ, and not only the God of abstract thought.

It remains true that Christian faith cannot escape from partnership with history, however many other partners it may choose. With this it has been mated and to this its loyalty belongs; the union is as indestructible as that of reason and sense experience in the natural sciences. But though this is true, the question remains: How can it be true? How can revelation mean both history and God?

II. History as Lived and as Seen

We may be helped toward a solution of the problem of history and faith by reflection upon the fact that the history to which we point when we speak of revelation is not the succession of events which an uninterested spectator can see from the outside but our own history. It is one thing to perceive from a safe distance the occurrences in a stranger's life and quite a different thing to ponder the path of one's own destiny, to deal with the why and whence and whither of one's own existence. Of a man who has been blind and who has come to see, two histories can be written. A scientific case history will describe what happened to his optic nerve or to the crystalline lens, what technique the surgeon used or by what medicines a physician wrought the cure, through what stages of recovery the patient passed. An autobiography, on the other hand, may barely mention these things but it will tell what happened to a self that had lived in darkness and now saw again trees and the sunrise, children's faces and the eyes of a friend. Which of these histories can be a parable of revelation, the outer history or the story of what happened to a self? When we speak of revelation in the Christian church we refer to *our* history, to the history of selves or to history as it is lived and apprehended from within.

The distinction between *our* history and events in impersonal time, or between history as lived and as contemplated from the outside, may be illustrated by contrasting parallel descriptions of the same social event. Lincoln's Gettysburg Address begins with history: "Fourscore and seven years ago our fathers brought forth on this continent, a new nation, conceived in Liberty, and dedicated to the proposition that all men are created equal." The same event is described in the *Cambridge Modern History* in the following fashion: "On July 4, 1776, Congress passed the resolution which made the colonies independent communities, issuing at the same time the well-known Declaration of Independence. If we regard the Declaration as the assertion of an abstract political theory, criticism and condemnation are easy. It sets out with a general proposition so vague as to be practically useless. The doctrine of the equality of men, unless it be qualified and conditioned by reference to special circumstance, is either a barren truism or a delusion."

The striking dissimilarity between these two accounts may be explained as being due merely to a difference of sentiment; the blind devotion of the patriot as opposed to the critical acumen and dispassionate judgment of the scientific historian. But the disparity goes deeper. The difference in sentiment is so profound because the beings about which the accounts speak differ greatly; the "Congress" is one thing, "our fathers" are almost another reality. The proposition that all men are created free and equal, to which the fathers dedicated their lives, their fortunes, and their sacred honor, and which for their children is to be the object of a new devotion, seems to belong to a different order of ideas than that to which the vague and useless, barren truism or delusion belongs. Though these various terms point to the same ultimate realities, the latter are seen in different aspects and apprehended in different contexts. Moreover it seems evident that the terms the external historian employs are not more truly descriptive of the things-in-themselves than those the statesman uses and that the former's understanding of what really happened is not more accurate than the latter's. In the one case the events of history are seen from the outside, in the other from the inside. Lincoln spoke of what had happened in *our* history, of what had made and formed us and to which we remain committed so long as we continue to exist as Americans; he spoke of purposes which lie in our enduring past and are therefore the purposes of our present life; he described the history of living beings and not data relating to dead things. It is a critical history, but the criticism of its author is not directed toward the general propositions so much as to the human beings who measure themselves and are measured by means of those general propositions; criticism is moral, directed toward selves and their community. The other account abstracts from living selves with their resolutions and commitments, their hopes and fears. It is not critical of men but of things; documents and propositions are its objects. The events it describes happened in impersonal time and are recorded less in the memories of persons than in books and monuments.

The example from American history may be duplicated in the history of every other community. Pericles' Funeral Oration appeals to memory and may be paralleled by many an external account of the rise of an empire "acquired by men who knew their duty . . . and who if they ever failed in an enterprise would not allow their virtues to be lost to their country, but freely gave their lives to her as the fairest offering they could present at her feast." Hosea's account of the childhood of Israel and the Psalmist's recall of what "we have heard and known and our fathers have told us" have their counterparts in ethnological descriptions of early Semitic tribal life. Shakespeare's invocations of memories clustering about "this royal throne of kings, this sceptred isle . . . this land of such dear souls, this dear, dear land," and Burke's reverential regard for a tradition in which the hand of God is visible may be matched by cool, aloof accounts of the rise of the British empire. The distinctions between the two types of history cannot be made by applying the value-judgment of true and false, but must be made by reference to differences of perspective. There are true and false appeals to memory as well as true and false external descriptions, but only uncritical dogmatism will affirm that truth is the prerogative of one of the points of view. Events may be regarded from the outside by a non-participating observer; then they belong to the history of things. They may be apprehended from within as items in the destiny of persons and communities; then they belong to a life-time and must be interpreted in a context of persons with their resolutions and devotions.

The differences between the outer history of things and the inner history of selves which appear in these illustrations need to be analyzed in a little more detail in preparation for our effort to understand the relation of revelation to history. It appears, first of all, that the data of external history are all impersonal; they are ideas, interests, movements among things. Even when such history deals with human individuals it seeks to reduce them to impersonal parts. Jesus becomes, from this point of view, a complex of ideas about ethics and eschatology, of psychological and biological elements. Other persons are dealt with in the same manner. One may look for an efficient factor among such impersonal elements, though its determination involves the peril of forsaking the objective point of view, as when a Marxist historian chooses economic elements or an intellectualist regards ideas in the mind as the motivating forces in history. Internal history, on the other hand, is not a story of things in juxtaposition or succession; it is personal in character. Here the final data are not elusive atoms of matter or thought but equally elusive selves. In such history it is not the idea of the soul which Socrates thought and communicated that is important but rather the soul of Socrates, "all glorious within," the soul of the "most righteous man of the whole age." In external history we deal with objects; in internal history our concern is with subjects. In the former, to use Professor Alexander's distinction, our data are "-eds," what is believed, sensed, conceived; but in the latter what is given is always an "-ing," a knowing, a willing, a believing, a feeling. Or, as Martin Buber put it, in external history all relations are between an "I" and an "it," while in the other they are relations between "I" and "Thou"; moreover the "I" in the "I-it" relation differs from the self in the "I-Thou" setting.

Speaking as critical idealists we might say that in external history all apprehension and interpretation of events must employ the category of individuality but in internal history it is the category of personality that must be used in perceiving and understanding whatever happens. In our history all events occur not to impersonal bodies but to selves in community with other selves, and they must be so understood. After the fashion of critical idealism we may distinguish external history as a realm of the pure reason from internal history as a sphere of the pure practical reason, though it is evident that Kantian reason must be understood in far more historical fashion than was the case in the eighteenth century when neither pure nor practical reason was thought to be socially and historically conditioned.

We may employ the method of critical realism rather than of critical idealism in making our distinction between external and internal history. From the realistic point of view, we are concerned in external history to abstract from all that is merely secondary, from subjective and partisan accounts of what happened; we seek to set forth the primary characteristics of each event as these may be defined by taking into account the reports of eye-witnesses, of contemporary documents and those "permanent possibilities of sensation," the enduring institutions, the constant movements of mind and will available to the experience of all percipients. In internal history, on the other hand, we are not concerned with the primary and secondary elements of external historical perception but with "tertiary qualities," with values. These are not private and evanescent as the secondary elements are, but common and verifiable in a community of selves; yet they are not objective in the sense in which the primary qualities of external perception are said to be objective. Critical realism, however, like critical idealism, is so strongly conditioned by its historic association with non-historically minded natural science and particularly with mathematics that its use in this realm of thinking about history requires a prior readjustment of all its concepts. It is enough to point out that the distinctions which appear in all critical philosophy as between knowledge of the external world and knowledge of the internal, which drive even the most dogmatic positivists to assert that ethics and religion belong to some other realm than that with which objective knowledge is concerned, must also be made in our understanding of history. There is a descriptive and there is a normative knowledge of history, and neither type is reducible to the terms of the other.

The distinction may be made clearer by noting the differences in the conceptions of value, time, and human association which are employed in the two contexts.

In external history value means valency or strength. The objective historian must measure the importance of an event or factor by the effect it has on other events or factors in the series. Though he is also a self, living in community, having a destiny, and so unable wholly to escape a moral point of view, as scientific historian he is bound to suppress his own value-judgments as much as possible. Not what is noblest in his sight but what is most effective needs to be treated most fully. So Alexander may have a larger place in his account than Socrates, though as a self the historian may elect to follow right to martyrdom rather than might to victory. Economic motives in the framing of the American Constitution may require far more attention than moral ideals, though the historian may be one who has abjured the ownership of property for himself and may live a semi-monastic life. Looking upon events in the manner of an impartial spectator, he seeks to suppress every response of love or repugnance and to apply a more or less quantitative measure of strength in determining the importance of persons or events.

In internal history, however, value means worth for selves; whatever cannot be so valued is unimportant and may be dropped from memory. Here the death of Socrates, the birth of Lincoln, Peter's martyrdom, Luther's reform, Wesley's conversion, the landing of the Pilgrims, the granting of Magna Charta are events to be celebrated; this history calls for joy and sorrow, for days of rededication and of shriving, for tragic participation and for jubilees. The valuable here is that which bears on the destiny of selves; not what is strongest is most important but what is most relevant to the lives of "I's" and "Thou's." Value here means quality, not power; but the quality of valued things is one which only selves can apprehend. In this context we do not measure the worth of even our own desires by their strength but by their relevance to the destiny of the self.

As with value so with time. In our internal history time has a different feel and quality from that of the external time with which we deal as esoteric historians. That latter time resembles that of physics. Physics knows a plain man's time, which has for him a valency like that of the "real" money of his province; it also knows a sophisticated time which is aware of its own relativity. So in external history there is the time of the naive chronicler with his acceptance of dynastic dates, his reckonings of years since creation, his A.D.'s and B.C.'s; or this history may think of time in the sophisticated way of a culture philosophy. But all these time-conceptions have one thing in common—they are all quantitative; all these times are numbered. Such time is always serial. In the series, past events are gone and future happenings are not yet. In internal history, on the other hand, our time is our duration. What is past is not gone; it abides in us as our memory; what is future is not non-existent but present in us as our potentiality. Time here is organic or it is social, so that past and future associate with each other in the present. Time in our history is not another dimension of the external space world in which we live, but a dimension of our life and of our community's being. We are not in this time, but it is in us. It is not associated with space in a unity of space-time, but it is inseparable from life in the continuity of life-time. We do not speak of it in precise numbers, but say in poetic fashion with Lincoln, "fourscore and seven years ago," meaning not eighty-seven but our remembered past. In humbler fashion we correlate, as gossips do, the lives and deaths and wars of kings with shocks and joys in our own history. Such time is not a number but a living, a stream of consciousness, a flow of feeling, thought, and will. It is not measurable by the hours and years of a planetary and solar rhythm; its ebb and flow, its pulsations and surges, its births and deaths and resurrections are incommensurable with lunar or atomic tides. If they are to be measured it must be done by a comparison with other inner alternations; in our history we do not correlate the death of the heart with the declining sun nor its rebirth with nature's spring but with a crucifixion of the son of God and with his rising to new life.

Human association also differs when regarded from the external or internal point of view. The external knower must see societies as made up of atomic individuals related to each other by external bonds. Yet even the human individuals are depersonalized, since they are understood as complexes of psychological and biological factors. Society, to his view, is a vast and intricate organization of interests, drives or instincts, beliefs, customs, laws, constitutions, inventions, geographic and climatic data, in which a critical and diligent inquiry can discover some intelligible structures and moving patterns of relation. In internal history, on the other hand, society is a community of selves. Here we do not only live among other selves but they live in us and we in them.

Relations here are not external but internal so that we are our relations and cannot be selves save as we are members of each other. When there is strife in this community there is strife and pain in us and when it is at peace we have peace in ourselves. Here social memory is not what is written in books and preserved in libraries, but what—not without the mediation of books and monuments, to be sure—is our own past, living in every self. When we become members of such a community of selves we adopt its past as our own and thereby are changed in our present existence. So immigrants and their children do, for whom Pilgrims become true fathers and the men of the Revolution their own liberators; so we do in the Christian community when the prophets of the Hebrews become our prophets and the Lord of the early disciples is acknowledged as our Lord. Not what is after the flesh—that is what is externally seen—but what is after the spirit—what has become a part of our own lives as selves—is the important thing in this internal view. In our history association means community, the participation of each living self in a common memory and common hope no less than in a common world of nature.

It may be said that to speak of history in this fashion is to try to think with poets rather than with scientists. That is what we mean, for poets think of persons, purposes, and destinies. It is just their Jobs and Hamlets that are not dreamt of in philosophies which rule out from the company of true being whatever cannot be numbered or included in an impersonal pattern. Drama and epic set forth pattern too, but it is one of personal relations. Hence we may call internal history dramatic and its truth dramatic truth, though drama in this case does not mean fiction.

The relevance of this distinction between two histories to the subject of revelation must now have become apparent. When the evangelists of the New Testament and their successors pointed to history as the starting point of their faith and of their understanding of the world, it was internal history that they indicated. They did not speak of events, as impersonally apprehended, but rather of what had happened to them in their community. They recalled the critical point in their own life-time when they became aware of themselves in a new way as they came to know the self on whom they were dependent. They turned to a past which was not gone but which endured in them as their memory, making them what they were. So for the later church, history was always the story of "our fathers," of "our Lord," and of the actions of "our God."

The inspiration of Christianity has been derived from history, it is true, but not from history as seen by a spectator; the constant reference is to subjective events, that is to events in the lives of subjects. What distinguishes such historic recall from the private histories of mystics is that it refers to communal events, remembered by a community and in a community. Subjectivity here is not equivalent to isolation, non-verifiability and ineffability; our history can be communicated, and persons can refresh as well as criticize each other's memories of what has happened to them in the common life; on the basis of a common past they can think together about the common future.

Such history, to be sure, can only be confessed by the community, and in this sense it is esoteric. One cannot point to historic events in the lives of selves as though they were visible to any external point of view. Isaiah cannot say that in the year King Uzziah died God became visible in the temple nor Paul affirm that Jesus the Lord appears to travelers on the Damascus road. Neither will any concentration of attention on Isaiah and Paul, any detailed understanding of their historical situation, enable the observer to see what they saw. One must look with them and not at them to verify their visions, participate in their history rather than regard it if one would apprehend what they apprehended. The history of the inner life can only be confessed by selves who speak of what happened to them in the community of other selves.

III. Faith in Our History

The distinction between history as known by the pure and as apprehended by the practical reason, though it raises difficulties that must be met, does assist us to understand how it is possible for the word "revelation" to point to history and yet point to God also. It cannot point to God, as we have noted, if the history to which it directs attention is the chain of events that an impersonal eye or mind apprehends. For such history, abstracting from human selves, must also abstract events from the divine self and, furthermore, while it may furnish motives for belief in the occurrence of certain happenings, it does not invite trust in a living God.

The error frequently made in the Christian community, which has been the occasion for the rise of many difficulties in understanding and propagating the historical faith, has been the location of revelation in external history or in history as known from the non-participating point of view. So revelation has been identified with some miracle, whether this was the single act of a person or his whole life or the life of a community, such as Israel or the church. In this way certain events in external history were set apart as sacred, or a sacred history of one community has been opposed to the secular histories of other societies.

Sacred events were inserted into a context otherwise secular and the continuity between the two types of events denied. It was denied that the events of holy history were subject to the same type of explanation which might be offered for secular happenings; that so-called secular events might have a sacred meaning for those who participated in them as selves was not thought possible.

Much so-called orthodoxy identified revelation with the Scriptures and regarded the latter as wholly miraculous, the product of an inspiration which suspended the ordinary processes of human thought and guaranteed inerrancy. But to validate the Scriptural miracle, another needed to be inserted into history, since that which stands completely alone is an impenetrable mystery no matter how much astonishment it calls forth. So miraculous Scriptures were related to miracles in the realm of nature, to a sun that stood still, a virgin-born child, to water turned by a word into wine. Furthermore the psychological miracle of prophecy as a supernatural foretelling of events, as though by second-sight, was introduced to validate the wonder of the Bible. The consequence of this method of argument was that two systems of reality on the same plane — a natural, historical, rational system and a supernatural, super-historical and super-rational system — were set beside each other. They were on the same plane, perceived by the same organs of sense and apprehended by the same minds, yet there was no real relation between them. Revelation took place within the supernatural and super-historical system; reason operated in the natural series of events. The distinction between the history in which revelation occurred and that in which there was no revelation was transferred to persons and things having history; there were natural and unnatural events, persons, and groups. It was assumed that the differences between nature and super-nature were due not to the beholder's situation but to the things viewed while the point of view remained constant. Hence arose the conflict between history and faith. For sacred events in a secular context must be secularly apprehended, and to demand of men that they should exempt certain events in the chain of perceived happenings from the application of the laws or principles with which they apprehend the others is to ask the impossible or to make everything unintelligible. How much the tendency to self-defensiveness and self-glorification in Christianity contributed to this effort to exempt the faith and its history from the judgments applicable to ordinary events it is not possible to say. But it must be noted that the consequences of the attempt to isolate sacred from secular history led not only to fruitless quarrels with natural and social science but also to internal conflict and inconsistency since it tended to substitute belief in the occurrence of miraculous events for faith in God and invited dispute about the relative importance of many wonders.

If the distinction between history as seen from without by a pure reason and from within by a practical reason, and if the denial of the exclusive validity of either view be allowed, we are enabled to understand not only how faith and history may be associated but how in the nature of the case they must be allied. An inner history, life's flow as regarded from the point of view of living selves, is always an affair of faith. As long as a man lives he must believe in something for the sake of which he lives; without belief in something that makes life worth living man cannot exist. If, as Tolstoy points out in his *Confession,* man does not see the temporality and futility of the finite he will believe in the finite as worth living for; if he can no longer have faith in the value of the finite he will believe in the infinite or else die. Man as a practical, living being never exists without a god or gods; there are some things to which he must cling as the sources and goals of his activity, the centers of value. As a rule men are polytheists, referring now to this and now to that valued being as the source of life's meaning. Sometimes they live for Jesus' God, sometimes for country, and sometimes for Yale. For the most part they make gods out of themselves or out of the work of their own hands, living for their own glory as persons and as communities. In any case the faith that life is worth living and the definite reference of life's meaning to specific beings and values is as inescapable a part of human existence as the activity of reason. It is no less true that man is a believing animal in this sense than that he is a rational animal. Without such faith men might exist, but not as selves. Being selves, they as surely have something for which to live as being rational they have objects to understand.

Such faith in gods or in values for which men live is inseparable from internal history. It is the gods that give unity to the events of personal life. A nation has an internal history so far as its members have some common center of reference, some good for which they live together, whether that be an abstract value, such as equality or democracy, which unites them in common devotion, or whether it be the personalized community itself, such as Athena, or Britannia, or Columbia. A man has one internal history so far as he is devoted to one value. For the most part persons and communities do not have a single internal history because their faiths are various and the events of life cannot be related to one continuing and abiding god. They have "too many selves to know the one," too many histories, too many gods; alongside their published and professed history there are suppressed but true stories of inner life concentrated about gods of whom they are ashamed. Without a single faith there is no real unity of the self or of a community, therefore no unified inner history but only a multiplicity of memories and destinies. Inner history and inner faith belong together, as the existence of self and an object of devotion for the sake of which the self lives are inseparable.

The relation is something like that of animal faith in the existence of an external world and the data of experience. By an unconquerable compulsion, given with life itself, we believe in the reality of the trees we see, the ground we walk upon, the table, chairs, and houses we touch and use, the food and drink we taste. We count upon enduring realities and are not usually put to shame. No matter how refined our skepticism grows, how far into infinity we pursue the constituent elements of our objects, how ethereal to the mind's eye the natural world becomes, we rely upon the enduring stuff of our environment and we continue to be nourished and to be borne up. "Nature," that is to say human nature, is sufficient to dispel the clouds of skepticism, as Hume himself pointed out. Without this animal faith in a dependable external world we literally would not live as bodies, for if we were true skeptics we would be errant fools to eat food made up of sense-data only, to breathe an unsubstantial air with unreal lungs, to walk with unreal feet upon a non-existent earth toward imaginary goals. By faith, by counting upon persistent factors in our environment, we live as bodies and with our brains think out this common world. But what the factors are on which we can count, what the permanent possibilities of sensation are on which we can depend in thought and act, that we cannot know save through repeated and common experience. The necessity of animal faith in objective reality may be prior to all experience, but concrete faith in any particular element in our world as dependable does not exist save as it is made possible by sense experience. Faith is inseparably connected with experience; but neither faith nor sense-experience can be substitutes for each other. So also the faith of selves in a source of value or in a god is inseparable from the inner experience of selves, from what happens to them in their history. They cannot but believe that these events, the joys and sorrows of the self, have meaning, but what the meaning is cannot be known apart from inner history. The necessity of believing in a god is given with the life of selves, but what gods are dependable, which of them can be counted on day after day, and which are idols—products of erroneous imagination—cannot be known save through the experiences of inner history.

The standpoint of faith, of a self directed toward gods or God, and the standpoint of practical reason, of a self with values and with a destiny, are not incompatible; they are probably identical. To be a self is to have a god; to have a god is to have history, that is, events connected in a meaningful pattern; to have one god is to have one history. God and the history of selves in community belong together in inseparable union.

IV. Relations of Internal and External History

Though we may be persuaded that there is a valid distinction between history as lived and history as observed by the external spectator; though we may recognize a relative validity in either type while noting the close relation of faith and the life of selves to the practical knowledge of our destiny; yet questions about the relations of the two types of history are bound to arise in our minds. When we have understood that revelation must be looked for in the events that have happened to us, which live in our memory, we cannot refrain from asking ourselves how this history is related to the external accounts of our life. To such questions we must give some attention before we can proceed to a closer definition of the meaning of revelation.

The two-aspect theory of history, like the two-aspect theory of body and mind, may be made necessary by the recognition that all knowing is conditioned by the point of view, that the exaltation of differences of understanding into differences of being raises more problems than it solves, that the intimate relations of subjective and objective truth require the rejection of every extreme dualism. But it is evident that the theory does not solve the problem of unity in duality and duality in unity. It only states the paradox in a new form, and every paradox is the statement of a dilemma rather than an escape from it. It is important, of course, that a paradox be correctly stated and that false simplicity be avoided. We have made some advance toward a correct statement of our dilemma, we believe, when we have recognized that the duality of the history in which there is revelation and of the history in which there is none is not the duality of different groups or communities, or when we have understood that this dualism runs right through Christian history itself. We are enabled to see why we can speak of revelation only in connection with our own history without affirming or denying its reality in the history of other communities, into whose inner life we cannot penetrate without abandoning ourselves and our community. The two-aspect theory allows us to understand how revelation can be in history and yet not be identifiable with miraculous events as visible to an external observer, and how events that are revelatory in our history, sources of unconquerable certainty for us, can yet be analyzed in profane fashion by the observer. But the paradox remains. It is but another form of the two-world thinking in which Christianity is forever involved, and we need not expect that in thinking about history we shall be able to escape the dilemma that confronts our faith in every other sphere. One-world thinking, whether as this-worldliness or as other-worldliness, has always betrayed Christianity into the denial of some of its fundamental convictions. It will do so in the case of history no less than in metaphysics and ethics. But how to think in two-worldly terms without lapsing into ditheism remains a problem of great import for faith.

There is no speculative escape from the dilemma; that is to say, we cannot absorb internal history into external history nor yet transcend both practical and objective points of view in such a way as to gain a knowledge of history superior to both and able to unite them into a new whole. If we begin with the spectator's knowledge of events, we cannot proceed to the participant's apprehension. There is no continuous movement from an objective inquiry into the life of Jesus to a knowledge of him as the Christ who is our Lord. Only a decision of the self, a leap of faith, a *metanoia* or revolution of the mind can lead from observation to participation and from observed to lived history. And this is true of all other events in sacred history.

It may be thought that the problem of the relation of inner and outer history can be solved by a determination of what the events, visible in two aspects, really are in themselves. But the idea of events-in-themselves like that of things-in-themselves is an exceedingly difficult one. The ultimate nature of an event is not what it is in its isolation but what it is in its connection with other events. Such knowledge of the nature of events is beyond the possibility of the finite point of view. Being finite souls with finite minds in finite bodies, men are confined to a double and partial knowledge which is yet not knowledge of double reality.

Though there be no metaphysical or meta-historical solution of the problem of historical dualism, there is a practical solution. Though we cannot speak of the way in which the two aspects of historical events are ultimately related in the event-for-God, we can describe their functional relationship for us. Such a description must once more be given confessionally, not as a statement of what all men ought to do but as a statement of what we have found it necessary to do in the Christian community on the basis of the faith which is our starting point.

In the first place, beginning with internal knowledge of the destiny of self and community, we have found it necessary in the Christian church to accept the external views of ourselves which others have set forth and to make these external histories events of spiritual significance. To see ourselves as others see us, or to have others communicate to us what they see when they regard our lives from the outside, is to have a moral experience. Every external history of ourselves, communicated to us, becomes an event in inner history. So the outside view of democracy offered by Marxists has become an event in the inner history of democracy. It has responded to that external view with defense but also with self-criticism and reformation. External histories of Christianity have become important events in its inner history. Celsus's description

of the sources of Christian belief and his criticism of miraculous super-
naturalism, Gibbon's, Feuerbach's, and Kautsky's accounts of Christianity, other surveys made from the points of view of idealistic or
positivistic philosophy, of Judaism or of the history of religion — these
have all been events in the internal history of Christianity. The church
has had to respond to them. Though it knew that such stories were not
the truth about it, it willingly or unwillingly, sooner or later, recognized
a truth about it in each one. In so far as it apprehended these events in
its history, these descriptions and criticisms of itself, with the aid of faith
in the God of Jesus Christ it discerned God's judgment in them and
made them occasions for active repentance. Such external histories have
helped to keep the church from exalting itself as though its inner life
rather than the God of that inner life were the center of its attention
and the ground of its faith. They have reminded the church of the earth-
en nature of the vessel in which the treasure of faith exists. In this practical way external history has not been incompatible with inner life but
directly contributory to it.

Secondly, just because the Christian community remembers the
revelatory moment in its own history, it is required to regard all events,
even though it can see most of them only from an external point of
view, as workings of the God who reveals himself, and so to trace with
piety and disinterestedness, so far as its own fate is concerned, the ways
of God in the lives of men. It is necessary for the Christian community, living in faith, to look upon all the events of time and to try to find
in them the workings of one mind and will. This is necessary because
the God who is found in inner history, or rather who reveals himself
there, is not only the God of spiritual life, but the universal God, the
creator not only of the events through which he discloses himself but
also of all other happenings. The standpoint of the Christian community is limited, being in history, faith, and sin. But what is seen from this
standpoint is unlimited. Faith cannot get to God save through historic
experience, just as reason cannot get to nature save through sense-experience. But as reason, having learned through limited experience an
intelligible pattern of reality, can seek the evidence of a like pattern in
all other experience, so faith, having apprehended the divine self in its
own history, can and must look for the manifestation of the divine self
in all other events. Thus prophets, for whom the revelation of God was
connected with his mighty acts in the deliverance of Israel from bondage,
found the marks of that God's working in the histories of all the nations.
The Christian community must turn in like manner from the revelation
of the universal God in a limited history to the recognition of his rule
and providence in all events of all times and communities. Such histories must be regarded from the outside to be sure; in events so

regarded the meeting of human and divine selves cannot be recorded, but all the secondary causes, all the factors of political and social life, can be approached with the firm conviction of an underlying unity due to the pervasive presence of the one divine self. It is not possible to describe external history by reference to miraculous deeds, but the revelation of the one God makes it possible and necessary to approach the multiplicity of all events in all times with the confidence that unity may be found, however hard the quest for it. Where faith is directed to many gods only pluralistic and unconnected histories can be written, if indeed there is any impulsion to understand or write history. Where, through a particular set of historical experiences, the conviction has been established that all events have one source and goal, it becomes possible to seek out the uniformities, the dependable patterns of process. That such history, though a product of piety, is not pious history, designed to exalt the inner life of the religious community or to emphasize the importance of religious factors in social life, must be evident. A faithful external history is not interested in faith but in the ways of God, and the more faithful it is the less it may need to mention his name or refer to the revelation in which he was first apprehended, or rather in which he first apprehended the believer. In this sense an external history finds its starting point or impulsion in an internal history.

Not only is the external history of other selves and communities a necessity and a possible work of faith on the part of Christians, but an external history of itself is its inescapable duty for two reasons. The revelation of God in history is, as we shall see, the revelation of a self. To know God is to be known of him, and therefore also to know the self as it is reflected in God. The church's external history of itself may be described as an effort to see itself with the eyes of God. The simultaneous, unified knowledge from within and from without that we may ascribe to God is indeed impossible to men, but what is simultaneous in his case can in a measure be successive for us. The church cannot attain an inclusive, universal point of view but it can attempt to see the reflection of itself in the eyes of God. What it sees in that reflection is a finite, created, limited, corporeal being, alike in every respect to all the other beings of creations. To describe that vision in detail, to see the limited, human character of its founder, the connections between itself and a Judaism to which it often, in false pride, feels superior, between its sacraments and mystery faiths, between Catholicism and feudalism, Protestantism and capitalism, to know itself as the chief of sinners and the most mortal of societies—all this is required of it by a revelation that has come to it through its history.

Moreover, though there is no transition from external observation to internal participation save by decision and faith, yet it is also true

43

that the internal life does not exist without external embodiment. The memory which we know within ourselves as pure activity must have some static aspect which an objective science, we may believe, will in time discover in the very structure of the neural system. What the neural system is to the memory of an individual self, books and monuments are to a common memory. Without the Bible and the rites of the institutional church the inner history of the Christian community could not continue, however impossible it is to identify the memory of the community with the documents. Though we cannot point to what we mean by revelation by directing attention to the historic facts as embodied and as regarded from without, we can have no continuing inner history through which to point without embodiment. "Words without thoughts never to heaven go" but thoughts without words never remain on earth. Moreover such is the alternation of our life that the thought which becomes a word can become thought again only through the mediation of the word; the word which becomes flesh can become word for us again only through the flesh. External history is the medium in which internal history exists and comes to life. Hence knowledge of its external history remains a duty of the church.

In all this we have only repeated the paradox of Chalcedonian christology and of the two-world ethics of Christianity. But it is necessary to repeat it in our time, especially in view of the all too simple definitions of history and revelation that fail to take account of the duality in union which is the nature of Christian life and history.

We have not yet succeeded in saying what we mean by revelation but have indicated the sphere in which revelation is to be found. That sphere is internal history, the story of what happened to us, the living memory of the community.

Apologetics, Criticism, and the Loss of Narrative Interpretation

Hans Frei

Biblical hermeneutics was theory of exegesis, Gottlob Wilhelm Meyer said. In the second half of the eighteenth century when general (non-theological) biblical hermeneutics developed rapidly in Germany, its principles of exegesis were pivoted between historical criticism and religious apologetics. The explicative meaning of the narrative texts came to be their ostensive or ideal reference. Their applicative meaning or religious meaningfulness was either a truth of revelation embodied in an indispensable historical event or a universal spiritual truth known independently of the texts but exemplified by them, or, finally, a compromise between the two positions amounting to the claim that while the historical fact is indispensable to revelation, the meaningfulness of revelation depends on its being set in some broader religious or moral context. No nonreferential explication existed until the mythical thesis was hesitantly applied to the biblical literature, but even "myth" as a critical-analytical category was not a complete change from meaning as ostensive reference. Almost everyone, a few of the Deists and Reimarus excepted, affirmed that explication harmonized with application. From left to right everybody thought that the Bible was religiously meaningful.

Hans Frei, "Apologetics, Criticism, and the Loss of Narrative Interpretation," in his *The Eclipse of Biblical Narrative* (New Haven: Yale University Press, 1974), pp. 124-142.

Hans Frei

I. The Gospel Story and the Hermeneutics of Mediating Theology

The chief beneficiary of this conservatism in general biblical hermeneutics was the New Testament story. Everyone who believed that
the sense of the gospel narratives is the history of Jesus the Messiah
believed also that the notion of historical salvation or revelation is itself
meaningful. On the other hand, people who believed that monotheism,
immortality, and the realization of man's happiness through altruism
are the substance of man's religion, equally available to all men at all
times without any special revelation, discerned this as the true sense of
the gospel narratives, the messianic history being merely their outward
trapping. Nobody said that the *real* sense of the narratives was religiously meaningless or anachronistic.

The first of these perspectives actually conceals two divergent
views. The Calvinist and Puritan inheritors in England and the Supernaturalists in Germany simply took it that all the narratives refer to actual events and describe them just as they happened. The mediating theologians who also commanded much of the biblical scholarship of the
eighteenth century, first the Latitudinarians in England and then the Neologians in Germany, agreed with them to some extent, specifically on the
necessity of a factual interpretation of the story of Jesus and a revealed
religion. Beyond that, however, they leaned in the other, more ratio-
nalistic, direction. Jesus was indeed the Messiah, so that a historical faith
is necessary for one's spiritual well-being. However, this faith has meaning only as an indispensable solution to a universally experienced moral
lack or dilemma. Thus the explicative sense of the narrative of Jesus the
Messiah is indeed that of ostensive reference, but its religious application or meaningfulness is derived in part from general moral experience
and religious principles and not only from the Bible itself.

Thinkers like Locke suggested that historical and spiritual faith
coincide. The story of man's creation and fall refers to mankind's general
religious and moral experience directly and not only by way of the historical incorporation of the experience into the specific factual history
of Adam. Sometimes this independent appeal to man's universal moral
need, which one may understand at least in part without awareness of
the biblical story, is quite direct, as in Conyers Middleton's allegorical
treatment of Genesis 1–3. Sometimes the appeal takes a more ambiguous
form as in Locke's *On the Reasonableness of Christianity*,[1] where the author
takes the story literally but still argues the case for the need of redemption on a more general basis.

1. Pages 1-9, 165f., passim.

In other words, the mediating theologians rejected the Calvinists', Puritans', and Supernaturalists' version of the notion of sin in which its meaningfulness was strictly dependent on its making specific ostensive, referential sense as history, told by the particular story of Adam and his progeny. These conservatives believed that the historical event of Adam's fall involves the guilt of all his descendants. The divine economy which has been at work in this historical sequence from eternity compensates for the disaster by condemning Adam's race to eternal punishment and misery, except for the salvation offered some in Jesus Christ's redeeming passion which had also been prepared from eternity.

The Latitudinarians and Neologians rejected this harsh version of sin based on the strict ostensive construal of the story in Genesis, and the consequent applicative interpretation of the story by a doctrine of original and ubiquitously inherited guilt and condemnation to eternal torment. But they turned their backs equally on the Deists' denial of the notion of human sinfulness in any form and on the concomitant need of a redeeming historical revelation. Mankind, it seemed to the mediating thinkers, having been gravely affected in its moral capacity and thus shorn of its natural immortality, proper moral understanding, and strength, needs a redeemer, a fact to which our natural experience in the world testifies. Redemption in history becomes intelligible from its natural context in our moral and religious experience, so that the wise man readily appreciates that rational, natural religion and morality need to be perfected from beyond themselves by a revealed religion which is above rather than against them. The mediating version of the concepts of sin and revelation may be sharper than that: the redeeming historical revelation may in large part contradict rather than perfect our natural religion and morality; but even then it remains certain that without our antecedent awareness, either positive or negative, of such morality and religion, the revelation has no applicative meaning. Without that antecedent context, the Bible's story of historical revelation would be religiously meaningless.

God's design of man's nature toward the realization of perfect happiness had been vitiated by man's action. One way or another the need and hiatus created by this situation are eventually met by the coming of Jesus. The historicity of Jesus, including his specific time and place, is obviously not deducible from the general human situation and experience. The fact that he lived and really was the Messiah would have to be demonstrated by external or factual evidence such as miracles, the probability of his resurrection from the dead, and the general reliability of the written witness to him. But the religious meaningfulness of historical redemption or revelation, in contrast to the factual reference or ostensive meaning of the gospel narratives, depends on there being an antecedent or concomitant religious context, independent of the narratives, within which to interpret them.

Among more conservative mediating thinkers it was customary to augment this argument from the religious appropriateness of the Redeemer for the human situation with an argument that historical conditions when he came were exactly ripe for his appearance. Mediating theology, firmly committed to the positivity of Christian religion, nonetheless succeeded in reversing the direction of the interpretation of the biblical stories from precritical days, so that they now made sense by their inclusion in a wider frame of meaning.

The religious sensibility and philosophical outlook to which mediating theologians appealed changed drastically after the eighteenth century, but the logic of the argument and its use of the Bible remained essentially the same. Instead of external evidence, there were appeals to a leap of faith in the miracle of historical redemption, with or without corroboration by scientific historical investigation of the actual life of the historical Jesus. Instead of man's moral imperfection, there were appeals to internal conditions such as despair and the longing for the paradox of grace, or external conditions such as mankind's unredeemed alienation from itself in the process of its history and the concomitant loss of man's true self-hood in alien social structures and institutions. But the mediating theological argument remained the same: the explicative meaning of the gospel narratives is their ostensive reference to Jesus the Messiah. The correlative, applicative, or religious meaningfulness of the narratives is at least in part provided by their answering a universal human condition or need of which we are all at least implicitly aware. Their explicative sense is quite distinct from, but in harmony with, their religious meaning. The principle of general hermeneutics applying to their *explication* is that meaning is logical coherence in the statement of a proposition, and also that meaning is reference. The principle of general hermeneutics for the *applicative* interpretation is the full or partial pertinence of mankind's general religious and moral experience to the biblical narratives at issue.

In these respects the theology and hermeneutics of the mediating theological thinkers remained constant down to the middle of the twentieth century. Whatever their differences, John Locke, Samuel Clarke, Joseph Butler, Johann Salomo Semler, Johann Joachim Spalding, Friedrich Schleiermacher, Albrecht Ritschl, Wilhelm Herrmann, Emil Brunner, Rudolf Bultmann, Karl Rahner, Gerhard Ebeling, Wolfhart Pannenberg, and Jürgen Moltmann all agreed on these principles. Most of them have disavowed that they were out to "prove" the truth of Christianity, chiefly the assertion that Jesus Christ is the Redeemer—the claim with which (as it seemed to them) all other Christian doctrines must harmonize. But they have all been agreed that one way or another the religious *meaningfulness* (as distinct from demonstration of the truth) of the claim could, indeed must, be perspicuous through its relation to other accounts of general human experience.

To the mediating theologians, the unique truth of Christianity is actually discoverable only by divine, self-communicating grace (or revelation). And this, in turn, has to be grasped through the venture of an act of faith which remains just as risky and uncertain as the grace or revelation, to which it refers, stays indemonstrable. But the possibility of such a miracle — for it is nothing less—and the meaningfulness of what is communicated by it, involve more than an appeal to divine authority. They involve an appeal to the appropriateness of this miracle to the human condition; and that condition is one that all right-thinking men can or should be able to recognize. In other words, there is an area of human experience on which the light of the Christian gospel and that of natural, independent insight shine at the same time, illumining it in the same way. The degree to and manner in which the one mode of insight has to be bolstered by the other is a matter of difference among various mediating theologians, and they have invented a wide variety of often very complex ways of stating their views on this subject. But on the substantive point that both modes must be present and correlated they are all agreed. There is no such thing as revelation without someone to receive it, and receive it, moreover, as a significant answer to or illumination of general life questions.

I have used the term apologetics to cover (among other things) this appeal to a common ground between analysis of human experience by direct natural thought and by some distinctively Christian thought. This has been the chief characteristic of the mediating theology of modernity. Usually, apologetic mediating theologians have accused their predecessors of wanting to "prove" or "secure" the Christian gospel (that saving truth for the human condition comes through Jesus Christ), while they themselves only wanted to indicate how it could be "meaningful" to "modern man." And when their successors came along, they in turn usually said the same two things. Modern mediating theology gives an impression of constantly building, tearing down, rebuilding, and tearing down again the same edifice. (Notable instances of this procedure are the revolt of nineteenth-century Christian liberals against the "evidence"-seeking theology of the eighteenth century, the revolt of the so-called dialectical or neo-orthodox theologians against nineteenth-century liberalism in the 1920s, and contemporary arguments in favor of the meaningfulness of a specific Christian "language game" among all the other language games people play.)

The mediating theologians have always said that given the pride and perversity of men, the belief that Jesus is Messiah may be an offense to them. Moreover, it may be difficult in view of the increasingly "secular," nonreligious thought of "modern man." But they also had to insist that it does make sense and is not experientially nonsensical. Furthermore, in regard to this central affirmation, at once historically factual and religiously true, the Bible meant what it said and is our indispensable source for the information. Even if the Bible generally no longer authorized what one believed—by providing either the reliably informative contents or the warrants for believing them — it had to provide and does provide the indispensable, factually informative, and religiously meaningful content in this instance.

II. Religious Apologetics and the Loss of Narrative Reading

The left-wing opponents of meditating and supernaturalist theology had of course to deny that these texts had to be read in this particular way, grounding religions in factual historical assertions. But mediating and left-wing parties were agreed that the criteria for what makes sense, as well as what can be religiously or morally significant, were general: whether or not the Bible provides us with reliable factual information, and whether or not this information is what the texts providing it are really all about, the Bible does not provide us with special canons by which religious ideas or claims become meaningful that wouldn't make sense in a wider context of meaning. It is no exaggeration to say that all across the theological spectrum the great reversal had taken place; interpretation was a matter of fitting the biblical story into another world with another story rather than incorporating that world into the biblical story.

No one who pretended to any sort of theology or religious reflection at all wanted to go counter to the "real" applicative meaning of biblical texts, once it had been determined what it was, even if one did not believe them on their own authority. Hence the right-wing and mediating theologians agreed that the New Testament made the affirmation about Jesus being Savior literally, and that it was to be understood that way (though this agreement did not always cover either the miracles he was reported to have performed or those with which he was purportedly associated, especially the virgin birth; nor, as we have noted, did it cover literal acceptance of such Old Testament accounts as the six-day creation or the fall, in the Book of Genesis). And those on the left of course denied that one either has to or can take this affirmation literally. Hence they denied that this is the real meaning of the texts, or they said it is impossible to find out from the texts the real shape of the occurrences to which they refer, e.g. what Jesus was really like or what he thought of himself, so that there is no way of checking the claim against the facts. Hence (once again) the texts must have meaning in some way other than literal or factual.

But almost no one, left, right, or center, wanted to be in the position of affirming at the same time that Jesus as the unique, indispensable Savior is the explicative sense of the texts, *and* that this affirmation is irrelevant or of merely anachronistic interest. If one affirmed the Messiahship of Jesus as the explicative sense of the story, one also affirmed it applicatively. If one denied this application one usually also denied it as the explicative sense. In this respect left-wing thinkers like Lessing and Strauss were apologists for the gospel narratives just as much as mediating or supernaturalist theologians: the explicative sense of the gospel stories is finally not their reference to a literal Messiah; this is only the stage of historical consciousness they represent. Their outward form or their real explicative sense is more general and harmonizes with universal religion. To have claimed otherwise would have meant saying not only that the *authority* of the Bible for belief is gone, but also that this portion of the Bible makes no religious sense at all, or else that its explication may have no carry-over whatever to application. It would have suggested that the truth claim cannot be affirmed and, additionally, that what it means is clear, and it is something that cannot have a negatively or positively significant religious meaning for anybody today. This position was universally rejected among theologians and non-theologians. One either claimed that the texts really do mean what they state, that salvation comes through Jesus Christ alone and that this is a significant and not an anachronistic statement; or else one said that this, taken literally, would be an insignificant statement and therefore cannot be what the texts mean. And so it has, by and large, remained to the present day among those who have thought about the matter.

The question is: Why should the possibility be ruled out that this is indeed the meaning of the texts, and that it may well be religiously anachronistic or at least without direct religious consequence for anyone today? At one level the answer is very simple: whereas historical criticism had had from its beginning a religiously neutral basis—no matter whether in fact any historian did, or for that matter can, keep his religious and moral convictions from interfering with the course and outcome of his investigations—the situation was very different in hermeneutics which was, as we have seen, apologetically implicated.

Certainly this was true for Protestant thought before the beginning of the period of our investigation, even though the cutting edge of the apologetics was different then, namely, to maintain against Roman Catholics that the Bible made sense (usually literal sense and/or figurative sense) without interpretive assistance either from the Church's magisterial office or from its accumulated doctrinal heritage. But it was true in a different sense in the eighteenth century. The specter now barely visible on the horizon was that important, indeed hitherto central portions of the Bible, no matter if they made referential sense, did not make abiding religious or moral sense at all, so that they are in effect really obsolete. And the accounts concerning Jesus as Messiah might be among these. What appeared, but not even sufficiently distinctly to be noticed by anyone but a few Deists who were mostly regarded as disgruntled cranks, was the suspicion that the accounts mean what they say, but that what they say is not only untrue or unverifiable but is an insignificant claim as well—except as an ancient superstition about miraculous and personal divine intervention. That is to say, for instance, that the texts concerning unique redemption exclusively through Jesus cannot (in the barbaric jargon of a twentieth-century school of theology) be demythologized, because they have no other meaning than what they say. And what they say may no longer mean anything religiously significant. To explicate them properly is to erect a formidable barrier to any possible applicative sense. That was the impossible option which no thinker across the religious spectrum would have countenanced then or, for that matter, today.

With regard to the gospel narratives, the apologetic impulse from left to right meant that they could finally be interpreted only in two ways. Either their explicative and applicative meaning (for Supernaturalist and mediating theologians) is that of reference to Jesus as the Messiah in historical fact, or (for Rationalists and their successors) this is only their mythological form, their substance being something else, e.g. the presentation of the individual, paradigmatic form of a message about true human life as God intended it. This message is rendered by way of a shape of life and a teaching authentic in quality and so compelling in authority that to grasp this possibility, to understand anything about it, is identical with deciding for or against the message.

Now two options were automatically eliminated by this apologetically motivated disjunctive alternative. First, there was Reimarus's claim that the story means what it says and is a lie. But second, the disjunction eliminates the explication of these accounts as primarily "narrative"— that they tell a story of salvation, an inalienable ingredient of which is the rendering of Jesus as Messiah, and that whether or not he was so in historical fact, or thought of himself as Messiah (i.e. whether the story refers or not), or whether the notion of a Messiah is still a meaningful notion, are different questions altogether. To the "narrative" perspective, these latter questions would have to do not with meaning or hermeneutics but with an entirely separable historical and theological judgment. Hermeneutically, it may well be the most natural thing to say that what these accounts are about is the story of Jesus the Messiah, even if there was no such person; or, if there was, he was not in fact the Messiah; and quite regardless of whether or not he (if he did exist) thought of himself as such; and regardless finally of the possible applicative significance of such a story and of the messianic concept to a modern context. Many elements may enter into the way a story makes sense, but its sheer narrative shape is an important and distinctive one which should not be confused with others—especially that of estimating its abiding religious meaning and that of assessing the narrative's cultural context or the reliability of the "facts" told in the story.

The apologetic urge from left to right, for which explication and application had to walk in harmony, was only one reason for the strange eclipse of the realistic narrative option in a situation in which many observers actually paid heed to that future. Hermeneutics stood between religious apologetics and historical criticism, and these two worked against the narrative option. The historical critics in particular were the beneficiaries of the definition of meaning as ostensive reference, an early triumph of which we observed in the conflict over the fulfillment of prophecy.

Unlike the religious apologist, the historian as such had no interest in applicative interpretation but only in explication. For the historian the meaning of historical or history-like statements is the spatio-temporal occurrences or conditions to which they refer. His business is to reconstruct the most likely course of these putative events or, if he finds evidence that there were none, to give credible historical explanations for the accounts having been written in their specific way. In the process he must appeal to the ordinary, i.e. nonmiraculous, experience of men, to the cultural conditions under which the accounts were written, to the most likely specific motives for writing them, to the process by which they came to be, and finally to any parallels he may discover to the specific writings he is analyzing. These are the explanatory procedures one applies in rendering what counts as a satisfactory historical explanation. The explication of the statements is either their ostensive reference or a historical situation accounting for, and in turn illumined by, the statements. The real history of the biblical narratives in which the historian is interested is not what is narrated or the fruit of its narrative shape; rather, it is that to which the story refers or the conditions that substitute for such reference. In short, he is interested not in the text as such but in some reconstructive context to which the text "really" refers and which renders it intelligible.

Hans Frei

It is well to recall the example of the debate over the fulfillment of prophecy. Its upshot was the sharp logical distinction of historical judgment from explicative (in particular, literal) sense, and the immediate reintegration of the two things under the dominance of an understanding of meaning as an ostensive reference. This is the philosophical context of historical criticism. Clearly, historical-critical analysis can be no more sympathetic than religious apologetics to an interpretation of the narrative text for which the narrative shape, theme, and course are of the greatest interest because they constitute the story's meaning, an interpretation that is not governed, as historical procedure is bound to be, by a theory of meaning either as ostensive (or ideal) reference or as an extension of such reference. This is not to say of course that historical explication is "wrong." It *is* to say, however, that the philosophical or conceptual apparatus, including the theory of meaning, underlying historical criticism of the gospel narratives tends to move it away from every explication of texts not directly governed by a referential theory of meaning or by the cognate identification of meaning with knowledge.

The situation has remained the same since the eighteenth century. The historical critic does something other than narrative interpretation with a narrative because he looks for what the narrative refers to or what reconstructed historical context outside itself explains it. He is not wrong when he does this, but unfortunately he is also not apt to see the logical difference between what he does and what a narrative interpretation might be and what it might yield. He is likely to think instead that a procedure that is neither a practical religious use of the narratives (a use which he sometimes though not always countenances), nor yet his own method with its particular conceptual tools, simply cannot exist; and certainly he does not believe that it can have the serious implications for a religious use of the narratives that he expects from the fruits of his own procedure. Nor would he easily tolerate the notion that his own procedure and narrative interpretation might have to live side by side without yielding a single overall fruit for a given narrative, that the two procedures might in given cases have divergent outcomes impossible to bring into harmonious balance.

In any case, whether one attributes it to the historical situation of the eighteenth-century interpreters or to their unhappy inability to make some appropriate logical distinctions, neither religious apologists nor historical critics were finally able to take proper and serious account of the narrative feature of the biblical stories. And this is all the more striking because all of them noted it and one way or another thought it significant. . . .

54

III. The English Novel, Its Cultural Context, and the Bible

Beyond the level of technical explanations for the lack of narrative interpretation, there are some interesting cultural considerations to explain this curious state of affairs. England and Germany were the two countries in which discussion of the biblical narratives was most intense in the eighteenth century. In England, where a serious body of realistic narrative literature and a certain amount of criticism of that literature was building up, there arose no corresponding cumulative tradition of criticism of the biblical writings, and that included no narrative interpretation of them. In Germany, on the other hand, where a body of critical analysis as well as general hermeneutics of the biblical writings built up rapidly in the latter half of the eighteenth century, there was no simultaneous development of realistic prose narrative and its critical appraisal.

In England, the novel was making an increasingly significant impact on a large section of the reading public. A critical literature began to develop about it in the latter part of the century, the critics noting the break of the genre with that of the romance from which it arose. *Don Quixote*, ridiculing the figure of the heroic knight of romantic tales, was usually held to signal the historical beginnings of the shift. Mrs. Clara Reeve, a minor but significant writer and critic of the day, distinguished between the novel and the whole variety of romances both in their character and their effect:

> The Romance is an heroic fable, which treats of fabulous persons and things.—The novel is a picture of real life and manners, and of the times in which it is written. The Romance in lofty and elevated language, describes what never happened nor is likely to happen.—The novel gives a familiar relation to such things, as pass every day before our eyes, such as may happen to our friend, or to ourselves; and the perfection of it, is to represent every scene, in so easy and natural a manner, and to make them appear so probable, as to deceive us into a persuasion (at least while we are reading) that all is real, until we are affected by the joys and distresses of the persons in the story, as if they were our own.[2]

The novel developed at the same time as a cognate change in the writing and estimate of historical narrative took place. Both were regarded as having great moral utility, instructing those who are capable of learning, among them especially the young and impressionable, in

---

2. Clara Reeve, *The Progress of Romance* (2 vols. in 1, 1785), vol. 1, p. 1111.

private virtue and public duty, and a due knowledge of human nature and character. Mrs. Reeve was rather defensive about the instructional value of the novel, knowing that the more toplofty among her gentle readers looked down on many a novel's Gothic weirdness and gossipy appeal to lust, greed, fashion, and vanity. All the same, she firmly maintained that this literary form is well suited to her obviously and uprightly moralistic view of life.[3]

David Hume, hardly given to pious moralizing, had no qualms in claiming that the study of history profited its perusers greatly because, in addition to amusing the fancy, "it improves the understanding, and . . strengthens virtue,"[4] although there is good reason to believe that he became progressively disenchanted about the lessons to be drawn from the past as he progressed in his own *History of England*.[5] Even so, Hume's earlier confident spirit was typical of the contemporary outlook on history writing, deeply influenced by the widely disseminated reading of the classical Greek and Roman historians, whose aim had been the inculcation of practical lessons from a knowledge of the human past.[6] Bolingbroke's famous phrase that history was "philosophy teaching by example" embodied the common view. The determined search for historical analogy made the tale an ancient historian told, as well as his purpose in writing, as contemporary to the present as was the customary historical setting of a novel, which usually was "of the times in which it is written" (as Mrs. Reeve said), and for the same didactic reason.

The practical usefulness common to history and the novel was but one aspect of the increasingly acknowledged similarity between them, including common procedures in the writing of both. One modern commentator on eighteenth-century writing distinguishes between the romance and the novel by attributing to the latter an awareness "of the ill-defined frontier between history and story, between truth and lie, between reality and fiction."[7]

It appeared that the frontier we cannot define we nonetheless

---

3. Ibid., vol. 2, pp. 77ff., 92ff.

4. Hume, "Of the Study of History," in *Of the Standard of Taste and Other Essays,* ed. S. W. Lenz (Indianapolis: Bobbs Merrill, 1965), p. 96.

5. See Leo Braudy, *Narrative Form in History and Fiction: Hume, Fielding, Gibbon* (Princeton: Princeton University Press, 1970), p. 85: "Hume's *History* purported at its outset to be a repository of political and moral philosophy. But in Hume's final state of mind the precepts for direct action that can be drawn from his work are few indeed."

6. See James William Johnson, *The Formation of English Neo-Classical Thought* (Princeton: Princeton University Press, 1967), ch. 2, esp. pp. 43ff.

7. Bruce Wardropper, quoted by Keith Stewart, "History, Poetry, and the Terms of Fiction in the Eighteenth Century," *Modern Philology* 66, 2 (Nov. 1968), p. 111n. 7.

know full well, so that consistency in ill-definition became important in maintaining the fiction that fiction is fact, to a degree that amounted to common and open conspiracy between writer and reader rather than to a mere willing suspension of disbelief on the part of the latter. So novels announced themselves as histories, not really intending to fool anybody for very long; and Samuel Richardson wrote to Bishop Warburton that he wished to maintain the fiction that Clarissa's letters were real, not because he wanted them to be "*thought* genuine," but, among other reasons, in order "to avoid hurting that kind of Historical Faith which Fiction itself is generally read with, tho' we know it to be Fiction."[8]

Fielding gave up part of the convention of pretense, but he maintained another and more significant part, that of *verisimilitude* to historical fact. He doubted the historians' ability to describe the real character of men from their public role and hence the explanation of historical movement from the description of public stance. He felt all the more keenly the responsibility of the novelist, precisely in his role as historian of private character:

> we who deal in private characters, who search into the most retired recesses and draw forth examples of virtue and vice from holes and corners of the world, are in a more dangerous situation. As we have no public notoriety, no concurrent testimony, no records to support and corroborate what we deliver, it becomes us not only to keep within the limits of possibility but of probability too; and this more especially in painting what is greatly good and amiable. Knavery and folly, though never so exorbitant, will more easily meet with assent, for ill nature adds great support and strength to faith.[9]

A. D. McKillop summarizes the mid-century development in fictional writing: "The emphasis shifted from a claim to actuality to a claim to probability, particularly as regards the possibilities of human nature."[10] But the pretense in either guise, actuality or verisimilitude, bespeaks a preference of "fact" over "fiction," if one equates fact with likelihood not only of character and occurrence but of broad societal and natural context as well. All of the novelist's techniques were designed to press that preference. As far as possible he wrote not episodes but continuous "historical" narrative, as life indeed is lived, even if he felt at liberty, as Fielding did, to lengthen or compress time spans in accordance with the intrinsic interest and importance of specific

---

8. Ibid., p. 111. See A. D. McKillop, *The Early Masters of English Fiction* (Lawrence: University of Kansas Press, 1956), p. 42.

9. Henry Fielding, *The History of Tom Jones* (New York: New American Library, 1963), Book 8, ch. 1, p. 338.

10. McKillop, *The Early Masters of English Fiction*, p. 42.

incidents. After all he, like the contemporary historian, was no mere chronicler or newspaper editor. He depicted neither heroic figures nor abstract qualities inherent in persons. He described recognizable sequences, and vices and virtues proceeding from credible motives on the part of recognizably human personalities. And these people were set within a specific (usually close to contemporary) historical time and within a definite and recognizable economic and social structure, interplay with which served to focus their character, station, and identity.

The writer's techniques did not merely express his preference for history-like reality over the incredible. He also used them to cross the obscure frontier from history to history-like fiction, while maintaining the integrity and similarity of the territory on either side. Richardson told his stories in letter form; most of the early novelists adopted the fictitious pose of editor, biographer, or historiographer. Fielding regarded his work as prose epic, deliberately reminding the reader at regular intervals that he, the reader, is not confronting reality immediately but only under the controlled guidance of the author, who remains a distinct and significant presence external to the narrative he holds before the reader as the image of reality.[11]

Once inside the territory of fiction, everything was depicted realistically or in history-like fashion. This does not mean that startling things might not be interspersed with the ordinary. On the contrary, of course; but they did not violate the rule of "familiarity." The novelists would have agreed with Diderot's dictum that the writer's art rejects the miraculous but not the marvelous since the natural order brings together the most extraordinary accidents. (It was up to the writer to see to it that the extraordinary did not appear contrived.) Fielding said substantially the same thing as Diderot:

> if the historian will confine himself to what really happened and utterly reject any circumstance which, though never so well attested, he must be well assured is false, he will sometimes fall into the marvellous, but never into the incredible. . . . It is by falling into fiction, therefore, that we generally offend against this rule of deserting probability, which the historian seldom if ever quits till he forsakes his character and commences a writer of romance.[12]

Unlike other forms of literature in England, this burgeoning tradition of prose fiction, hewing close to worldly reality—its logic not sim-

---

11. See R. A. Donovan, *The Shaping Vision: Imagination in the English Novel from Defoe to Dickens* (Ithaca: Cornell University Press, 1966), pp. 245f.; also Braudy, ch. 4, who contrasts Fielding favorably with Hume because the latter in his *History* does not speak enough in his own voice.

12. Fielding, *Tom Jones*, p. 338.

ply that of illustrated theme or system but that of cumulative rendering of persons and reality through narrative continuity in time—suffered no interruption during the romantic era. "Scott and Jane Austen are doubtless just what they would have been had the Preface to *Lyrical Ballads* not been written, and neither one gives any apparent indication of belonging to the same century as Byron, Delacroix, and Berlioz."[13] (But even the contrast between romantic lyricism and realistic depiction, clear though it is, ought not to be exaggerated: Wordsworth in the *Preface* and Coleridge in *Biographia Literaria* both draw attention to the imitation of real life, rusticity in particular in Wordsworth's poetry, though in the controversy between them Coleridge clearly works against and draws back from Wordsworth's tendency to idealize or universalize rustic speech and character, and from Wordsworth's belief that poetry can be a direct embodiment of such speech.[14])

In England the development toward the full scope of what Erich Auerbach called serious modern realism proceeded neither so dramatically nor so completely as it did in France in the nineteenth century. But basically the development was similar.[15] The difference (as Auerbach saw the matter) was awareness of the agitated movement of the overall historical background, which furnished the French novel's ultimate frame. The sense of the massive fluidity of that background allowed the lower classes to emerge as genuine agents and bearers of reality in their own right within the novel, and not merely as isolated individual characters interesting in their contrapuntal effect. On the other hand, the awareness of powerful, shifting historical forces and their infrastructures (as we might say today) transformed the novel's moralistic and individualistic perspective. Reality was instead constituted by the fateful depth portrayed in the transaction between these forces and the "random" individuals whom they engulf "as it were accidentally" and force to react one way or another.[16]

No doubt the English novel, much more than the French, continued to present social structures as given and eternally fixed. But even if the development was not so complete as it was in France, there was a steadily expanding tradition of English literature, seriously depicting the relation of society and the individual and of people within the conventions set by given social structures. Imaginative expression imposed order on the perception of reality as the close interaction between or-

13. Donovan, *The Shaping Vision*, p. 248.

14. See S. T. Coleridge, "Biographia Literaria," ch. 17 in *The Portable Coleridge*, ed. I. A. Richards (New York: Viking Press, 1961), pp. 535ff.

15. Auerbach, *Mimesis: The Representation of Reality in Western Literature*, trans. by W. R. Trask (Princeton: Princeton University Press, 1953), pp. 491f.

16. Ibid., p. 44.

dinary persons, held together by common temporal experience and by the conventions of a political, economic, and social structure significant enough to generate serious moral existence.

This form of writing was neither a slavish imitation of the perceived external world nor simple moral didacticism about it. Governing themes, particularly of a moral or characterological kind, were indeed present; but they could not be at odds with or force the rest of the artist's world in its verisimilitude to the temporally connected world of mundane reality. Such themes therefore had to be rendered in the process of the narrated world's cumulative chronological presentation, and not by an external ready-made imposition. Novels were not moral tales but renderings of a temporally connected world in which interpersonal and social experience was related to moral existence in a way that was as intimate as it was ambiguous. The ambiguity was the fruit of locating temporally sequential personal life within a broader, inescapably social rather than merely ethical context. This location made all the difference because it made the field of action amenable as much to historical narration and social—not to say informal sociological—observation as to moral description of behavior.

Gradually the impact of a locally quite diverse but nonetheless nationally coherent society with significant unifying foci of a moral, political, economic, and social kind made itself felt in writing as in other aspects of the common life. The novel reflected that coherence as well as the drastic changes within it which, despite their massiveness, still left a single national life. The shift in social makeup in which personal life and awareness were caught up as a result of the Industrial Revolution permeated the awareness of the middle-class readership, which was not only the novel's initial clientele but remained its natural readership no matter what the changes within the middle class itself or in the upper and lower levels of Britain's social structure. It is fascinating that this art form remained essentially the same and retained its hold on a large reading public's imagination when it mirrored a world in which the landed squire and his family and retainers formed the center and scope of reality, and later when it reflected a world in which rural cottage industries had been supplanted by towns and factories, and when the Enclosure Acts had done the rest to create a new reality by driving the rural poor into the new, burgeoning cities and slums.

By the close of the first third of the nineteenth century, England, unlike Germany, had undergone not only its religious and philosophical but also its political, scientific, and economic revolutions. Even if the dust had not settled completely on all these great upheavals, between them they had shaped the nation. They created a climate favorable to this literary form which remained the same when other forms experienced the break of the romantic era. Indeed, the multiplex revolution enhanced the novelist's sense of the appropriateness of mundane reality for imaginative representation and scrutiny, and his moral and aesthetic concern with the quality of human life which is so firmly set within this mundane social and natural matrix. The continuity of political and legal institutions through all the changes no doubt contributed heavily to that sense of an unchanging historical order in the English novel on which Auerbach and others have commented.

Much of the Bible consists of realistic narration, so much so that there is no surprise in its being subjected again and again, in this era of burgeoning realism, to inquiry as to whether it was *really* true to reality. How probable were the things that were told? Unlike other story traditions of the ancient world (the comparison with Homer becoming increasingly common among scholars as the century wore on), *this* story tradition appeared to be true and to have the marks of verisimilitude and of probable factuality. This was the case most especially if one left out of account all miracle stories. But even they seemed to have the marks of realism about them. It was often asked what other explanation than the genuine resurrection of Jesus would account for the startling but seemingly genuine and believable change of outlook among the disciples who, on their own admission, had been so cowardly and discouraged at the time of Jesus' trial and death.

But the new tradition of a *literary* realism was never applied to the technical task of biblical interpretation, so that speculation about the possible fruits of such a procedure at the time are as useless as they are fascinating. For reasons already mentioned, it was not to be: the debate over the factuality of the biblical reports was far too central and crucial. On apologetic as well as historical grounds, the question of the factuality of biblical reports, and the cognate debate over whether its putative factuality or the recognition of some central ideational themes was really the important thing about the Bible, prevented any serious attention to narrative shape in its own right.

In both cases what the biblical narratives are all about is something other than their character as cumulatively or accretively articulated stories whose themes emerge into full shape only through the narrative rendering and deployment itself. The curious, unmarked frontier between history and realistic fiction allows easy transition if one's interest is the rendering and exploration of a temporal framework through their logically similar narrative structure, perhaps most of all in the case of the biblical stories where the question of fact or fiction is so problematical. But when prime interest is concentrated on the fact issue—and it could hardly be otherwise in eighteenth-century examination of the Bible—the unmarked frontier is no longer merely real. Now it becomes impenetrable; one is either on one side of it or the other, and the decision between them is the crucial issue. The peculiar and intricate logic of narration is pushed into the background, and the similarity between the two kinds of writing is no longer significant except in a purely decorative sense. Empirical historical investigation into what most probably happened, together with supporting hypotheses and arguments, is a different enterprise from the endeavor to set forth a temporal world, which is the peculiar way in which realistic narrative means or makes sense. Not that one is more legitimate than the other. It is simply the case that one cannot do both at once, nor will the one kind of analysis do duty for the other.

In England, the interest in the historical factuality and/or the general themes of the biblical narratives subverted more than the technical appreciation of these writings as realistic narratives. Also pushed out of the way was all concern with what kinds of writings these narratives might be. Their narrative structure and their literary-historical origin and development were largely ignored. Whatever else the fruits of the deist debates, interest was concentrated from that day forward largely on criticism of the facts and not of the writings of the Bible. It was a procedure similar to that which F. C. Baur was later to pinpoint so accurately in the assumptions and procedures of D. F. Strauss's *The Life of Jesus.*[17] Although Bishop Lowth's *De sacra poesi Hebraeorum* and his commentary on Isaiah exercised some influence, they did not succeed in establishing a historical or literary-critical tradition of the biblical writings in the author's native land. T. K. Cheyne and more recent commentators have observed that only Warburton and Lowth—bitter antagonists as they were—and Alexander Geddes showed any talent for Old Testament criticism. The situation was essentially the same in the study of the New Testament.[18] Neither narratively nor historically-critically did the Bible as writing become the object of a tradition of scholarly commentary.

The burgeoning realistic outlook, increasingly embodied in the middle class of which men like David Hume were so proud for its contribution to political freedom and to the republic of the sciences, arts, and letters, was indeed reflected in common perspectives on the Bible. But it never shaped in the study of the Bible the same kind of imagina-

17. "Strauss is concerned not with the criticism of the writing but only with the criticism of the history." F. C. Baur, *Kritische Untersuchungen über die kanonischen Evangelien* (Tübingen: Fues, 1847), p. 40. (See Baur's discussion of Strauss, ibid., pp. 40-76.)

18. See *The Cambridge History of the Bible* (New York: Cambridge University Press, 1963), vol. 3, ch. 8; W. Neil, "Critical and Theological Use of the Bible 1700-1950," pp. 271f.

tive and analytical grasp applied to the writing and reading of the novel. Realism in regard to the Bible meant the discussion of the fact question or else its treatment in the spirit of Bolingbroke's dictum about history, "philosophy teaching by example." In the latter case, the Bible's perennial themes were taken to be descriptive of the solid, real, and mundane world and its God taught by eighteenth-century science, and of the solid, real, and mundane virtues inculcated by history and philosophy. (Those like Gibbon, who were persuaded of the grandeur both of the well-being and the decay of past epochs conveyed by properly written history, were always a trifle contemptuous of the Bible's level of teaching.)

Like history and the novel, much biblical narrative in explicative interpretation is not "system" or pure factual description but the cumulative rendering of a temporal framework through small impact on either pious use or technical scholarly analysis of the Bible. The argument from prophecy and its fulfillment, the logic of which rested in large part on just such a cumulative connection, receded from view early in the century. Its disappearance, as noted earlier, was due to its forced transfer from a formal narrative world of figural and literal interconnection to the arena of debate about the evidence for and against its factual claims. Its logic was basically altered, indeed destroyed, as a result of this shift from one world to another.

Such sense of a narrative framework as continued to exist among religious (and not merely scholarly) readers was now no longer chiefly that of providentially governed biblical history. In that scheme, earlier and later depictions within the Bible had been connected as type and antitype; but in addition, every present moral and historical experience had been fitted into it by bestowing on the present experience a figural interpretation that adapted it into the governing biblical narrative. All this had now changed. Such narrative sense as remained in the reading of the Bible found the connective narrative tissue which served simultaneously as its own effective thread to present experience in the history of the soul's conversion and perfection. This theme and transfer of narrative continuity took place either directly, as in the Methodists' devout use of the Bible to aid in tracing and treading the path from sin to perfection, or indirectly, as in the allegory of Christian's journey to Mount Zion with the aid and admonition of Evangelist and Interpreter in *The Pilgrim's Progress.*

Wesley's and Whitefield's preaching testified with powerful eloquence to their belief in the redeeming death of Christ and its efficacy for the Christian. In other words, it is not a lack of appreciation for the importance of the occurrence character (the "objectivity") of certain crucial events which makes the piety of the evangelical awakening in England something other than realistic. They are objective and objectively transforming events, though the crucial evidence by which they become religiously certain is not external but internal to the soul. (Christ is not reduced, as people often claim about early Methodism, to a subjective experience.) It is not the lack of an objective savior but the location of the cumulative narrative bond which indicates how loose and tentative is the hold of this profound religious movement on a context or world, temporal, eternal, or both, in which one may feel at home. The crucial and indispensable continuity or linkage in the story is the journey of the Christian person from sin through justification to sanctification or perfection.[19]

In figural interpretation the figure itself is real in its own place, time, and right, and without any detraction from that reality it prefigures the reality that will fulfill it. This figural relation not only brings into coherent relation events in biblical narration, but also allows the fitting of each present occurrence and experience into a real, narrative framework or world. Each person, each occurrence is a figure of that providential narrative in which it is also an ingredient. In that fashion all experience belongs in a real world.

In evangelical piety that relation is reversed; the atoning death of Jesus is indeed real in its own right and both necessary and efficacious for the redemption of the sinner. Nonetheless, though real in his own right, the atoning Redeemer is at the same time a figure or type of the Christian's journey; for this is the narrative framework, the meaningful pattern within which alone the occurrence of the cross finds its applicative sense. What is real, and what therefore the Christian really lives, is his own pilgrimage; and to its pattern he looks for the assurance that he is really living it.

19. For a survey of religious practice including biblical preaching in the evangelical revival, see Horton Davies, *Worship and Theology in England from Watts and Wesley to Maurice, 1690-1850* (Princeton: Princeton University Press, 1961), pt. 2, pp. 143-240.

The Narrative Quality of Experience

Stephen Crites

*La narration est toute l'épopée; elle est toute l'historie;
elle enveloppe le drame et le sous-entend.*

—Balzac

The *forms* of cultural expression are not historical accidents. They are not products of culture, much less products of individual choice and contrivance, although actual cultural expressions are to some extent both. The *way* people speak, dance, build, dream, embellish, is to be sure always culturally particular: it bears the imprint of a time and a place. A people speaks a particular language, not the same as that spoken in another land nor quite the same as that spoken by their fathers, and each person adapts it with some originality to his own use. But the fact that people speak some language is no historical accident. It is a necessary mark of being human, i.e., being capable of having a history. That is also true of other persistent forms of cultural expression. They are the *conditions* of historical existence; their expressions are moulded in the historical process itself into definite *products* of particular cultures.

I do not know how to go about proving any such grandiose thesis. To me, I confess, it seems self-evident, in the sense that once the ap-

Stephen Crites, "The Narrative Quality of Experience," *Journal of the American Academy of Religion*, XXXIX, 3 (September 1971): 291-311.

propriate distinctions are made it becomes obvious. Be that as it may, I propose here to illustrate the point in relation to storytelling, which I take to be one of the most important cultural expressions. I want to argue that the formal quality of experience through time is inherently narrative.[1]

I introduce this thesis by briefly posing another, to which it is intimately related: The style of action through time is inherently musical. The relation of the two theses can be stated in an equation of positively luminous simplicity: Narrative quality is to experience as musical style is to action. And action and experience interpenetrate. Let us see about that.

We speak of the things we do as having a particular style. There is a style in the way a person writes and speaks. An artist paints in a certain style. A farmer exhibits a style in the way he plows his field; a dealer, in the way he keeps his store and arranges his wares. A man's style is formed by the way he is brought up, by the people among whom he has lived, by his training: by his experience. Westerners have, collectively, a different style from Easterners and Californians. Yet in its details a man's style is idiomorphic—as the ringmaster says, inimitable. What is style?

Suppose I walk with unbroken stride across a room. It is a single complex movement. If I were a dancer I could, perhaps, cross the room at a single leap. But even for a dancer the action involves not only a steady change of position in the space of the room, but a divisible duration. There are variations on a joke about a runner so fast that he can turn and see himself still at the starting line. The point of the joke is that however single and swift a movement is there is always before and after.[2] An action is altogether temporal. Yet it has a unity of form through time, a form revealed only in the action as a whole. That temporal form is what we mean by style. My gait has a particular style—an ungainly one, as it happens, of a sort developed in walking through cornfields. But you could not detect it in a still photograph, because the style is in the movement. The same is true of gestures, mannerisms, the putting together of words, the modulations of the voice in speaking the words. All of these are actions, conscious movements in time, and it is appropriate in each case to speak of their having a particular style.

Why conscious movements? Actions are the movements of

1. That is to say that I conceive my undertaking to be phenomenological. It will not, however, be larded with citations from the great German and French phenomenologists. The phenomenology will be homemade.

2. Though not as if, like Zeno's arrow, one passed through a series of quasi-mathematical points in time. The temporality of which we speak is constituted by the movement itself, and not by the (essentially spatial) units of its measure.

bodies, but unlike other movements they are performed by bodies that are both the subjects of experience and purposive agents. It does not occur to us, in common speech, to attribute style to unconscious bodies.[3] Movements must be conscious to have a style. Yet that does not imply that one necessarily attends consciously to these movements or to their style. One may do so, and may even attempt to change or to perfect his style. But he has a style, regardless of whether he ever concerns himself with it. Typically, the style is formed quite unconsciously by an agent intent on the various projects to which he directs his action. I cross the room to look out the window or talk to a friend, not in order to perfect my style of walking. The formation of style is seldom the conscious intent or point of an action, except when someone is deliberately training himself, say, as an artist or an athlete. But it is in any case the inner concomitant of an action, whatever its aim: whatever the product of the action, its style is a by-product, or, as we may say in anticipating our comments on its musicality, it is its accompaniment.

It is no coincidence that musical performance exhibits the formal properties of style generally. The rhythms and melodic lines of music are inherently temporal. We do not hear them all at once, but in a succession of pulses and pitched vibrations; yet we experience them as a unity, a unity through time. The reality of a musical phrase, being inherently temporal, implies the evanescence of all its elements. So it is with style. Its elements, too, are evanescent, yet the style of an action exists in the rhythms and the varying pattern of intensities found in it as a whole. To say that my gait in crossing the room has a style is to say that it expresses certain antic rhythms, that it is a crude kind of dance. Similarly, there is something in the cadences and modulations of a voice in speech that is struggling to become a song. Even this essay, turbid as it is, does, after all, have a style, and if you would have to say that its style is flat compared to your favorite books of poems, I think that in the end you would be indulging in a kind of musical criticism of the two productions.

Style is, of course, musical only in a rudimentary sense. It is not yet music, is—so to speak—below the threshold of music. Yet there is a definite relation between music and style, and not merely a strained analogy. If style is the form of conscious movement, music is that form

3. However poetically we may express our appreciation for, say, the revolutions of the moon, we would not normally attribute style to it, nor even to the "song" of a bird. And while we do speak of the style of a painting, I take it that that is an oblique way of referring to the style of the artist in his act of painting it: the "painting" and not the artifact as such has style. Again, when people are asleep their style slumbers also; "What style!" would be a nice comic caption for a cartoon picturing a woman pointing at her snoring husband.

purified: to the extent that it becomes conscious art it is purged of any inherent relation to a moving body, except as its mere "instrument." The music itself is pure action, not the movement of any thing but simply movement itself: invisible, light as air, freed from the weight of a body and the confinements of space. It exists in time alone, and is, therefore, experienced in the only way we could experience an altogether temporal reality: as something heard, as sound. It must, to be sure, be produced by a body, by someone singing or someone beating, strumming, blowing an instrument. So it, too, will have a style. Yet in itself, as it sounds forth, it is the aesthetic idealization of style; it is, so to speak, the style of style. In music, style is no longer ancillary to an action with some other aim, but is itself the sole aim of the action.

But style generally, the form of all action, is the source of music, its basis in ordinary life. Because it has its source in an ineluctable feature of human existence, music is one of the universal cultural forms of which we spoke at the outset. It is not an arbitrary contrivance, but is a purified form of the incipient musicality of style itself. People take such satisfaction in music because it answers to a powerful if seldom noticed aspect of everything they do, of every gesture, every footstep, every utterance; answers to it and gives it a purified expression. Courtship, worship, even violent conflict, call forth musical expressions in order to give these activities a certain ideality, a specific ideality rooted in the activities themselves. That is why the music of a culture or subculture has such a vital connection, so revealing yet so hard to define, with its whole style of life. The music of a people, or even a cohesive group, is peculiarly its own. It is the particular musical style that permits a group's lifestyle, its incipient musicality, to express itself in full dance and song. The connection is of course reciprocal: the musical style in turn molds the lifestyle. But it cannot be an altogether alien mold. There is a beautiful paradox in the peculiar intensity with which a person responds to music which is "his own": even if he has not heard it before, it is familiar, as though something is sounding in it that he has always felt in his bones; and yet it is really new. It is his own style, revealed to him at an otherwise unimaginable level of clarity and intensity.

Now I want to suggest that stories have a similar resonance for us. But the comments on the musical style of action are not merely for the sake of establishing an analogy with the narrative quality of experience. Narrative, after all, is the other cultural form capable of expressing coherence through time, though its temporality is not so pure as that of music. Particularly important for our purposes, furthermore, are the kinds of stories that have strong musical overtones, for which verse would be the most appropriate form. So let our comments on style sound quietly and perhaps even musically in the background of what follows.

I. Mundane Stories and Sacred Stories

There are powerful grounds for thinking that narrative form is artifice; that it is simply one of the ways we organize a life of experience that is in itself inchoate. We are being reminded nowadays that stories are fictions after all.[4] Of course there have been many forms of narrative— epic, drama, history, the novel, and so on—and our knowledge of the origins and development of such genres has given us a keen impression of their cultural and historical relativity. Furthermore, among some of the most important modern writers there has occurred a determined reaction against all standard narrative forms, partly on the grounds that such forms represent a subtle falsification of the immediacies of experience, of the modern experience in particular. Even writers who retain recognizably narrative forms have experimented with them freely. The great storytellers of our time as well as those who refuse to tell stories have made us aware of how much art is involved in all storytelling. It no longer appears natural and innocent in our eyes.

The study of traditional folk cultures has also made us aware that there is more to narrative form than meets the eye (or the ear), and at least it raises the question whether that may also be true even for a culture as fragmented, sophisticated, and anti-traditional as ours. For within the traditional cultures there have been some stories that were told, especially on festal occasions, that had special resonance. Not only told but ritually re-enacted, these stories seem to be allusive expressions of stories that cannot be fully and directly told, because they live, so to speak, in the arms and legs and bellies of the celebrants. These stories lie too deep in the consciousness of a people to be directly told: they form consciousness rather than being among the objects of which it is directly aware. As such they are intimately related to what we have called "style," and so it is not surprising that these stories can hardly be expressed at all without an integral fusion of music with narrative. Every serious attempt to express them creates poetry. The expressions admit of great variation in detail, but no variation fully grasps the story within these diverse stories.

We sometimes apply our ambiguous term *myth* to this "story within the story." But it is not identical with the "myths" or legends we

4. The point is brilliantly argued and elaborated in Frank Kermode, *The Sense of an Ending: Studies in the Theory of Fiction* (New York: Oxford University Press, 1968). Professor Kermode warns that "If we forget that fictions are fictive we regress to myth. . . ." (p. 41). My argument may well illustrate what he is warning against. I do deny that all narratives are merely fictive, and I go on to deny that myth, or what I call sacred story, is a mere regression from a fiction. But it is ungrateful to single out my disagreements with a book from which I have derived uncommon profit in pondering my theme.

are able to read in ancient books, although these give us valuable access to those stories which have so powerfully formed a civilization's sense of itself and its world. We might also call these stories "religious," except that this designation implies modern distinctions between religious forms and secular, artistic, political forms, and these distinctions are misleading as applied to traditional cultures. Certainly these mythopoeic stories function quite differently in traditional cultures from the way conscious art does in what we are pleased to call higher cultures. They are anonymous and communal. None of our individualized conceptions of authorship are appropriate to them, and while rich powers of imagination may be expressed in them they are certainly not perceived as conscious fictions. Such stories, and the symbolic worlds they project, are not like monuments that men behold, but like dwelling-places. People live in them. Yet even though they are not directly told, even though a culture seems rather to be the telling than the teller of these stories, their form seems to be narrative. They are moving forms, at once musical and narrative, which inform people's sense of the story of which their own lives are a part, of the moving course of their own action and experience.

I propose, with some misgivings, to call these fundamental narrative forms sacred stories, not so much because gods are commonly celebrated in them, but because men's sense of self and world is created through them. For that matter, only the musical stories that form men's living image of themselves and their world have been found fit to celebrate the powers on which their existence depends. For these are stories that orient the life of people through time, their life-time, their individual and corporate experience and their sense of style, to the great powers that establish the reality of their world. So I call them sacred stories, which in their secondary, written expressions may carry the authority of scripture for the people who understand their own stories in relation to them.

The stories that are told, all stories directly seen or heard, I propose to call mundane stories. I am uneasy about that term also, although it is not meant to be in the least depreciatory. It simply implies a theory about the objectified images that fully articulated stories must employ, i.e., about words, scenes, roles, sequences of events within a plot, and other narrative devices: that such images, to be capable of being plausible objects of consciousness, must be placed within that world, that phenomenological *mundus,* which defines the objective horizon of a particular form of consciousness. In order to be told, a story must be set within a world. It may not be an everyday world, i.e., it may be an imaginatively augmented world. But even the most fanciful stories have their proprieties. We speak of a universe of discourse, and this too has its limiting firmament above and below, beyond which nothing can be conceived to happen. Historically there have been a variety of such worlds, correlative to the historical forms of consciousness. The stories of an age or a culture take place within its world. Only in that sense are they necessarily mundane. Here, in some world of consciousness, we find stories composed as works of art as well as the much more modest narrative communications that pass between people in explaining where they have been, why things are as they are, and so on. Set within a world of consciousness, the mundane stories are also among the most important means by which people articulate and clarify their sense of that world. In order to initiate their children in "the ways of the world," parents tell them stories — although in recent times, particularly, the problem has arisen that the children find themselves having to make their way in quite a different world, for which they have to devise quite different kinds of stories than those their parents taught them.

Sacred stories, too, are subject to change, but not by conscious reflection. People do not sit down on a cool afternoon and think themselves up a sacred story. They awaken to a sacred story, and their most significant mundane stories are told in the effort, never fully successful, to articulate it. For the sacred story does not transpire within a conscious world. It forms the very consciousness that projects a total world horizon, and therefore informs the intentions by which actions are projected into that world. The style of these actions dances to its music. One may attempt to name a sacred story, as we shall try to do in our conclusion. But such naming misleads as much as it illuminates, since its meaning is contained—and concealed—in the unutterable cadences and revelations of the story itself. Yet every sacred story is creation story: not merely that one may name creation of world and self as its "theme" but also that the story itself creates a world of consciousness and the self that is oriented to it.

Between sacred and mundane stories there is distinction without separation. From the sublime to the ridiculous, all a people's mundane stories are implicit in its sacred story, and every mundane story takes soundings in the sacred story. But some mundane stories sound out greater depths than others. Even the myths and epics, even the scriptures, are mundane stories. But in these, as well as in some works of literary art, and perhaps even in some merry little tales that seem quite content to play on the surface, the sacred stories resonate. People are able to feel this resonance, because the unutterable stories are those they know best of all.

It is possible for such resonances to sound in poetic productions that seem to defy all traditional forms of storytelling. For the surface of conventional narrative forms may have become so smooth and hard that it is necessary to break it in order to let a sacred story sound at all. Such

71

a necessity may signalize that the sacred story is altogether alive, transforming itself in the depths. Break the story to tell a truer story! But there are also darker possibilities in this situation, as we shall see.

II. The Inner Form of Experience

A. The Chronicle of Memory

Between sacred story and the mundane stories there is a mediating form: the form of the experiencing consciousness itself. For consciousness is moulded by the sacred story to which it awakens, and in turn it finds expression in the mundane stories that articulate its sense of reality. But consciousness itself is not a blank. Consciousness has a form of its own, without which no coherent experience at all would be possible.[5] Aside from that formidable inconvenience, it is difficult to see how a consciousness, itself entirely formless, could be the fulcrum that I have suggested it is between sacred and mundane stories. I want further to propose that the form of active consciousness, i.e., the form of its experiencing, is in at least some rudimentary sense narrative. That is why consciousness is able to mediate between the sacred and mundane stories through which it orients itself in a world.[6] A square peg would not fit into a round hole. The stories give qualitative substance to the form of experience because it is itself an incipient story.

That is the central thesis of this essay. Of all the unlikely things that have been said thus far, it perhaps seems the least plausible. In attempting to explain and support it I want to do the usual thing in such straits, and appeal for the help of a favorite teacher. The teacher is Augus-

---

5. As Kant argued in *The Critique of Pure Reason*, though of course reaching quite different conclusions about the constitution of this necessary form. To make at the level of *strenge Wissenschaft* my case that the primary forms of possible experience are narrative, I should also have to follow Kant's lead by providing a transcendental deduction of these incipient narrative forms. But I content myself with the gestures in that direction contained in this and the following section.

6. There is an implicit circularity here that may as well be made explicit, since I am sure to be found out anyway: I appeal to the form of sacred and mundane story to suggest that the structure of experience informed by such stories must itself be in some sense narrative. But I have not really proven that what I have called sacred story is in any acceptable sense narrative itself, and among the reasons that make me think it is, the most important is that experience has at root a narrative form: experience can derive a specific sense of its own temporal course in a coherent world only by being informed by a qualifying structure that gives definite contours to its own form. Very well. The points are mutually supportive, i.e., the argument is in the end circular, as any good philosophical argument is. And in the end it has only the explanatory power of this particular circle to commend it.

tine of Hippo. Not that he would necessarily subscribe to my thesis. But being a good teacher, he has helped me find my way to my own notions, and even when I have pursued my own follies he has only given me help when I knew I needed it.

The help in this case is offered in his brooding reflections on memory and time in the tenth and eleventh books of the *Confessions*. Whether or not he succeeded in establishing the subjectivity of time in that famous discussion, whether indeed that is what he was trying to do, I want to invert the problem and suggest that he did succeed in establishing the temporality of the subject. Consciousness grasps its objects in an inherently temporal way, and that temporality is retained in the unity of its experience as a whole.

Augustine ponders the paradox that the future, which does not yet exist, should pass into the past which no longer exists, through a present that is difficult to *conceptualize* as more than a vanishing quasi-mathematical point. The paradox is resolved when past, present, and future are considered to be not necessarily independent metaphysical modalities, but unavoidable modalities of experience in the mind or experiencing consciousness *(anima)*. For consciousness "anticipates and attends and remembers, so that what it anticipates passes through what it attends into what it remembers" (XI:xxviii).[7] We will consider in the next section the highly developed temporality implicit in this three-fold function of consciousness. But already in memory alone there is the simpler temporality of sequence, of before and after.

Without memory, in fact, experience would have no coherence at all. Consciousness would be locked in a bare, momentary present, i.e., in a disconnected succession of perceptions which it would have no power to relate to one another. It might be argued that that would already imply a temporality of the most elemental sort. It is already significant that experience has, in its present, this sheer momentary quality. But it is memory that bestows the sense of temporal succession as well as the power to abstract coherent unities from this succession of momentary percepts.

In Book X Augustine singles out this capacity of memory for analysis, and also for a kind of awe—Augustine is a thinker for whom awe and close analysis are intensified together:

> Great is this power of memory, excessively great, my God, a vast and infinite interior space: who has plumbed it to the depths? Yet this is a power of my mind and pertains to my nature, so that I myself do not grasp all that I am. (X:viii)

7. I take responsibility for the translation of extracts from *The Confessions* quoted here.

Yet, Augustine muses, people take this prodigy within themselves for granted. Ignoring this interior space, they are amazed by the great dimensions of mountains, oceans, rivers, the orbits of the stars. But greater than the wonder of these external, natural wonders is the simple fact that he himself can speak of these things even though he does not at the moment see them. That is possible because he sees "inwardly in my memory" these things he had once seen outwardly with his eyes—yet it is not the very things themselves that appear in this inner vision: For

> still I did not absorb these things [into myself] in seeing them . . . nor are they themselves attached to me, but their images only, and I know by what sense of the body each was impressed upon me. (X:viii)

Detached from things and lodged in memory, along with inner impressions of feeling and mood, these images are susceptible to the uses of thought and the play of imagination. Called up by the activities of the mind, they can be dismantled and reassembled or combined in original ways. When we do not attend to them they are "submerged and they slide down, as it were, into the remote interior spaces" of memory. But from this "dispersion" they can always be "collected" again by our thought, i.e., literally, by our cogitations. Augustine likes to play on the etymological connection between *cogo*—collect—and *cogito*. (X:xi)

So there is an important distinction between memory and recollection that goes back at least to Augustine. All the sophisticated activities of consciousness literally re-collect the images lodged in memory into new configurations, reordering past experience. But that would be impossible were it not for the much more naive functioning of memory itself, preserving the images drawn from experience. But I venture to suggest that memory does not contain its images quite so "scatteredly and confusedly" as Augustine suggests in the passage cited above. The memory also has its order, not the recollected order formed by thought and imagination, but a simple order of succession. This succession is the order in which the images of actual experience through time have been impressed upon the memory. It constitutes a kind of lasting chronicle, fixed in my memory, on the temporal course of my experience. This chronicle does not need to be recollected strictly, but merely to be recalled: I need only call up again the succession of images which stand waiting in memory in the order in which I experience them. Of course the recall is not total, the chronicle is not without lacunae. In fact, it is for great stretches quite fragmentary. But what we do succeed in calling up we find differentiated into fairly clear sequence. We are aware of what comes before and what comes after. When we are uncertain, or feel that a crucial scene is missing, we have the sense of "consulting" our memory. The recall is not infallible, but we have the sense that this "consultation" is possible, that the chronicle is "there," in memory, to be consulted, that if we concentrate intensely on our remembering we will be able to recall a sequence of events accurately. I consult my memory in this way, for example, when I mentally retrace my steps in the effort to recall where I may have lost something.

Yet that odd consultation is not strictly an act of recollection. We must consult our memory in order to recollect its images, to reorganize them for the more sophisticated purposes of the mind. But remembering is not yet knowing. Its chronicle is too elemental, too fixed to be illuminating. Experience is illuminated only by the more subtle processes of recollection. At least in this sense, all knowledge is recollection! So is all art, including the art of storytelling. It is an act. It has style. But mere remembering as such has no style, if we could isolate it from the process of recollection that in practice generally accompanies it.

Yet storytelling is not an arbitrary imposition upon remembered experience, altogether alien to its own much simpler form. Images do not exist in memory as atomic units, like photographs in an album, but as transient episodes in an image-stream, cinematic, which I must suspend and from which I must abstract in order to isolate a particular image. The most direct and obvious way of recollecting it is by telling a story, though the story is never simply the tedious and unilluminating recital of the chronicle of memory itself. And, of course, I can manipulate the image-stream in other ways. I can abstract general features and formal elements of it for purposes of theory, or suspend it in order to draw a picture, or splice episodes from it in a way that gives them new significance. I can contemplate a whole segment of the image-stream in a single glance of inner vision, then fragment it so that its elements are left twinkling in isolation like stars—yet even then memory is not shattered. Indeed, I can do such things because the original chronicle, the image stream, is always at hand, needing only to be recalled. I can even measure out its segments into long times and short times, recalling some episodes as having occurred a long time ago, others more recently (a phenomenon that Augustine ponders with great care in XI:xv-xxviii).[8]

I recall, for example, a sequence from my own memory. In telling it, of course, recollection already intervenes, but I recollect in a way as faithful as possible to the memory itself. I measure out "a long time" and recall an episode from my childhood. I have not thought about it for many years, and yet I find its chronicle in good condition, extremely detailed

---

8. In recognizing the importance of this strange measurement of what no longer exists, Augustine does implicitly acknowledge the primitive order of succession within memory. Memory is not simply a vast interior space in which images tumble at random.

and in clear sequence. In an impetuous fit of bravado I threw a rock through a garage window. I recall the exact spot on the ground from which I picked up the rock, I recall the wind-up, the pitch, the rock in mid-air, the explosive sound of the impact, the shining spray of glass, the tinkling hail of shards falling on the cement below, the rough, stony texture of the cement. I recall also my inner glee at that moment, and my triumph when a playmate, uncertain at first how to react, looked to me for his cue and then broke into a grin. Now I could cut and splice a bit, passing over hours not so clearly recalled anyway, except that my mood underwent drastic change. Then I recall that moment in the evening when I heard my father's returning footsteps on the porch and my guilty terror reached a visceral maximum the very memory of which wrenches a fat adult belly—for remembering is not simply a process in the head! The details of the scene that ensued are likewise very vivid in my memory.

Now it would be quite possible for me to tell this story very differently. My perspective on it has been changed, partly by the death of my father and the fact that I am now myself the father of children, partly, too, by my reading in the *Confessions* a story about a wanton theft of pears and by some reading in Freud on the rivalry of fathers and sons, and so forth. So I have many insights into this chronicle that I could not have had at the time its events occurred. Yet the sophisticated new story I might tell about it would be superimposed on the image-stream of the original chronicle. It could not replace the original without obliterating the very materials to be recollected in the new story. Embedded in every sophisticated retelling of such a story is this primitive chronicle preserved in memory. Even conscious fictions presuppose its successive form, even when they artfully reorder it.

B. A Dramatic Tension

In the chronicle of memory there is the simple temporality of succession, duration, of before and after, but not yet the decisive distinction between past, present, and future, that provides the tension of experience and therefore demands the tenses of language. Memory, containing the past, is only one modality of experience, that never exists in isolation from those that are oriented to the present and the future. To understand the relation of the three we may again refer to Augustine.

He points out that past, present, and future cannot be three distinct realities or spheres of being that somehow coexist. Only the present exists.

> But perhaps it might properly be said: there are three times, a present of things past, a present of things present, a present of things future. (XI:xx)

Only the present exists, but it exists only in these tensed modalities. They are inseparably joined in the present itself. Only from the standpoint of present experience could one speak of past and future. The three modalities are correlative to one another, in every moment of experience.

> For these are in the mind as a certain triadic form, and elsewhere I do not see them: the present of things past is memory, the present of things present is direct attention, the present of things future is anticipation. (XI:xx)

I want to suggest that the inner form of any possible experience is determined by the union of these three distinct modalities in every moment of experience. I want further to suggest that the tensed unity of these modalities requires narrative forms both for its expression (mundane stories) and for its own sense of the meaning of its internal coherence (sacred stories). For this tensed unity has already an incipient narrative form.

The chronicle of memory, with its simple successiveness, its before and after, is in actual experience always already taken up into the more sophisticated temporality of tense. If we would attempt to isolate anticipation as we did memory we would again discover a very elemental narrative form. We might call it the scenario of anticipation.[9] I have in mind our guesses and predictions about what may happen, hunches generally formulated in the attempt to lay some plans about our own projected courses of action. Projected action often dominates this modality of experience, though one may simply worry about the future or indulge in euphoric dreams about it. But whether anticipation takes the passive form of dreams, worries, and wishes, or is instrumental in laying plans or making resolutions for projected actions, it seems intuitively clear that we anticipate by framing little stories about how things may fall out. As the term *scenario* implies, these anticipatory stories are very thin and vague as compared with the dense, sharp detail of the chronicle of memory. It is also clear that the course of events generally turns out quite differently from what we had anticipated. But the experience of thwarted expectations, or the comic situation when parties to an encounter come to it with very different scenarios in mind—e.g., she prepared for political discussion, he for romantic rendezvous—simply serve to show that we do orient ourselves to the future by means

9. I have discussed such anticipatory scenarios in some detail in an essay to which the present one is in many ways a sequel: "Myth, Story, History," published in a symposium entitled *Parable, Myth and Language* (Cambridge, Mass.: The Church Society for College Work, 1968), p. 68.

of such scenarios. Though they are generally vague they are not altogether formless. However freely our action may improvise upon the scenario, it is never simply random.

Now it is not as though the scenario of anticipation were set alongside the chronicle of memory, as two quite separate stories. Our sense of personal identity depends upon the continuity of experience through time, a continuity bridging even the cleft between remembered past and projected future. Even when it is largely implicit, not vividly self-conscious, our sense of ourselves is at every moment to some extent integrated into a single story. That on the one hand.

On the other hand, the distinction between memory and anticipation is absolute. The present is not merely an indifferent point moving along a single unbroken and undifferentiated line, nor is the temporality of experience such a line. Nor do past and future simply "meet" in the present. Memory and anticipation, the present of things past and the present of things future, are tensed modalities of the present itself. They are the tension of every moment of experience, both united in that present and qualitatively differentiated by it. For precisely in this momentary present which embraces my whole experience, the past remembered is fixed, a chronicle that I can radically reinterpret but cannot reverse or displace: what is done cannot be undone! And within this same present the future is, on the contrary, still fluid, awaiting determination, subject to alternative scenarios.[10] Precisely as modalities of the present of experience, the past remembered is determinate, the future anticipated is indeterminate, and the distinction between them is intuitively clear and absolute.

But how can the present contain such tension, on the one hand unifying, on the other hand absolutely distinguishing its tensed modalities? It can do so because the whole experience, as it is concentrated in a conscious present, has a narrative form. Narrative alone can contain the full temporality of experience in a unity of form. But this incipient story, implicit in the very possibility of experience, must be such that it can absorb both the chronicle of memory and the scenario of anticipation, absorb them within a richer narrative form without effacing the difference between the determinacy of the one and the indeterminacy of the other.

We can define such a narrative form a little more fully by reminding ourselves that the conscious present has a third modality: the present of things present. This *praesens de praesentibus* Augustine designates

10. The fluidity of the future from the standpoint of consciousness has nothing to do with the truth or falsity of deterministic theories. The point is phenomenological, not metaphysical.

as *contuitus*—direct attention. True enough, but there is something more. If discussion of the aetherial-seeming objects of memory and anticipation may have tempted us to speak of consciousness itself as if it were an invisibility suspended in a void, mention of its direct present must sharply remind us that consciousness is a function of an altogether bodily life. The conscious present is that of a body impacted in a world and moving, in process, in that world. In this present, action and experience meet. Memory is its depth, the depth of its experience in particular; anticipation is its trajectory, the trajectory of its action in particular. The *praesens de praesentibus* is its full bodily reality.

It is, moreover, the moment of decision within the story as a whole. It is always the *decisive* episode in the story, its moment of crisis between the past remembered and the future anticipated but still undetermined. The *critical* position of this modality gives the story a dramatic character as a whole. And since action and experience join precisely at this decisive and critical juncture in the drama, the whole drama vibrates with the musicality of personal style.

Still, it is a drama of a rudimentary sort. Life is not, after all, a work of art. An artistic drama has a coherence and a fullness of articulation that are never reached by our rudimentary drama. But the drama of experience is the crude original of all high drama. High drama can only contrive the appearance of that crisis which the conscious present actually is. The difference between a fixed past and a future still to be resolved, which in experience is an absolute difference, must be artfully contrived on a stage by actors who know the outcome as well as they know the beginning. The art of drama imitates the life of experience, which is the true drama.

Life also imitates art. The stories people hear and tell, the dramas they see performed, not to speak of the sacred stories that are absorbed without being directly heard or seen, shape in the most profound way the inner story of experience. We imbibe a sense of the meaning of our own baffling dramas from these stories, and this sense of its meaning in turn affects the form of a man's experience and the style of his action. Such cultural forms, both sacred and mundane, are of course socially shared in varying degrees, and so help to link men's inner lives as well as orienting them to a common public world. Both the content and the form of experience are mediated by symbolic systems which we are able to employ simply by virtue of awakening within a particular culture in which those symbolic systems are the common currency. Prevailing narrative forms are among the most important of such symbolic systems. It is not as though a man begins as a purely individual consciousness with the incipient story and musicality of his private experience, and then casts about for a satisfying tale to lend it some higher significance. People

79

Stephen Crites

awaken to consciousness in a society, with the inner story of experience and its enveloping musicality already infused with cultural forms. The vitalities of experience itself may in turn make a man feel that some of the old stories have a hollow ring and may be the source of originality in the formation of new stories, or even new kinds of stories. But the *way* we remember, anticipate, and even directly perceive, is largely social. A sacred story in particular infuses experience at its root, linking a man's individual consciousness with ultimate powers and also with the inner lives of those with whom he shares a common soil.

There is an entrancing half-truth that has gained wide currency, particularly among American undergraduates. It is that time itself is a cultural product, e.g., the creation of certain grammatical forms.[11] Presumably we could be rid of it if we played our cards right, say, with a non-Western deck. The kernel of truth in this idyllic vision is that particular conceptions of times are indeed imbibed from cultural forms, not only from the structures of a language but from the kinds of stories being told. For the temporality that I have argued is necessary for the very possibility of experience does not of itself imply any particular conception of time. The connections among its episodes or moments is not necessarily, for example, either magical, causal, logical, or teleological. Least of all does it imply any theory regarding the metaphysical status of time. The temporality of lived experience as such, with its inherent tensions and crises, can only, so to speak, raise questions about the reality and meaning of time. For the answers to these questions it must, as it were, turn to the sacred and mundane cultural forms lying at hand.

11. This view is usually linked with a loveable primitivism now in vogue. Students who make this link often seize upon the theories of Benjamin Lee Whorf, who had observed, for example, that characteristically Western notions of time could not be expressed at all in the language of the Hopi Indians. See "An American Indian Model of the Universe," in the collection of Whorf's writings entitled *Language, Thought, and Reality* (Cambridge, Mass.: M.I.T. Press, 1956). Cf. Richard M. Gale, *The Language of Time* (London: Routlege & Kegan Paul, 1968), pp. 45-48, for a critique of some of the general claims Whorf's observations led him to make. Those who cite Whorf are often less cautious than he is in claiming that time is the product of a particular culture, and therefore holding out the possibility that there are or might be peoples blessedly free of the conflicts and traumas of temporal existence. Among some of my favorite students it comes out like this:

> O happy hippy Hopis
> of peyote buds and herbs:
> No tensions in their teepees,
> no tenses in their verbs.

Far removed from this idyllic vision is the fine work of Georges Poulet, *Studies in Human Time*, trans. by Elliott Coleman (Baltimore: Johns Hopkins Press, 1956). Poulet points up the radical developments and the subtle modulations in the sense of time within Western culture itself, particularly in the works of a succession of important French and American writers.

In fact, the answers precede and sometimes preclude the questions! Stories, in particular, infuse the incipient drama of experience with a definite sense of the way its scenes are connected. They reveal to people the kind of drama in which they are engaged, and perhaps its larger meaning. So the fact that there are very different notions of time implicit in the cultural forms of different historical traditions does not contradict the inherent temporality of all possible experience. There is only one absolute limit to that diversity: it is impossible that a culture could offer no interpretation of this temporality at all.

In principle, we can distinguish between the inner drama of experience and the stories through which it achieves coherence. But in any actual case the two so interpenetrate that they form a virtual identity, which, if we may pun a little, is in fact a man's very sense of his own personal identity. The sacred story in particular, with its musical vitality, enables him to give the incipient drama of his experience full dramatic dimensions and allows the incipient musicality of his style to break forth into real dance and song. Hence the powerful inner need for expressive forms, the music played and sung and danced, the stories told and acted, projected within the world of which men are conscious.

So the narrative quality of experience has three dimensions, the sacred story, the mundane stories, and the temporal form of experience itself: three narrative tracks, each constantly reflecting and affecting the course of the others.

And sometimes the tracks cross, causing a burst of light like a comet entering our atmosphere. Such a luminous moment, in which sacred, mundane, and personal are inseparably conjoined, we call *symbolic* in a special sense. Of course, there is a more general sense in which every element in a story is a symbol, an imaginative representation conveying a meaning; but even in that sense the symbol is partly constituted by its position in the story. A story is not a mere assembly of independently defined symbols. Still less is a symbol in the more pregnant sense, e.g., a religious symbol, an atomic capsule of meaning that drops from the heavens or springs from the unconscious in isolated splendor.[12] The cross, or a holy mountain, receive their meaning from the stories in which they appear. Such a symbol imports into any icon or life situation or new story in which it appears, the significance given it

12. It has been widely assumed that symbols are in some sense primitive in experience, and that myths and other narrative forms are secondary constructions that assemble the primal symbolic material into stories. That view, for example, in a highly sophisticated form, seems to be an important premise of Paul Ricoeur's fine studies in this field, e.g., *The Symbolism of Evil*, trans. by Emerson Buchanan (New York: Harper & Row, 1967). But such a view seems to presuppose an atomism of experience that I think is quite impossible.

in a cycle of mundane stories, and also the resonances of a sacred story. The shock of its appearance is like the recurrence in daylight of an episode recalled from dreams. For a religious symbol becomes fully alive to consciousness when sacred story dramatically intersects both an explicit narrative and the course of a man's personal experience. The symbol is precisely that double intersection.

Narrative form, and not the symbol as such, is primitive in experience. But narrative form is by no means innocent. It acknowledges and informs only what is contained in its own ordering of events. Even the most naive tale begins "once upon a time"—a time prior to which there is only darkness, no time so far as the temporality constituted by the story is concerned. That time begins with this "once . . ." and when the tale has run its course there is nothing left. Its characters disappear into a timeless "happily ever after." It is meaningless to ask whether they really do. For they live only within the tensions and crises which constitute the significant time of the story, the narrative "tick-tock,"[13] between the tick of "once upon a time" and the tock of happy resolution. Of course, the resolution may not be happy. We may leave our characters in a state of horror also outside all time and, therefore, pure and unambiguous. This happiness, this horror, are both beyond the possibilities of recognizable human experience. Only narrative form can contain the tensions, the surprises, the disappointments and reversals and achievements of actual, temporal experience. The vague yet unambiguous, uncanny happiness and horror are "beyond." The story itself may, to be sure, contain symbolic accents that refer to such a beyond, e.g., the resurrection, or images of eternal blessedness or torment, or descents into a nether region that is strangely familiar. Such symbolic accents are not necessarily intimations of immortality. Imagination is projected by them beyond any possible experience, and yet the projection itself takes place within the contingencies of experience. It belongs to the story. However deep into the bowels of hell Dante leads us, however high into heaven, it is remarkable how he and his sinners and saints keep our attention fixed on the little disk of earth, that stage on which the drama of men's moral struggles in time is enacted. Far from reducing the significance of this time-bound story in which we are embroiled, such visions of happiness and horror make it all the more portentous. Even in secularized projections beyond the ambiguity of history into social utopia or doomsday, a particular sense of the histori-

13. Frank Kermode ingeniously treats "tick-tock" as a model of plot, contrasting the organized duration between the "humble genesis" of tick and the "feeble apocalypse" of tock with the "emptiness," the unorganized blank that exists between our perception of "tock" and the next "tick." *The Sense of an Ending*, pp. 44-46.

cal drama itself is implicit. For the meaning of both happiness and horror is derived, even in the uttermost leap of the imagination beyond our story, from our conception of the story itself.

If experience has the narrative quality attributed to it here, not only our self-identity but the empirical and moral cosmos in which we are conscious of living is implicit in our multidimensional story. It therefore becomes evident that a conversion or a social revolution that actually transforms consciousness requires a traumatic change in a man's story. The stories within which he has awakened to consciousness must be undermined, and in the identification of his personal story through a new story both the drama of his experience and his style of action must be reoriented. Conversion is reawakening, a second awakening of consciousness. His style must change steps, he must dance to a new rhythm. Not only his past and future, but the very cosmos in which he lives is strung in a new way.

The point is beautifully made in a passage from the *Protreptikos* of Clement of Alexandria, selections from which, in verse translation, are among the last things we have from the pen of Thomas Merton. Clement, himself a convert to Christianity, is writing at the time Christianity first emerged in a serious way into a classical culture already become decadent. In a passage entitled "The New Song," he retells an old Greek legend but glosses it in a way that gives it a radical new turn. A bard named Eunomos was singing, to his own accompaniment of the lyre, a hymn to the death of the Pythian dragon. Meanwhile, unnoticed by the pagan assembly, another performance is under way.

> Crickets were singing among the leaves all up the
>   mountainside, burning in the sun.
> They were singing, not indeed for the death of the dragon,
>   the dead Pythian, but
> They hymned the all-wise God, in their own mode, far
>   superior to that of Eunomos.
> A harp string breaks on the Locrian.
> A cricket flies down on top of the lyre. She sings on the
>   instrument as though on a branch. The singer, harmonizing
>   with the cricket's tune, goes on without the lost string.
> Not by the song of Eunomos is the cricket moved, as the
>   myth supposes, or as is shown by the bronze statue the
>   Delphians erected, showing Eunomos with his harp and his
>   companion in the contest!
> The cricket flies on her own and sings on her own.

The subversive cricket sings the new song, to Clement old as creation yet newly come to human lips, of the Christian logos.

See what power the new song has!
From stones, men,
From beasts it has made men.
Those otherwise dead, those without a share in life that is
  really life
At the mere sound of this song
Have come back to life. . . .
Moreover He has structured the whole universe musically
And the discord of elements He has brought together in an
  ordered symphony
So that the whole Cosmos is for Him in harmony.[14]

III. Modernity and Revolution: An Intemperate Conclusion

The form of consciousness to which we apply the name *modernity* seems to represent a transformation as radical, though of a different sort, as that celebrated by Clement. Some have even suggested the emergence of a yet new sensibility, so new and inchoate that it can only be designated "post-modern." All this is too close to us to speak of it with much assurance, but I yield to the temptation to offer some suggestions that bear on our theme.

I have argued that experience is molded, root and branch, by narrative forms, that its narrative quality is altogether primitive. At the same time, expression is obviously not limited to storytelling. Mind and imagination are capable of recollecting the narrative materials of experience into essentially non-narrative forms. Indeed there seems to be a powerful inner drive of thought and imagination to overcome the relentless temporality of experience. One needs more clarity than stories can give us, and also a little rest. The kind of pure spatial articulation we find in painting and sculpture, with all movement suspended, gratifies this deep need. Also in meditation and in theoretical endeavors we are a little less completely at the mercy of our own temporality. Traditional myths, stories dominated by timeless archetypes, have functioned in this way: by taking personal and historical time up into the archetypal story, they give it a meaning which in the end is timeless, cosmic, absolute.

14. Clement of Alexandria, Selections from *The Protreptikos,* an essay and translation by Thomas Merton (New York: New Directions, 1962), pp. 15-16, 17. It is significant that the early Christian preaching was largely a story-telling mission, offering people a new story, the Christian kerygma, to reorient their sense of the meaning both of historical time and of their own personal life-time.

But an important feature of the modern situation is the employ-ment of quite different strategies for breaking the sense of narrative time. At a very general level, these strategies fall into two opposite and indeed mutually antagonistic types: one is the strategy of abstraction, in which images and qualities are detached from experience to become data for the formation of generalized principles and techniques. Such abstraction enables us to give experience a new, non-narrative and atemporal coher-ence. It is an indispensable strategy for conducting many of the practi-cal affairs of life in our society; we are all technicians, like it or not. In its more elaborated forms, the strategy of abstraction is the basis for all science. Its importance in the formation of modern institutions can hardly be exaggerated. But strategies of the other type seem almost equally im-portant in the formation of "modern" consciousness. This other type we may call the strategy of contraction. Here narrative temporality is again fragmented, not by abstraction to systems of generality, but by the con-striction of attention to dissociated immediacies: to the particular image isolated from the image stream, to isolated sensation, feeling, the flash of the overpowering moment in which the temporal context of that mo-ment is eclipsed and past and future are deliberately blocked out of con-sciousness. It is commonly assumed that this dissociated immediacy is what is concrete and irreducible in experience.

But the sweat and grit of the moment, which some so highly prize, is in fact a contraction of the narrative movement that is really concrete in experience, as generality is the abstraction from it. The point can perhaps best be made indirectly, by noticing that these two time-defying strategies have projected a distinctively modern version of a dualism in the idea of the self: the dualism of mind and body. We state the matter backwards if we say that something called *mind* abstracts from experience to produce generality, or if we say that "the body" has feel-ings and sensations. It is the activity of abstracting from the narrative concreteness of experience that leads us to posit the idea of mind as a distinct faculty. And it is the concentration of consciousness into feel-ing and sensation that gives rise to the idea of body. Both mind and body are reifications of particular functions that have been wrenched from the concrete temporality of the conscious self. The self is not a composite of mind and body. The self in its concreteness is indivisible, temporal, and whole, as it is revealed to be in the narrative quality of its experience. Neither disembodied minds nor mindless bodies can ap-pear in stories. There the self is given whole, as an activity in time.

Yet criticism alone cannot dissolve this mind-body dualism. The very fact of its stubborn persistence in our ordinary sense of ourselves, even though we know better (in theory!), testifies to the very great im-portance in the modern world of the two strategies on which it is based.

Stephen Crites

The power to abstract makes explanation, manipulation, control possible. On the other hand we seek relief and release in the capacity to contract the flow of time, to dwell in feeling and sensation, in taste, in touch, in the delicious sexual viscosities. So "the mind" dwells in the light, clear, dry, transparent, unmessy. "The body" dwells in the damp privacy of a friendly darkness created by feeling and sensation. In principle, the powers of consciousness to abstract and to contract need no more be in conflict than day and night. But day and night form a rhythm within the continuum of time. If the abstraction and contraction of consciousness were merely temporary suspensions of the narrative quality of experience there would be no crisis.

But the modern world has seen these two strategies played off ever more violently against one another. One could show how the reification of mind and body has killed modern metaphysics by leading it into arid controversies among dualistic, materialistic, and idealistic theories. But this comparatively harmless wrangle among post-Cartesian metaphysicians is only a symptom of the modern bifurcation of experience. Its more sinister expression is practical: the entrapment of educated subcultures in their own abstract constructions, and the violent reaction against this entrapment, a reaction that takes the form of an equally encapsulating constriction of experience into those warm, dark, humid immediacies. One thinks of Faust in his study where everything is so dry that a spark would produce an explosion, and then Faust slavering and mucking about on the bracken. Against the inhumanly dry and abstract habitations of the spirit that have been erected by technological reason, the cry goes up, born of desperation, to drop out and sink into the warm stream of immediacy. Within the university the reaction and counterreaction have been especially violent in the humanities.

And that is ironical. For the material with which the humanities have traditionally dealt is predominantly narrative. There have been deep conflicts among different kinds of stories and divergent interpretations. Still, the humanities have kept the story alive in the university; and it is precisely the story, with its underlying musicality, that provides generality and immediacy their humanly fruitful functions. So long as the story retains its primary hold on the imagination, the play of immediacy and the illuminating power of abstraction remain in productive tension. But when immediacy and abstract generality are wrenched out of the story altogether, drained of all musicality, the result is something I can only call, with strict theological precision, demonic. Experience becomes demonically possessed by its own abstracting and contracting possibilities, turned alien and hostile to experience itself. When the humanities give up the story, they become alternately seized by desiccated abstractions and scatological immediacies, the light of the mind becoming a blinding and withering glare, the friendly darkness deepening into the chaotic night of nihilism. Ethical authority, which is always a function of a common narrative coherence of life, is overthrown by a naked show of force exercised either in the name of reason or in the name of glandular vitality. Contrary to the cynical theory that violent force is the secret basis of authority, it is in fact always the sign that authority has dissolved.

So much for modernity. Now one speaks, perhaps wistfully, of the emergence of a "post-modern" sensibility. This new sensibility is sometimes called "revolutionary," a term that sounds less empty than "post-modern," but is still obscure enough. Certainly it is often discussed in terms of the same dualisms and wearisome strategies of abstraction and contraction that have plagued the "modern" period. Some envision a "revolution" that would consist in extending the control of abstract, technological reason to the whole life of society; maximum manipulation justified on the high moral ground that it would improve behavior—down to the least flicker of an eyelash. Others appear to hope for a society perpetually turned on and flowing with animal juices. The utopia schemed in the crystal palace, or that plotted in the cellar of the underground man: the lure of either of these utopias or any all-purpose combination of them can lead one to nothing more than a variation on an all too familiar refrain. Neither appears to catch the cadences of the new song that I think is struggling to be heard when people speak seriously of revolution.

I think that "revolution" is the name that a post-modern consciousness gives to a new sacred story. I realize that if this essay has ever strayed into the sphere of sober theory, it has with this suggestion abandoned it altogether in favor of testimony. But if we really are talking about a sacred story, what can we do but testify? Certainly the sacred story to which we give this name cannot be directly told. But its resonances can be felt in many of the stories that are being told, in songs being sung, in a renewed resolution to act. The stories being told do not necessarily speak of gods in any traditional sense, yet there seem to be living continuities in this unutterable story with some of the sacred stories of the past. Certainly, too, revolution is more than the name for an idea or a program, though it is giving rise to many ideas and programs, some no doubt half-baked and quixotic—anything radically serious seems to gather a penumbra of lunacy—but also some that actively express the most intense needs of our times.[15] This revolutionary story has united

15. There are also, of course, theories of revolution itself. But it is significant that the most important theories of revolution are dialectical. For a dialectical theory is that form of generality that preserves in itself the vital pulse of a temporal movement. A dialectical theory of revolution is not an alternative to a study of revolution, but is its exegesis.

the angry children of poverty and the alienated children of abundance in a common moral passion and a common sense of the meaning of their experience. Among those for whom the story is alive there is a revival of ethical authority otherwise almost effaced in our society. For it establishes on a new basis the coherency of social and personal time. It makes it possible to recover a living past, to believe again in the future, to perform acts that have significance for the person who acts. By so doing, it restores a human form of experience.

The Virtues, the Unity of a Human Life, and the Concept of a Tradition

Alasdair MacIntyre

Any contemporary attempt to envisage each human life as a whole, as a unity, whose character provides the virtues with an adequate *telos*, encounters two different kinds of obstacle, one social and one philosophical. The social obstacles derive from the way in which modernity partitions each human life into a variety of segments, each with its own norms and modes of behavior. So work is divided from leisure, private life from public, the corporate from the personal. So both childhood and old age have been wrenched away from the rest of human life and made over into distinct realms. And all these separations have been achieved so that it is the distinctiveness of each and not the unity of the life of the individual who passes through those parts in terms of which we are taught to think and to feel.

The philosophical obstacles derive from two distinct tendencies, one chiefly, though not only, domesticated in analytical philosophy and one at home in both sociological theory and in existentialism. The former is the tendency to think atomistically about human action and to analyze complex actions and transactions in terms of simple components. Hence the recurrence in more than one context of the notion of "a basic action." That particular actions derive their character as parts of larger

---

Alasdair MacIntyre, "The Virtues, the Unity of a Human Life and the Concept of a Tradition," in his *After Virtue* (Notre Dame: University of Notre Dame Press, 1981), pp. 190-209.

wholes is a point of view alien to our dominant ways of thinking and yet one which it is necessary at least to consider if we are to begin to understand how a life may be more than a sequence of individual actions and episodes.

Equally the unity of a human life becomes invisible to us when a sharp separation is made either between the individual and the roles that he or she plays—a separation characteristic not only of Sartre's existentialism, but also of the sociological theory of Ralf Dahrendorf—or between the different role—and quasi-role—enactments of an individual life so that life comes to appear as nothing but a series of unconnected episodes—a liquidation of the self characteristic, as I noticed earlier, of Goffman's sociological theory. I already also suggested in Chapter 3 that both the Sartrian and the Goffmanesque conceptions of selfhood are highly characteristic of the modes of thought and practice of modernity. It is perhaps therefore unsurprising to realize that the self as thus conceived cannot be envisaged as a bearer of the Aristotelian virtues.

For a self separated from its roles in the Sartrian mode loses that arena of social relationships in which the Aristotelian virtues function if they function at all. The patterns of a virtuous life would fall under those condemnations of conventionality which Sartre put into the mouth of Antoine Roquentin in *La Nausée* and which he uttered in his own person in *L'Être et le Néant*. Indeed the self's refusal of the inauthenticity of conventionalized social relationships becomes what integrity is diminished into in Sartre's account.

At the same time the liquidation of the self into a set of demarcated areas of role-playing allows no scope for the exercise of dispositions which could genuinely be accounted virtues in any sense remotely Aristotelian. For a virtue is not a disposition that makes for success only in some one particular type of situation. What are spoken of as the virtues of a good committee man or of a good administrator or of a gambler or a pool hustler are professional skills professionally deployed in those situations where they can be effective, not virtues. Someone who genuinely possesses a virtue can be expected to manifest it in very different types of situations, many of them situations where the practice of a virtue cannot be expected to be effective in the way that we expect a professional skill to be. Hector exhibited one and the same courage in his parting from Andromache and on the battlefield with Achilles; Eleanor Marx exhibited one and the same compassion in her relationship with her father, in her work with trade unionists, and in her entanglement with Aveling. And the unity of a virtue in someone's life is intelligible only as a characteristic of a unitary life, a life that can be conceived and evaluated as a whole. Hence just as in the discussion of the changes in and fragmentation of morality which accompanied the rise of modernity in the earlier parts of this book, each stage in the emergence of the characteristically modern views of the moral judgment was accompanied by a corresponding stage in the emergence of the characteristically modern conceptions of selfhood; so now, in defining the particular pre-modern concept of the virtues with which I have been preoccupied, it has become necessary to say something of the concomitant concept of selfhood, a concept of a self whose unity resides in the unity of a narrative which links birth to life to death as narrative beginning to middle to end.

Such a conception of the self is perhaps less unfamiliar than it may appear at first sight. Just because it has played a key part in the cultures which are historically predecessors of our own, it would not be surprising if it turned out to be still an unacknowledged presence in many of our ways of thinking and acting. Hence it is not inappropriate to begin by scrutinizing some of our most taken-for-granted, but clearly correct conceptual insights about human actions and selfhood in order to show how natural it is to think of the self in a narrative mode.

It is a conceptual commonplace, both for philosophers and for ordinary agents, that one and the same segment of human behavior may be correctly characterized in a number of different ways. To the question "What is he doing?" the answers may with equal truth and appropriateness be "Digging"; "Gardening"; "Taking exercise"; "Preparing for winter"; or "Pleasing his wife." Some of these answers will characterize the agent's intentions, others unintended consequences of his actions, and of these unintended consequences some may be such that the agent is aware of them and others not. What is important to notice immediately is that any answer to the questions of how we are to understand or to explain a given segment of behavior will presuppose some prior answer to the question of how these different correct answers to the question "What is he doing?" are related to each other. For if someone's primary intention is to put the garden in order before the winter and it is only incidentally the case that in so doing he is taking exercise and pleasing his wife, we have one type of behavior to be explained; but if the agent's primary intention is to please his wife by taking exercise, we have quite another type of behavior to be explained and we will have to look in a different direction for understanding and explanation.

In the first place the episode has been situated in an annual cycle of domestic activity, and the behavior embodies an intention which presupposes a particular type of household-cum-garden setting with the peculiar narrative history of that setting in which this segment of behavior now becomes an episode. In the second instance the episode has

Alasdair MacIntyre

been situated in the narrative history of a marriage, a very different, even if related, social setting. We cannot, that is to say, characterize behavior independently of intentions, and we cannot characterize intentions independently of the settings which make those intentions intelligible both to agents themselves and to others.

I use the word "setting" here as a relatively inclusive term. A social setting may be an institution, it may be what I have called a practice, or it may be a milieu of some other human kind. But it is central to the notion of a setting as I am going to understand it that a setting has a history, a history within which the histories of individual agents not only are, but have to be, situated, just because without the setting and its changes through time the history of the individual agent and his changes through time will be unintelligible. Of course one and the same piece of behavior may belong to more than one setting. There are at least two different ways in which this may be so.

In my earlier example the agent's activity may be part of the history both of the cycle of household activity and of his marriage, two histories which have happened to intersect. The household may have its own history stretching back through hundreds of years, as do the histories of some European farms, where the farm has had a life of its own, even though different families have in different periods inhabited it, and the marriage will certainly have its own history, a history which itself presupposes that a particular point has been reached in the history of the institution of marriage. If we are to relate some particular segment of behavior in any precise way to an agent's intentions and thus to the settings which that agent inhabits, we shall have to understand in a precise way how the variety of correct characterizations of the agent's behavior relate to each other, first by identifying which characteristics refer us to an intention and which do not, and then by classifying further the items in both categories.

Where intentions are concerned, we need to know which intention or intentions were primary, that is to say, of which it is the case that, had the agent intended otherwise, he would not have performed that action. Thus if we know that a man is gardening with the self-avowed purposes of healthful exercise and of pleasing his wife, we do not yet know how to understand what he is doing until we know the answer to such questions as whether he would continue gardening if he continued to believe that gardening was healthful exercise, but discovered that his gardening no longer pleased his wife, *and* whether he would continue gardening, if he ceased to believe that gardening was healthful exercise, but continued to believe that it pleased his wife, *and* whether he would continue gardening if he changed his beliefs on both points. That is to say, we need to know both what certain of his beliefs are and which of them are causally effective; and, that is to say, we need to know whether certain contrary-to-fact hypothetical statements are true or false. And until we know this, we shall not know how to characterize correctly what the agent is doing.

Consider another equally trivial example of a set of compatibly correct answers to the question "What is he doing?": "Writing a sentence"; "Finishing his book"; "Contributing to the debate on the theory of action"; "Trying to get tenure." Here the intentions can be ordered in terms of the stretch of time to which reference is made. Each of the shorter-term intentions is, and can only be made, intelligible by reference to some longer-term intentions; and the characterization of the behavior in terms of the longer-term intentions can only be correct if some of the characterizations in terms of shorter-term intentions are also correct. Hence the behavior is only characterized adequately when we know what the longer- and longest-term intentions invoked are and how the shorter-term intentions are related to the longer. Once again we are involved in writing a narrative history.

Intentions thus need to be ordered both causally and temporally and both orderings will make references to settings, references already made obliquely by such elementary terms as "gardening," "wife," "book," and "tenure." Moreover the correct identification of the agent's beliefs will be an essential constituent of this task; failure at this point would mean failure in the whole enterprise. (The conclusion may seem obvious; but it already entails one important consequence. There is no such thing as "behavior," to be identified prior to and independently of intentions, beliefs, and settings. Hence the project of a science of behavior takes on a mysterious and somewhat outré character. It is not that such a science is impossible; but there is nothing for it to be but a science of uninterpreted physical movement such as B. F. Skinner aspires to. It is no part of my task here to examine Skinner's problems; but it is worth noticing that it is not at all clear what a scientific experiment could be, if one were a Skinnerian, since the conception of an experiment is certainly one of intention- and belief-informed behavior. And what would be utterly doomed to failure would be the project of a science of, say, *political* behavior, detached from a study of intentions, beliefs, and settings. It is perhaps worth noting that when the expression "the behavioral sciences" was given its first influential use in a Ford Foundation Report of 1953, the term "behavior" was defined so as to include what were called "such subjective behavior as attitudes, beliefs, expectations, motivations and aspirations" as well as "overt acts." But what the Report's wording seems to imply is that it is cataloguing two distinct sets of items, available for independent study. If the argument so far is correct, then there is only one set of items.)

Alasdair MacIntyre

Consider what the argument so far implies about the inter-relationships of the intentional, the social, and the historical. We identify a particular action only by invoking two kinds of context, implicitly if not explicitly. We place the agent's intentions, I have suggested, in causal and temporal order with reference to their role in his or her history; and we also place them with reference to their role in the history of the setting or settings to which they belong. In doing this, in determining what causal efficacy the agent's intentions had in one or more directions, and how his short-term intentions succeeded or failed to be constitutive of long-term intentions, we ourselves write a further part of these histories. Narrative history of a certain kind turns out to be the basic and essential genre for the characterization of human actions.

It is important to be clear how different the standpoint presupposed by the argument so far is from that of those analytical philosophers who have constructed accounts of human actions which make central the notion of "a" human action. A course of human events is then seen as a complex sequence of individual actions, and a natural question is: How do we individuate human actions? Now there are contexts in which such notions are at home. In the recipes of a cookery book, for instance, actions are individuated in just the way that some analytical philosophers have supposed to be possible of all actions. "Take six eggs. Then break them into a bowl. Add flour, salt, sugar, etc." But the point about such sequences is that each element in them is intelligible as an action only as a-possible-element-in-a-sequence. Moreover even such a sequence requires a context to be intelligible. If in the middle of my lecture on Kant's ethics I suddenly broke six eggs into a bowl and added flour and sugar, proceeding all the while with my Kantian exegesis, I have *not*, simply in virtue of the fact that I was following a sequence prescribed by Fanny Farmer, performed an intelligible action.

To this it might be retorted that I certainly performed an action or a set of actions, if not an intelligible action. But to this I want to reply that the concept of an intelligible action is a more fundamental concept than that of an action as such. Unintelligible actions are failed candidates for the status of intelligible action; and to lump unintelligible actions and intelligible actions together in a single class of actions and then to characterize action in terms of what items of both sets have in common is to make the mistake of ignoring this. It is also to neglect the central importance of the concept of intelligibility.

The importance of the concept of intelligibility is closely related to the fact that the most basic distinction of all embedded in our discourse and our practice in this area is that between human beings and other beings. Human beings can be held to account for that of which they are the authors; other beings cannot. To identify an occurrence as an action is in the paradigmatic instances to identify it under a type of description which enables us to see that occurrence as flowing intelligibly from a human agent's intentions, motives, passions, and purposes. It is therefore to understand an action as something for which someone is accountable, about which it is always appropriate to ask the agent for an intelligible account. When an occurrence is apparently the intended action of a human agent, but nonetheless we cannot so identify it, we are both intellectually and practically baffled. We do not know how to respond; we do not know how to explain; we do not even know how to characterize minimally as an intelligible action; our distinction between the humanly accountable and the merely natural seems to have broken down. And this kind of bafflement does indeed occur in a number of different kinds of situations; when we enter alien cultures or even alien social structures within our own culture, in our encounters with certain types of neurotic or psychotic patients (it is indeed the unintelligibility of such patients' actions that leads to their being treated as patients; actions unintelligible to the agent as well as to everyone else are understood—rightly—as a kind of suffering), but also in everyday situations. Consider an example.

I am standing waiting for a bus and the young man standing next to me suddenly says: "The name of the common wild duck is *Histrionicus histrionicus histrionicus*." There is no problem as to the meaning of the sentence he uttered: the problem is how to answer the question, what was he doing uttering it? Suppose he just uttered such sentences at random intervals; this would be one possible form of madness. We would render his action of utterance intelligible if one of the following turned out to be true. He has mistaken me for someone who yesterday had approached him in the library and asked: "Do you by any chance know the Latin name of the common wild duck?" *Or* he has just come from a session with his psychotherapist who has urged him to break down his shyness by talking to strangers. "But what shall I say?" "Oh, anything at all." *Or* he is a Soviet spy waiting at a prearranged rendezvous and uttering the ill-chosen code sentence which will identify him to his contact. In each case the act of utterance becomes intelligible by finding its place in a narrative.

To this it may be replied that the supplying of a narrative is not necessary to make such an act intelligible. All that is required is that we can identify the relevant type of speech act (e.g., "He was answering a question") or some purpose served by his utterance (e.g., "He was trying to attract your attention"). But speech acts and purposes too can be intelligible or unintelligible. Suppose that the man at the bus stop explains his act of utterance by saying "I was answering a question." I reply: "But I never asked you any question to which that could have been the answer." He says, "Oh, I know *that*." Once again his action becomes unintelligible. And a parallel example could easily be constructed to show that the mere fact that an action serves some purposes of a recognized type is not sufficient to render an action intelligible. Both purposes and speech-acts require contexts.

The most familiar type of context in and by reference to which speech-acts and purposes are rendered intelligible is the conversation. Conversation is so all-pervasive a feature of the human world that it tends to escape philosophical attention. Yet remove conversation from human life and what would be left? Consider then what is involved in following a conversation and finding it intelligible or unintelligible. (To find a conversation intelligible is not the same as to understand it; for a conversation which I overhear may be intelligible, but I may fail to understand it.) If I listen to a conversation between two other people, my ability to grasp the thread of the conversation will involve an ability to bring it under some one out of a set of descriptions in which the degree and kind of coherence in the conversation is brought out: "a drunken, rambling quarrel," "a serious intellectual disagreement," "a tragic misunderstanding of each other," "a comic, even farcical misconstrual of each other's motives," "a penetrating interchange of views," "a struggle to dominate each other," "a trivial exchange of gossip."

The use of words such as "tragic," "comic," and "farcical" is not marginal to such evaluations. We allocate conversations to genres, just as we do literary narratives. Indeed a conversation is a dramatic work, even if a very short one, in which the participants are not only the actors, but also the joint authors, working out in agreement or disagreement the mode of their production. For it is not just that conversations belong to genres in just the way that plays and novels do; but they have beginnings, middles, and endings just as do literary works. They embody reversals and recognitions; they move towards and away from climaxes. There may within a longer conversation be digressions and subplots, indeed digressions within digressions and subplots within subplots.

But if this is true of conversations, it is true also *mutatis mutandis* of battles, chess games, courtships, philosophy seminars, families at the dinner table, businessmen negotiating contracts—that is, of human transactions in general. For conversation, understood widely enough, is the form of human transactions in general. Conversational behavior is not a special sort or aspect of human behavior, even though the forms of language-using and of human life are such that the deeds of others speak for them as much as do their words. For that is possible only because they are the deeds of those who have words.

I am presenting both conversations in particular, then, and human actions in general as enacted narratives. Narrative is not the work of poets, dramatists, and novelists reflecting upon events which had no narrative order before one was imposed by the singer or the writer; narrative form is neither disguise nor decoration. Barbara Hardy has written that "we dream in narrative, day-dream in narrative, remember, anticipate, hope, despair, believe, doubt, plan, revise, criticize, construct, gossip, learn, hate and love by narrative" in arguing the same point.[1]

At the beginning of this chapter I argued that in successfully identifying and understanding what someone else is doing we always move towards placing a particular episode in the context of a set of narrative histories, histories both of the individuals concerned and of the settings in which they act and suffer. It is now becoming clear that we render the actions of others intelligible in this way because action itself has a basically historical character. It is because we all live our narratives in our lives and because we understand our own lives in terms of the narratives that we live out that the form of narrative is appropriate for understanding the actions of others. Stories are lived before they are told—except in the case of fiction.

This has of course been denied in recent debates. Louis O. Mink, quarrelling with Barbara Hardy's view, has asserted: "Stories are not lived but told. Life has no beginnings, middles, or ends; there are meetings, but the start of an affair belongs to the story we tell ourselves later, and there are partings, but final partings only in the story. There are hopes, plans, battles and ideas, but only in retrospective stories are hopes unfulfilled, plans miscarried, battles decisive, and ideas seminal. Only in the story is it America which Columbus discovers and only in the story is the kingdom lost for want of a nail."[2]

What are we to say to this? Certainly we must agree that it is only retrospectively that hopes can be characterized as unfulfilled or battles as decisive and so on. But we so characterize them in life as much as in art. And to someone who says that in life there are no endings, or that final partings take place only in stories, one is tempted to reply, "But have you never heard of death?" Homer did not have to tell the tale of Hector before Andromache could lament unfulfilled hope and final parting. There are countless Hectors and countless Andromaches whose lives embodied the form of their Homeric namesakes, but who never came to the attention of any poet. What is true is that in taking an event as a beginning or an ending we bestow a significance upon it which may be debatable. Did the Roman republic end with the death

1. Barbara Hardy, "Towards a Poetics of Fiction: An Approach through Narrative," *Novel*, 2 (1968): 5.

2. Louis O. Mink, "History and Fiction as Modes of Comprehension," *New Literary History*, 1 (1970): 557-558.

of Julius Caesar, or at Philippi, or with the founding of the principate? The answer is surely that, like Charles II, it was a long time a-dying; but this answer implies the reality of its ending as much as do any of the former. There is a crucial sense in which the principate of Augustus, or the taking of the oath in the tennis court, or the decision to construct an atomic bomb at Los Alamos constitute beginnings; the peace of 404 B.C., the abolition of the Scottish Parliament, and the battle of Waterloo equally constitute endings; while there are many events which are both endings and beginnings.

As with beginnings, middles, and endings, so also with genres and with the phenomenon of embedding. Consider the question of to what genre the life of Thomas Becket belongs, a question which has to be asked and answered before we can decide how it is to be written. (In Mink's paradoxical view this question could not be asked until *after* the life had been written.) In some of the medieval versions, Thomas's career is presented in terms of the canons of medieval hagiography. In the Icelandic *Thomas Saga* he is presented as a saga hero. In David Knowles's modern biography the story is a tragedy, the tragic relationship of Thomas and Henry II, each of whom satisfies Aristotle's demand that the hero be a great man with a fatal flaw. Now it clearly makes sense to ask who is right, if anyone: the monk William of Canterbury, the author of the saga, or the Cambridge Regius Professor Emeritus? The answer appears to be clearly the last. The true genre of the life is neither hagiography nor saga, but tragedy. So of such modern narrative subjects as the life of Trotsky or that of Lenin, of the history of the Soviet Communist Party or the American presidency, we may also ask: To what genre does their history belong? And this is the same question as: What type of account of their history will be both true and intelligible?

Or consider again how one narrative may be embedded in another. In both plays and novels there are well-known examples: the play within the play in *Hamlet,* Wandering Willie's Tale in *Redgauntlet,* Aeneas' narrative to Dido in book 2 of the *Aeneid,* and so on. But there are equally well-known examples in real life. Consider again the way in which the career of Becket as archbishop and chancellor is embedded within the reign of Henry II, or the way in which the tragic life of Mary Stuart is embedded in that of Elizabeth I, or the history of the Confederacy within the history of the United States. Someone may discover (or not discover) that he or she is a character in a number of narratives at the same time, some of them embedded in others. Or again, what seemed to be an intelligible narrative in which one was playing a part may be transformed wholly or partly into a story of unintelligible episodes. This last is what happened to Kafka's character K. in both *The Trial* and *The Castle.* (It is no accident that Kafka could not end his novels, for the notion of an ending, like that of a beginning, has its sense only in terms of intelligible narrative.)

I spoke earlier of the agent as not only an actor, but an author. Now I must emphasize that what the agent is able to do and say intelligibly as an actor is deeply affected by the fact that we are never more (and sometimes less) than the co-authors of our own narratives. Only in fantasy do we live what story we please. In life, as both Aristotle and Engels noted, we are always under certain constraints. We enter upon a stage which we did not design and we find ourselves part of an action that was not of our making. Each of us being a main character in his own drama plays subordinate parts in the dramas of others, and each drama constrains the others. In my drama, perhaps, I am Hamlet or Iago or at least the swineherd who may yet become a prince, but to you I am only A Gentleman or at best Second Murderer, while you are my Polonius or my Gravedigger, but your own hero. Each of our dramas exerts constraints on each other's, making the whole different from the parts, but still dramatic.

It is considerations as complex as these which are involved in making the notion of intelligibility the conceptual connecting link between the notion of action and that of narrative. Once we have understood its importance, the claim that the concept of an action is secondary to that of an intelligible action will perhaps appear less bizarre and so too will the claim that the notion of "an" action, while of the highest practical importance, is always a potentially misleading abstraction. An action is a moment in a possible or actual history or in a number of such histories. The notion of a history is as fundamental a notion as the notion of an action. Each requires the other. But I cannot say this without noticing that it is precisely this that Sartre denies—as indeed his whole theory of the self, which captures so well the spirit of modernity, requires that he should. In *La Nausée*, Sartre makes Antoine Roquentin argue not just what Mink argues, that narrative is very different from life, but that to present human life in the form of a narrative is always to falsify it. There are not and there cannot be any true stories. Human life is composed of discrete actions which lead nowhere, which have no order; the story-teller imposes on human events retrospectively an order which they did not have while they were lived. Clearly if Sartre/Roquentin is right—I speak of Sartre/Roquentin to distinguish him from such other well-known characters as Sartre/Heidegger and Sartre/Marx—my central contention must be mistaken. There is nonetheless an important point of agreement between my thesis and that of Sartre/Roquentin. We agree in identifying the intelligibility of an action with its place in a narrative sequence. Only Sartre/Roquentin takes it that human actions are as such unintelligible occurrences: it is to a realization of the metaphysical implications of this that Roquentin is brought in the course of the novel and the practical effect upon him is to bring to an end his own project of writing an historical biography. This project no longer makes sense. Either he will write what is true or he will write an intelligible history, but the one possibility excludes the other. Is Sartre/Roquentin right?

We can discover what is wrong with Sartre's thesis in either of two ways. One is to ask: What would human actions deprived of any falsifying narrative order be like? Sartre himself never answers this question; it is striking that in order to show that there are no true narratives, he himself writes a narrative, albeit a fictional one. But the only picture that I find myself able to form of human nature *an-sich,* prior to the alleged misinterpretation by narrative, is the kind of dislocated sequence which Dr. Johnson offers us in his notes of his travels in France: "There we waited on the ladies—Morville's.—Spain. Country towns all beggars. At Dijon he could not find the way to Orleans.—Cross roads of France very bad.—Five soldiers.—Woman.—Soldiers escaped.—The magistrate cannot seize a soldier but by the Colonel's permission, etc., etc."[3] What this suggests is what I take to be true, namely that the characterization of actions allegedly prior to any narrative form being imposed upon them will always turn out to be the presentation of what are plainly the disjointed parts of some possible narrative.

We can also approach the question in another way. What I have called a history is an enacted dramatic narrative in which the characters are also the authors. The characters of course never start literally *ab initio*; they plunge *in medias res,* the beginnings of their story already made for them by what and who has gone before. But when Julian Grenfell or Edward Thomas went off to France in the 1914-18 war, they no less enacted a narrative than did Menelaus or Odysseus when *they* went off. The difference between imaginary characters and real ones is not in the narrative form of what they do; it is in the degree of their authorship of that form and of their own deeds. Of course just as they do not begin where they please, they cannot go on exactly as they please either; each character is constrained by the actions of others and by the social settings presupposed in his and their actions, a point forcibly made by Marx in the classical, if not entirely satisfactory, account of human life as enacted dramatic narrative, *The Eighteenth Brumaire of Louis Bonaparte.*

I call Marx's account less than satisfactory partly because he wishes to present the narrative of human social life in a way that will be compatible with a view of the life as law-governed and predictable in a particular way. But it is crucial that at any given point in an enacted

3. Philip Hobsbaum, *A Reader's Guide to Charles Dickens* (1973), p. 32.

dramatic narrative we do not know what will happen next. The kind of unpredictability for which I argued in Chapter 8 of *After Virtue* is required by the narrative structure of human life, and the empirical generalizations and explorations which social scientists discover provide a kind of understanding of human life which is perfectly compatible with that structure.

This unpredictability coexists with a second crucial characteristic of all lived narratives, a certain teleological character. We live out our lives, both individually and in our relationships with each other, in the light of certain conceptions of a possible shared future, a future in which certain possibilities beckon us forward and others repel us, some seem already foreclosed and others perhaps inevitable. There is no present which is not informed by some image of some future and an image of the future which always presents itself in the form of a *telos*—or a variety of ends or goals—towards which we are either moving or failing to move in the present. Unpredictability and teleology therefore coexist as part of our lives; like characters in a fictional narrative we do not know what will happen next, but nonetheless our lives have a certain form which projects itself towards our future. Thus the narratives which we live out have both an unpredictable and a partially teleological character. If the narrative of our individual and social lives is to continue intelligibly—and either type of narrative may lapse into unintelligibility— it is always both the case that there are constraints on how the story can continue *and* that within those constraints there are indefinitely many ways that it can continue.

A central thesis then begins to emerge: man is in his actions and practice, as well as in his fictions, essentially a story-telling animal. He is not essentially, but becomes through his history, a teller of stories that aspire to truth. But the key question for men is not about their own authorship; I can only answer the question "What am I to do?" if I can answer the prior question "Of what story or stories do I find myself a part?" We enter human society, that is, with one or more imputed characters—roles into which we have been drafted—and we have to learn what they are in order to be able to understand how others respond to us and how our responses to them are apt to be construed. It is through hearing stories about wicked stepmothers, lost children, good but misguided kings, wolves that suckle twin boys, youngest sons who receive no inheritance but must make their own way in the world, and eldest sons who waste their inheritance on riotous living and go into exile to live with the swine, that children learn or mislearn both what a child and what a parent is, what the cast of characters may be in the drama into which they have been born and what the ways of the world are. Deprive children of stories and you leave them unscripted, anxious

101

stutterers in their actions as in their words. Hence there is no way to give us an understanding of any society, including our own, except through the stock of stories which constitute its initial dramatic resources. Mythology, in its original sense, is at the heart of things. Vico was right and so was Joyce. And so too of course is that moral tradition from heroic society to its medieval heirs according to which the telling of stories has a key part in educating us into the virtues.

I suggested earlier that "an" action is always an episode in a possible history: I would now like to make a related suggestion about another concept, that of personal identity. Derek Parfit and others have recently drawn our attention to the contrast between the criteria of strict identity, which is an all-or-nothing matter (*either* the Tichborne claimant *is* the last Tichborne heir *or* he is not; *either* all the properties of the last heir belong to the claimant *or* the claimant is not the heir—Leibniz's Law applies) and the psychological continuities of personality which are a matter of more or less. (Am I the same man at fifty as I was at forty in respect of memory, intellectual powers, critical responses? More or less.) But what is crucial to human beings as characters in enacted narratives is that, possessing only the resources of psychological continuity, we have to be able to respond to the imputation of strict identity. I am forever whatever I have been at any time for others—and I may at anytime be called upon to answer for it—no matter how changed I may be now. There is no way of *founding* my identity—or lack of it—on the psychological continuity or discontinuity of the self. The self inhabits a character whose unity is given as the unity of a character. Once again there is a crucial disagreement with empiricist or analytical philosophers on the one hand and with existentialists on the other.

Empiricists, such as Locke or Hume, tried to give an account of personal identity solely in terms of psychological states or events. Analytical philosophers, in so many ways their heirs as well as their critics, have wrestled with the connection between those states and events and strict identity understood in terms of Leibniz's Law. Both have failed to see that a background has been omitted, the lack of which makes the problems insoluble. That background is provided by the concept of a story and of that kind of unity of character which a story requires. Just as a history is not a sequence of actions, but the concept of an action is that of a moment in an actual or possible history abstracted for some purpose from the history, so the characters in a history are not a collection of persons, but the concept of a person is that of a character abstracted from a history.

What the narrative concept of selfhood requires is thus twofold. On the one hand, I am what I may justifiably be taken by others to be in the course of living out a story that runs from my birth to my death;

I am the *subject* of a history that is my own and no one else's, that has its own peculiar meaning. When someone complains—as do some of those who attempt or commit suicide—that his or her life is meaningless, he or she is often and perhaps characteristically complaining that the narrative of their life has become unintelligible to them, that it lacks any point, any movement towards a climax or a *telos*. Hence the point of doing any one thing rather than another at crucial junctures in their lives seems to such persons to have been lost.

To be the subject of a narrative that runs from one's birth to one's death is, I remarked earlier, to be accountable for the actions and experiences which compose a narratable life. It is, that is, to be open to being asked to give a certain kind of account of what one did or what happened to one or what one witnessed at any earlier point in one's life than the time at which the question is posed. Of course someone may have forgotten or suffered brain damage or simply not attended sufficiently at the relevant time to be able to give the relevant account. But to say of someone under some one description ("The prisoner of the Chateau d'If") that he is the same person as someone characterized quite differently ("The Count of Monte Cristo") is precisely to say that it makes sense to ask him to give an intelligible narrative account enabling us to understand how he could at different times and different places be one and the same person and yet be so differently characterized. Thus personal identity is just that identity presupposed by the unity of the character which the unity of a narrative requires. Without such unity there would not be subjects of whom stories could be told.

The other aspect of narrative selfhood is correlative: I am not only accountable. I am one who can always ask others for an account, who can put others to the question. I am part of their story, as they are part of mine. The narrative of any one life is part of an interlocking set of narratives. Moreover this asking for and giving of accounts itself plays an important part in constituting narratives. Asking you what you did and why, saying what I did and why, pondering the differences between your account of what I did and my account of what I did and *vice versa*, these are essential constituents of all but the very simplest and barest of narratives. Thus without the accountability of the self those trains of events that constitute all but the simplest and barest of narratives could not occur; and without that same accountability narratives would lack that continuity required to make both them and the actions that constitute them intelligible.

It is important to notice that I am not arguing that the concepts of narrative or of intelligibility or of accountability are *more* fundamental than that of personal identity. The concepts of narrative, intelligibility and accountability presuppose the applicability of the concept of personal identity, just as it presupposes their applicability and just as indeed each of these three presupposes the applicability of the two others. The relationship is one of mutual presupposition. It does follow of course that all attempts to elucidate the notion of personal identity independently of and in isolation from the notions of narrative, intelligibility, and accountability are bound to fail. As all such attempts have.

It is now possible to return to the question from which this enquiry into the nature of human action and identity started: In what does the unity of an individual life consist? The answer is that its unity is the unity of a narrative embodied in a single life. To ask "What is the good for me?" is to ask how best I might live out that unity and bring it to completion. To ask "What is the good for man?" is to ask what all answers to the former question must have in common. But now it is important to emphasize that it is the systematic asking of these two questions and the attempt to answer them in deed as well as in word which provide the moral life with its unity. The unity of a human life is the unity of a narrative quest. Quests sometimes fail, are frustrated, abandoned, or dissipated into distractions; and human lives may in all these ways also fail. But the only criteria for success or failure in a human life as a whole are the criteria of success or failure in a narrated or to-be-narrated quest. A quest for what?

Two key features of the medieval conception of a quest need to be recalled. The first is that without some at least partly determinate conception of the final *telos* there could not be any beginning to a quest. Some conception of the good for man is required. Whence is such a conception to be drawn? Precisely from those questions which led us to attempt to transcend that limited conception of the virtues which is available in and through practices. It is in looking for a conception of *the* good which will enable us to order other goods, for a conception of *the* good which will enable us to extend our understanding of the purpose and content of the virtues, for a conception of *the* good which will enable us to understand the place of integrity and constancy in life, that we initially define the kind of life which is a quest for the good. But secondly it is clear the medieval conception of a quest is not at all that of a search for something already adequately characterized, as miners search for gold or geologists for oil. It is in the course of the quest and only through encountering and coping with the various particular harms, dangers, temptations, and distractions which provide any quest with its episodes and incidents that the goal of the quest is finally to be understood. A quest is always an education both as to the character of that which is sought and in self-knowledge.

The virtues therefore are to be understood as those dispositions which will not only sustain practices and enable us to achieve the goods internal to practices, but which will also sustain us in the relevant kind of quest for the good, by enabling us to overcome the harms, dangers, temptations, and distractions which we encounter, and which will furnish us with increasing self-knowledge and increasing knowledge of the good. The catalogue of the virtues will therefore include the virtues required to sustain the kind of households and the kind of political communities in which men and women can seek for the good together, and the virtues necessary for philosophical enquiry about the character of the good. We have then arrived at a provisional conclusion about the good life for man: the good life for man is the life spent in seeking for the good life for man, and the virtues necessary for the seeking are those which will enable us to understand what more and what else the good life for man is. We have also completed the second stage in our account of the virtues, by situating them in relation to the good life for man and not only in relation to practices. But our enquiry requires a third stage.

For I am never able to seek for the good or exercise the virtues only *qua* individual. This is partly because what it is to live the good life concretely varies from circumstance to circumstance even when it is one and the same conception of the good life and one and the same set of virtues which are being embodied in a human life. What the good life is for a fifth-century Athenian general will not be the same as what it was for a medieval nun or a seventeenth-century farmer. But it is not just that different individuals live in different social circumstances; it is also that we all approach our own circumstances as bearers of a particular social identity. I am someone's son or daughter, someone else's cousin or uncle; I am a citizen of this or that city, a member of this or that guild or profession; I belong to this clan, that tribe, this nation. Hence what is good for me has to be the good for one who inhabits these roles. As such, I inherit from the past of my family, my city, my tribe, my nation, a variety of debts, inheritances, rightful expectations, and obligations. These constitute the given of my life, my moral starting point. This is in part what gives my life its own moral particularity.

This thought is likely to appear alien and even surprising from the standpoint of modern individualism. From the standpoint of individualism I am what I myself choose to be. I can always, if I wish to, put in question what are taken to be the merely contingent social features of my existence. I may biologically be my father's son; but I cannot be held responsible for what he did unless I choose implicitly or explicitly to assume such responsibility. I may legally be a citizen of a certain country; but I cannot be held responsible for what my country does or has done unless I choose implicitly or explicitly to assume such responsibility. Such individualism is expressed by those modern Americans who deny any responsibility for the effects of slavery upon black

Americans, saying "I never owned any slaves." It is more subtly the standpoint of those other modern Americans who accept a nicely calculated responsibility for such effects measured precisely by the benefits they themselves as individuals have indirectly received from slavery. In both cases "being an American" is not in itself taken to be part of the moral identity of the individual. And of course there is nothing peculiar to modern Americans in this attitude: the Englishman who says, "*I never did any wrong to Ireland; why bring up that old history as though it had something to with me?*" or the young German who believes that being born after 1945 means that what Nazis did to Jews has no moral relevance to his relationship to his Jewish contemporaries, exhibits the same attitude, that according to which the self is detachable from its social and historical roles and statuses. And the self so detached is of course a self very much at home in either Sartre's or Goffman's perspective, a self that can have no history. The contrast with the narrative view of the self is clear. For the story of my life is always embedded in the story of those communities from which I derive my identity. I am born with a past; and to try to cut myself off from that past, in the individualist mode, is to deform my present relationships. The possession of an historical identity and the possession of a social identity coincide. Notice that rebellion against my identity is always one possible mode of expressing it.

Notice also that the fact that the self has to find its moral identity in and through its membership in communities such as those of the family, the neighborhood, the city, and the tribe does not entail that the self has to accept the moral *limitations* of the particularity of those forms of community. Without those moral particularities to begin from there would never be anywhere to begin; but it is in moving forward from such particularity that the search for the good, for the universal, consists. Yet particularity can never be simply left behind or obliterated. The notion of escaping from it into a realm of entirely universal maxims which belong to man as such, whether in its eighteenth-century Kantian form or in the presentation of some modern analytical moral philosophies, is an illusion and an illusion with painful consequences. When men and women identify what are in fact their partial and particular causes too easily and too completely with the cause of some universal principle, they usually behave worse than they would otherwise do.

What I am, therefore, is in key part what I inherit, a specific past that is present to some degree in my present. I find myself part of a history and that is generally to say, whether I like it or not, whether I recognize it or not, one of the bearers of a tradition. It was important when I characterized the concept of a practice to notice that practices always have histories, and that at any given moment what a practice is depends on a mode of understanding it which has been transmitted often through many generations. And thus, insofar as the virtues sustain the relationships required for practices, they have to sustain relationships to the past—and to the future—as well as in the present. But the traditions through which particular practices are transmitted and reshaped never exist in isolation from larger social traditions. What constitutes such traditions?

We are apt to be misled here by the ideological uses to which the concept of a tradition has been put by conservative political theorists. Characteristically such theorists have followed Burke in contrasting tradition with reason and the stability of tradition with conflict. Both contrasts obfuscate. For all reasoning takes place within the context of some traditional mode of thought, transcending through criticism and invention the limitations of what had hitherto been reasoned in that tradition; this is as true of modern physics as of medieval logic. Moreover when a tradition is in good order it is always partially constituted by an argument about the goods the pursuit of which gives to that tradition its particular point and purpose.

So when an institution—a university, say, or a farm, or a hospital—is the bearer of a tradition of practice or practices, its common life will be partly, but in a centrally important way, constituted by a continuous argument as to what a university is and ought to be or what good farming is or what good medicine is. Traditions, when vital, embody continuities of conflict. Indeed when a tradition becomes Burkean, it is always dying or dead.

The individualism of modernity could of course find no use for the notion of tradition within its own conceptual scheme except as an adversary notion; it therefore all too willingly abandoned it to the Burkeans, who, faithful to Burke's own allegiance, tried to combine adherence in politics to a conception of tradition which would vindicate the oligarchical revolution of property of 1688 and adherence in economics to the doctrine and institutions of the free market. The theoretical incoherence of this mismatch did not deprive it of ideological usefulness. But the outcome has been that modern conservatives are for the most part engaged in conserving only older rather than later versions of liberal individualism. Their own core doctrine is as liberal and as individualist as that of self-avowed liberals.

A living tradition then is an historically extended, socially embodied argument, and an argument precisely in part about the goods which constitute that tradition. Within a tradition the pursuit of goods extends through generations, sometimes through many generations. Hence the individual's search for his or her good is generally and characteristically conducted within a context defined by those traditions of which the individual's life is a part, and this is true both of those goods which are internal to practices and of the goods of a single life. Once again the narrative phenomenon of embedding is crucial: the history of a practice in our time is generally and characteristically embedded in and made intelligible in terms of the larger and longer history of the tradition through which the practice in its present form was conveyed to us; the history of each of our own lives is generally and characteristically embedded in and made intelligible in terms of the larger and longer histories of a number of traditions. I have to say "generally and characteristically" rather than "always," for traditions decay, disintegrate, and disappear. What then sustains and strengthens traditions? What weakens and destroys them?

The answer in key part is: the exercise or the lack of exercise of the relevant virtues. The virtues find their point and purpose not only in sustaining those relationships necessary if the variety of goods internal to practices are to be achieved, and not only in sustaining the form of an individual life in which that individual may seek out his or her good as the good of his or her whole life, but also in sustaining those traditions which provide both practices and individual lives with their necessary historical context. Lack of justice, lack of truthfulness, lack of courage, lack of the relevant intellectual virtues—these corrupt traditions, just as they do those institutions and practices which derive their life from the traditions of which they are the contemporary embodiments. To recognize this is of course also to recognize the existence of an additional virtue, one whose importance is perhaps most obvious when it is least present, the virtue of having an adequate sense of the traditions to which one belongs or which confront one. This virtue is not to be confused with any form of conservative antiquarianism; I am not praising those who choose the conventional conservative role of *laudator temporis acti*. It is rather the case that an adequate sense of tradition manifests itself in a grasp of those future possibilities which the past has made available to the present. Living traditions, just because they continue a not-yet-completed narrative, confront a future whose determinate and determinable character, so far as it possesses any, derives from the past.

In practical reasoning the possession of this virtue is not manifested so much in the knowledge of a set of generalizations or maxims which may provide our practical inferences with major premises; its presence or absence rather appears in the kind of capacity for judgment which the agent possesses in knowing how to select among the relevant stack of maxims and how to apply them in particular situations. Cardinal Pole possessed it, Mary Tudor did not; Montrose possessed it, Charles I did not. What Cardinal Pole and the Marquis of Montrose possessed were in fact those virtues which enable their possessors to pursue both their own good and the good of the tradition of which they are the bearers, even in situations defined by the necessity of tragic, dilemmatic choice. Such choices, understood in the context of the tradition of the virtues, are very different from those which face the modern adherents of rival and incommensurable moral premises in the debates about which I wrote in Chapter 2 of *After Virtue*. Wherein does the difference lie?

It has often been suggested—by J. L. Austin, for example—that *either* we can admit the existence of rival and contingently incompatible goods which make incompatible claims to our practical allegiance *or* we can believe in some determinate conception of *the* good life for man, but that these are mutually exclusive alternatives. No one can consistently hold both these views. What this contention is blind to is that there may be better or worse ways for individuals to live through the tragic confrontation of good with good. And that to know what the good life for man is may require knowing what are the better and what are the worse ways of living in and through such situations. Nothing *a priori* rules out this possibility: and this suggests that within a view such as Austin's there is concealed an unacknowledged empirical premise about the character of tragic situations.

One way in which the choice between rival goods in a tragic situation differs from the modern choice between incommensurable moral premises is that *both* of the alternative courses of action which confront the individual have to be recognized as leading to some authentic and substantial good. By choosing one I do nothing to diminish or derogate from the claim upon me of the other, and therefore, whatever I do, I shall have left undone what I ought to have done. The tragic protagonist, unlike the moral agent as depicted by Sartre or Hare, is not choosing between allegiance to one moral principle rather than another, nor is he or she deciding upon some principle of priority between moral principles. Hence the "ought" involved has a different meaning and force from that of the "ought" in moral principles understood in a modern way. For the tragic protagonist cannot do everything that he or she ought to do. This "ought," unlike Kant's, does not imply "can." Moreover any attempt to map the logic of such "ought" assertions on to some modal calculus so as to produce a version of deontic logic has to fail.[4]

Yet it is clear that the moral task of the tragic protagonist may be performed better or worse, independently of the choice between alternatives that he or she makes—*ex hypothesi* he or she has no *right* choice

---

4. See, from a very different point of view, Bas C. Van Fraasen, "Values and the Heart's Command," *Journal of Philosophy*, 70 (1973): 5-19.

to make. The tragic protagonist may behave heroically or unheroically, generously or ungenerously, gracefully or gracelessly, prudently or imprudently. To perform his or her task better rather than worse will be to do both what is better for him or her *qua* individual and *qua* parent or child or *qua* citizen or member of a profession, or perhaps *qua* some or all of these. The existence of tragic dilemmas casts no doubt upon and provides no counter-examples to the thesis that assertions of the form "To do this in this way would be better for X and/or for his or her family, city or profession" are susceptible of objective truth and falsity, any more than the existence of alternative and contingently incompatible forms of medical treatment casts doubt on the thesis that assertions of the form "To undergo his medical treatment in this way would be better for X and/or his or her family" are susceptible of objective truth and falsity.[5]

The presupposition of this objectivity is of course that we can understand the notion of "good for X" and cognate notions in terms of some conception of the unity of X's life. What is better or worse for X depends upon the character of that intelligible narrative which provides X's life with its unity. Unsurprisingly it is the lack of any such unifying conception of a human life which underlies modern denials of the factual character of moral judgments and more especially of those judgments which ascribe virtues or vices to individuals.

I argued earlier that every moral philosophy has some particular sociology as its counterpart. What I have tried to spell out in this chapter is the kind of understanding of social life which the tradition of the virtues requires, a kind of understanding very different from those dominant in the culture of bureaucratic individualism. Within that culture conceptions of the virtues become marginal and the tradition of the virtues remains central only in the lives of social groups whose existence is on the margins of the central culture. Within the central culture of liberal or bureaucratic individualism, new conceptions of the virtues emerge and the concept of a virtue is itself transformed. To the history of that transformation I therefore now turn; for we shall only understand the tradition of the virtues fully if we understand to what kinds of degeneration it has proved liable.

5. See, from a different point of view, the illuminating discussion of Samuel Guttenplan, "Moral Realism and Moral Dilemmas," *Proceedings of the Aristotelian Society* (1979-80): 61-80.

II: NARRATIVE AS A CRITICAL TOOL

Ideology, Metaphor, and Analogy

Nicholas Lash

Introduction

Theologians are more frequently charged with flight from reality than with strenuous engagement in its obdurate complexity. If "it is the fault of the idealist always to seek escape from the authority of the tragic,"[1] then it must be admitted that much Christian preaching and theological writing, appealing as it does to "ultimate reality," or to a "higher truth," in a manner that depreciates or trivializes the urgency and agony of particular choice and particular circumstance, provides ample warrant for Donald MacKinnon's contention that "idealism remains a besetting temptation of the theological understanding."[2] "Idealism," he wrote twenty-five years earlier, "is always in the end the acceptance of the realm of ideas as somehow self-justifying, of man's spiritual experience as the real motor force of historical change."[3] It is hardly surprising that one who thus character-

---

1. Donald M. MacKinnon, "The Conflict Between Realism and Idealism," *Explorations in Theology* 5 (London, 1979), p. 164.
2. MacKinnon, "Absolute and Relative in History," *Explorations*, p. 57. In the same volume, cf. "Lenin and Theology," p. 22.
3. Donald M. MacKinnon, "Christian and Marxist Dialectic," in *Christian Faith and Communist Faith*, ed. Donald M. MacKinnon (London, 1953), p. 236.

Nicholas Lash, "Ideology, Metaphor, and Analogy," from his *Theology on the Way to Emmaeus* (London: SCM Press, 1986), pp. 95-119.

ized idealism should insist that "There are deep lessons to be learnt by the contemporary theologian from serious engagement with the Marxist rejection of idealism."[4] And if, for Marx and for most Marxists, religious discourse is presumed to be inescapably idealist in character, MacKinnon himself is one of many contemporary Christian theologians who would agree with the late Michael Foster that "Christianity is itself opposed to idealism," and that "the Christian should agree with almost all the criticism which the Marxist brings against idealism."[5]

Any such agreement would entail accepting many fundamental features of the Marxist critique of "ideology." I have attempted elsewhere to indicate some of the senses in which the practice of Christian belief, and Christian theology, are appropriately characterized as "ideological."[6] I suggested that both the practice of faith and theological reflection are "ideological" in the non-pejorative sense that they are aspects of the general process of the production of meanings and ideas. The practice of faith and theological enquiry are, moreover, frequently more or less "ideological" both in the sense that they reflect patterns of social relationship and dominance, and in the sense that believers in general and theologians in particular are frequently unaware of or unable to perceive the extent to which this is so, and hence fail to recognize the ways in which their discourse concerning man, the world, and God is subject to that element of illusion and distortion described, in the Marxist tradition, as "false consciousness." And if, from this point of view, the responsibility for the "critique of ideology" devolves partly upon the social scientist, I would wish to resist his claim to be the sole executant of this critical function, and to insist that it falls to the theologians, also, to seek to make problematic the grounds of religious practice and theological enquiry.

In the present paper, I want to indicate some of the ways in which Christian theological enquiry, or some aspects of that enquiry, might contribute to the "critique of ideology." I propose to do this by making some tentative suggestions concerning the relationship between "metaphor" and "analogy" in religious and theological discourse. By way of introduction, however, it will be convenient to return to Donald MacKinnon's reflections on the controversy between "idealism" and "realism."

The epistemological dimension of this controversy is indicated

4. MacKinnon, *Explorations*, p. 57.
5. Michael B. Foster, "Historical Materialism," in MacKinnon, *Christian Faith*, p. 90. The meaning of terms descriptive of philosophical positions or strategies undergoes, in the course of their history, bewildering shifts and diversifications. I hope that, in this paper, the contexts will sufficiently indicate the sense in which the term "idealism" is being used.
6. Cf. Nicholas L. A. Lash, "Theory, Theology and Ideology," in *The Sciences and Theology in the Twentieth Century*, ed. A. R. Peacocke (New York: Routledge, Chapman & Hall, 1981).

by MacKinnon's characterization of Kant's refutation of idealism as "a necessary part of his subtle and strenuous effort . . . to hold together a view which treated learning about the world as a finding, with one that regarded such learning as a constructive act."[7] The complexity of the relationship between "finding" and "fashioning,"[8] between discovery and construction, may be indicated by reminding ourselves that—in myth, parable, the writing of history and of the novel—*narrative* forms are not the least important of the modes of discourse that we employ in our attempts to "discover," to lay bare, something of what is the case concerning the world in which we are, and concerning the ways in which we are and may be "located" in a world that sets objective limits to our attempts to fashion it to our desires and fancies.

Even though Archimedes leaping from his bath could be said to have "made" a discovery, it would still seem more immediately apparent of narrative than it is of the language of scientific discovery that we *construct* our apprehension of reality, and that in this sense construction (with its attendant risks of fantasy and illusion) is the form of all "invention."[9] We should, however, remember Einstein's insistence "on the extent to which fundamental scientific progress must wait on the development, by spontaneous intellectual creativity, of more powerful branches of mathematics."[10] Nevertheless, there does seem to be a sense in which narrative construction is more patently a "work of art" than is the elaboration of scientific theory. And if this is so, then that sense may be closely connected with the apparently more pervasive presence of the *metaphorical* in narrative than in theoretical discourse.

Already, several questions are suggested which should be of some interest to students of Christian theology; and they are questions which raise issues concerning the "ideological" character of religious practice and theological reflection. In the first place, there is the question of divine revelation. A form of Christian faith which had surrendered all attempt to speak of our perception of meaning, our apprehension of hope, as fundamentally "given" in revelation, would have surrendered, without a struggle, to Feuerbach's perceptive but partial critique. And yet the way is now barred to any theology of revelation which attempts, "positivistically," to see, in the sources and grounds of Christian hope, exceptions to the rule that it is only in risking the construction of a story that human beings have given content,

---

7. MacKinnon, "Idealism and Realism: An Old Controversy Renewed," *Explorations*, p. 138.

8. Cf. Donald M. MacKinnon, *The Problem of Metaphysics* (Cambridge, 1974), p. 7.

9. The restless ambivalence of that term is not, I think, without significance.

10. MacKinnon, *Explorations*, p. 153.

shape, and specificity to their hopes and fears. The narrative that declares our hope to be "received" and not "invented" is itself an interpretative and, in *that* sense, a "constructive" enterprise. And we cannot avoid taking personal responsibility for the tale that we tell, even while acknowledging that the truth of the tale ultimately depends upon a fulfillment of conditions, the manner of which is beyond our observation and understanding.[11]

But, with that acknowledgment, is not any possibility of the Christian legitimately laying claim to *knowledge* of the truth of the tale that he tells automatically excluded? This is no new question. Aquinas attempted to tackle it in the first question of the *Summa Theologiae*. Its contemporary exploration would demand the kind of close attention to problems concerning the relationship of "knowledge" to "belief" which many contemporary writers, from Christians (cheerfully disclaiming any suggestion that they "know" that of which they speak) to Althusserian Marxists (arbitrarily restricting the range of use of the concept of "knowledge" to the products of their "theoretical practice"), prefer either to evade or disastrously to oversimplify.[12]

In the second place, if, as I propose to argue, there are forms of narrative discourse which have an irreducible centrality in the practice of Christianity, is not Christian religious discourse thereby rendered unavoidably "ideological," at least in the sense that the "truthfulness" of a tale told is partly determined by the circumstances of its production — in respect both of the "point of view" from which it is told, and of the linguistic and imaginative resources available for its construction? In other words, does not narrative discourse lack that aspiration to universality and timelessness of expression which is characteristic of "theoretical" or "scientific" discourse?

In the third place, if the Christian wishes to urge that there are tales to be told which, for all the particularity of their production and symbolic content, nevertheless "embody" or "signify" "universal" truths, is he not obliged to consider questions concerning the relationship of myth, history, and poetry to metaphysics? Donald MacKinnon has suggested that metaphysics sometimes emerges as "the attempt to convert poetry into the logically admissible."[13] In what circumstances could such "conversion" hope to be successful? And what

11. Cf. MacKinnon, *Explorations,* p. 165.

12. It is disappointing to find as sophisticated a philosopher of religion as Anthony Kenny apparently taking for granted a sharp disjunction between "knowledge" and "belief": "I suppose that few people claim to know that there is a God; most believe it as a matter of faith" (Anthony Kenny, *The God of the Philosophers* [Oxford, 1979], p. 127).

13. Donald M. MacKinnon, "Metaphysical and Religious Language," *Borderlands of Theology and Other Essays* (London, 1968), p. 214.

forms of metaphysical discourse are available, today, that are not fatally infected by idealism?

Brian Wicker, on whose stimulating study *The Story-Shaped World* I shall shortly be drawing, argues that "Metaphor . . . raises questions that only analogy . . . can answer, while conversely analogy can only answer questions that are raised in a metaphorical form."[14] In the light of my earlier remarks on the epistemological dimension of the controversy between idealism and realism, I suggest that Wicker's proposal might be expanded along the following lines.

The metaphysician traditionally conducts his enquiry along the "way of analogy." He supposes himself to be in some sense set on a voyage of discovery, at least inasmuch as only the boldest of bad metaphysicians would cheerfully admit that he was arbitrarily imposing patterns on the world of our experience. However, set on such a voyage, the theological metaphysician is prey to scepticism and discouragement in view of the fact that, appropriately mindful of the interrogative, heuristic character of his analogical extension of familiar usage, discovery is always indefinitely postponed.

The story-teller explores in a different direction. Conscious of his responsibility to help his audience to "shape" their experience, to "make sense" of their world, he journeys along the way, not of analogy, but of metaphor. But the attempt to "make sense" of the world elides with dangerous ease into the attempt to make the world, in our imagination, conform to how we would have it be. The narrator is prey not so much to discouragement as to the illusion that the human quest for meaning and truth is a quest for appropriate construction.

The forms of Christian discourse are set between the poles of metaphor and analogy, of narrative and metaphysics. How, then, may the relationship between these poles be negotiated in practice and characterized in theory? And what steps can be taken to minimize the twin risks of scepticism and illusion? These are some of the issues on which, after this protracted introduction, I wish tentatively to offer some reflections.

I. Metaphor and Autobiography

The tension between the story-teller and the philosopher, between metaphor and analogy, expression and analysis, between "the logic of the

---

14. Brian Wicker, *The Story-Shaped World* (London, 1975), p. 27. In context, this thesis is far from being as uninformatively abstract as it appears here. It arises from an interpretation of the relationship between the octet and sestet in Gerard Manley Hopkins' sonnet, "God's Grandeur."

heart" and a cooler, more dispassionate set of logical tools, is ancient and intractable. And if, in the nineteenth century, Newman attempted to sustain the tension in his exploration of the relationships between "real" and "notional" assent, between "religion" and "theology," today, in theological circles in Britain, the tension is in danger of slackening into mutual indifference. It is not that the conflict has been resolved, or even significantly clarified, but rather, as Brian Wicker suggests, that the battleground has shifted from theology to literary criticism.[15]

Wicker illuminatingly contrasts the divergent assessments of the metaphorical in two contemporary traditions of criticism, represented by Norman Mailer and Alain Robbe-Grillet. Both men see their task as "helping to free the individual from a system of emotional and cultural constraint . . . rooted in the inherited ideology of their respective societies."[16] Mailer would free us from the "one-dimensionality" of technologism through "a return to an older poetic and metaphorical way of looking at the world."[17] According to Robbe-Grillet, the anthropomorphism that is endemic to metaphorical discourse perpetuates our enslavement to "Nature," itself a construct of bourgeois Romanticism. He sees it as the job of the novelist to cleanse our language of anthropomorphism by banishing all metaphor.

Epistemologically, a central issue concerns the cognitive status of literary and artistic experience and expression.[18] And if, in philosophy and the social sciences, an ancient rationalism still frequently depreciates the cognitive capacity of metaphorical discourse,[19] Gadamer's study of *Truth and Method* and Ricoeur's study of *The Rule of Metaphor* signal a redressing of the balance.[20] Gadamer has sought to rehabilitate the Romantic recognition that "art is knowledge and the experience of the work of art is a sharing of this knowledge."[21]

15. Cf. Wicker, *Story-Shaped World*, p. 7.

16. Wicker, loc. cit.

17. Wicker, *Story-Shaped World*, p. 2.

18. "Mr. Moore," said a writer in the first number of the *Westminster Review*, in 1824, "is a poet, and therefore is *not* a reasoner" (cited with disapproval in John Stuart Mill, *Autobiography* [Oxford, 1971], p. 68). As Gadamer puts it: "It is not now said that poets tell lies, but that they are incapable of saying anything true" (Hans-Georg Gadamer, *Truth and Method* [London, 1975], p. 243).

19. As, for example, in the Althusserian manner of distinguishing between "science" and "ideology," according to which only the former can furnish knowledge, or in the epistemological strategy for which Ernest Gellner pleads so eloquently in *Legitimation of Belief* (Cambridge, 1974). For a brief discussion of the Althusserian distinction, cf. Lash, "Theory, Theology and Ideology," in Peacocke, *Sciences and Theology*.

20. Cf. Paul Ricoeur, *The Rule of Metaphor* (London, 1978). For an historical sketch of the erosion of metaphor from the cognitive to the merely expressive or decorative, cf. Ricoeur's discussion of "the decline of rhetoric" (pp. 44-64).

21. *Truth and Method*, p. 87.

Mailer would surely agree. But perhaps we should say, more cautiously, that art *may* be knowledge, because "the recurring temptation to self-indulgence and even dishonesty that goes with a dedication to metaphorical language is far from conquered today."[22] Robbe-Grillet's attempt to "cleanse" our language of metaphor represents one form of the struggle against this temptation. "We need," says Wicker, "the corrective presence of the not-human . . . of that which is impervious to linguistic manipulation."[23] The theological overtones are clear. But how can that which is "impervious to linguistic manipulation," *sive Deus sive natura,* be brought to speech? Where non-human empirical reality is concerned, the answer might be sought in the quest of scientific discourse for a formal purity as little "infected" as possible by the anthropormorphism of the metaphorical. Where the mystery of God is concerned, however, it is less clear what linguistic strategy, if any, could meet this demand. We shall return to such questions later on. I have mentioned them at this stage only to suggest that the "corrective presence" to which Wicker refers cannot make its appearance exclusively *within* the narrative mode of discourse. Narrative without metaphor (in so far as it is possible at all) merely depicts a world devoid of meaning, and to be left alone with one's own meaninglessness is "an ironic kind of 'liberation.'"[24] Are these the only options available: the construction of meaning or the recognition of meaninglessness? Or is there also meaning that is not, in the last analysis, fashioned but found? Even the form of the question is, significantly, metaphysical. Thus it is that reflection on metaphor raises questions which cannot be answered metaphorically (because anthropomorphism cannot be anthropomorphically transcended) and which receive, in narrative discourse from which metaphor has—so far as possible—been banished, only the bleakest of negative responses.

I suggest that the distinction between narrative, metaphorical discourse, and those non-narrative modes of discourse to which reflection on the metaphorical gives rise appears, within Christianity, as a distinction between religious practice and critical reflection on that practice: between "religion" and "theology." This is only a first approximation demanding further specification which I shall try to give to it as the argument proceeds.

The distinction between religious and theological discourse, too often obscured or elided in the work of theologians, philosophers, and social scientists alike is, nevertheless, fundamental and irreducible. It is, however, formal and heuristic in character, and to insist that it must be

22. Wicker, *Story-Shaped World,* p. 12.
23. Wicker, loc. cit.
24. Wicker, *Story-Shaped World,* p. 190.

kept in mind is not to issue a warrant for employing it with that insensitivity to the complex variety of particular instances which is the besetting sin of so many attempts at classifying or "mapping" our linguistic usage.

Having issued that warning against mistaking the map for the countryside, I now want to suggest that the paradigm or "focal" forms of Jewish and Christian religious discourse are not simply narrative but are, more specifically, autobiographical. They are autobiographical both in the sense that they are "self-involving" (although this will be shown in their performance, and will not necessarily appear in their grammatical form) and in the sense that, as self-involving, they "locate" the speaker (or the group of which he is a spokesman) in a particular cultural, historical tradition: "My father was a wandering Aramean." Whether the "audience" addressed is God (in acts of supplication and worship) or other people (in acts of witness), the Christian is the teller of a tale, the narrator of a story which he tells as *his* story, as a story in which he acknowledges himself to be a participant.

From this elementary observation, a number of things follow. In the first place, Christian religious discourse, as autobiographical, will always be shaped and influenced more deeply than we know by the circumstances of its production. However "truthfully" we try to tell our story, the narrative that we produce is always subject to ideological distortion.

In the second place, Christian religious discourse, as autobiographical, tends to attribute an unwarranted universality to the particular forms in which, in particular circumstances, it finds expression. Convinced that the tale that we tell is truly told, Christians tend to assume that the way they tell it is the way it has ever been and must ever be told.

In the third place, the construction of an autobiography, as of any narrative, entails selection, planning, the imposition of order. We do not "merely" remember. We seek to construct, to *"make"* sense of our lives and of our history. Unless we construct the narrative, we can make no sense of our temporally ordered existence. But the very fact that the sense has to be "made," the narrative constructed, threatens the veracity of the tale.

In the fourth place, every narrative has a beginning, a middle, and an end. But "end" ambiguously signifies both conclusion and goal, both terminus and purpose. And the Christian, like any autobiographer, stands in the middle of the history to which he seeks to give narrative expression. He is therefore tempted, for the sake of the coherence of the story (which is the coherence of his human and Christian experience) to claim a clearer apprehension of the "plot" than the evidence warrants. Living in hope of resurrection, he is tempted to reduce past and present suffering to the status of necessary conditions of a "happy ending." "The temptation of Hegelian and utilitarian alike," says Donald MacKinnon, "is to find always the justification of the present in the future."[25] And he adds: "But the Cross utterly prevents such a trivializing of the past."[26] The dark facticity of particular deeds and particular tragedy may not be obliterated for the sake of the coherence of the narrative. Not the least insidious of the forms of idealism by which Christian religious discourse is threatened is that which, springing from the conviction that there *is* a sense which it all makes, seeks prematurely to give to that sense unified narrative expression.

I have been trying to sketch some of the ways in which, as autobiographical (and hence as metaphorical) discourse, Christian religious speech is threatened by "self-indulgence and even dishonesty." Are there countervailing influences to hand which might discipline and purify faith's tendency to construct a significance which, *as* constructed, is at best distorted and, at worst, illusory? There are, I suggest, at least two such corrective influences.

I have already insisted on the importance of the distinction between "religion" and "theology," between the practice of faith, in worship and witness, and critical reflection on that practice. Thus the first corrective influence, or set of such influences, arises from the interaction of practice and reflection. There will be a variety of forms of reflection (or "theological disciplines") corresponding to the variety of aspects under which the practice of faith may be critically considered. Thus, for example, because Christian religious discourse is *discourse* it demands "grammatical" or philosophical consideration (in the next section of this essay, I shall therefore consider "theology as metaphysics"). Because Christian religious discourse is paradigmatically *narrative,* it demands literary-critical consideration. And because Christian narrative is in some sense autobiographical, it demands historical consideration.

The tendency, in contemporary English biblical studies, is to consider literary-critical and historical aspects of theological reflection as sharply distinct and to concentrate on the latter to the neglect of the former. This tendency derives from a period when positivistic conceptions of historical understanding went hand-in-hand with non-cognitive accounts of literary and poetic statement (which carried the implication that the fruit of literary-critical reflection on the biblical narratives could only be "subjective" in character). But if it has sometimes been

25. MacKinnon, "Prayer, Worship, and Life," *Christian Faith,* p. 248.
26. MacKinnon, loc. cit.

assumed (in theology and elsewhere) that there is "a natural tension between the historian and the literary critic,"[27] there is no timeless validity to this assumption. Thus, for example, Gadamer has power-fully argued the case for recovering a sense of the fundamental unity of the hermeneutical disciplines. From such a standpoint, it makes sense to say that "historical understanding proves to be a kind of literary criti-cism writ large."[28] Gadamer, at least as I understand him, is not seek-ing to obliterate the distinction between historical truth and the truth of metaphorical fiction. He is calling to our attention connections and similarities that have been too long obscured from view. At least where Christian theology is concerned, it is surely worth remembering that the New Testament historian, for example, is dealing with narratives whose adequate elucidation demands (though it does not always re-ceive) the most sophisticated use of literary-critical skills. And whether what those narratives express is, in the last resort, construction or dis-covery is, arguably, a question whose resolution is constitutive of the decision of Christian faith.

My first suggestion, then, is that Christian religious discourse is subject to purificatory and corrective criticism from the historian and the literary critic, as well as from the sociologist and psychologist of religion (to mention two other disciplines whose right to be heard is increasingly acknowledged even in the more cobwebbed theological debating-chambers). And if the tensions between practice and reflec-tion are frequently destructive, rather than creative, this is partly be-cause exegetes and historians have sometimes been invited to establish the grounds of belief, rather than critically to reflect upon its past and present performance and, when they have shown themselves incapable of executing this function, it has been concluded that belief has no grounds. But this is to raise questions of verification on which I shall briefly comment later on.

I have said that there are two sets of corrective influences upon the tendency of Christian belief to undergo ideological distortion. I now want to suggest, therefore, that in addition to those external correctives some of which have just been indicated, Christian religious practice also contains *internal* correctives to its own anthropomorphism. If the history of Christian faith and spirituality is a history of exuberant metaphor (verbal, ritual, and iconographic), it is—just as insistently—a history of silence, simplicity, and iconoclasm: of a sense that what needs to be said cannot be said. Not the least powerful of the pressures generating this apophantic dimension in Christian history has been the experience of

27. Gadamer, *Truth and Method*, p. 301.
28. Gadamer, *Truth and Method*, p. 304.

suffering. If "ideology . . . dulls the tragic vision's alertness to limits,"[29] the experience of tragedy can sharpen that vision or (to change the metaphor) can constitute the hard rock on which the exuberance of affirmation is broken. Suffering corrupts and disfigures. And yet, it can also purify. Any description of Christian belief as "merely ideological," as self-indulgent construction of satisfying narrative, inexcusably ignores the silent witness of that simplicity and realism which has sometimes been the fruit of a practically sustained "alertness to limits."

If it is true that one of the most important features of any metaphor is that we must deny its literal truth if we are to understand its metaphorical significance,[30] and hence perceive the truth which metaphor expresses, then it is perhaps not fanciful to suggest that the dialectic of affirmation and denial, which is so striking a feature of the history of Christian spirituality, amounts to a practical recognition of the metaphorical status of those narrative forms which I have described as paradigmatic for Christian religious discourse.

In the performance of that dialectic, Christians have been motivated by the conviction that they were responding to the "corrective presence" of that which is "impervious to linguistic manipulation." This conviction, married to that unquenchable intellectual curiosity, that "pure . . . desire simply to know,"[31] which has been one of the hallmarks of Western consciousness, has sometimes provoked Christian believers to forms of reflection, of philosophical enquiry, which transcend the practical dialectic of metaphor and its negation.[32] There are questions which the recognition of paradox and, indeed, silence itself provokes rather than stifles. Metaphorical discourse, I have suggested, raises questions which cannot be answered metaphorically. In various ways, in the past, such questions have been explored along "the way of analogy," to which we now therefore turn.

---

29. Alvin W. Gouldner, *The Dialectics of Ideology and Technology* (London, 1976), p. 75.

30. Cf. Wicker, *Story-Shaped World*, p. 26.

31. B. J. F. Lonergan, *Insight* (London, 1957), p. 74. "Deep within us all, emergent when the noise of other appetites is stilled, there is a desire to know, to understand, to see why, to discover the reason, to find the cause, to explain" (ibid., p. 4). This pursuit of truth "for its own sake," and the practical and moral dilemmas to which it today gives rise, formed the theme of Professor George Steiner's Bronowski lecture, *Has Truth a Future?* (London: BBC Publications, 1978), which I have elsewhere attempted to "read" theologically: cf. Nicholas L. A. Lash, "Christology and the Future of Truth," *Incarnation and Myth: The Debate Continued*, ed. Michael Gouldner (London, 1979), pp. 224-232.

32. This is one way of reading the phenomenon of so-called "hellenization": cf. Wolfhart Pannenberg, "The Appropriation of the Philosophical Concept of God as a Dogmatic Problem of Early Christian Theology," *Basic Questions in Theology*, vol. 2 (London, 1971), pp. 119-183.

Nicholas Lash

II. Analogy: *Voie* sans Issue?

In the previous section I raised the question: how can that which is "impervious to linguistic manipulation" be brought to speech? When the intended referent of this question is the transcendent mystery of God, there are several reasons for supposing that metaphysical discourse (where metaphysics is conceived as that branch of philosophy the logic of whose procedures focuses on analogical usage of unrestricted generality) cannot provide the answer.

Firstly, there are those who insist that the "way of analogy" is closed, and that it is only in metaphor that we can hope to speak of God. If this were the case, then there would be no way past the Feuerbachian critique, because we would be unable to discriminate between the "models" of God that we fashion in metaphor and the discovered mystery signified by such constructions. All that we say of God, affirmatively, is indeed "projected" from our human experience, is anthropomorphic in character, and we would have no way of showing the sense of such language to be other than "merely" projective.

Secondly, there are those who, in various ways, assimilate the logic of analogy to that of metaphor, using the two concepts more or less interchangeably.[33] On this account, the "way of analogy" is apparently open, but the appearance is illusory, because "analogy" turns out to be either a sub-class of metaphor or the "common heading" under which "the family of metaphor" is subsumed.[34]

Thirdly, recent studies of metaphor, standing in varied relations of dependence on Aristotle's *Poetics*, lay the emphasis on dissimilarity. Thus Ricoeur: "Enigma lives on in the heart of metaphor. In metaphor, 'the same' operates *in spite of* 'the different.'"[35] So far, so good. But not the least of the reasons why I hesitated before deciding to risk using the term "analogy" in this essay is that it has become increasingly common to lay the emphasis, when speaking of analogy, on *similarity*: as if, along the way of analogy, "the different" operated *in spite of* "the same." This is emphatically *not* the case with Aquinas's use of analogy, although it has sometimes been made to appear so in neoscholastic apologetics searching for a "direct route," philosophically, to the knowledge of God.

In the fourth place, it could be suggested that the "no entry" sign across the way of analogy was most firmly planted by Kant. It is,

33. This happens even in Pannenberg's interesting essay, "Analogy and Doxology," *Basic Questions in Theology*, vol. 1 (London, 1970), pp. 211-238; cf. e.g. pp. 212, 228.
34. Cf. Ricoeur, *Metaphor*, p. 260.
35. Ibid., p. 196.

however, at least worth asking *which* route it was that he blocked in so apparently insurmountable a manner.

According to Donald MacKinnon, Kant "raised a problem which by dexterous use of Aristotelian analogy [the scholastics] had tried to bypass."[36] This bypass consisted in exploiting the ontological conviction that, since "Being . . . was an analogically participated transcendental,"[37] it was possible to move from negation to affirmation, from speech concerning the conditioned to speech concerning the unconditioned ground of all conditions. "When the schoolmen insist that agnosticism comes before anthropomorphism, we are with them all the time. But, alas, their device for allowing assertion on the basis of negation demands assumptions that we cannot make. For we have to admit in knowledge a kind of intuitive awareness of analogically participated being which we do not seem to have."[38]

Who are these "schoolmen," who employ this device? They undoubtedly include many of those seventeenth- and eighteenth-century scholastics against whose views Kant was reacting. But, here as elsewhere, we need to remember the sea-change undergone by late scholasticism in the seventeenth century. Thrown newly on the defensive, proof rather than enquiry became the dominant concern. Theology "replaced the inquiry of the *quaestio* by the pedagogy of the thesis."[39]

Nevertheless, even if the conviction that human beings had, or could have, "a kind of intuitive awareness of analogically participated being" was of considerable assistance to a theology nervously contracting into apologetic, apologetic concerns alone can hardly have accounted for its emergence. Is the presumption of such intuitive awareness to be found further back, in thirteenth-century scholasticism? Or, since that question is impossibly large, is it to be found in Aquinas' treatment in the first thirteen Questions of the first part of his *Summa Theologiae?* For centuries, at least since Cajetan, the answer has appeared to be "yes," and that affirmative reply is still frequently given in such neoscholasticism as survives

36. MacKinnon, *Borderlands*, p. 209.

37. MacKinnon, loc. cit.

38. MacKinnon, *Borderlands*, p. 210. Where the Kantian sources of Barth's rejection of that "invention of Antichrist" (*Church Dogmatics* 1/1 [Edinburgh, 1936], p. x), the *analogia entis*, are concerned, it is worth comparing MacKinnon's comments with Barth's sketch of Kant's rejection of the possibility of metaphysics, "if one understands by it a theoretical knowledge of objects, the concepts of which must be devoid of corresponding *intuitions*" (*Protestant Theology in the Nineteenth Century* [London, 1972], p. 275, my stress).

39. B. J. F. Lonergan, "Theology in its New Context," *A Second Collection* (London, 1974), p. 57.

even today.[40] In recent decades, however, historical studies of medieval thought on the one hand, and philosophical developments on the other, have made possible a reading of Aquinas that is not filtered through the systematizing transformations wrought in post-seventeenth-century scholasticism. It is beyond my competence to resolve the historical issue. I can only record the fact that I am persuaded by those whose interpretation of Aquinas's procedures gives us an account of his treatment of analogy which does not involve any recourse to that "device" against which Kant protested.[41]

One of the central targets of Lonergan's *Insight* is those who persist in assuming that "knowing consists in taking a look." On this assumption, terms such as "essence" and "existence" are taken to refer to mysterious objects which "need an extraordinary language to articulate or a superior faculty to apprehend them. Possession of such a faculty then becomes the prerequisite for being a metaphysician. Call it superior insight or the intuition of being."[42] This model of metaphysical enquiry is in striking contrast to that with which Aquinas worked. For him, "the mode of metaphysics is not intuitive . . . but logical."[43] The metaphysician is distinguished from the logician "not in possessing an arcane method but simply by the power of his intelligence."[44] On this account there is a certain irony in H. P. Owen's criticism of G. E. M. Anscombe and P. T. Geach for being preoccupied, in their treatment of

40. Thus, for example, according to Professor Eric Mascall, "St. Thomas's doctrine, because it is rooted in the act of being which is analogically common to God and his creatures, gives us a process by which we can transform the *via negativa* into the *via eminentiae* and . . . can achieve a real knowledge of God in this life" (Eric L. Mascall, *He Who Is*, rev. ed. [London, 1966], pp. 225-226). For Mascall, the "intuition" whereby this achievement is realized is a matter of "penetrating to the ontological depths" of "finite beings" so as to "know them as the creatures of God" (ibid., pp. 91, 85). Armed with this curious metaphor, Mascall elsewhere brings off the most complete misdescription of the "fundamental thesis" of Lonergan's *Insight* that I have come across: "knowing always consists in penetrating beneath the immediately apprehended surface of an object into its intelligible *being*. Insight is *in*-sight, seeing *into* the observed object" (E. L. Mascall, *The Openness of Being* [London, 1971], p. 84, his stresses).

41. My justification for relying so heavily, in the following pages, on David Burrell's detailed discussion of this text is, therefore, that—although his reading of the Questions confirms my own impression of what Aquinas was "up to"—I am less concerned with the historical issue than with sketching an account of the "way of analogy" which coheres with the general account of the critical function of theological reflection which I am offering in this essay, and which does not entail having recourse to an epistemological theory of "intuitions" of "being."

42. David B. Burrell, *Aquinas: God and Action* (London, 1979), p. 47.

43. Ibid., p. 48.

44. Burrell, *Aquinas*, p. 6, paraphrasing a favorite passage in Aquinas's commentary on Aristotle's *Metaphysics*: "Philosophus [differt] a dialectico secundum potentiam" (cf. Burrell, *Aquinas*, pp. 48, 176).

analogy, "with logic at the expense of metaphysics."[45] And it is significant that Owen, in common with most neoscholastics, supposes that the metaphysician's explorations along the way of analogy can furnish us with a doctrine of God.

To discover what Aquinas is up to in these Questions, it is necessary to attend to his performance, and not to be misled by the fact that the tools he uses are not those which a modern logician would employ. Thus, in spite of Aquinas's insistence that he is concerned to show "what God is not,"[46] generations of commentators have been misled by his use of "object-language constructions to do metalinguistic jobs"[47] into supposing that he is offering a doctrine of God, at least in the sense that he is constructing a catalogue of divine attributes. In fact, "Aquinas is not attempting to describe God at all,"[48] and "a perceptive reader would think twice before identifying a deliberate consideration of what God is not with a teaching presuming to say what God is."[49] His treatment is resolutely grammatical and, "while a grammatical account cannot pretend to offer a proper account of the subject in question, it can discourage improper ones."[50] Thus, although in these Questions there are few instances of Aquinas indicating the connections between "the more austere grammatical discipline of theology"[51] and religious discourse, a view of the relationship between religion and theology is implicit in the procedures he adopts. Theology neither reinforces nor supplants the "image" of God built up through Christian living—in prayer, work, suffering, relationship—an image which, for the Christian, finds its focus in consideration of the person, words, work, and death of Jesus the Christ. The role of theology, as Aquinas conceives it, is to "exercise critical control" over this image, and over the narratives in which it finds expression, "now unravelling confusions and inconsistencies that arise from it, now checking it with *praxis* to offset its stereotypical drift, now challenging it as a lazy simplification."[52] In this account, then, meta-

---

45. H. P. Owen, *The Christian Knowledge of God* (London, 1979), p. 211.

46. "Quia de Deo scire non possumus quit sit sed quid non sit, non possumus considerare de Deo quomodo sit sed potius quomodo non sit. Primo ergo considerandum est quomodo non sit, secundo quomodo a nobis cognoscatur, tertio quomodo nominetur" (Aquinas, *Summa Theologiae*, vol. 2; *Existence and Nature of God*, Ia, 2-11 [London, 1964], p. 18). In other words, the *entire* discussion of God's "attributes" in Questions 3-11 is under the rubric of what God is *not*, the other two topics being considered in Questions 12 and 13.

47. Burrell, *Aquinas*, p. 17.

48. Ibid., p. 16.

49. Ibid., p. 13.

50. Ibid., p. 22.

51. Ibid., p. 27.

52. Ibid., p. 178.

Nicholas Lash

physical theology stands in a critical relationship to religious practice similar to that which I have already suggested obtains between the "hermeneutical" theological disciplines and the practice of religion.[53]

If Burrell is justified in thus interpreting Aquinas' insistence that he is concerned, by reflecting "grammatically" on the limits of language, to elucidate what cannot be said of God, then the gulf between Aquinas and Kant is perhaps not so wide, at this point, as has usually been supposed. But if "we cannot pretend to offer a description of a transcendent object without betraying its transcendence,"[54] does it follow that there is nothing which we can truly say of God? It would seem so, for even the discussion, in Question 13, of those predicates which *are* acceptably used of God remains under the rubric of God's "simpleness," his "non-compositeness," according to which "all statements formed of subject and object—that is to say, all discourse—will falsify the reality which God is."[55] It is at this point that the question of whether or not Aquinas sought to provide the outlines of a "doctrine of God" is most closely linked with the question of analogy, for it has often been supposed, as we have seen, that the way of analogy provided a route by which the *via negativa* could be transcended, giving rise to a set of positive affirmations sufficiently firm and informative as to constitute the elements of a doctrine of God.[56]

---

53. Because "being that can be understood is language," hermeneutics, according to Gadamer, is "a universal aspect of philosophy, and not just the methodological basis of the so-called human sciences" (*Truth and Method,* pp. 432, 433). Thus "hermeneutics is not to be viewed as a mere subordinate discipline within the arena of the *Geisteswissenschaften*" (Hans-Georg Gadamer, "On the Scope and Function of Hermeneutical Reflection," *Philosophical Hermeneutics* [London, 1977], p. 19). I endorse Gadamer's insistence on this universality of "the hermeneutic *phenomenon*" (*Truth and Method,* p. xi, my stress) and therefore acknowledge that there is a hermeneutical "aspect" to all linguistic activity. However, by distinguishing between "hermeneutical" and "metaphysical" theological disciplines I intend to indicate that there are, nevertheless, distinct tasks to be undertaken not all of which are appropriately described, from the methodological point of view, as "hermeneutic": cf. B. J. F. Lonergan's comments on "hermeneutics" in general and Gadamer in particular, in *Method in Theology* (London, 1972), pp. 155, 212. The issue here is closely related to that which is central to the debate between Gadamer and Habermas (on which, cf. Thomas McCarthy, *The Critical Theory of Jürgen Habermas* [London, 1978], pp. 170-193).

54. Burrell, *Aquinas,* p. 7.

55. Ibid., p. 25. In Aquinas's account, to say that God is radically "simple" is not to "name a characteristic of God" but is "a short-hand way of remarking that no articulated form of expression can succeed in stating anything about God" (Burrell, *Aquinas,* p. 18).

56. The debate between "Thomists" and those highly critical of "Thomist" views of these matters is of little interest due to the persistent failure of both parties either to submit "Aquinas" texts to detailed and philosophically serious examination or seriously to discriminate between the logical and the substantive issues. Cf. e.g., amongst the critics, Keith Ward, *The Concept of God* (Oxford, 1974), pp. 131-158.

128

In view of Burrell's insistence that Aquinas's grammatical reflections on language and its limits do not provide us with a "doctrine of God," it comes as little surprise to find him insisting that, although Aquinas is perhaps best known for his theory of analogy, on "closer inspection it turns out that he never had one."[57] And Burrell's comment on Cajetan and, following him, the host of others who have tried to construct such a theory from Aquinas' scattered and unsystematic observations on analogy is somewhat caustic: "The misunderstanding resulted in the usual way: the philosophical activity of the master became doctrine in the hands of his disciples."[58]

In fact, the situation is more interesting than that negative comment indicates. Neoscholasticism supposed that, on the basis of a theory of analogy, it was able to construct a doctrine of God. Whereas, if Aquinas *had* had a "theory" of analogy he would thereby have been prevented from using analogy to speak of God at all. That remark is, I hope, sufficiently provocative to deserve unpacking a little.

Metaphor functions with recognition of differences: "the metaphorical statement captures its sense as metaphorical midst the ruins of the literal sense."[59] Aquinas's distinction between metaphor and analogy stems from this recognition that, if we are to apprehend the truth which metaphor expresses, we must first deny its literal truth. There are, however, some expressions of which this denial is unnecessary, because we do not know and cannot specify the limits of their literal applicability.[60] Thus, for example, to understand what is meant by a "living" tradition, we have not first got to deny that cultural processes are organisms. Nor, if we describe a friend as having a "wise expression," do we have to add hurriedly: "Of course, it's not really his *expression* that is wise." In both cases, our usage is "analogical." In contrast, if we describe a talented gardener as having "green fingers," it is necessary implicitly to deny the literal truth of the description.[61] Terms like "*wise,*

---

57. Burrell, *Aquinas*, p. 55. Burrell's reading is here very close to Herbert McCabe's, according to whom "analogy," for Aquinas, "is not a way of getting to know about God, nor is it a theory of the structure of the universe, it is a comment on our use of certain words" (H. McCabe, ed., *Summa Theologiae*, vol. 3: *Knowing and Naming God*, Ia, 12-13 [London, 1964], p. 106).

58. Burrell, *Aquinas*, p. 55.

59. Burrell, *Aquinas*, p. 221.

60. "No metaphor is the best possible metaphor — you can always say 'I didn't really mean that.' But some things we say of God even though they are imperfect cannot be improved on by denying them; their imperfection lies in our understanding of what we are trying to mean" (McCabe, *Knowing and Naming God*, p. 107).

61. There are, I appreciate, problems concerning the relationship between analogy and "dead metaphor," but I do not think that they affect the point at issue. Cf. Ricoeur's discussion of Derrida, in *Metaphor*, pp. 284-295.

good, and *living* are used . . . in contexts so widely divergent that they defy comparison. . . . How are such expressions related? That we cannot say."[62] We learn how to use such terms appropriately, not by applying a theoretical maxim, but through the practical discipline of developing a sensitive appreciation of appropriate usage. Linguistic usage is an art, not a science. And, if we *were* able theoretically to formulate the way in which the contexts in which we use such terms are related, then we would be unable to use them of "a God who transcends all our contexts."[63] It is in this sense that it is true to say that, if Aquinas had had a *theory* of analogical predication he would thereby have been prevented from using analogy to speak of God. Those who have constructed "theories" of analogy have usually construed "analogy" as itself a univocal term, whereas Aquinas wisely refrained from making this move: in his hands, the notion of "analogy" is itself highly analogical.

But what is Aquinas's justification for assuming that even terms such as "wise," "good," and "living" can be applied non-metaphorically to God? The first thing to notice is that the terms selected are "perfection terms" which occur, as a matter of fact, in the religious activity of praising God.[64] Aquinas's remarks about the applicability of such terms to radically diverse contexts, the limits of which we cannot specify, at least indicate that the believer, in thus articulating his praise of God, is not manifestly talking nonsense. We cannot specify the limits of the applicability of such terms; therefore we cannot specify the limits of their literal applicability; therefore these terms (which believers, as a matter of fact, apply to God) cannot be said to be not literally applicable to God.

At this point, however, it is necessary to notice the part played by those considerations of causality which reflect Aquinas's enduring neo-Platonism. His heuristic definition of God as the "source" of all things affords "the formal license to use [perfection terms] *in divinis.*"[65] As the source of all that is, God is the source of all "perfections."[66] It

---

62. Burrell, *Aquinas,* p. 10.

63. Burrell, loc. cit.

64. Cf. Burrell, *Aquinas,* pp. 59-60.

65. Burrell, *Aquinas,* p. 66, commenting on Question 13, art. 5: "Non enim possumus nominare Deum nisi ex creaturis. . . . Et sic quidquid dicitur de Deo et creaturis, dicitur secundum quod est aliquis ordo creaturae ad Deum ut ad principium et causum."

66. "It is creative causality, therefore, that establishes between being and God the bond of participation that makes the relation by analogy ontologically possible" (Ricoeur, *Metaphor,* p. 276). Ricoeur rightly insists on the importance of the fact that, in his mature works, Aquinas pursued the enquiry *not* in terms of "formal" causality, or "likeness," but of *dependence in act.* Hence it is, also, that Burrell devotes the second half of his study to an elucidation of Aquinas's "inherently analogous" (p. 116) notion of *"actus."* For an admirably lucid summary of Aquinas's extension of the notion of causality for God, cf. McCabe's appendix on "Causes," with its insistence that "God, for St. Thomas, is not a

follows, according to Aquinas, that if such terms as "wise" and "good" and "living" *were* to be used literally, they would be used primarily of God and only secondarily of whatever else it is to which they are variously applicable. "The obvious implication is that we are never in a position to employ these terms literally."[67] By applicability, Aquinas, having begun by sharply distinguishing metaphorical from analogical usage, has ended by acknowledging that there is an "irreducibly metaphorical dimension to analogous expressions."[68] Or, to put the point anthropomorphically (and thus metaphorically), only God would be in a position to use analogical terms without any touch of metaphor. However, to interpret this recognition as amounting to a concession that, at the end of the day, "analogy" had been subsumed into "metaphor" would be to ride roughshod over significant grammatical distinctions which Aquinas was at pains to elucidate.[69] After all, many philosophers of science today would be willing to recognize an irreducibly metaphorical dimension in scientific discourse. But few of them would suppose that they were thereby admitting that all scientific discourse was "merely metaphorical."

The philosopher, as Aquinas conceives his task, cannot show the believer *how* to use of God even those terms which are literally (and not "merely" metaphorically) applicable to God. Just as the philosopher does not *initiate* the quest for God, "the source and goal of all things," so also the philosopher cannot teach us the appropriate use of religious language. That use will be learnt, in religion as in cookery and politics, by disciplined practice: "in religious matters, as in others, a philosopher can at best help to discriminate sense from nonsense."[70]

The way of analogy serves neither as a substitute for nor, in any direct sense, as a confirmation of the way of discipleship. At most, by shedding some light on the logically peculiar character of the linguistic

---

causal explanation of the world . . . what we know of him does not serve to explain the world, all that we know of him is that he must exist if the world is to have explanation" (*Knowing and Naming God*, p. 102).

67. Burrell, *Aquinas*, p. 70, commenting on Question 13, art. 6. This implication is far from obvious to Don Cupitt who, contrasting Aquinas and Kant, claims that, according to the argument of Question 13, "we can transcend our own subjectivity and see the world as it were from God's point of view" (*The Nature of Man* [London, 1979], p. 51). This is grossly misleading. For a more nuanced account of the similarities and differences between Kant and Aquinas on these matters, cf. Karl Rahner, "Thomas Aquinas on Truth," *Theological Investigations*, vol. xiii (London, 1975), pp. 13-31, esp. p. 25.

68. Burrell, *Aquinas*, p. 56.

69. Cf. Ricoeur, *Metaphor*, pp. 277-280.

70. Burrell, *Aquinas*, p. 69.

Nicholas Lash

dimension of our quest for God, it may "help us through the temptation to think that reality is unintelligible."[71]

Aquinas has often been described as "agnostic," and my emphasis on the extent to which, in these opening Questions of the *Summa Theologiae*, he resolutely refrains from offering a "doctrine of God," contenting himself with paying sustained logical attention to what can *not* be said of God, would seem to underline the appropriateness of that description. There are, however, at least two points of view from which the description is misleading. In the first place, Aquinas is not the only great metaphysician to have supposed that there is a sense, however obscure and indirect, in which a disciplined attention to linguistic usage can *show* us something of the character of the objects of our discourse[72] (and therefore, possibly, something of the character of our relationship to God). Of course, grammatical reflection cannot "directly tell us whether or not there are any such objects,"[73] but then it is abundantly clear from the first Question of the *Summa Theologiae* that Aquinas is not concerned to attempt to demonstrate that God exists.[74] It is no business of the philosophical theologian to seek to verify religious truth-claims. It does not follow that such verification is nobody's business either: "Wittgenstein did not after all say in his parenthesis '*Religion* as grammar.'"[75]

In the second place, I suggest that we need to distinguish between agnosticism as a religious attitude (the practical attitude of one who refrains from worship because of his suspicion that songs of praise are sung not merely into silence but into emptiness) and as a theological policy aimed at insistently reminding the believer of the limits both of his language and of his theoretical understanding. The knowledge born of human love is frequently incapable of finding adequate expression. Lovers, and not only those with weak digestions, have been known to "sigh and groan." The lover does not, however, infer from his inability to "capture the beloved in language" that the beloved is not, after all, known. The "reticence" of the lover, his continual negation of expressions perceived as inadequate to their object, does not argue ne-

71. Ibid., p. 75.

72. Is this not true of Aristotle, Kant, and Hegel? Burrell is fond of appealing to Wittgenstein's remark: "*Essence* is stressed by grammar. . . . Grammar tells what kind of object anything is. (Theology as grammar.)" (*Philosophical Investigations*, I, Paragraphs 371, 373). Cf. Burrell, *Aquinas*, pp. 17, 74, 76.

73. Renford Bambrough, "Introduction," *Reason and Religion*, ed. S. C. Brown (London, 1977), p. 13.

74. This *first* Question is ignored with tedious regularity by philosophers of religion commenting on the second.

75. Bambrough, "Introduction," p. 16.

science, but a more penetrating knowledge than that contained in those "neutral" descriptions of the beloved that are also available to casual acquaintances, and are found in the files of the family doctor and the social historian. On what *logical* grounds could the possibility be excluded that there is available, within human experience, a "dark knowledge" of that transcendent mystery of which such neutral descriptions are precisely *not* available (and that they are not is part of the drift of Aquinas' grammatical reflections)? That is, of course, a dangerous line of thought because, if human love is always threatened by illusion, how much more so is man's personal knowledge of the unknown God? If love, any love, is to be responsible, it needs continual submission to a process of verification, of the correlative purification of illusion. But husband and wife do not usually set private detectives (the social equivalent of the "natural theologian," in the sense in which Karl Barth was rightly suspicious of him?) onto each other, even though there may be circumstances in which resort to this desperate expedient is appropriate. But it is significant that these will be circumstances in which, love having grown cold, personal knowledge has been called radically into question. Burrell nearly captures the sense in which it is and is not appropriate to describe Aquinas as "agnostic" when he says that "Aquinas displays his religious discipline more clearly by the ease with which he is able to endure so unknown a God."[76]

III. A Note on "Verification"

It is fashionable to characterize the strategies available for the testing of religious truth-claims as lying between the limits of "rationalism" on the one hand and "fideism" on the other. By "rationalism," I understand an approach according to which the practice of faith is judged at best irresponsible and at worst superstitious, except in so far as its grounds

---

76. Burrell, *Aquinas*, p. 67. Two further comments are in order. Firstly, Aquinas sought to moderate the even more radical agnosticism of a "long tradition of devotion and theology" (T. Gilby, *Knowing and Naming God*, p. xxxii) represented by the Pseudo-Denys (cf. Q. 13, art. 1, 1; art. 3, 2; art. 12, 1) and, in the generation preceding his own, by Alain de Lille (cf. Q. 13, art. 2, c; art. 6, c) and Maimonides (cf. Q. 13, art. 2, c; art. 5, c).

Secondly, although "Thomist" treatments of the "doctrine of analogy" have, in their quest for descriptions of divine attributes, supposed themselves to be far less "agnostic" than the account of Aquinas's use of analogy offered here, it is by no means clear that they succeeded. This I take to be the drift of Campbell's comments on E. L. Mascall's *Existence and Analogy* (London, 1949); cf. C. A. Campbell, "The Doctrine of Analogy," *On Selfhood and Godhood* (London, 1957), pp. 427-433. For drawing my attention to Campbell's study, and for many perceptive comments on earlier drafts of this paper, I am greatly indebted to J. A. Bradley.

have been established and secured by techniques of verification that are independent of specifically religious considerations. By "fideism," I understand an approach which, insisting that appropriate criteria of assessment are only available *within* particular patterns of experience, or "ways of life," refuses to submit the claims of faith to "external" assessment, whether by the historian, the social scientist, or the philosopher.

Christianity has, at one time or another, invested heavily in forms of rationalism in an attempt to ensure its integrity and respectability as an aspect of the human quest for truth. Thus, for example, the burgeoning of "natural theologies" in the eighteenth century (especially in the form of "arguments from design") represented an acceptance, by philosophers of religion, of responsibility for securing the theistic ground of Christian belief. It was not, of course, the theistic grounds alone that needed to be secured. From the eighteenth century onwards, biblical scholars and historians of doctrine came to accept responsibility for securing, by techniques of "secular" or "scientific" historiography, the historical ground of Christian belief.

In our day, both philosophers of religion and historians of Christian origins have increasingly come to admit their inability to fulfill their allotted tasks. But the apparent vulnerability to which their failure exposes Christian belief may yet be beneficial. For the rationalist strategy presupposed that, except in so far as we have succeeded in "securing" reality *theoretically*, our patterns of action and policy are irresponsible. There is, however, an alternative and perhaps more fruitful strategy which, recognizant of the primacy of action in respect of reflection, of "social existence" in respect of "consciousness,"[77] supposes that unless we risk seeking responsibly to live and act in the world, any theoretical "purchase" that we imagine ourselves to have upon reality is fragile and suspect. And if this alternative strategy was put to theological use by Newman, especially in his *University Sermons,* it was put to rather different use, by a contemporary of his, as a central characteristic of Marx's "materialism."

The account that I have tried to give, in this essay, of the relation between religious practice and theological reflection—whether historical, literary-critical, or metaphysical—is, in this sense, "materialist."

To paraphrase Marx, the question whether objective truth can be attributed to Christian believing is a practical question. The Christian must prove the truth, i.e. the reality and power, the this-sidedness of his believing in practice.[78] "If the Christian faith is true (and unless its truth-

---

77. Karl Marx, 1859 Preface to "A Contribution to the Critique of Political Economy," *Early Writings* (London, 1975), p. 425.

78. Cf. Marx's second thesis on Feuerbach, *Early Writings,* p. 422.

claims can be sustained we had better have done with it for ever), its truth is constituted by the correspondence of its credenda with harsh, human reality."[79] That correspondence eludes theoretical demonstration. It can, however, be practically, imperfectly, partially, and provisionally *shown* by the character and quality of Christian engagement in patterns of action and suffering, praise and endurance, that refuse to short-cut the quest by the erection of conceptual or institutional absolutes. The absolutization of contingent particulars is always idolatrous: the denial of divine transcendence.

Thus pragmatically to characterize the practical procedures by which Christian truth-claims are to be submitted to continual "verification" is not, however, to endorse the strategy of the "fideist." For if Christian truth-claims cannot—in any straightforward sense—be confirmed by theological reflection, whether historical or philosophical, they are nevertheless such as to demand continual exposure to *dis*confirmation. Thus, for example, I should wish to argue, firstly, that there are constitutive features of Christian belief which are such as to be permanently exposed to historical falsification; secondly, that the narrative forms in which Christian belief finds primary expression are permanently threatened by that illusory self-indulgence the diagnosis of which is the responsibility of literary criticism; thirdly, that Christian faith in divine transcendence is permanently threatened by that incoherence in its discourse the detection of which is the responsibility of the metaphysician, or "theological grammarian."

In brief: the testing of Christian truth-claims occurs, or should occur, in the interplay between their practical verification and their exposure to historical, literary, and philosophical criticism.

My justification for offering so outrageously oversimplified a sketch of problems of enormous complexity is that it seemed incumbent upon me to indicate, in however summary a fashion, that approach to problems of verification and falsification which is, I believe, implied by the account of what I have offered in this essay of the relationship between theology and religion.

IV. Conclusion

It has sometimes been suggested that Christians both can and should opt either for "the God of Abraham, Isaac, and Jacob," or for "the God of the philosophers"; either for narrative or for metaphysics; either for "making sense" of experience or for seeking to discover the truth-con-

79. MacKinnon, "Lenin and Theology," *Explorations*, p. 21.

Nicholas Lash

ditions of those assertions characteristic of Christian confession. In this essay I have attempted, perhaps too obliquely, to indicate some of the reasons why none of these options is, in fact, available.

To suppose that narrative is an alternative to metaphysics, metaphor an alternative to analogy, is to overlook the fact that "Metaphor . . . raises questions that only analogy . . . can answer, while conversely analogy can only answer questions that are raised in a metaphorical form."[80] Similarly, to suppose that construction is an alternative to discovery is either, if one opts for construction, to settle for a Feuerbachian account of the "essence of Christianity" (and there are surely less cumbersome ways of being an atheist than to use the paraphernalia of Christian language and imagery simply to express the form of our alienation?), or to suppose that we have access to the mystery of God other than through the hazardous enterprise of fashioning our human history.

If nothing is gained by attempting partial solutions, neither is anything to be gained by settling back into that benign pluralism ("of course we always need *both*") which mistakes the diagnosis of a problem for its solution. I have suggested that there are two senses in which the story-teller comes first, and two senses in which, if he were left to himself, the integrity and truthfulness of Christianity would be compromised.

Thus, on the one hand, the story-teller comes first inasmuch as Christian religious discourse, as a constitutive element in the practice of Christianity, is paradigmatically narrative (and, more specifically, autobiographical) in form. From this point of view, to "leave the story-teller to himself" would be to leave Christian practice—unconstrained by historical, literary, and philosophical criticism—exposed to the risk, endemic to all autobiography, of "self-indulgence and even dishonesty." (And this, even though, as I have indicated, Christian practice also embodies certain *internal* correctives.) There is thus a sense in which the indispensability of theology is the indispensability of criticism for all forms of theology.

On the other hand, theology's hermeneutical disciplines (historical and literary-critical) also employ narrative, and hence metaphorical, modes of discourse. The historian of Christian origins, and the literary critic, are thus also "story-tellers" after their fashion. As such, their products invite the logical attention of the metaphysician: in this sense they, too, cannot be "left to themselves." But yet, as story-tellers, they "come first" inasmuch as the metaphysician, proceeding along the way of analogy, can only answer questions that are "raised in a metaphorical form."

80. Wicker, *Story-Shaped World*, p. 27. I find it interesting that this "slogan" of Wicker's should closely echo the thrust of Ricoeur's more massively learned story, which appeared in the same year.

The picture that emerges, I suggest, is one that would set the dialectic between construction and the disciplined quest for discovery, between narrative and metaphysics, between making sense and assessing the cost of the operation, along not one axis, but two: the "vertical" axis of the relationship between religion and theology, and the "horizontal" axis of the relationship between hermeneutical and philosophical disciplines.

The schematic character of my remarks in these concluding paragraphs may have given the impression that I have sought to construct yet another "satisfying model" of theological method with which to distract us from the harder task of tackling, both practically and theoretically, the substantive issues. That has not been my intention. Exercises in theological method that lose sight of their essentially heuristic, exploratory character are yet another form in which the temptation of idealism insinuates itself into the theologian's work.

The dialectic between narrative and nescience, anthropomorphism and agnosticism, vision and darkness, autobiographical enactment and the suffering that breaks our constructed identity, is constitutive both of Christian religious practice and of the relationships that obtain between the various patterns of theological enquiry in which that practice is critically reflected. If there are safeguards against illusion and scepticism, they are not, in the last resort, subject to our control. We can, at most, seek to take appropriate precautions.

Epistemological Crises, Dramatic Narrative, and the Philosophy of Science

Alasdair MacIntyre

I

What is an epistemological crisis? Consider, first, the situation of ordinary agents who are thrown into such crises. Someone who has believed that he was highly valued by his employers and colleagues is suddenly fired; someone proposed for membership of a club whose members were all, so he believed, close friends is blackballed. Or someone falls in love and needs to know what the loved one *really* feels; someone falls out of love and needs to know how he or she can possibly have been so mistaken in the other. For all such persons the relationship of *seems* to *is* becomes crucial. It is in such situations that ordinary agents who have never learned anything about academic philosophy are apt to rediscover for themselves versions of the other-minds problem and the problem of the justification of induction. They discover, that is, that there is a problem about the rational justification of inferences from premises about the behavior of other people to conclusions about their thoughts, feelings, and attitudes and of inferences from premises about how individuals have acted in the past to conclusions expressed as generalizations about their behavior — generalizations which would enable us to make reasonably reliable predications about their future behavior. What

Alasdair MacIntyre, "Epistemological Crises, Dramatic Narrative, and the Philosophy of Science," *Monist* 60, 4 (October 1977): 453-472.

they took to be evidence pointing unambiguously in some one direction now turns out to have been equally susceptible of rival interpretations. Such a discovery is often paralysing, and were we all of us all of the time to have to reckon with the multiplicity of possible interpretations open to us, social life as we know it could scarcely continue. For social life is sustained by the assumption that we are, by and large, able to construe each others' behavior—that error, deception, self-deception, irony and ambiguity, although omnipresent in social life, are not so pervasive as to render reliable reasoning and reasonable action impossible. But can this assumption in any way be vindicated?

Consider what it is to share a culture. It is to share schemata which are at one and the same time constitutive of and normative for intelligible action by myself and are also means for my interpretations of the actions of others. My ability to understand what you are doing and my ability to act intelligibly (both to myself and to others) are one and the same ability. It is true that I cannot master these schemata without also acquiring the means to deceive, to make more or less elaborate jokes, to exercise irony and utilize ambiguity, but it is also, and even more importantly, true that my ability to conduct any successful transactions depends on my presenting myself to most people most of the time in unambiguous, unironical, undeceiving, intelligible ways. It is these schemata which enable inferences to be made from premises about past behavior to conclusions about future behavior and present inner attitudes. They are not, of course, empirical generalizations; they are prescriptions for interpretation. But while it is they which normally preserve us from the pressure of the other-minds problem and the problem of induction, it is precisely they which can in certain circumstances thrust those very problems upon us.

For it is not only that an individual may rely on the schemata which have hitherto informed all his interpretations of social life and find that he has been led into radical error or deception, so that for the first time the schemata are put in question—perhaps for the first time they also in this moment become visible to the individual who employs them—but it is also the case that the individual may come to recognise the possibility of systematically different possibilities of interpretation, of the existence of alternative and rival schemata which yield mutually incompatible accounts of what is going on around him. Just this is the form of epistemological crisis encountered by ordinary agents and it is striking that there is not a single account of it anywhere in the literature of academic philosophy. Perhaps this is an important symptom of the condition of that discipline. But happily we do possess one classic study of such crises. It is Shakespeare's *Hamlet*.

Hamlet arrives back from Wittenberg with too many schemata

available for interpreting the events at Elsinore of which already he is a part. There is the revenge schema of the Norse sagas; there is the Renaissance courtier's schema; there is a Machiavellian schema about competition for power. But he not only has the problem of which schema to apply; he also has the other ordinary agents' problem: whom now to believe? His mother? Rosencrantz and Guildenstern? His father's ghost? Until he has adopted some schema he does not know what to treat as evidence; until he knows what to treat as evidence he cannot tell which schema to adopt. Trapped in this epistemological circularity, the general form of his problem is: "What is going on here?" Thus Hamlet's problem is close to that of the literary critics who have asked: "What is going on in *Hamlet*?" And it is close to that of directors who have asked: "What should be cut and what should be included in my production so that the audience may understand what is going on in *Hamlet*?"

The resemblance between Hamlet's problem and that of the critics and directors is worth noticing, for it suggests that both are asking a question which could equally well be formulated as: "What is going on in *Hamlet*?" or "How ought the narrative of these events to be constructed?" Hamlet's problems arise because the dramatic narrative of his family and of the kingdom of Denmark through which he identified his own place in society and his relationships to others has been disrupted by radical interpretative doubts. His task is to reconstitute, to rewrite that narrative, reversing his understanding of past events in the light of present responses to his probing. This probing is informed by two ideals, truth and intelligibility, and the pursuit of both is not always easily coherent. The discovery of a hitherto unsuspected truth is just what may disrupt a hitherto intelligible account. And of course while Hamlet tries to discover a true and intelligible narrative of the events involving his parents and Claudius, Gertrude and Claudius are trying to discover a true and intelligible narrative of Hamlet's investigation. To be unable to render oneself intelligible is to risk being taken to be mad—is, if carried far enough, to be mad. And madness or death may always be the outcomes which prevent the resolution of an epistemological crisis, for an epistemological crisis is always a crisis in human relationships.

When an epistemological crisis is resolved, it is by the construction of a new narrative which enables the agent to understand *both* how he or she could intelligibly have held his or her original beliefs *and* how he or she could have been so drastically misled by them. The narrative in terms of which he or she at first understood and ordered experiences is itself made into the subject of an enlarged narrative. The agent has come to understand how the criteria of truth and understanding must be reformulated. He has had to become epistemologically self-conscious

and at a certain point he may have come to acknowledge two conclusions: the first is that his new forms of understanding may themselves in turn come to be put in question at any time; the second is that,
because in such crises the criteria of truth, intelligibility, and rationality
may always themselves be put in question—as they are in *Hamlet*—we
are never in a position to claim that now we possess the truth or now
we are fully rational. The most that we can claim is that this is the best
account which anyone has been able to give so far, and that our beliefs
about what the marks of "a best account so far" are will themselves
change in what are at present unpredictable ways.

Philosophers have often been prepared to acknowledge this historical character in respect of scientific theories; but they have usually
wanted to exempt their own thinking from the same historicity. So, of
course, have writers of dramatic narrative; *Hamlet* is unique among plays
in its openness to reinterpretation. Consider, by contrast, Jane Austen's
procedure in *Emma*. Emma insists on viewing her protégée, Harriet, as a
character in an eighteenth-century romance. She endows her, deceiving
both herself and Harriet, with the conventional qualities of the heroine
of such a romance. Harriet's parentage is not known; Emma converts her
into the foundling heroine of aristocratic birth so common in such romances. And she designs for Harriet precisely the happy ending of such
a romance, marriage to a superior being. By the end of *Emma* Jane Austen
has provided Emma with some understanding of what it was in herself
that had led her not to perceive the untruthfulness of her interpretation
of the world in terms of romance. *Emma* has become a narrative about
narrative. But Emma, although she experiences moral reversal, has only
a minor epistemological crisis, if only because the standpoint which she
now, through the agency of Mr. Knightly, has come to adopt, is presented
as though it were one from which *the* world as it is can be viewed. False
interpretation has been replaced not by a more adequate interpretation,
which itself in turn may one day be transcended, but simply by the truth.
We, of course, can see that Jane Austen is merely replacing one interpretation by another, but Jane Austen herself fails to recognise this and
so has to deprive Emma of this recognition too.

Philosophers have customarily been Emmas and not Hamlets,
except that in one respect they have often been even less perceptive
than Emma. For Emma it becomes clear that her movement towards the
truth necessarily had a moral dimension. Neither Plato nor Kant would
have demurred. But the history of epistemology, like the history of ethics
itself, is usually written as though it were not a moral narrative, that is,
in fact as though it were not a narrative. For narrative requires an evaluative framework in which good or bad character helps to produce unfortunate or happy outcomes.

One further aspect of narratives and their role in epistemological crises remains to be noticed. I have suggested that epistemological progress consists in the construction and reconstruction of more adequate narratives and forms of narrative and that epistemological crises are occasions for such reconstruction. But if this were really the case then two kinds of questions would need to be answered. The first would be of the form: How does this progress begin? What are the narratives from which we set out? The second would be of the form: How comes it, then, that narrative is not only given so little place by thinkers from Descartes onwards, but has so often before and after been treated as a merely aesthetic form? The answers to these questions are not entirely unconnected.

We begin from myth, not only from the myths of primitive peoples, but from those myths or fairy stories which are essential to a well-ordered childhood. Bruno Bettelheim has written: "Before and well into the oedipal period (roughly, the ages between three and six or seven), the child's experience of the world is chaotic. . . . During and because of the oedipal struggles, the outside world comes to hold more meaning for the child and he begins to try to make some sense of it. . . . As a child listens to a fairy tale, he gets ideas about how he may create order out of the chaos that is his inner life."[1] It is from fairy tales, so Bettelheim argues, that the child learns how to engage himself with and perceive an order in social reality; and the child who is deprived of the right kind of fairy tale at the right age later on is apt to have to adopt strategies to evade a reality he has not learned how to interpret or to handle.

"The child asks himself, 'Who am I? Where did I come from? How did the world come into being? Who created man and all the animals? What is the purpose of life?' . . . He wonders who or what brings adversity upon him and what can protect him against it. Are there benevolent powers in addition to his parents? *Are* his parents benevolent powers? How should he form himself, and why? Is there hope for him, though he may have done wrong? Why did all this happen to him? What will it mean to his future?"[2] The child originally requires answers that are true to his own experience, but of course the child comes to learn the inadequacy of that experience. Bettelheim points out that the young child told by adults that the world is a globe suspended in space and spinning at incredible speeds may feel bound to repeat what they say, but would find it immensely more plausible to be told that the earth is held up by a giant. But in time the young child learns that what the

---

1. Bruno Bettelheim, *The Uses of Enchantment* (New York: Alfred A. Knopf, 1976), pp. 74-75.
2. Ibid., p. 47.

adults told him is indeed true. And such a child may well become a Descartes, one who feels that all narratives are misleading fables when compared with what he now takes to be the solid truth of physics.

Yet to raise the question of truth need not entail rejecting myth or story as the appropriate and perhaps the only appropriate form in which certain truths can be told. The child may become not a Descartes, but a Vico or a Hamann who writes a story about how he had to escape from the hold which the stories of his childhood and the stories of the childhood of the human race originally had upon him in order to discover how stories can be true stories. Such a narrative will be itself a history of epistemological transitions and this narrative may well be brought to a point at which questions are thrust upon the narrator which make it impossible for him to continue to use it as an instrument of interpretation. Just this, of course, happens to Descartes, who having abjured history as a means to truth, recounts to us his own history as the medium through which the search for truth is to be carried on. For Descartes and for others this moment is that at which an epistemological crisis occurs. And all those questions which the child has asked of the teller of fairy tales arise in a new adult form. Philosophy is now set the same task that had once been set for myth.

II

Descartes' description of his own epistemological crisis has, of course, been uniquely influential. Yet Descartes radically misdescribes his own crisis and thus has proved a highly misleading guide to the nature of epistemological crises in general. The agent who is plunged into an epistemological crisis knows something very important: that a schema of interpretation which he has trusted so far has broken down irremediably in certain highly specific ways. So it is with Hamlet. Descartes, however, starts from the assumption that he knows nothing whatsoever until he can discover a presuppositionless first principle on which all else can be founded. Hamlet's doubts are formulated against a background of what he takes to be — rightly—well-founded beliefs; Descartes' doubt is intended to lack any such background. It is to be contextless doubt. Hence also that tradition of philosophical teaching arises which presupposes that Cartesian doubts can be entertained by anyone at any place or time. But of course someone who really believed that he knew nothing would not even know how to begin on a course of radical doubt; for he would have no conception of what his task might be, of what it would be to settle his doubts and to acquire well-founded beliefs. Conversely, anyone who knows enough to know *that* does indeed possess a set of extensive epistemological beliefs which he is not putting in doubt at all.

Descartes' failure is complex. First of all he does not recognise that among the features of the universe which he is not putting in doubt is his own capacity not only to use the French and the Latin languages, but even to express the same thought in both languages; and as a consequence he does not put in doubt what he has inherited in and with these languages, namely, a way of ordering both thought and the world expressed in a set of meanings. These meanings have a history; seventeenth-century Latin bears the marks of having been the language of scholasticism, just as scholasticism was itself marked by the influence of twelfth- and thirteenth-century Latin. It was perhaps because the presence of his languages was invisible to the Descartes of the *Discours* and the *Meditationes* that he also did not notice what Gilson pointed out in detail: how much of what he took to be the spontaneous reflections of his own mind was in fact a repetition of sentences and phrases from his school textbooks. Even the *Cogito* is to be found in Saint Augustine.

What thus goes unrecognised by Descartes is the presence not only of languages, but of a tradition—a tradition that he took himself to have successfully disowned. It was from this tradition that he inherited his epistemological ideals. For at the core of this tradition was a conception of knowledge as analogous to vision: the mind's eye beholds its objects by the light of reason. At the same time this tradition wishes to contrast sharply knowledge and sense-experience, including visual experience. Hence there is metaphorical incoherence at the heart of every theory of knowledge in this Platonic and Augustinian tradition, an incoherence which Descartes unconsciously reproduces. Thus Descartes also cannot recognise that he is responding not only to the timeless demands of scepticism, but to a highly specific crisis in one particular social and intellectual tradition.

One of the signs that a tradition is in crisis is that its accustomed ways for relating *seems* and *is* begin to break down. Thus the pressures of scepticism become more urgent and attempts to do the impossible, to refute scepticism once and for all, become projects of central importance to the culture and not mere private academic enterprises. Just this happens in the late middle ages and the sixteenth century. Inherited modes of ordering experience reveal too many rival possibilities of interpretation. It is no accident that there are a multiplicity of rival interpretations of both the thought and the lives of such figures as Luther and Machiavelli in a way that there are not for such equally rich and complex figures as Abelard and Aquinas. Ambiguity, the possibility of alternative interpretations, becomes a central feature of human character and activity. *Hamlet* is Shakespeare's brilliant mirror to the age, and the difference between Shakespeare's account of epistemological crises and Descartes' is now clear. For Shakespeare invites us to reflect on the crisis of the self as a crisis in the tradition which has formed the self; Descartes by his attitude to history and to fable has cut himself off from the possibility of recognising himself; he has invented an unhistorical, self-endorsed self-consciousness and tried to describe his epistemological crisis in terms of it. Small wonder that he misdescribes it.

Consider by contrast Galileo. When Galileo entered the scientific scene he was confronted by much more than the conflict between the Ptolemaic and Copernican astronomies. The Ptolemaic system was itself inconsistent both with the widely accepted Platonic requirements for a true astronomy and with the perhaps even more widely accepted principles of Aristotelian physics. These latter were in turn inconsistent with the findings of over two centuries of scholars at Oxford, Paris, and Padua about motion. Not surprisingly, instrumentalism flourished as a philosophy of science and Osiander's instrumentalist reading of Copernicus was no more than the counterpart to earlier instrumentalist interpretations of the Ptolemaic system. Instrumentalism, like attempts to refute scepticism, is characteristically a sign of a tradition in crisis.

Galileo resolves the crisis by the threefold strategy. He rejects instrumentalism; he reconciles astronomy and mechanics; and he redefines the place of experiment in natural science. The old mythological empiricist view of Galileo saw him appealing to the facts against Ptolemy and Aristotle; what he actually did was to give a new account of what an appeal to the facts had to be. Wherein lies the superiority of Galileo to his predecessors? The answer is that he, for the first time, enables the work of all his predecessors to be evaluated by a common set of standards. The contributions of Plato, Aristotle, the scholars at Merton College, Oxford, and at Padua, the work of Copernicus himself at last all fall into place. Or, to put matters in another and equivalent way: the history of late medieval science can finally be cast into a coherent narrative. Galileo's work implies a rewriting of the narrative which constitutes the scientific tradition. For it now became retrospectively possible to identify those anomalies which had been genuine counterexamples to received theories from those anomalies which could justifiably be dealt with by ad hoc explanatory devices or even ignored. It also became retrospectively possible to see how the various elements of various theories had fared in their encounters with other theories and with observations and experiments, and to understand how the form in which they had survived bore the marks of those encounters. A theory always bears the marks of its passage through time and the theories with which Galileo had to deal were no exception.

Let me cast the point which I am trying to make about Galileo in a way which, at first sight, is perhaps paradoxical. We are apt to suppose that because Galileo was a peculiarly great scientist, therefore he had his own peculiar place in the history of science. I am suggesting instead that it is because of his peculiarly important place in the history of science that he is accounted a particularly great scientist. The criterion of a successful theory is that it enables us to understand its predecessors in a newly intelligible way. It, at one and the same time, enables us to understand precisely why its predecessors have to be rejected or modified and also why, without and before its illumination, past theory could have remained credible. It introduces new standards for evaluating the past. It recasts the narrative which constitutes the continuous reconstruction of the scientific tradition.

This connection between narrative and tradition has hitherto gone almost unnoticed, perhaps because tradition has usually been taken seriously only by conservative social theorists. Yet those features of tradition which emerge as important when the connection between tradition and narrative is understood are ones which conservative theorists are unlikely to attend to. For what constitutes a tradition is a conflict of interpretations of that tradition, a conflict which itself has a history susceptible of rival interpretations. If I am a Jew, I have to recognise that the tradition of Judaism is partly constituted by a continuous argument over what it means to be a Jew. Suppose I am an American: the tradition is one partly constituted by a continuous argument over it means to be an American and partly by continuous argument over what it means to have rejected tradition. If I am a historian, I must acknowledge that the tradition of historiography is partly, but centrally, constituted by arguments about what history is and ought to be, from Hume and Gibbon to Namier and Edward Thompson. Notice that all three kinds of tradition—religious, political, intellectual— involve epistemological debate as a necessary feature of their conflicts. For it is not merely that different participants in a tradition disagree; they also disagree as to how to characterize their disagreements and as to how to resolve them. They disagree as to what constitutes appropriate reasoning, decisive evidence, conclusive proof.

A tradition then not only embodies the narrative of an argument, but it is only to be recovered by an argumentative retelling of that narrative which will itself be in conflict with other argumentative retellings. Every tradition therefore is always in danger of lapsing into incoherence and when a tradition does so lapse it sometimes can only be recovered by a revolutionary reconstitution. Precisely such a reconstitution of a tradition which had lapsed into incoherence was the work of Galileo.

It will now be obvious why I introduced the notion of tradition by alluding negatively to the viewpoint of conservative theorists. For they, from Burke onwards, have wanted to counterpose tradition and reason and tradition and revolution. Not reason, but prejudice; not revolution, but inherited precedent; these are Burke's key oppositions. Yet if the present arguments are correct it is traditions which are the bearers of reason, and traditions at certain periods actually require and need revolutions for their continuance. Burke saw the French Revolution as merely the negative overthrow of all that France had been and many French conservatives have agreed with him, but later thinkers as different as Péguy and Hilaire Belloc were able retrospectively to see the great revolution as reconstituting a more ancient France, so that Jeanne D'Arc and Danton belong within the same single, if immensely complex, tradition.

Conflict arises, of course, not only within, but between traditions and such a conflict tests the resources of each contending tradition. It is yet another mark of a degenerate tradition that it has contrived a set of epistemological defences which enable it to avoid being put in question or at least to avoid recognising that it is being put in question by rival traditions. This is, for example, part of the degeneracy of modern astrology, of some types of psychiatric thought, and of liberal Protestantism. Although, therefore, any feature of any tradition, any theory, any practice, any belief can always under certain conditions be put in question, the practice of putting in question, whether within a tradition or between traditions, itself always requires the context of a tradition. Doubting is a more complex activity than some skeptics have realized. To say to oneself or to someone else "Doubt all your beliefs here and now" without reference to historical or autobiographical context is not meaningless; but it is an invitation not to philosophy, but to mental breakdown, or rather to philosophy as a means of mental breakdown. Descartes concealed from himself, as we have seen, an unacknowledged background of beliefs which rendered what he was doing intelligible and sane to himself and others. But suppose that he had put that background in question too—what would have happened to him then?

We are not without clues, for we do have the record of the approach to breakdown in the life of one great philosopher. "For I have already shown," wrote Hume,

> that the understanding, when it acts alone, and according to its most general principles, entirely subverts itself, and leaves not the lowest degree of evidence in any proposition, either in philosophy or common life. . . . The *intense* view of these manifold contradictions and imperfections in human reason has so wrought upon me, and heated my brain, that I am ready to reject all belief and reasoning, and can look upon no opinion even as more probable or likely than another. Where am I, or what? From what causes do I derive my existence, and to what condi-

147

tion shall I return? Whose favour shall I court, and whose anger must I dread? What beings surround me? and on whom have I any influence? I am confronted with all these questions, and begin to fancy myself in the most deplorable condition imaginable, inviron'd with the deepest darkness and utterly depriv'd of the use of every member and faculty.[3]

We may note three remarkable features of Hume's cry of pain. First, like Descartes, he has set a standard for the foundations of his beliefs which could not be met; hence all beliefs founder equally. He has not asked if he can find good reasons for preferring in respect of the best criteria of reason and truth available some among others of the limited range of possibilities of belief which actually confront him in his particular cultural situation. Secondly, he is in consequence thrust back without any answers or possibility of answers upon just that range of questions that, according to Bettelheim, underlie the whole narrative enterprise in early childhood. There is indeed the most surprising and illuminating correspondence between the questions which Bettelheim ascribes to the child and the questions framed by the adult, but desperate, Hume. For Hume by his radical skepticism has lost any means of making himself—or others—intelligible to himself, let alone to others. His very skepticism itself becomes unintelligible.

There is perhaps a possible world in which "empiricism" would have become the name of a mental illness, while "paranoia" would be the name of a well-accredited theory of knowledge. For in this world empiricists would be consistent and unrelenting—unlike Hume—and they would thus lack any means to order their experience of other people or of nature. Even a knowledge of formal logic would not help them; for until they knew how to order their experiences they would possess neither sentences to formalize nor reasons for choosing one way of formalizing them rather than another. Their world would indeed be reduced to that chaos which Bettelheim perceives in the child at the beginning of the oedipal phase. Empiricism would lead not to sophistication, but to regression. Paranoia by contrast would provide considerable resources for living in the world. The empiricist maxim "Believe only what can be based upon sense-experience" or Occam's razor, would leave us bereft of all generalizations and therefore of all attitudes towards the future (or the past). They would isolate us in a contentless present. But the paranoid maxims "Interpret everything which happens as an outcome of envious malice" and "Everyone and everything will let you down" receive continuous confirmation for those who adopt them. Hume cannot answer the question: "What beings surround me?"

3. David Hume, *Treatise on Human Nature*, ed. L. A. Selby-Bigge (London: Oxford University Press, 1941), Bk. I, iv, vii, pp. 267-269.

But Kafka knew the answer to this very well: "In fact the clock has certain personal relationships to me, like many things in the room, save that now, particularly since I gave notice—or rather since I was given notice . . .—they seem to be beginning to turn their backs on me, above all the calendar. . . . Lately it is as if it had been metamorphosed. Either it is absolutely uncommunicative—for example, you want its advice, you go up to it, but the only thing it says is 'Feast of the Reformation'—which probably has a deeper significance, but who can discover it?—or, on the contrary, it is nastily ironic."[4]

So in this possible world they will speak of Hume's Disease and of Kafka's Theory of Knowledge. Yet is this possible world so different from that which we inhabit? What leads us to segregate at least some types of mental from ordinary, sane behavior is that they presuppose and embody ways of interpreting the natural and social world which are radically discordant with our customary and, as we take it, justified modes of interpretation. That is, certain types of mental illness seem to presuppose rival theories of knowledge. Conversely every theory of knowledge offers us schemata for accepting some interpretations of the natural and social world rather than others. As Hamlet discovered earlier, the categories of psychiatry and of epistemology must be to some extent interdefinable.

III

What I have been trying to sketch are a number of conceptual connections which link such notions as those of an epistemological crisis, a narrative, a tradition, natural science, skepticism, and madness. There is one group of recent controversies in which the connections between these concepts has itself become a central issue. I refer, of course, to the debates which originated from the confrontation between Thomas Kuhn's philosophy of science and the views of those philosophers of science who in one way or another are the heirs of Sir Karl Popper. It is not surprising therefore that the positions which I have taken should imply conclusions about those controversies, conclusions which are not quite the same as those of any of the major participants. Yet it is perhaps because the concepts which I have examined—such as those on epistemological crisis and of the relationship of conflict to tradition—have provided the largely unexamined background to the recent debates that their classification may in fact help to resolve some of the issues.

4. Letter to his sister Valli, in *I Am a Memory Come Alive,* ed. Nahum N. Glatzer (New York: Schocken Books, 1974), p. 235.

In particular I shall want to argue that the positions of some of the most heated antagonists—notably Thomas Kuhn and Imre Lakatos—can be seen to converge once they are emended in ways towards which the protagonists themselves have moved in their successive reformulations of their positions.

One very striking new conclusion will however also emerge. For I shall want to reinforce my thesis that dramatic narrative is the crucial form for the understanding of human action and I shall want to argue that natural science can be a rational form of enquiry if and only if the writing of a true dramatic narrative—that is, of history understood in a particular way—can be a rational activity. Scientific reason turns out to be subordinate to, and intelligible only in terms of, historical reason. And if this is true of the natural sciences, *a fortiori* it will be true also of the social sciences.

It is therefore sad that social scientists have all too often treated the work of writers such as Kuhn and Lakatos as it stood. Kuhn's writing in particular has been invoked time and again—for a period of ten years or so, a ritual obeisance towards Kuhn seems almost to have been required in presidential addresses to the American Political Science Association—to license the theoretical failures of social science. But while Kuhn's work uncriticised — or for that matter Popper or Lakatos uncriticised — represents a threat to our understanding, Kuhn's work criticised provides an illuminating application for the ideas which I have been defending.

My criticisms of Kuhn will fall into three parts. In the first I shall suggest that his earlier formulations of his position are much more radically flawed than he himself has acknowledged. I shall then argue that it is his failure to recognise the true character of the flaws in his earlier formulations which leads to the weakness of his later revisions. Finally I shall suggest a more adequate form of revision.

What Kuhn originally presented was an account of epistemological crises in natural science which is essentially the same as the Cartesian account of epistemological crises in philosophy. This account was superimposed on a view of natural science which seems largely indebted to the writings of Michael Polanyi (Kuhn nowhere acknowledges any such debt). What Polanyi had shown is that all justification takes place within a social tradition and that the pressures of such a tradition enforce often unrecognised rules by means of which discrepant pieces of evidence or difficult questions are often put on one side with the tacit assent of the scientific community. Polanyi is the Burke of the philosophy of science, and I mean this analogy with political and moral philosophy to be taken with great seriousness. For all my earlier criticisms of Burke now become relevant to the criticism of Polanyi.

Polanyi, like Burke, understands tradition as essentially conservative and essentially unitary. (Paul Feyerabend—at first sight so different from Polanyi—agrees with Polanyi in his understanding of tradition. It is just because he so understands the scientific tradition that he rejects it and has turned himself into the Emerson of the philosophy of science; not "Every man his own Jesus," but "Every man his own Galileo.") He does not see the omnipresence of conflict—sometimes latent—within living traditions. It is because of this that anyone who took Polanyi's view would find it very difficult to explain how a transition might be made from one tradition to another or how a tradition which had lapsed into incoherence might be reconstructed. Since reason operates only *within* traditions and communities according to Polanyi, such a tradition or a reconstruction could not be a work of reason. It would have to be a leap in the dark of some kind.

Polanyi never carried his argument to this point. But what is a major difficulty in Polanyi's position was presented by Kuhn as though it were a discovery. Kuhn did of course recognise very fully how a scientific tradition may lapse into incoherence. And he must have (with Feyerabend) the fullest credit for recognising in an original way the significance and character of incommensurability. But the conclusions which he draws, namely that "proponents of competing paradigms must fail to make complete contact with each other's viewpoints" and that the transition from one paradigm to another requires a "conversion experience" do not follow from his premises concerning incommensurability. These last are threefold: adherents of rival paradigms during a scientific revolution disagree about what set of problems provide the test for a successful paradigm in that particular scientific situation; their theories embody very different concepts; and they "see different things when they look from the same point in the same direction." Kuhn concludes that "just because it is a transition between incommensurables" the transition cannot be made step by step; and he uses the expression "gestalt switch" as well as "conversion experience." What is important is that Kuhn's account of the transition requires an additional premise. It is not just that the adherents of rival paradigms disagree, but that *every* relevant area of rationality is invaded by that disagreement. It is not just that threefold incommensurability is present, but rationality apparently cannot be present in any other form. Now this additional premise would indeed follow from Polanyi's position and if Kuhn's position is understood as presupposing something like Polanyi's, then Kuhn's earlier formulations of his positions become all too intelligible; and so do the accusations of irrationalism by his critics, accusations which Kuhn professes not to understand.

What follows from the position thus formulated? It is that scientific revolutions are epistemological crises understood in a Cartesian way. Everything is put in question simultaneously. There is no rational continuity between the situation at the time immediately preceding the crisis and any situation following it. To such a crisis the language of evangelical conversation would indeed be appropriate. We might indeed begin to speak with the voice of Pascal, lamenting that the highest achievement of reason is to learn what reason cannot achieve. But of course, as we have already seen, the Cartesian view of epistemological crises is false; it can never be the case that everything is put in question simultaneously. That would indeed lead to large and unintelligible lacunas, not only in the history of practices, such as those of the natural sciences, but also in the personal biographies of scientists.

Moreover Kuhn does not distinguish between two kinds of transition experience. The experience which he is describing seems to be that of the person who, having been thoroughly educated into practices defined and informed by one paradigm, has to make the transition to a form of scientific practice defined and informed by some radically different paradigm. Of this kind of person what Kuhn asserts may well on occasion be true. But such a scientist is always being invited to make a transition that has already been made by others; the very characterization of his situation presupposes that the new paradigm is already operative while the old still retains some power. But what of the very different type of transition made by those scientists who first invented or discovered the new paradigm? Here Kuhn's divergences from Polanyi ought to have saved him from his original Polanyi-derived conclusion. For Kuhn does recognise very fully and insightfully how traditions lapse into incoherence. What some, at least, of those who are educated into such a tradition may come to recognise is the gap between its *own* epistemological ideals and its actual practices. Of those who recognise this some may tend towards skepticism and some towards instrumentalism. Just this, as we have already seen, characterized late medieval and sixteenth-century science. What the scientific genius, such as Galileo, achieves in his transition, then, is not only a new way of understanding nature, but also and inseparably a new way of understanding the old science's way of understanding nature. It is because only from the standpoint of the new science can the inadequacy of the old science be characterized that the new science is taken to be more adequate than the old. It is from the standpoint of the new science that the continuities of narrative history are re-established.

Kuhn has of course continuously modified his earlier formulations and to some degree his position. He has in particular pointed out forcefully to certain of his critics that it is they who have imputed to him the thesis that scientific revolutions are nonrational or irrational events, a conclusion which he has never drawn himself. His own position is "that, if history or any other empirical discipline leads us to believe that the development of science depends essentially on behavior that we have previously thought to be irrational, then we should conclude not that science is irrational, but that our notion of rationality needs adjustment here and there."

Feyerabend however, beginning from the same premises as Kuhn, has drawn on his own behalf the very conclusion which Kuhn so abhors. And surely if scientific revolutions were as Kuhn describes them, if there were nothing more to them than such features as the threefold incommensurability, Feyerabend would be in the right. Thus if Kuhn is to, as he says, "adjust" the notion of rationality, he will have to find the signs of rationality in some feature of scientific revolutions to which he has not yet attended. Are there such features? Certainly, but they belong precisely to the history of these episodes. It is more rational to accept one theory or paradigm and to reject its predecessor when the later theory or paradigm provides a stand-point from which the acceptance, the life-story, and the rejection of the previous theory or paradigm can be recounted in more intelligible historical narrative than previously. An understanding of the concept of the superiority of one physical theory to another requires a prior understanding of the concept of the superiority of one historical narrative to another. The theory of scientific rationality has to be embedded in a philosophy of history.

What is carried over from one paradigm to another are epistemological ideals and a correlative understanding of what constitutes the progress of a single intellectual life. Just as Descartes' account of his own epistemological crisis was only possible by reason of Descartes' ability to recount his own history, indeed to live his life as a narrative about to be cast into a history—an ability which Descartes himself could not recognise without falsifying his own account of epistemological crises—so Kuhn and Feyerabend recount the history of epistemological crises as moments of almost total discontinuity without noticing the historical continuity which makes their own intelligible narratives possible. Something very like this position, which I have approached through a criticism of Kuhn, was reached by Lakatos in the final stages of his journey away from Popper's initial positions.

If Polanyi is the Burke of the philosophy of science and Feyerabend the Emerson, then Popper himself or at least his disciples inherit the role of J. S. Mill—as Feyerabend has already noticed. The truth is to be approached through the free clash of opinion. The logic of the moral sciences is to be replaced by *Logik der Forschung*. Where Burke sees reasoning only within the context of tradition and Feyerabend sees the tradition as merely repressive of the individual, Popper has rightly tried to make something of the notion of rational tradition. What hindered this attempt was the Popperian insistence on replacing the false methodology of induction by a new methodology. The history of Popper's own thought and of that of his most gifted followers was for quite a number of years the history of successive attempts to replace Popper's original falsificationism by some more adequate version, each of which in turn fell prey to counterexamples from the history of science. From one point of view the true heir of these attempts is Feyerabend; for it is he who has formulated the completely general thesis that all such attempts were doomed to failure. There is *no* set of rules as to how science *must* proceed and all attempts to discover such a set founder in their encounter with actual history of science. But when Lakatos had finally accepted this, he moved on to new ground.

In 1968, while he was still a relatively conservative Popperian, Lakatos had written: "the appraisal is rather of a *series of theories* than of an isolated *theory*." He went on to develop this notion into that of a research program. The notion of a research program is of course oriented to the future and there was therefore a tension between Lakatos's use of this notion and his recognition that it is only retrospectively that a series of theories can be appraised. In other words what is appraised is always a history; for it is not just a series of theories which is appraised, but a series of theories which stand in various complex relationships to each other through time which is appraised. Indeed what we take to be a single theory is always "a growing developing entity, one which cannot be considered as a static structure."[5] Consider for example the kinetic theory of gases. If we read the scientific textbooks for any period we shall find presented an entirely ahistorical account of the theory. But if we read all the successive textbooks we shall learn not only that the kinetic theory of 1857 was not quite that of 1845 and that the kinetic theory of 1901 is neither that of 1857 nor that of 1965. Yet at each stage the theory bears the marks of its previous history, of a series of encounters with confirming or anomalous evidence, with other theories, with metaphysical points of view, and so on. The kinetic theory not merely has, but is a history, and to evaluate it is to evaluate how it has fared in this large variety of encounters. Which of these have been victories, which defeats, which compounds of victory and defeat, and which not classifiable under any of these headings? To evaluate a theory, just as to evaluate a series of theories, one of Lakatos's research programs, is precisely to write that history, that narrative of defeats and victories.

5. Richard M. Burian, "More than a Marriage of Convenience: On the Inextricability of History and Philosophy of Science," unpublished paper, p. 38.

This is what Lakatos recognised in his paper on "History of Science and Its Rational Reconstructions."[6] Methodologies are to be assessed by the extent to which they satisfy historiographical criteria; the best scientific methodology is that which can supply the best rational reconstruction of the history of science, and for different episodes, different methodologies may well be successful. But in talking not about history, but about rational reconstructions Lakatos has still not exorcised the ghosts of the older Popperian belief in methodology; for he was quite prepared to envisage the rational reconstruction as "a caricature" of actual history. Yet it matters enormously that our histories should be true, just as it matters that our scientific theories make truth one of their goals.

Kuhn interestingly and perhaps oddly insists against Lakatos on truth in history (he accuses Lakatos of replacing genuine history by "philosophy fabricating examples"), but yet denies any notion of truth to natural science other than that truth which attaches to solutions, to puzzles, and to concrete predictions. In particular he wants to deny that a scientific theory can embody a true ontology, that it can provide a true representative of what is "really there." "There is, I think no theory-independent way to reconstruct phrases like 'really there'; the notion of a match between the ontology of a theory and its 'real' counterpart in nature now seems to me illusive in principle."[7]

This is very odd; because science has certainly shown us decisively that some existence-claims are false just because the entities in question are *not* really there—whatever *any* theory may say. Epicurean atomism is not true, there are no humors, nothing with negative weight exists; phlogiston is one with the witches and the dragons. But other existence-claims have survived exceptionally well through a succession of particular theoretical positions: molecules, cells, electrons. Of course our beliefs about molecules, cells, and electrons are by no means what they once were. But Kuhn would be put into a very curious position if he adduced this as a ground for denying that some existence-claims still have excellent warrant and others do not.

What worries Kuhn, however, is something else: "in some important respects, though by no means in all, Einstein's general theory of relativity is closer to Aristotle's mechanics than either of them is to Newton's."[8] He therefore concludes that the superiority of Einstein to Newton is in puzzle solving and not in an approach to a true ontology. But what

6. I. Lakatos, "History of Science and Its Rational Reconstructions," in *Boston Studies in the Philosophy of Science*, Vol. VIII, ed. Roger C. Buch and Robert S. Cohen (Dordrecht-Holland: D. Reidel Publishing Co., 1974).
7. Thomas S. Kuhn, *The Structure of Scientific Revolutions*, 2d ed. (Chicago: University of Chicago Press, 1970), p. 206.
8. Ibid., pp. 206-207.

an Einstein ontology enables us to understand is why *from the standpoint of an approach to truth* Newtonian mechanics is superior to Aristotelian. For Aristotelian mechanics as it lapsed into incoherence could never have led us to the special theory; construe them how you will, the Aristotelian problems about time will not yield the questions to which special relativity is the answer. A history which moved from Aristotelianism directly to relativistic physics is not an imaginable history.

What Kuhn's disregard for ontological truth neglects is the way in which the progress toward truth in different sciences is such that they have to converge. The easy reductionism of some positivist programs for science was misleading here, but the rejection of such a reductionism must not blind us to the necessary convergence of physics, chemistry, and biology. Were it not for a concern for ontological truth, the nature of our demand for a coherent and convergent relationship between all the sciences would be unintelligible.

Kuhn's view may, of course, seem attractive simply because it seems consistent with a fallibilism which we have every reason to accept. *Perhaps* Einsteinian physics will one day be overthrown just as Newtonian was; perhaps, as Lakatos in his more colorfully rhetorical moments used to suggest, all our scientific beliefs are, always have been, and always will be false. But it seems to be a presupposition of the way in which we do natural science that fallibilism has to be made consistent with the regulative ideal of an approach to a true account of the fundamental order of things and not vice versa. If this is so, Kant is essentially right; the notion of an underlying order—the kind of order that we would expect if the ingenious, unmalicious god of Newton and Einstein had created the universe—*is* a regulative ideal of physics. We do not need to understand this notion quite as Kant did, and our antitheological beliefs may make us uncomfortable in adopting it. But perhaps discomfort at this point is a sign of philosophical progress.

I am suggesting, then, that the best account that can be given of why some scientific theories are superior to others presupposed the possibility of constructing an intelligible dramatic narrative which can claim historical truth and in which such theories are the subject of successive episodes. It is because and only because we can construct better and worse histories of this kind, histories which can be rationally compared with each other, that we can compare theories rationally too. Physics presupposes history and history of a kind that invokes just those concepts of tradition, intelligibility, and epistemological crisis for which I argued earlier. It is this that enables us to understand why Kuhn's account of scientific revolutions can in fact be rescued from the charges of irrationalism levelled by Lakatos and why Lakatos's final writings can be rescued from the charges of evading history levelled by Kuhn.

Without this background, scientific revolutions become unintelligible episodes; indeed Kuhn becomes—what in essence Lakatos accused him of being—the Kafka of the history of science. Small wonder that he in turn felt that Lakatos was not a historian, but a historical novelist.

A final thesis can now be articulated. When the connection between narrative and tradition on the one hand, and theory and method on the other, is lost sight of, the philosophy of science is set insoluble problems. Any set of finite observations is compatible with any one out of an infinite set of generalizations. Any attempt to show the rationality of science, once and for all, by providing a rationally justifiable set of rules for linking observations and generalizations breaks down. This holds, as the history of the Popperian school shows, for falsification as much as for any version of positivism. It holds, as the history of Rudolph Carnap's work shows, no matter how much progress may be made on detailed, particular structures in scientific inference. It is only when theories are located in history, when we view the demands for justification in highly particular contexts of a historical kind, that we are freed from either dogmatism or capitulation to skepticism. It therefore turns out that the program which dominated the philosophy of science from the eighteenth century onwards, that of combining empiricism and natural science, was bound to break down either at worst in irrationalism or at best in a set of successively weakened empiricist programs whose driving force was a deep desire not to be forced into irrationalist conclusions. Hume's Disease is, however, incurable and ultimately fatal, and even backgammon (or that type of analytical philosophy which is often the backgammon of the professional philosopher) cannot stave off its progress indefinitely. It is, after all, Vico, and neither Descartes nor Hume, who has turned out to be in the right in approaching the relationship between history and physics.

From System to Story: An Alternative Pattern for Rationality in Ethics

Stanley Hauerwas and David Burrell

I. Narrative, Ethics, and Theology

In the interest of securing a rational foundation for morality, contemporary ethical theory has ignored or rejected the significance of narrative for ethical reflection. It is our contention that this has been a profound mistake resulting in a distorted account of moral experience. Furthermore, the attempt to portray practical reason independent of narrative contexts has made it difficult to assess the value which convictions characteristic of Christians or Jews might have for moral existence. As a result, we have lost sight of the ways these traditions might help us deal with the moral issues raised by modern science and medicine.[1]

---

1. For example, James Gustafson ends his recent Marquette Lecture, "The Contributions of Theology to Medical Ethics," by saying "For most persons involved in medical care and practice, the contribution of theology is likely to be of minimal importance, for the moral principles and values needed can be justified without reference to God, and the attitudes that religious beliefs ground can be grounded in other ways. From the standpoint of immediate practicality, the contribution of theology is not great, either in its extent or in its importance" (p. 94). While we have no wish to challenge this as a descriptive statement of what pertains today, we think we can show that even though "moral principles can be justified without reference to God," how they are accounted for still makes a difference for

---

Stanley Hauerwas and David Burrell, "From System to Story: An Alternative Pattern for Rationality in Ethics," from *Truthfulness and Tragedy: Further Investigations in Christian Ethics* by Stanley Hauerwas (Notre Dame: University of Notre Dame Press, 1977), pp. 15-39.

We will develop two independent but interrelated theses in order to illustrate and substantiate these claims. First, we will try to establish the significance of narrative for ethical reflection. By the phrase "the significance of narrative," we mean to call attention to three points:[2] (1) that character and moral notions only take on meaning in a narrative; (2) that narrative and explanation stand in an intimate relationship, and therefore moral disagreements involve rival histories of explanation; and (3) that the standard account of moral objectivity is the obverse of existentialist ethics, since the latter assumes that the failure to secure moral objectivity implies that all moral judgments must be subjective or arbitrary. Ironically, by restricting the meaning of "rationality" the standard account has unwarrantedly expanded the realm of the irrational. This has led some to the mistaken idea that the only way to be free from the tyranny and manipulative aspect of "reason" is to flee into the "irrational." By showing the way narrative can function as a form of rationality we hope to demonstrate that these represent false alternatives.

Second, we will try to show how the convictions displayed in the Christian story have moral significance. We will call particular attention to the manner in which story teaches us to know and do what is right under definite conditions. For at least one indication of the moral truthfulness of a particular narrative is the way it enables us to recognize the limits of our engagements and yet continue to pursue them.

II. The Standard Account of Moral Rationality

At least partly under the inspiration of the scientific ideal of objectivity,[3] contemporary ethical theory has tried to secure for moral judgments an

---

the meaning of the principle and how it works to form institutions and ways of life that may have practical importance. To be sure, Christians may have common moral convictions with non-Christians, but it seems unwise to separate a moral conviction from the story that forms its context of interpretation. Moreover, a stance such as Gustafson's would seem to assume that medicine as it is currently formed is the way it ought to be. In this respect we at least want to leave open the possibility of a more reformist if not radical stance.

2. We wish to thank Professor MacIntyre for helping us clarify these issues. As will be obvious to anyone acquainted with his work, we are deeply influenced by his argument that the "conflict over how morality is to be defined is itself a moral conflict. Different and rival definitions cannot be defended apart from defending different and rival sets of moral principles." "How To Identify Ethical Principles," unpublished paper prepared for the National Commission for the Protection of Human Subjects of Biomedical and Behavioral Research, p. 8.

3. The search for ethical objectivity, of course, is also a response to the social and political diversity of our day. Thus the search for a "foundation" for ethics involves the

Stanley Hauerwas and David Burrell

objectivity that would free such judgments from the subjective beliefs, wants, and stories of the agent who makes them. Just as science tries to insure objectivity by adhering to an explicitly disinterested method, so ethical theory tried to show that moral judgments, insofar as they can be considered true, must be the result of an impersonal rationality. Thus moral judgments, whatever else they may involve, must at least be non-egoistic in the sense that they involve no special pleading from the agent's particular history, community identification, or otherwise particular point of view to establish their truthfulness.

Thus the hallmark of contemporary ethical theory, whether in a Kantian or utilitarian mode, has been to free moral behavior from the arbitrary and contingent nature of the agent's beliefs, dispositions, and character. Just as science strives to free the experiment from the experimenter, so ethically, if we are to avoid unchecked subjectivism or relativism, it is thought that the moral life must be freed from the peculiarities of agents caught in the limits of their particular histories. Ethical rationality assumes it must take the form of science if it is to have any claim to being objective.[4]

There is an interesting parallel to this development in modern medical theory. Eric Cassell has located a tension between the explanation of a disease proper to science and the diagnosis a clinician makes

---

attempt to secure rational agreement short of violence. That attraction of the ideal of science for ethicists may be due partly to science appearing to be the last form of universal culture we have left. Of course, this strategy comes to grief on the diversity of activity and disciplines that constitute what we generally call science. For example, see Ernest Becker's reflection on this in his *The Structure of Evil* (New York: Braziller, 1968). The desire for "objectivity" in ethics, moreover, is part of the irrepressible human desire to think that what we have done or had to do is the right thing to do. The quest for certainty, both intellectually and morally, is the need to secure our righteousness in an ambiguous world.

4. We do not mean to claim the actual practice of science involves this sense of objectivity. Indeed we are very sympathetic with Toulmin's analysis of science, not as a tight and coherent logical system, but "as a conceptual aggregate, or 'population,' within which there are—at most—localized pockets of logical systematicity." *Human Understanding* (Princeton: Princeton University Press, 1972), p. 128. It is exactly his stress on necessity of understanding the history of the development of a discipline in order to understand its sense of "rationality" that we feel must be recovered in science as well as, though with different significance, in ethics. As he suggests, "In science as much as in ethics the historical and cultural diversity of our concepts gives rise to intractable problems, only so long as we continue to think of 'rationality' as a character of particular systems of propositions or concepts, rather than in terms of the procedures by which men change from one set of concepts and beliefs to another" (ibid., p. 478). Rather, what must be seen is that rationality "is an attribute, not of logical or conceptual systems as such, but of the human activities or enterprises of which particular sets of concepts are the temporary cross-sections" (ibid., p. 133).

for a particular patient.[5] The latter is well-described by Tolstoy in *War and Peace:*

> Doctors came to see Natasha, both separately and in consultation. They said a great deal in French, in German, and in Latin. They criticised one another, and prescribed the most diverse remedies for all the diseases they were familiar with. But it never occurred to one of them to make the simple reflection that they could not understand the disease from which Natasha was suffering, as no single disease can be fully understood in a living person; for every living person has his complaints unknown to medicine—not a disease of the lungs, of the kidneys, of the skin, of the heart, and so on, as described in medical books, but a disease that consists of one out of the unnumerable combinations of ailments of those organs.[6]

The scientific form of rationality is represented by B. F. Skinner's commentary on this quote. Skinner suggests that Tolstoy was justified in calling every sickness a unique event during his day, but uniqueness no longer stands in the way of the development of the science of medicine since we can now supply the necessary general principles of explanation. Thus happily, according to Skinner, "the intuitive wisdom of the old-style diagnostician has been largely replaced by the analytic procedures of the clinic, just as a scientific analysis of behavior will eventually replace the personal interpretation of unique instances."[7]

Even if we were competent to do so, it would not be relevant to our argument to try to determine whether Tolstoy or Skinner, or some combination of both, describes the kind of explanation most appropriate to medical diagnosis (though our hunch lies with Tolstoy). Rather it is our contention that the tendency of modern ethical theory to find a

5. Eric Cassel, "Preliminary Exploration of Thinking in Medicine," *Ethics in Science and Medicine* C, 2, 1 (1975): 1-12. MacIntyre's and Gorovitz's "Toward a Theory of Medical Error" also obviously bears on this issue. See it in H. T. Engelhardt and D. Callahan, eds., *Science, Ethics and Medicine* (Hastings-on-Hudson: Hastings Center Publication, 1976).

6. Quoted by B. F. Skinner in *Science and Human Behavior* (New York: Macmillan, 1953), pp. 18-19. Eric Cassell's "Illness and Disease" (*Hastings Center Report,* 6, 2 [April 1976]: 27-37) is extremely interesting in this respect. It is his contention that we as yet have failed to appreciate the obvious fact that doctors do not treat diseases but patients who have diseases.

7. Skinner, *Science and Human Behavior,* p. 19. In the light of Skinner's claim it is interesting to reflect on John Wisdom's observation in *Paradox and Discovery* (New York: Philosophical Library, 1965). "It is, I believe, extremely difficult to breed lions. But there was at one time at the Dublin zoo a keeper by the name of Mr. Flood who bred many lion cubs without losing one. Asked the secret of his success, Mr. Flood replied, 'Understanding lions.' Asked in what consists the understanding of lions, he replied, 'Every lion is different.' It is not to be thought that Mr. Flood, in seeking to understand an individual lion, did not bring to bear his great experience with other lions. Only he remained free to see each lion for itself" (p. 138). We are indebted to Professor Ed Erde for the Tolstoy and Wisdom quotes.

functional equivalent to Skinner's "scientific analysis" has distorted the nature of practical reason. Ethical objectivity cannot be secured by retreating from narrative, but only by being anchored in those narratives that best direct us toward the good.

Many have tried to free the objectivity of moral reason from narrative by arguing that there are basic moral principles, procedures, or points of view to which a person is logically or conceptually committed when engaged in moral action or judgment. This logical feature has been associated with such titles as the categorical imperative, the ideal observer, universalizability, or more recently, the original position. Each of these in its own way assumes that reasons, if they are to be morally justified, must take the form of judgments that can and must be made from anyone's point of view.[8] All of the views assume that "objectivity" will be attained in the moral life only by freeing moral judgments from the "subjective" story of the agent.

This tradition has been criticized for the formal nature of its account of moral rationality, i.e., it seems to secure the objectivity of moral judgment exactly by vacating the moral life of all substantive content. Such criticism fails to appreciate, however, that these accounts of moral rationality are attempts to secure a "thin" theory of the moral life in order to provide an account of moral duty that is not subject to any community or tradition. Such theories are not meant to tell us how to be good in relation to some ideal, but rather to insure that what we owe to others as strangers, not as friends or sharers in a tradition, is nonarbitrary.

---

8. We are aware that this judgment would need to be qualified if each of these positions were considered in detail. Yet we think that this does characterize a tendency that these positions share. For each position is attempting to establish what Frankena calls the "institution of morality," that is, to show that morality is an institution that stands on its own, separate from other human activities such as politics, religion, etiquette. (We suspect connected with this attempt to establish the independence of ethics is the desire to give ethics a disciplinary character like that of the sciences. For an excellent discussion of ethics as a "quasi-discipline" see Toulmin, *Human Understanding*, pp. 406-411.) The language of obligation tends to become central for these interpretations of the moral life as they trade on our feeling that we ought to do our duty irrespective of how it affects or relates to our other interests and activities. Obligation and rationality are thus interpreted in interdependent terms as it is assumed that an ethics of obligation can provide the standpoint needed to establish the independence of moral discourse from all the relativities of interests, institutions, and commitments save one, the interests of being rational. That is, the moral life, at least as it involves only those obligations that we owe one another apart from any special relationships, needs no further grounding apart from our common rationality. It should be obvious that our criticisms of this approach have much in common with such thinkers as Foot, MacIntyre, Toulmin, and Hampshire. For a critique of the emphasis on obligation to the exclusion of virtue in contemporary accounts of the moral life see Hauerwas, "Obligation and Virtue Once More," *Journal of Religious Ethics*, 3, 1 (Spring 1975): 27-44, and the response and critique by Frankena in the same issue.

What I am morally obligated to do is not what derives from being a father, or a son, or an American, or a teacher, or a doctor, or a Christian, but what follows from my being a person constituted by reason. To be sure all these other roles or relations may involve behavior that is good to do, but such behavior cannot be required except as it can be based upon or construed as appropriate to rationality itself. This is usually done by translating such role-dependent obligations as relations of promise-keeping that are universalizable. (Of course, what cannot be given are any moral reasons why I should become a husband, father, teacher, doctor, or Christian in the first place.)

It is our contention, however, that the standard account of moral rationality distorts the nature of the moral life by: (1) placing an unwarranted emphasis on particular decisions or quandaries; (2) by failing to account for the significance of moral notions and how they work to provide us skills of perceptions; and (3) by separating the agent from his interests. We will briefly spell out each of these criticisms and suggest how each stems in part from the way standard accounts avoid acknowledging the narrative character of moral existence.

A. Decisions, Character, and Narrative

In his article, "Quandary Ethics," Edmund Pincoffs has called attention to the way contemporary ethics concentrates on problems — situations in which it is hard to know what to do — as paradigmatic concerns for moral analysis.[9] In such a model, ethics becomes a decision procedure for resolving conflict-of-choice situations. This model assumes that no one faces an ethical issue until they find themselves in a quandary: should I or should I not have an abortion, etc. Thus the moral life appears to be concerned primarily with "hard decisions."

This picture of the moral life is not accidental, given the standard account of moral rationality. For the assumption that most of our moral concerns are "problems" suggests that ethics can be construed as a rational science that evaluates alternative "solutions." Moral decisions should be based on rationally derived principles that are not relative to any one set of convictions. Ethics becomes a branch of decision theory. Like many of the so-called policy sciences, ethics becomes committed to those descriptions of the moral life that will prove relevant to its mode of analysis, that is, one which sees the moral life consisting of dilemmas open to rational "solutions."

By concentrating on "decisions" about "problems," this kind of

9. *Mind,* 80 (1971): 552-571. For similar criticism, see Hauerwas, *Vision and Virtue: Essays in Christian Ethical Reflection* (Notre Dame: Fides, 1974).

ethical analysis gives the impression that judgments can be justified apart from the agent who finds himself or herself in the situation. What matters is not that David Burrell or Stanley Hauerwas confronts a certain quandary, but that anyone may or can confront X or Y. The only intentions or reasons for our behavior that are morally interesting are those that anyone might have. So in considering the question of abortion, questions like Why did the pregnancy occur? What kind of community do you live in? What do you believe about the place of children? may be psychologically interesting but cannot be allowed to enter into the justification of the decision. For such matters are bound to vary from one agent to another. The "personal" can only be morally significant to the extent that it can be translated into the "impersonal."

(Though it is not central to our case, one of the implications of the standard account of rationality is its conservative force. Ethical choice is always making do in the societal framework we inherit, because it is only in such a framework that we are able to have a problem at all. But often the precise problem at issue cannot arise or be articulated given the limits of our society or culture. We suspect that this ineptness betrays a commitment of contemporary ethical theory to political liberalism: one can concentrate on the justification of moral decisions because one accepts the surrounding social order with its moral categories. In this sense modern ethical theory is functionally like modern pluralist democratic theory: it can afford to be concerned with incremental social change, to celebrate "issue" politics, because it assumes the underlying social structures are just.)[10]

By restricting rationality to choices between alternative courses

---

10. To our mind one of the most disastrous aspects of the standard account of rationality is the resulting divorce of ethical reflection from political theory. It may be objected that the works of Rawls and Nozick are impressive counters to such a claim. However, it is interesting to note that the political theory they generate exists in a high level of abstraction from the actual workings of the modern state. It is only when ethicists turn their attention to C. B. MacPherson's challenge to the liberal democratic assumptions that Rawls and Nozick presuppose that they will address questions that are basic, for liberal political theory and the objectivist's account of moral rationality share the assumption that morally and politically we are strangers to one another. Thus any common life can only be built on our willingness to qualify our self-interest in order to increase our long-term satisfaction. From this perspective the standard account can be viewed as an attempt to secure a basis for national politics for a society that shares no interests beyond each individual increasing his chance for survival. It is our hunch that historically the disputes and disagreements in ethical theory such as that between Rawls and Hare will appear as scholastic debates within a liberal framework, for the disputants agree on far more than they disagree. For MacPherson's critique of these assumptions see his *Democratic Theory* (Oxford: Clarendon Press, 1973). For a radical critique of liberal democracy both in terms of the liberal understanding of rationality and the self similar to our own, see Roberto Unger's *Knowledge and Politics* (New York: Free Press, 1975).

of action, the various normative theories formed in accordance with the standard account have difficulty explaining the moral necessity to choose between lesser evils.[11] Since rational choice is also our moral duty, it must also be a good duty. Otherwise one would be obliged rationally to do what is morally a lesser evil. There is no place for moral tragedy; whatever is morally obligatory must be good, even though the consequences may be less than happy. We may subjectively regret what we had to do, but it cannot be a moral regret. The fact that modern deontological and teleological theories assume that the lesser evil cannot be a moral duty witnesses to their common commitment to the standard view of moral rationality.

The problem of the lesser evil usually refers to tragic choices externally imposed, e.g., the necessity of killing civilians in order to halt the manufacture of weapons. Yet the language of "necessity" is often misleading, for part of the "necessity" is the character of the actors, whether they be individuals or nations. Because moral philosophy under the influence of the standard account has thought it impossible to discuss what kind of character we should have—that, after all, is the result of the accident of birth and psychological conditioning—it has been as-

11. For a critique of this assumption see Michael Walzer, "Political Action: The Problem of Dirty Hands," *Philosophy and Public Affairs*, 2, 2 (Winter 1973): 160-180. He is responding to Hare's "Rules of War and Moral Reasoning," *Philosophy and Public Affairs*, 1, 2 (Winter 1972): 161-181. Hare argued that though one might wrongly think he was faced with a moral dilemma, this could not be the case if a course of action suggested itself that was moral. See also John Ladd's very useful discussion of this issue in his "Are Science and Ethics Compatible?" in Engelhardt and Callahan, eds., *Science, Ethics and Medicine*. This is also the issue that lies behind the theory of double effect in Roman Catholic moral theology, though it is seldom explicitly discussed in these terms. For example, see Richard McCormick's, *Ambiguity in Moral Choice* (Marquette Theology Lectures: Marquette University, 1973). See Hauerwas, "Natural Law, Tragedy, and Theological Ethics," in his *Truthfulness and Tragedy* (Notre Dame: University of Notre Dame, 1977), for a different perspective.

For a fascinating study of the problem of moral evil in terms of the economic category of scarcity, see Vivian Walsh, *Scarcity and Evil* (Englewood Cliffs: Prentice-Hall, 1961). Ms. Walsh argues that we are often mistaken in trying to ascribe responsibility for actions that are the result of scarcity even when the scarcity is not the result of the "external" limits but of the person doing the action. What we often must do is the lesser good because of our own limits, but we must learn to know it is a lesser good without implying that we are morally blameworthy. Even though we are sympathetic with Ms. Walsh's analysis, we think the concept of character provides a way to suggest what is an inappropriate "scarcity" for anyone to lack in their character given the form of their engagements. Albert Speer lacked political sense that became morally blameworthy because of his political involvement, but that does not mean morally there is no way to indicate that his character should have provided him with the skills to know what kind of politics he was involved with. In classical terms the concept of character gives the means to assess in what ways we are blameworthy or praiseworthy for what we have omitted as for what we have "done."

sumed that moral deliberation must accept the limits of the decision required by his or her character. At best, "character" can be discussed in terms of "moral education"; but since the "moral" in education is determined by the standard account, it does not get us very far in addressing what kind of people we ought to be.

As a result, the standard account simply ignores the fact that most of the convictions that charge us morally are like the air we breathe — we never notice them. We never notice them precisely because they form us not to describe the world in certain ways and not to make certain matters subject to decision. Thus we assume, without good reason, that it is wrong to kill children. Or even more strongly, we assume that it is our duty to provide children (and others who cannot protect themselves) with care that we do not need to give the stranger. These are not matters that we need to articulate or decide about; their force lies rather in their not being subject to decision. And morally we must have the kind of character that keeps us from subjecting them to decision.

(What makes "medical ethics" so difficult is the penchant of medical care to force decisions that seem to call into question aspects of our life that we assumed not to be matters of decision, e.g., should we provide medical care for children who are born with major disabilities such as meningomyelocele.[12] In this respect, the current interest in "medical ethics" does not simply represent a response to issues arising in modern medicine, but also reflects the penchant of the standard account to respond to dilemmas.)

Another way to make this point is that the standard account, by concentrating on a decision, fails to deal adequately with the formation of a moral self, i.e., the virtues and character we think it important for moral agents to acquire. But the kind of decisions we confront, indeed the very way we describe a situation, is a function of the kind of character we have. And character is not acquired through decisions, though it may be confirmed and qualified there; rather, it is acquired through the beliefs and dispositions we have come to possess.

But from the perspective of the standard account, beliefs and dispositions cannot be subject to rational deliberation and formation.[13]

12. For a discussion of these issues see Hauerwas, "The Demands and Limits of Care: Ethical Reflections on the Moral Dilemma of Neonatal Intensive Care," in *Truthfulness and Tragedy.*

13. It is not just Prichard that argues in this way but, as Henry Veatch suggests, Kant is the primary inspiration behind those that would make interest, desires, and beliefs, in principle, unjustifiable. This, of course, relates to the matter discussed in note 4, as Kant wanted to provide a basis for morality not dependent on any theological or anthropological assumption — except that of man's rational capacity. That is why Kant's principle of univer-

Positions based on the standard account do not claim that our dispositions, or our character, are irrelevant to how we act morally. But these
aspects of our self are rational only as they enter into a moral decision.
It is our contention, however, that it is character, inasmuch as it is displayed by a narrative, that provides the context necessary to pose the
terms of a decision, or to determine whether a decision should be made
at all.[14]

We cannot account for our moral life solely by the decisions we
make; we also need the narrative that forms us to have one kind of
character rather than another. These narratives are not arbitrarily acquired, although they will embody many factors we might consider
"contingent." As our stories, however, they will determine what kind of
moral considerations — that is, what reasons — will count at all. Hence
these narratives must be included in any account of moral rationality
that does not unwarrantedly exclude large aspects of our moral existence, i.e., moral character.[15]

The standard account cannot help but view a narrative account
as a retreat from moral objectivity. For if the individual agent's intentions and motives — in short, the narrative embodied in his or her character — are to have systematic significance for moral judgment, then it

---

salizability, which has so often been misinterpreted, applies only to men as rational beings
and not to just all human beings. As Veatch points out in this latter case, "the maxim of
one's action would be based on a regard simply for certain desires and likings characteristic of human nature — albeit desires that all human beings happen to share in. But any mere
desire of inclination or liking or sentiment of approbation, even if it be shared by the entire human race, would still not be universalizable in the relevant sense, simply because it
was something characteristic of and peculiar to human kind, and hence not truly universal." "Justification of Moral Principles," *Review of Metaphysics*, 29, 2 (December 1975): 225.

14. For example, witness this exchange between Lucy and Linus as Lucy walks
by while Linus is preparing a snowball for launching.

> Lucy: Life is full of Choices.
> You may choose, if you so wish, to throw that snowball at me.
> You may also choose, if you so wish, not to throw that snowball
> at me.
> Now, if you choose to throw that snowball at me, I will pound you
> right into the ground.
> If you choose not to throw that snowball at me, your head will be
> spared.
>
> Linus: (Throwing the snowball to the ground) Life is full of choices,
> but you never get any.

15. For a more extended analysis of the concept of character, see Hauerwas,
Character and the Christian Life: A Study in Theological Ethics (San Antonio: Trinity University Press, 1975). For a similar critique of the Kantian inspired moral philosophy, see Bernard Williams, "Persons, Character, and Morality," in Amelie Rorty, ed., *The Identities of
Persons* (Berkeley: University of California Press, 1976), pp. 197-215.

seems that we will have to give preference to the agent's interpretation of what he has done. So the dreaded first person singular, which the standard account was meant to purge from moral argument, would be reintroduced. To recall the force of 'I,' however, does not imply that we would propose "because I want to" as a moral reason. The fact is that the first person singular is seldom the assertion of the solitary 'I,' but rather the narrative of that I. It is exactly the category of narrative that helps us to see that we are forced to choose between some universal standpoint and the subjectivistic appeals to our own experience. For our experiences always come in the form of narratives that can be checked against themselves as well as against others' experiences. I cannot make my behavior mean anything I want it to mean, for I have learned to understand my life from the stories I have learned from others.

The language the agent uses to describe his behavior, to himself and to others, is not uniquely his; it is *ours,* just as the notions we use have meanings that can be checked for appropriate or inappropriate use. But what allows us to check the truthfulness of these accounts of our behavior are the narratives in which our moral notions gain their paradigm uses. An agent cannot make his behavior mean anything he wants, since at the very least it must make sense within his own story, as well as be compatible with the narrative embodied in the language he uses. All our notions are narrative-dependent, including the notion of rationality.

B. Moral Notions, Language, and Narrative

We can show how our very notion of rationality depends on narrative by noting how the standard account tends to ignore the significance and meaning of moral notions. For the standard account pictures our world as a *given* about which we need to make decisions. So terms like "murder," "stealing," "abortion," although admitted to be evaluative, are nonetheless regarded as descriptive. However, as Julius Kovesi has persuasively argued, our moral notions are not descriptive in the sense that "yellow" is, but rather describe only as we have purposes for such descriptions.[16] Moral notions, in other words, like many of our nonmoral notions (though we are not nearly so sure as the standard account how this distinction should be made) do not merely describe our activity; they also form it. Marx's claim that the point of philosophy should be not to analyze the world but to change it, is not only a direc-

16. Julius Kovesi, *Moral Notions* (New York: Humanities Press, 1967), and Hauerwas, *Vision and Virtue,* pp. 11-29. For a detailed account of how the meaning of a word depends on its history, see Raymond Williams, *Keywords* (New York: Oxford, 1976).

tive to ethicists but also an astute observation about the way our grammar displays the moral direction of our lives. For the notions that form our moral perception involve skills that require narratives, that is, accounts of their institutional contexts and purposes, which we must know if we are to know how to employ them correctly. In other words, these notions are more like skills of perception which we must learn how to use properly.

The standard account's attempt to separate our moral notions from their narrative context, by trying to ground or derive their meaning from rationality itself, has made it difficult to explain why moral controversies are so irresolvable. The standard account, for example, encourages us to assume that the pro- and anti-abortion advocates mean the same thing by the word "abortion." So it is assumed that the moral disagreement between these two sides must involve a basic moral principle such as "all life is sacred," or be a matter of fact such as whether the fetus is considered human life. But this kind of analysis fails to see that the issue is not one of principle or fact, but one of perception determined by a history of interpretation.

Pro- and anti-abortion advocates do not communicate on the notion "abortion," since each group holds a different story about the purpose of the notion. At least so far as "abortion" is concerned, they live in conceptually different worlds. This fact does not prohibit discussion. But if it takes place, it cannot begin with the simple question of whether abortion is right or wrong. It is rather more like an argument between a member of the PLO and an Israeli about whether an attack on a village is unjustified terrorism. They both know the same "facts" but the issue turns on the story each holds, and within which those "facts" are known.

The advocates of the standard account try to train us to ignore the dependence of the meaning and use of notions on their narrative contexts, by providing normative theory for the derivation and justification of basic moral notions. But to be narrative-dependent is not the same as being theory-dependent, at least in the way that a utilitarian or deontological position would have us think. What makes abortion right or wrong is not its capacity to work for or against the greatest good of the greatest number in a certain subclass. What sets the context for one's moral judgment is rather the stories we hold about the place of children in our lives, or the connection one deems ought or ought not to hold between sexuality and procreation, or some other such account. Deontological or utilitarian theories that try to free moral notions from their dependence on examples and the narratives that display them prove to be too monochromatic to account for the variety of our notions and the histories on which they are dependent.

169

Stanley Hauerwas and David Burrell

There can be no normative theory of the moral life that is sufficient to capture the rich texture of the many moral notions we inherit.
What we actually possess are various and sometimes conflicting stories
that provide us with the skills to use certain moral notions. What we
need to develop is the reflective capacity to analyze those stories, so
that we better understand how they function. It is not theory-building
that develops such a capacity so much as close attention to the ways
our distinctive communities tell their stories. Furthermore, an analysis
of this sort carries us to the point of assessing the worth these moral
notions have for directing our life projects and shaping our stories.

The standard account's project to supply a theory of basic moral
principles from which all other principles and actions can be justified
or derived represents an attempt to make the moral life take on the
characteristics of a system. But it is profoundly misleading to think that
a rational explanation needs to be given for holding rational beliefs,[17]
for to attempt to provide such an account assumes that rationality itself
does not depend on narrative. What must be faced, however, is that our
lives are not and cannot be subject to such an account, for the consistency necessary for governing our lives is more a matter of integrity
than one of principle. The narratives that provide the pattern of integrity
cannot be based on principle, nor are they engaging ways of talking
about principles. Rather, such narratives are the ones which allow us to
determine how our behavior "fits" within our ongoing pattern.[18] To be

17. For example, R. S. Downie and Elizabeth Telfer attempt to argue that "the ordinary rules and judgments of social morality presuppose respect for persons as their ultimate ground . . . [and] that the area of private or self-referring morality also presuppose
respect for persons as its ultimate ground." *Respect for Persons* (New York: Schocken, 1970),
p. 9. They interpret respect for persons in a Kantian fashion of respecting the claim another
rational capacity—that is, capable of self- determining and rule-governing behavior—can
demand. It never seems to occur to them that the "ordinary rules of social morality" or
"self-referring morality" may not need an "ultimate ground." Moreover, they have a good
deal of trouble explaining why we owe respect to children or "idiots" on such grounds.
They simply assert that there "are sufficient resemblances between them and persons" to
justify extending respect to them (ibid., p. 35). For a different perspective on this issue,
see Hauerwas, "The Retarded and the Criteria for the Human," in his *Truthfulness and
Tragedy.* It is Downie's and Telfer's contention that "respect for persons" is the basis of
such Christian notions as agape. It is certainly true that much of what a "respect for persons" ethic represents has been assumed by Christian morality, but we think that it is misleading to assume that the story that informs the latter can be translated into the former.
One of the places to see this is how each construes the relationship between obligation
and super-erogation. The Christian ethic of charity necessarily makes obligatory what a
follower of "respect for persons," can see only as super-erogation. For an analysis of agape
in terms of equal regard, see Gene Outka, *Agape: An Ethical Analysis* (New Haven: Yale
University Press, 1972).

18. For an account of the moral life that makes "fittingness" central, see H. R. Niebuhr, *The Responsible Self* (New York: Harper and Row, 1963).

170

sure, fittingness cannot have the necessitating form desired by those who want the moral life to have the "firmness" of some sciences, but it can exhibit the rationality of a good story.

C. Rationality, Alienation, and the Self

The standard account also has the distressing effect of making alienation the central moral virtue. We are moral exactly to the extent that we learn to view our desires, interests, and passions as if they could belong to anyone. The moral point of view, whether it is construed in a deontological c- teleological manner, requires that we view our own projects and life as if we were outside observers. This can perhaps be seen most vividly in utilitarianism (and interestingly in Rawls's account of the original position) as the utilitarian invites us to assume that perspective toward our projects which will produce the best consequences for anyone's life plan. So the standard account obligates us to regard our life as an observer would.

But, paradoxically, what makes our projects valuable to us (as Bernard Williams has argued) is that they are ours. As soon as we take the perspective of the standard account we accept the odd position of viewing our stories as if they were anyone's or at least capable of being lived out by anyone. Thus we are required to alienate ourselves from the projects that make us interested in being anything at all.

The alienation involved in the standard account manifests itself in the different ways the self is understood by modern ethical theory. The self is often pictured as consisting of reason and desire, with the primary function of reason being to control desire. It is further assumed that desire or passion can give no clues to the nature of the good, for the good can only be determined in accordance with "reason." Thus the standard account places us in the odd position of excluding pleasure as an integral aspect of doing the good. The good cannot be the satisfaction of desire, since the morality of reason requires a sharp distinction between universal rules of conduct and the "contingent" appetites of individuals.

Not only are we taught to view our desires in contrast to our reason, but the standard account also separates our present from our past. Morally, the self represents a collection of discontinuous decisions bound together only in the measure to which they approximate the moral point of view. Our moral capacity thus depends on our ability to view our past in discontinuity with our present. The past is a limit, as it can only prevent us from embodying more fully the new opportunities always guaranteed by the moral point of view. Thus our moral potentiality depends on our being able to alienate ourselves from our past in order to grasp the timelessness of the rationality offered by the standard account.[19]

(In theological terms the alienation of the self is a necessary consequence of sinful pretensions. When the self tries to be more than it was meant to be, it becomes alienated from itself and all its relations are disordered. The view of rationality offered by the standard account is pretentious exactly as it encourages us to try to free ourselves from history. In effect, it offers us the possibility of being like God. Ironically enough, however, this is not the God of the Jews and the Christians since, as we shall see, that God does not will himself to be free from history.)

In fairness, the alienation recommended by the standard account is motivated by the interest of securing moral truthfulness. But it mistakenly assumes that truthfulness is possible only if we judge ourselves and others from the position of complete (or as complete as possible)

---

19. It would take us too far afield to explore this point further, but surely it is Kant that stands behind this understanding of the self. It is impossible to document this, but it is at least worthwhile calling attention to two passages from *Religion Within the Limits of Reason Alone*, translated by Theodore Green (New York: Harper, 1960). "In the search for the rational origins of evil action, every such action must be regarded as though the individual had fallen into it directly from a state of innocence. For whatever his previous deportment may have been, whatever natural causes may have been influencing him, and whatever these causes were to be found within or outside him, his action is yet free and determined by none of these causes; hence it can and must always be judged as an original use of his will. . . . Hence we cannot inquire into the temporal origins of this deed, but solely into its rational origin, if we are thereby to determine and, whereby possible, to elucidate the propensity, if it exists, i.e., the general subjective ground of the adoption of transgression into our maxim" (p. 36). In case it is objected that Kant is only dealing with moral evil, consider "To reconcile the concept of freedom with the idea of God as a *necessary* Being raises no difficulty at all: for freedom consists not in the contingency of the act, i.e., not in indeterminism, but rather in absolute spontaneity. Such spontaneity is endangered only by predeterminism, where the determining ground of the act is in *antecedent time*, with the result that, the act being now no longer in my power but in the hands of nature, I am irresistibly determined; but since in God no temporal sequence is thinkable, this difficulty vanishes" (p. 45). It is, of course, the possibility of the moral law that Kant thinks gives men the possibility to be like God — timeless. It is not a far distance from Kant to the existentialist in this respect. Of course it is true that the Kantian outlook, as Williams suggests, makes less of an abstraction of the individual than utilitarianism. But the question arises "of whether the honourable instincts of Kantianism to defend the individuality of individuals against the agglomerative indifference of Utilitarianism can in fact be effective granted the impoverished and abstract character of persons as moral agents which the Kantian view seems to impose. . . . It is a real question, whether the conception of the individual provided by the Kantian theories is in fact enough for others who, while equally rejecting Utilitarianism, want to allow more room than Kantianism can allow for the importance of individual character and personal relations in moral experience." Bernard Williams, "Persons, Character, and Morality," in A. Rorty, ed., *The Identities of Persons*, pp. 200-201.

disinterest. Even if it were possible to assume such a stance, however, it would not provide us with the conditions for truthfulness. For morally there is no neutral story that insures the truthfulness of our particular stories. Moreover, any ethical theory that is sufficiently abstract and universal to claim neutrality would not be able to form character. For it would have deprived itself of the notions and convictions which are the necessary conditions for character. Far from assuring truthfulness, a species of rationality which prizes objectivity to the neglect of particular stories distorts moral reasoning by the way it omits the stories of character formation. If truthfulness (and the selflessness characteristic of moral behavior) is to be found, it will have to occur in and through the stories that tie the contingencies of our life together.

It is not our intention to call into question the significance of disinterestedness for the moral life, but rather to deny that recent accounts of "universality" or the "moral point of view" provide adequate basis for such disinterest. For genuine disinterest reflects a non-interest in the self occasioned by the lure of a greater good or a more beautiful object than we can create or will into existence.[20] In this sense we are not able to choose to conform to the moral point of view, for it is a gift. But as a gift it depends on our self being formed by a narrative that provides the conditions for developing the disinterest required for moral behavior.

D. The Standard Account's Story

None of the criticisms above constitutes a decisive objection to the standard account, but taken together they indicate that the standard account is seriously inadequate as a description of our moral existence. How then are we to account for the continued dominance of the standard account for contemporary ethical theory? If our analysis has been right, the explanation should be found in the narrative that provides an apparent cogency for the standard account in spite of its internal and external difficulties.[21]

But it is difficult to identify any one narrative that sets the context for the standard account. For it is not one but many narratives that sustain its plausibility. The form of some of these stories is of recent

20. For this point and much else that is involved in this paper, see Iris Murdoch, *The Sovereignty of the Good Over Other Concepts* (Cambridge: Cambridge University Press, 1967).

21. We have not based our criticism of the standard account on the debates between those who share its presuppositions. It is, of course, true that as yet no single theory of the standard account has proved to be persuasive to those who share its presuppositions. We still find Kant the single most satisfying statement of the program implied by the standard account.

origin, but we suspect that the basic story underlying the standard account is of more ancient lineage, namely, humankind's quest for certainty in a world of contingency.

It seems inappropriate to attribute such a grand story to the standard account, since one of its attractions is its humility; it does not pretend to address matters of the human condition, for it is only a method. As a method it does not promise truth, only clarity.

Yet the process of acculturating ourselves and others in the use of this method requires a systematic disparaging of narrative. For by teaching us to prefer a "principle" or a "rational" description (just as science prefers a statistic description) to a narrative description, the standard account not only fails to account for the significance of narrative but also sets obstacles to any therapy designed to bring that tendency to light. It thus fails to provide us with the critical skills to know the limits of the narrative which currently has us in its grasp.

The reason for this lack of critical perspective lies in the narrative born of the Enlightenment. The plot was given in capsule by Auguste Comte: first came religion in the form of stories, then philosophy in the form of metaphysical analysis, and then science with its exact methods.[22] The story he tells in outline is set within another elaborated by Hegel, to show us how each of these ages supplanted the other as a refinement

---

22. Ernest Becker, however, argues that Comte has been misunderstood as his purpose was not to free science from morality but to call attention to what kind of moral activity science involved. Thus Becker suggests, "Comte's Positivism, in sum, solved the problem of science and morals by using science to support a man-based morality. With all the force at his command he showed that life is a moral problem, and science only a tool whose unity would serve the larger unity of life. Like de Maistre and de Bonald, and like Carlyle in England, he looked approvingly on the Middle Ages. But he did not pine nostalgically for their institutions; he saw the Middle Ages as possessing what man needed most, and has since lost: a critical, unitary world view by which to judge right and wrong, good and bad, by which to subordinate personal desire to social interest. But instead of basing this knowledge on theological fiat, man could now settle it firmly on science. In this way, the Enlightenment could achieve what the Middle Ages almost possessed; but it could do this on a much sounder footing than could ever have been possible during the earlier time, namely, it could achieve the subordination of politics to morality on a scientific rather than on a theological basis. Social order and social harmony would be a call of the new day, and human progress could then be progress in social feeling, community, and love—all of it based on the superordinate science of man in society, serving man, elevating humanity." *The Structure of Evil,* p. 50.

In this respect, consider Simone Weil's observation that "The criticism of religion is always, as Marx said, the condition for all progress; but what Marx and the Marxists have not clearly seen is that, in our day, everything that is most retrograde in the spirit of religion has taken refuge, above all, in science itself. A science like ours, essentially closed to the layman, and therefore to scientists themselves, because each is layman outside his narrow specialism, is the proper theology of an ever increasingly bureaucratic society."

in the progressive development of reason. So stories are pre-scientific, according to the story legitimizing the age which calls itself scientific. Yet if one overlooks that budding contradiction, or fails to spell it out because everyone knows that stories are out of favor anyway, then the subterfuge has been worked and the exit blocked off.

Henceforth, any careful or respectable analysis, especially if it is moral in intent, will strike directly for the problem, leaving the rest for journalists who titillate or novelists who entertain. Serious folk, intent on improving the human condition, will have no time for that (except maybe after hours), for they must focus all available talent and resources on solving the problems in front of them. We all recognize the crude polarities acting here, and know how effectively they function as blinders. It is sufficient for our interests to call attention only to the capacity stories hold for eliciting critical awareness, and how an awareness of story enhances that approach known as scientific by awakening it to its presuppositions. Hence, we have argued for a renewed awareness of stories as an analytic tool, and only especially adopted to our moral existence, since stories are designed to effect critical awareness as well as describe a state of affairs.

By calling attention to the narrative context of the standard account, we are not proposing a wholesale rejection of that account or of the theories formed under its inspiration. In fact, the efforts expended on developing contrasting ethical theories (like utilitarianism or formalism) have become part of our legacy, and offer a useful way to introduce one to ethical reasoning. Furthermore, the manner of proceeding which we associate with the standard account embodies concerns which any substantive moral narrative must respect: a high regard for public discourse, the demand that we be able to offer reasons for acting that are at once cogent and appropriate, and a way to develop critical skills of discrimination and judgment. Finally, any morality depends on a capacity to generate and to articulate moral principles that can set boundaries for proper behavior and guide our conduct.

Our emphasis on narrative need not militate against any of these distinctive concerns. Our difficulty rather lies with the way the standard account attempts to express and to ground these concerns in a manner of accounting which is narrative-free. So we are given the impression that moral principles offer the actual ground for conduct, while in fact they present abstractions whose significance continues to depend on original narrative contexts. Abstractions play useful roles in reasoning, but a continual failure to identify them as abstractions becomes systematically misleading: a concern for rationality thereby degenerates into a form of rationalism.

Our criticism of the standard account has focused on the anomalies which result from that rationalism. We have tried to show how the hegemony of the standard account in ethics has in fact ignored or distorted significant aspects of moral experience. We do not wish to gainsay the importance of rationality for ethics; only to expose a pretentious form of rationalism. Though the point can be made in different ways, it is no accident that the stories which form the lives of Jews and Christians make them peculiarly sensitive to any account which demands that human existence fit a rational framework. The legitimate human concern for rationality is framed by a range of power of quite another order. It is this larger contingent context which narrative is designed to order in the only manner available to us.

In this way, we offer a substantial explication of narrative as a constructive alternative to the standard account. Our penchant has been to rely upon the standard account as though it were the only lifeboat in a sea of subjective reactions and reductive explanations. To question it would be tantamount to exposing the leaks in the only bark remaining to us. In hearkening to the narrative context for action, we are trying to direct attention to an alternative boat available to us. This one cannot provide the security promised by the other, but in return it contains instructions designed to equip us with the skills required to negotiate the dangers of the open sea.

III. Stories and Reasons for Acting

Ethics deals explicitly with reasons for acting. The trick lies in turning reasons into a form proper to acting. The normal form for reasoning requires propositions to be linked so as to display how the conclusion follows quite naturally. The very skills which allow us to form statements lead us to draw other statements from them as conclusions. The same Aristotle who perfected this art, however, also reminded us that practical syllogisms must conclude in an action rather than another proposition.[23] As syllogisms, they will display the form proper to reasoning, yet they must do so in a way that issues in action.

This difference reflects the fact that practical wisdom cannot claim to be a science, since it must deal with particular courses of action (rather than recurrent patterns); nor can it call itself an art, since "action and making are different kinds of thing." The alternative Aristotle settles for is "a true and reasoned . . . capacity to act with regard to the things that

23. Cf. G. E. M. Anscombe, "Thought and Action in Aristotle," in R. Bambrough, ed., *New Essays on Plato and Aristotle* (New York: Humanities Press, 1965), pp. 151-152. See also Hauerwas, *Character and the Christian Life*, Chapter II.

are good or bad for man" (*Nicomachean Ethics,* 1140b5). We have suggested that stories in fact help us all to develop that capacity as a reasoned capacity. This section will focus on the narrative form as a form of rationality; the following section will show how the act of discriminating among stories develops skills for judging truly what is "good or bad for man." Using Aristotle's discriminations as a point of reference is meant to indicate that our thesis could be regarded as a development of his; in fact, we would be pleased to find it judged to be so.

(Our argument put in traditional terms is that the moral life must be grounded in the "nature" of man. However, that "nature" is not "rationality" itself, but the necessity of having a narrative to give our life coherence. The truthfulness of our moral life cannot be secured by claims of "rationality" in itself but rather by the narrative that forms our need to recognize the many claims on our lives without trying to subject them to a false unity of coherence.)

A. Narrative Form as Rational Discourse

There are many kinds of stories, and little agreement on how to separate them into kinds. We distinguish short stories from novels, while acknowledging the short novel as well. We recognize that some stories offer with a particular lucidity patterns or plots which recur in countless other stories. We call these more archetypal stories "myths," and often use them as a shorthand for referring to a typical tangle or dilemma which persons find themselves facing, whether in a story or in real life. That feature common to all stories which gives them their peculiar aptitude for illuminating real-life situations is their narrative structure.

Experts will want to anatomize narrative as well, of course, but for our purposes let it be the connected description of action and of suffering which moves to a point. The point need not be detachable from the narrative itself; in fact, we think a story better that does not issue in a determinate *moral.* The "point" we call attention to here has to do with that form of connectedness which characterizes a novel. It is not the mere material connection of happenings to one individual, but the connected unfolding that we call *plot.* Difficult as this is to characterize— independently of displaying it in a good story!—we can nonetheless identify it as a connection among elements (actions, events, situations) which is neither one of logical consequence nor one of mere sequence. The connection seems rather designed to move our understanding of a situation forward by developing or unfolding it. We have described this movement as gathering to a point. Like implication, it seeks to make explicit what would otherwise remain implicit; unlike implication, the rules of development are not those of logic but stem from some more mysterious source.

The rules of development are not logical rules because narrative connects contingent events. The intelligibility which plot affords is not a necessary one, because the events connected do not exhibit recurrent patterns. Narrative is not required to be explanatory, then, in the sense in which a scientific theory must show necessary connections among occurrences. What we demand of a narrative is that it display how occurrences are actions. Intentional behavior is purposeful but not necessary. We are not possessed of the theoretical capacities to predict what will happen on the basis of what has occurred. Thus a narrative moves us on to answer the question that dogs us: What happened next? It cannot answer that question by arbitrary statement, for our inquiring minds are already involved in the process. Yet the question is a genuine one precisely because we lack the capacity for sure prediction.

It is the intentional nature of human action which evokes a narrative account. We act for an end, yet our actions affect a field of forces in ways that may be characteristic yet remain unpredictable. So we can ask, What would follow from our hiring Jones?, as though certain events might be deduced from his coming on board. Yet we also know that whatever follows will not do so deductively, but rather as a plot unfolds. Nevertheless, we are right in inquiring into what might *follow from* our hiring him, since we must act responsibly. By structuring a plausible response to the question, And what happened next?, narrative offers just the intelligibility we need for acting properly.

B. What the Narrative Unfolds

But what makes a narrative plausible? The field of a story is actions (either deeds or dreams) or their opposite, sufferings. In either case, what action or passion is seen to unfold is something we call "character." *Character*, of course, is not a theoretical notion, but merely the name we give to the cumulative source of human actions. Stories themselves attempt to probe that source and discover its inner structure by trying to display how human actions and passions connect with one another to develop a character. As we follow the story, we gain some insight into recurrent connecting patterns, and also some ability to assess them. We learn to recognize different configurations and to rank some characters better than others.

Gradually, then, the characters (or ways of unifying actions) that we can recognize offer patterns for predicting recurring ways of acting. Expectations are set up, and the way an individual or others deal with those expectations shows us some of the capacities of the human spirit.

In this way, character can assume the role of an analytic tool even though it is not itself an explanatory notion. Character is neither explanatory in origin nor in use, for it cannot be formulated prior to nor independently of the narrative which develops it. Yet it can play an illuminating or analytic role by calling attention to what is going on in a narrative as the plot unfolds: a character is being developed. Moreover, this character, as it develops, serves as a relative baseline for further developing itself or other characters, as we measure subsequent actions and responses against those anticipated by the character already developed. In this way, character plays an analytic role by offering a baseline for further development. That the baseline itself will shift represents one more way of distinguishing narrative development from logical implication.

We may consider the set of expectations associated with a developing character as a "language," a systematic set of connections between actions which offers a setting or syntax for subsequent responses. Since character cannot be presented independently of the story or stories that develop it, however, the connection between a syntactical system and use, or the way in which a language embodies a form of life, becomes crystal clear. By attending to character, stories will display this fact to us without any need for philosophical reminders.

Similarly, we will see how actions, like expressions, accomplish what they do as part of a traditional repertoire. What a narrative must do is to set out the antecedent actions in such a way as to clarify how the resulting pattern becomes a tradition. In this way, we will see why certain actions prove effective and others fail, much as some expressions succeed in saying what they mean while others cannot. Some forms of story, like the three-generation Victorian novel, are expressly designed to display how a grammar for actions develops, by adopting a deliberately historical (even explicitly generational) structure. Lawrence's *Rainbow*, for example, shows how the shaping habits of speech and personal interaction are altered over three generations in response to industrial development. As he skilfully displays this alteration in grammar over against a traditional syntax, we can grasp something of the capacities latent in us as human beings. In articulating the characters, Lawrence succeeds in making explicit some reaches of the human spirit as yet unexplored.

Stories, then, certainly offer more than entertainment. What they do offer, however, cannot be formulated independently of our appreciating the story, so seeking entertainment is less distracting than looking for a moral. The reason lies with the narrative structure, whose plot cannot be abstracted without banality, yet whose unity does depend on its having a point. Hence it is appropriate to speak of a plot, to call attention to the ordering peculiar to narrative. It is that ordering, that capacity to unfold or develop character, and thus offer insight into the human conditions, which recommends narrative as a form of rationality especially appropriate to ethics.

C. How a Narrative Unfolds

If a narrative becomes plausible as it succeeds in displaying a believable character, we may still ask how *that* achievement offers us an intelligibility appropriate to discriminating among courses of action. Using Aristotle's language, how can stories assist in the formation of a practical wisdom? How can stories themselves develop a capacity for judging among alternatives? And further, how does discriminating among stories make that capacity even keener? Since reading stories for more than mere entertainment is usually described as "appreciating" them, some skills for assessing among them are already implied in one's appreciating any single story.

We often find ourselves quite unable, however, to specify the grounds for preferring one story to another. Critics, of course, develop a language for doing this, trying to formulate our normally inchoate criteria. Yet these criteria themselves are notoriously ambiguous. They must be rendered in utterly analogous terms, like "unity," "wholeness," "consistency," "integrity," etc. So we cannot hope to grasp the criteria without a paradigm instance, yet how can we present an exemplary instance without telling a story?[24] So criticism can only conceive itself as disciplining our native capacity to appreciate a good story.

A complete account of the way narrative functions, then, would be a narrative recounting how one came to judge certain stories better than others. Since this narrative would have to be autobiographical, we would have a vantage for judgment beyond the intrinsic merit of the narrative itself, in the perceived character of its author. If stories are designed to display how one might create and relate to a world and so offer us a paradigm for adopting a similar posture, this autobiographical story would have to show how a person's current manner of relating himself to the world itself represents a posture towards alternative stances. The narrative will have to recount why — and do so in the fashion proper to narrative — one stance comes after another, preferably by improving upon it.[25]

24. For an account of the way analogous terms can be used once they are effectively linked to a paradigm instance, cf. Burrell, *Analogy and Philosophical Language* (New Haven and London: Yale University Press, 1973).

25. It may of course happen that one cannot sustain a particular relationship and "fails." Again, the way he deals with that becomes a story. Stories often seem better the more they overturn conventional assessments and challenge settled attitudes.

Augustine's *Confessions* offers just such an account by showing how Augustine's many relationships, all patterned on available stories, were gradually relativized to one overriding and ordering relationship with God revealing himself in Jesus. Augustine's life-story is the story of that process of ordering.

D. Augustine's **Confessions**: *A Narrative Assessment of Life Stories*

Writing ten years after the decisive moment in the garden, Augustine sees that event as culminating a quest shaped by two questions: How to account for evil? How to conceive of God? That quest was also dogged by demands much more immediate than questions, of course. These needs were symbolically ordered in the experience recounted in Book 9, and monitored sense by sense, passion by passion, in Book 10. What interests us here, however, is the step-wise manner in which Augustine relates himself relating to the shaping questions: How explain evil? How conceive divinity?

The pear-tree story allows him to telegraph to the reader how he was able to discriminate one question from the other early on, even though the skills developed to respond to one would help him meet the other. For his own action, reflected upon, allowed him to glimpse an evil deed as wanton or pointless (2.4-10). From the perspective displayed by the *Confessions,* he formulates clearly an intimation which guided his earlier quest: what makes an action evil is not so much a reason as the lack of one. So we would be misled to attribute evil to the creator who orders all things, since ordering and giving reasons belong together.

By separating in this way the query into the source of evil from the attempt to conceive divinity, Augustine took a categorical step. That is, he was learning how to slip from the grip in which Manichean teaching held him, as he came to realize that nothing could properly explain the presence of evil in the world. Nothing, that is, short of a quality of human freedom which allowed us to act for no reason at all. Since explanations offer reasons, and evil turns on the lack of reasons, some form other than a causal explanation must be called for. The only form which can exhibit an action without pretending to explain it is the very one he adopted for the book itself: narrative. So Augustine took his first decisive step towards responding to the shaping question by eschewing the pretense of explanation in favor of a reflective story.

Categorical discriminations are not usually made all at once, of course. If we are set to turn up an explanation, we will ordinarily keep trying to find a satisfactory one. We cannot give up the enterprise of looking for an explanation unless our very horizon shifts. (It is just such a horizon shift or paradigm change which we identify as a categorical discrimination.) Yet horizons form the stable background for inquiry, so normally we cannot allow them to shift. In Augustine's case, as in many, it only occurred to him to seek elsewhere after repeated attempts at explaining proved fruitless. Furthermore, the specific way in which the Manichean scheme failed to explain the presence of evil also suggested why seeking an explanation was itself a fruitless tack.

To be sure, the Manichean accounts to which Augustine alludes strike us as altogether too crude to qualify as explanations. In fact, it sounds odd to identify his rejection of Manichean teachings with the explicit adoption of a story-form, since it is their schemes which sound to us like "stories." The confusion is understandable enough, of course; it is the very one this essay addresses: stories are fanciful, while explanations are what offer intelligibility. Yet fanciful as they appear to us, the Manichean schemes are explanatory in form. They postulate causes for behavior in the form of diverse combinations of "particles" of light or darkness. The nature of the particles is less relevant, of course, than the explanatory pretense. What first struck Augustine was the scheme's inability to explain diverse kinds of behavior coherently (5.10, 7.1-6). What he came to realize, however, was that *any* explanatory scheme would in principle undermine a person's ability to repent because it would remove whatever capacity we might have for assuming responsibility for our own actions (6.5, 7.12-13, 8.10). This capacity to assume responsibility would not always suffice to accomplish what we (or at least a part of us) desire (8.8-9); but such a capacity is logically necessary if we are to claim our actions as our own—and so receive praise or blame for them. If our contrary actions could be explained by contrary substances within us, then we would not be able to own them. And if we cannot own our actions, then we have no self to speak of. So the incoherence of the explanations offered led Augustine to see how the very quest for explanation itself failed to cohere with the larger life project belonging to every person.

As the narrative of Augustine's own life project displays, this deliberate shift away from the explanatory modes of the Manichees or the astrologers led to adopting a form which would also help him better to conceive divinity. If evil is senseless, we cannot attribute it to the one who creates with order and reason. If we commit evil deeds, we must be able to own up to them, to confess them, if we want to open ourselves to a change of heart. And the more we examine that self which can act responsibly—in accomplishing deeds or in judging among opinions—the more we come into possession of a language for articulating divinity. It was a language of inwardness, as practiced by the

Platonists of his day (7.10). It assumed a scheme of powers of the soul, but made its point by transcendental argument: if we are to make the discriminations we do, we must do so by virtue of an innate light or power (7.17). This way of articulating the power by which we act responsibly, then, becomes the model for expressing divinity. The path which led away from seeking an explanation for evil offers some promise for responding to the second question as well.

Augustine must take one more step, however, lest he forfeit the larger lesson of his struggle with the Manichees, and simply substitute a Platonist explanatory scheme for theirs.[26] The Platonists appeal to formal facts by way of transcendental argument. His life, however, was framed by facts of another kind: of rights and wrongs dealt to others (6.15); of an order to which he now aspired to conform, but which he found himself unable to accomplish (8.11). What he misses in the Platonists' book is "the mien of the true love of God. They make no mention of the tears of confession" (7.21). He can read there "of the Word, God . . . but not read in them that 'the Word was made flesh and came to dwell among us' (John 1:14)" (7.9). While they speak persuasively of the conditions for acting and judging aright, they do not tell us how to do what we find ourselves unable to do: to set our hearts aright.

The key to that feat Augustine finds not in the books of the Platonists, but in the gospels. Or better, he finds it in allowing the stories of the gospels to shape his story. The moment of permission, as he records it, is preceded by stories of others allowing the same to happen to them, recounting how they did it and what allowing it to happen did to them. The effect of these stories is to insinuate a shift in grammar tantamount to the shift from explanation to narrative, though quite in line with that earlier shift. Since we think of stories as relating accomplishments, Augustine must use these stories together with his own to show us another way of conceiving them.

It is not a new way, for it consciously imitates the biblical manner of displaying God's great deeds in behalf of his people. Without ceasing to be the story of Israel, the tales of the Bible present the story of God. Similarly, without ceasing to be autobiography, Augustine's *Confessions* offer an account of God's way with him. The language of will and of struggle is replaced by that of the heart: "As I came to the end

---

26. Peter Brown shows how this choice represented an existential decision as well. The *Platonici* formed an identifiable group of noble humanists, and as such offered a viable alternative to Christianity. While they were not formed into a church, their common aspirations could well be imagined to constitute a community of like-minded persons. See his *Augustine of Hippo* (Berkeley: University of California Press, 1967).

of the sentence, it was as though the light of confidence flooded into my heart and all the darkness of doubt was dispelled" (8.12). Yet the transformation is not a piece of magic; the narrative testifies to that. And his narrative will give final testimony to the transformation of that moment in the measure that it conforms to the life story of the "Word made flesh." So the answer to his shaping questions is finally received rather than formulated, and that reception is displayed in the narrative we have analyzed.

IV. Truthfulness as Veracity and Faithfulness

The second step which Augustine relates is not a categorial one. It no longer has to do with finding the proper form for rendering a life project intelligible. The narrative Augustine tells shows us how he was moved to accept the gospel story by allowing it to shape his own. In more conventional terms, this second step moves beyond philosophical therapy to a judgment of truth. That is why recognizable arguments surround the first step, but not this one. Assent involves more subtle movements than clarification—notably assent of this sort, which is not an assent *to* evidence but an assent *of* faith. Yet we will grasp its peculiar warrants better if we see how it moves along the same lines as the categorial discrimination.

Accepting a story as normative by allowing it to shape one's own story in effect reinforces the categorial preference for story over explanation as a vehicle of understanding. Augustine adumbrates the way one step leads into the other towards the beginning of Book 6:

> From now on I began to prefer the Catholic teaching. The Church demanded that certain things should be believed even though they could not be proved. . . . I thought that the Church was entirely honest in this and far less pretentious than the Manichees, who laughed at people who took things on faith, made rash promises of scientific knowledge, and then put forward a whole system of preposterous inventions which they expected their followers to believe on trust because they could not be proved. (6.5)

The chapter continues in a similar vein, echoing many contemporary critiques of modern rationalist pretensions.

A. Criteria for Judging among Stories

The studied preference for story over explanation, then, moves one into a neighborhood more amenable to what thirteenth-century theologians called an "assent of faith," and, in doing so, helps us to develop a set of criteria for judging among stories. Books 8, 9, and 10 of the *Confessions* record the ways in which this capacity for discriminating among stories is developed. It is less a matter of weighing arguments than of displaying how adopting different stories will lead us to become different sorts of persons. The test of each story is the sort of person it shapes. When examples of diverse types are offered to us for our acceptance, the choices we make display in turn our own grasp of the *humanum*. Aristotle presumed we could not fail to recognize a just man, but also knew he would come in different guises (*Nicomachean Ethics* 1097b6-1098b7).

The criteria for judging among stories, then, will most probably not pass an impartial inspection. For the powers of recognition cannot be divorced from one's own capacity to recognize the good for human kind. This observation need not amount to a counsel of despair, however. It is simply a reminder that on matters of judgment we consult more readily with some persons than others, because we recognize them to be in a better position to weigh matters sensibly. Any account of that "position" would have to be autobiographical, of course. But it is not an account we count on; it is simply our recognition of the person's integrity.

Should we want to characterize the story which gives such coherence to a person's life, however, it would doubtless prove helpful to contrast it with alternatives. The task is a difficult one, however, either for oneself or for another. For we cannot always identify the paths we have taken; Augustine continued to be engaged in mapping out the paths he was actually traversing at the very time of composing the *Confessions* (see Book 10). Yet we can certainly formulate a list of working criteria, provided we realize that any such list cannot pretend to completeness nor achieve unambiguous expression.

Any story which we adopt, or allow to adopt us, will have to display:

(1) power to release us from destructure alternatives;
(2) ways of seeing through current distortions;
(3) room to keep us from having to resort to violence;
(4) a sense for the tragic: how meaning transcends power.

It is inaccurate, of course, to list these criteria as features which a story must display. For they envisage rather the effect which stories might be expected to have on those who allow them to shape their lives. The fact that stories are meant to be read, however, forces one to speak of them as relational facts. So we cannot help regarding a story as something which (when well-constructed) will help us develop certain skills of perception and understanding. This perspective corresponds exactly to the primary function of narratives by contrast with explanatory schemes: to relate us to the world, including our plans for modifying it. Those plans have consequences of their own, but their shape as well as their execution depends on the expectations we entertain for planning.

Those expectations become a part of the plans themselves, but they can be articulated independently. And when they are, they take the form of stories, notably of heroes. Thus the process of industrialization becomes the story of tycoons, as the technology we know embodies a myth of man's dominating and transforming the earth. Not that industrial processes are themselves stories, or technological expertise a myth. In fact, we are witnessing today many attempts to turn those processes and that expertise to different ends by yoking them to a different outlook. Stories of these experiments suggest new ways of using some of the skills we have developed, and illustrate the role of narrative in helping us to formulate and to practice new perspectives.[27]

Stories, then, help us, as we hold them, to relate to our world and our destiny: the origins and goals of our lives, as they embody in narrative form specific ways of acting out that relatedness. So in allowing ourselves to adopt and be adopted by a particular story, we are in fact assuming a set of practices which will shape the ways we relate to our world and destiny. Lest this sound too instrumental, we should remind ourselves that the world is not simply waiting to be seen, but that language and institutions train us to regard it in certain ways.[28] The criteria listed above assume this fact; let us consider them in greater detail.

B. Testing the Criteria

Stories which (2) offer ways to see through current distortions can also (1) empower us to free ourselves from destructive alternatives, for we can learn how to see a current ideology as a distortion by watching what it can do to people who let it shape their story. The seduction of Manichean doctrine for Augustine and his contemporaries lay precisely in its offering itself as a *story* for humankind — much as current problem-solving techniques will invariably also be packaged as a set of practices leading to personal fulfillment. So Augustine's subsequent discrimination between explanation and story first required an accurate

27. This is the point of Peter Winch's oft-cited analysis: "Understanding a Primitive Society," reprinted in Bryan R. Wilson, ed., *Rationality* (Oxford: Blackwell, 1970).

28. For further elaboration of this, see Iris Murdoch, *The Sovereignty of the Good Over Other Concepts*.

identification of Manichean teaching as explanatory pretense in the guise of a story.

To judge an alternative course to be destructive, of course, requires some experience of its effects on those who practice the skills it embodies. It is the precise role of narrative to offer us a way of experiencing those effects without experimenting with our own lives as well. The verisimilitude of the story, along with its assessable literary structure, will allow us to ascertain whether we can trust it as a vehicle of insight, or whether we are being misled. In the absence of narratives, recommendations for adopting a set of practices can only present themselves as a form of propaganda, and be judged accordingly.[29] Only narrative can allow us to take the measure of a scheme for human improvement, granting that we possess the usual skills for discriminating among narratives as well.

The last two criteria also go together: (3) providing room to keep us from having to resort to violence, and (4) offering a sense for the tragic: how meaning transcends power. We can watch these criteria operate if we contrast the story characteristic to Christians and Jews with one of the prevailing presumptions of contemporary culture: that we can count on technique to offer eventual relief from the human condition. This conviction is reflected in the penchant of consequential ethical theories not only to equate doing one's duty with the greatest good for all, but also to presume that meeting our obligations will provide the satisfaction we seek. Surely current medical practice is confirmed by the conviction that harnessing more human energies into preventing and curing disease will increasingly free our lives from tragic dilemmas.[30] Indeed, science as a moral enterprise has provided what Ernest Becker has called an "anthropodicy," as it holds out the possibility that our increased knowledge serves human progress toward the creation of a new human ideal, namely, to create a mankind free of suffering.[31]

But this particular ethos has belied the fact that medicine, at least

29. Cf. James Cameron's efforts to offer perspective to current writing on the "sexual revolution," in *New York Review of Books,* 23 (May 13, 1976):19-28.

30. MacIntyre's argument in "Towards a Theory of Medical Error" (cited in note 5), that medicine must necessarily deal with explanations of individuals, only makes this claim more poignant. For the attempt to claim that the only errors in medicine were those characteristic of a science of universals was necessary if medicine was to make good its claim to be the means to free mankind of the limits of disease. To recognize that medical explanation and prediction is subject to the same limits as explanation and prediction of individuals will require a radical reorientation of the story that morally supports and directs medical care.

31. Becker, *The Structure of Evil,* p. 18. "The central problem posed by the Newtonian revolution was not long in making itself felt. This was the momentous new problem; it is still ours today—I mean of course the problem of a new theodicy. If the new

as characterized by its moral commitment to the individual patient, is a tragic profession. For to attend to one in distress often means that many others cannot be helped. Or to save a child born retarded may well destroy the child's family and cause unnecessary burdens on society. But the doctor is pledged to care for each patient because medicine does not aim at some ideal moral good, but at caring for the needs of the patient whom the doctor finds before him. Because we do not know how to regard medicine as a tragic profession, we tend of course to confuse caring with curing. The story which accompanies technology—of setting nature aright—results in the clinical anomalies to which we are subjecting others and ourselves in order to avoid the limits of our existence.[32]

The practice of medicine under the conditions of finitude offers an intense paradigm of the moral life. For the moral task is to learn to continue to do the right, to care for this immediate patient, even when we have no assurance that it will be the successful thing to do. To live morally, in other words, we need a substantive story that will sustain moral activity in a finite and limited world. Classically, the name we give such stories is tragedy. When a culture loses touch with the tragic, as ours clearly has done, we must redescribe our failures in acceptable terms. Yet to do so *ipso facto* traps us in self-deceiving accounts of what we have done.[33] Thus our stories quickly acquire the characteristics of a policy, especially as they are reinforced by our need to find self-justifying reasons for our new-found necessities.

This tactic becomes especially troublesome as the policy itself assumes the form of a central story that gives our individual and collective lives coherence. This story then becomes indispensable to us, as it provides us with a place to be. Phrases like "current medical practice," "standard hospital policy," or even "professional ethics," embody ex-

---

nature was so regular and beautiful, then why was there evil in the human world? Man needs a new theodicy, but this time he could not put the burden on God. Man had to settle for a new limited explanation, an anthropodicy which would cover only those evils that allow for human remedy." Science naturally presented itself as the "remedy."

32. It is tempting to try to make, as many have, the ethic of "respect for persons" sufficient as a moral basis for medical care. (Cf. Paul Ramsey's *The Patient as Person*.) But if, as we suggest, medicine is necessarily involved in tragic choices, a more substantive story than that is needed to sustain and give direction to medical care. Without such a story we will be tempted to make technology serve as a substitute as it allows us to delay further decisions of life and death that we must make in one or another arena. For a critique of the way "person" is being used as a regulative moral notion in medical ethics, see Hauerwas, "Must a Patient Be a 'Person' To Be a Patient? Or, My Uncle Charlie is Not Much of a Person But He Is Still my Uncle Charlie," in his *Truthfulness and Tragedy*.

33. For an analysis of the concept of self-deception, see Burrell and Hauerwas, "Self-Deception and Autobiography: Reflections on Speer's *Inside the Third Reich*," in *Truthfulness and Tragedy*.

emplary stories which guide the way we use the means at hand to care for patients. Since we fail to regard them as stories, however, but must see them as a set of principles, the establishment must set itself to secure them against competing views. If the disadvantaged regard this as a form of institutional violence, they are certainly correct.

Such violence need not take the form of physical coercion, of course. But we can detect it in re-descriptions which countenance coercion. So, for example, an abortion at times may be a morally necessary, but sorrowful, occurrence. But our desire for righteousness quickly invites us to turn what is morally unavoidable into a self-deceiving policy, e.g., the fetus, after all, is just another piece of flesh. It takes no mean skill, certainly, to know how to hold onto a description that acknowledges significant life, while remaining open to judging that it may have to be destroyed. Yet medical practice and human integrity cannot settle for less. Situations like these suggest, however, that we do not lie because we are evil, but because we wish to be good or to preserve what good we already embody.[34]

We do not wish to claim that the stories with which Christians and Jews identify are the only stories that offer skills for truthfulness in the moral life. We only want to identify them as ways to countenance a posture of locating and doing the good which must be done, even if it does not lead to human progress. Rather than encourage us to assume

---

34. Jules Henry's analysis of the phenomenon of "sham" is perhaps the most graphic depiction of this. He says,

> Children in our culture cannot avoid sham, for adults cannot escape depression, hostility and so on. Since sham consists in one person's withholding information, while implying that the other person should act as if he had it all; since sham consists also in giving false information while expecting the other person to act as if the information were true; since sham consists in deriving advantage from withholding or giving information—and since, on the whole, our culture is sham-wise, it might seem that the main problem for the mental health of children is to familiarize them with the edges of sham. Yet, if we were to do that, they would be "shot" for Albee is right. Our main problem, then, is to tell them the world lies but they should act as if it told the truth. But this, too, is impossible, for if one acted as if all sham were truth he might not be shot, but he certainly would lose all his money and marry the wrong person though he would have lots of friends. What then is the main problem; or rather, what does mankind do? People do not like children who lack innocence, for they hold the mirror up to adults. If children could not be deceived, they would threaten adults beyond toleration, they would never be orderly in elementary school and they clearly could not be taught the rot-gut dished out to them as truth. Personally I do not know what to do; and I anticipate a geometric increase in madness, for sham is at the basis of schizophrenia and murder itself. (*On Sham, Vulnerability, and Other Forms of Self-Destruction* [New York: Vintage Books, 1973], pp. 123-124).

See also his *Pathways to Madness* (New York: Vintage Books, 1971), pp. 99-187.

that the moral life can be freed from the tragedies that come from living in a limited and sinful world, these stories demand that we be faithful to God as we believe he has been faithful to us through his covenant with Israel and (for Christians) in the cross of Christ.[35]

C. A Canonical Story

Religious faith, on this account, comes to accepting a certain set of stories as canonical. We come to regard them not only as meeting the criteria sketched above, along with others we may develop, but find them offering ways of clarifying and expanding our sense of the criteria themselves. In short, we discover our human self more effectively through these stories, and so use them in judging the adequacy of alternative schemes for humankind.

In this formal sense, one is tempted to wonder whether everyone does not accept a set of stories as canonical. To identify those stories would be to discover the shape one's basic convictions take. To be unable to do so would either mark a factual incapacity or an utterly fragmented self. Current discussion of "polytheism" leads one to ask whether indiscriminate pluralism represents a real psychic possibility for a contemporary person.[36] In our terms, arguing against the need for a canonical story amounts to questioning "why be good?" Just as we do not require ethics to answer that question, so we need not demand a perspicuously canonical story. But we can point to the endemic tendency of men and women to allow certain stories to assume that role, just as ethicists remind us of the assessments we do in fact count on to live our lives.

35. For a fuller development of the issues in this last section see Hauerwas, "Natural Law, Tragedy and Theological Ethics," in *Truthfulness and Tragedy*. Moreover, for a perspective similar to this see Ernest Becker, *The Denial of Death* (New York: Free Press, 1975). In a broad sense Becker suggests man's situation is tragic because, "Man has a symbolic identity that brings him sharply out of nature. He is a symbolic self, a creature with a name, a life history. He is a creator with a mind that soars to speculate about atoms and infinity, who can place himself imaginatively at a point in space and contemplate bemusedly his own planet . . . yet at the same time man is a worm and food for worms. This is the paradox: He is out of nature and hopeless in it; he is dual, up in the stars and yet housed in a heart-pumping, breath-grasping body that once belonged to a fish. Man literally is split in two: he has awareness of his own splendid uniqueness in that he sticks out of nature with a towering majesty, and yet he goes back into the ground a few feet in order blindly to rot and disappear forever. It is a terrifying dilemma to be in and to have to live with" (p. 26).

36. In his *Revisioning Psychology* (New York: Harper & Row, 1975), chapter 1, James Hillman questions whether psychic integration has not been conceived in too "monotheistic" a manner. His discussion is flawed by failing to see how an analogical "reference to one" offers a feasible way of mediating between an ideal which is too confining and a *laissez faire* program which jettisons ideals altogether.

System, Story, Performance: A Proposal about the Role of Narrative in Christian Systematic Theology

David F. Ford

This paper concerns three basic categories through which human and Christian identity can be conceived: system, story, performance. It is suggested that in Christian systematic theology "story" has a key role, inseparable from the form and content of the Christian stories, especially the Gospels. These are realistic narratives with a "middle distance" (cf. J. P. Stern, *On Realism*) perspective on reality, and this is the primary perspective for Christian community, worship, revelation, history, eschatology, and ethics. This implies a critique of any position in which primacy is given to the other categories or to another type of story. It also is congruent with, while also raising critical questions about, Lindbeck's "cultural-linguistic" theory of religion. Yet both "system" and "performance" must be in continual, critical interaction with "story" if it is to maintain its rational, moral, and spiritual integrity, and in this exchange apologetics takes place. The "performance," at the cutting edge of the story, has three main dynamics: praise and prayer; community life; and prophecy in word and action. Each of these is accompanied by "journeys of intensification" in theology. Systematic theology tries to take account of all this in focusing on the traditional "loci" of theology, in which it seeks to arrive at a systematic particularity of the story—past, present, and future.

Originally published as David F. Ford, "'The Best Apologetics is Good Systematics': A Proposal about the Place of Narrative in Christian Systematic Theology," *Anglican Theological Review* LXVII, 3 (July 1985): 232-254.

David F. Ford

I. System, Story, Performance

Miss Murdoch's plea that she is not a philosophical novelist is a variant of Beckett's: an attempt to forestall the tactical reductionism of critics, who need to isolate a theme and gain a point of vantage on the work. Hence her repudiation of "readings" which merely catch allusions, deploy appropriate names, seek out contexts from her own philosophical essays, and exaggerate her affinity with the existentialists.

What is side-stepped in such readings is the problem of philosophically evaluating a Murdoch novel's "strong, agile realism" (to use her own phrase). That realism is an attempt, subject to the formal constraints without which the novel could not be a work of art, to capture truth in all its contingency, and to avoid the consoling artifice of theory, myth or dream. It is an attempt to tear aside the net which necessarily allows us only an impoverished view of the world. Yet for Miss Murdoch the writing of the novel does not resemble the philosopher's attempt to arrive at truth. In its multiplicity of functions, its characteristic style, its sensuality and indirectness, the novel is wholly different from the philosophical treatise.

This does not mean that her novels have no worthwhile philosophy. It means rather that they are best equipped to incarnate a philosophy which a treatise could not adequately set down. For Murdoch novels convey the theory that no theory (including those in her own philosophical essays) is ever adequate. The struggle to arrive at truth, or at the Good (a Platonic vocabulary is inevitable here) is mainly a struggle to discern, accurately and lovingly, the detail of how things are. Neither truth nor goodness are susceptible of prior specification; and the "dryness" Miss Murdoch finds in much contemporary philosophy and literature reflects the impoverished preconception of human agency which they share.[1]

Peregrine Horden's account of Iris Murdoch's position as a professional philosopher and novelist has within it an indication of the basic categories of this paper: system or theory; realistic narrative; and human agency or performance. Murdoch's way of interrelating system, story, and performance is also broadly in line with what will be proposed later, and her philosophy and novels are part of the ecology that sustains this paper.

Thomas Mann's novels raise similarly profound questions about those interrelationships, which are elucidated by J. P. Stern in a paper entitled "Relativity in and around *The Magic Mountain*":

If we now try to answer the central question of this paper—What is radically new about *The Magic Mountain*?—we get three closely con-

---

1. "Philosophical Fictions," Introduction to *The Novelist as Philosopher: Modern Fiction and the History of Ideas*, ed. Peregrine Horden, Chichele Lectures 1982 (Oxford: All Souls College, 1983), p. xi.

nected answers, all intimately bound up with Mach's critique of false abstractions and Einstein's notion of relativity. The relativizing of the concept of absolute time is, first, part of the theorizing conducted by the characters in the novel; secondly, it is part of the experience recounted; and, thirdly—and here we are moving from physics and philosophy back into literary criticism—relativity enters the narrative structure of the story itself."[2]

There is theorizing within the novel, and theory also informs the narrative structure; experience and the decision of living are recounted, and the whole novel mediates to the reader the possibility of a transformation of knowledge into experience and action; and the narrative incorporates a double-movement, one offering a consecutive story-line of events *nacheinander,* the other offering a simultaneous, *nebeneinander* view. Informing all of this, Stern suggests, is a sophisticated understanding of time which, with the help of Einstein and other contemporary influences, combines the linear and the simultaneous. Yet the time of the novel is relative to two "fictionally achieved absolutes," the moral strength and spirit of Hans Castorp, and his dutiful response to the course of contemporary history.

I will return to Mann later; for the present, the relevant point is that, in his own very different way, he is concerned with issues tackled by Murdoch and that these may be appropriately categorized under the headings of system, story, and performance. Both also suggest that "story" might have a certain primacy, albeit relative, inclusive, and coinherent with other modes. Each of the categories is clearly relevant to the rendering of human identity. A person may be described in systematic, theoretical terms using the natural or human sciences or some other approach through linguistic analysis, epistemology, ontology, or theology. Some of these are highly selective and specialist in their interest, others are more synthetic and concerned to unite a variety of approaches as systematically as possible.

The same person who has been the subject of physical, biochemical, genetic, psychological, sociological, anthropological, economic, political, ecological, philosophical, and theological interest may also be indicated through telling stories. These too have many possible levels and aspects, ranging from a focus on the "stream of consciousness," through varieties of realism and of fantasy focusing on an individual, to the larger stories of family, community, culture, nation, religion, civilization, species, and even cosmos.

Yet there is also the "cutting edge" of the person's story, the living of a life now in which the factors described by systematic and narrative

2. Ibid., p. 63.

David F. Ford

means are taken up into new speech, action, suffering, and events. This "performance" of life is often characterized by concentration on key relationships, commitments, visions, and particular experiences in such a way that, while the systems and the narratives help to inform and direct, these are overflowed and opened up for a different "ecology" of life and a new future.

The main ways of conceiving Christian identity can be related to the same categories and their interrelations. Christian theologians could also be "typed" according to them—some take story or history as their leading category, others specialize in systematic theoretical understanding, and others are rigorously existential in their focus on present performance. Most systematic theologians try to combine the three in some sort of synthesis, but, within that, need to take crucial decisions about their relative importance and modes of interaction. My paper is one proposal about how this should be done.

II. Christianity's Middle-Distance Realism

Traditionally, Christian systematic theology has been deeply involved with narrative. Each major locus can be seen as an attempt to do justice to the whole overarching story from the standpoint of one event or stage within it: election as God's conception of the story, followed by creation, sin and evil, providence, redemption (including christology and soteriology), pneumatology, ecclesiology, and eschatology. The doctrine of the Trinity embraces the whole, pointing to knowledge and love of God as the *raison d'être* of it all. The Bible was understood typologically, with everything converging on the life, death, and resurrection of Jesus Christ, and that central, inclusive story was at the heart of Christian life, worship, creeds, and doctrine.

In much narrative theology, there has been a great deal of discussion of the contention that the "realistic narrative" form of the Gospels is inseparable from their meaning. The meaning is, it is claimed, an inextricable combination of form and content, in which characters and events are rendered cumulatively in temporal sequence through words, actions, sufferings, and occurrences, and their complexity, individuality, and particularity can only be grasped as they unfold through the story.[3] As Horden says of Murdoch, they try "to capture truth in all

---

3. See my own discussion, *Barth and God's Story: Biblical Narrative and the Theological Method of Karl Barth in "The Church Dogmatics"* (Frankfurt: Verlag Peter Lang, 1981, 1985), esp. chap. 4; also David Ford, "Barth's Interpretation of the Bible," in *Karl Barth: Studies of His Theological Method*, ed. S. W. Sykes (Oxford: Clarendon Press, 1979), pp. 55-87.

its contingency," and Christianity has accorded to their message about contingent events a remarkable importance. George Lindbeck has proposed a "cultural-linguistic" theory of religion that allows one to do justice both to this distinctive feature of Christianity and also to the distinctiveness of other religions and ways of living, without in the process becoming committed to an extreme relativism as regards truth.[4] I want to explore some of the consequences for Christian systematic theology of taking seriously both Lindbeck's theory of religion and the centrality in Christianity of the testimony to Jesus Christ in realistic narrative form.

My way into this is through trying to conceptualize something of the distinctiveness that results from the Gospels playing the role they do in Christianity. The key concept is borrowed from J. P. Stern's intense and elegant work *On Realism*.[5] It is the idea of the "middle distance" perspective. This is the primary perspective of literary realism as Stern (here in the tradition of Auerbach's *Mimesis*) defines it. The middle distance is that focus which best does justice to the ordinary social world of people in interaction. It portrays them acting, talking, suffering, thinking, and involved in institutions, societies, and networks of relationships over time; in general this perspective renders, in the words of my opening quotation, "the detail of how things are."[6] The perspective and the content go together. If one moves too close and allows the dominant perspective to become, for example, one person's inner world or stream of consciousness, then the middle distance has been supplanted. Likewise, if one takes too broad an overview and subsumes the particular people, words, and actions into a generalization, a trend, or a theory, the middle distance loses its own integrity and becomes, at best, evidence or supportive illustration. This is by no means to imply that interiority or generalization or many other perspectives are incompatible with the middle-distance perspective. Rather it is a matter of primacy and balance, which writers as diverse as the Evangelists, Iris Murdoch, and Thomas Mann all observe in their various ways.

There are also epistemological implications of the concept of the middle distance. One of these concerns is the level of precision appropriate to conveying the truth about people in their social world. The truth that matters most is not usually that of detailed information of an

---

4. See George Lindbeck, *The Nature of Doctrine* (London: SPCK, 1984; Philadelphia: Westminster, 1983).

5. (London: Routledge and Kegan Paul, 1973).

6. Although, of course, the status of this "are" is open to endless possible qualification and even subversion—Iris Murdoch's eminently realistic novel *The Black Prince* (London: Penguin, 1975), for example, concludes with a set of postscripts that throw radical suspicion on the way the reader was led to understand the story in the course of reading it. Cf. p. 197 (in this essay) on the "realism of assessment."

exactness appropriate to other investigations (such as precise medical description — though Mann shows with what effect this can be used when subsumed into the realism of *The Magic Mountain*), but is the sort of portrayal that neither loses the wood through examining each tree too closely nor embarks on a systematic ecology of the whole region. It is quite possible to convey truth adequately with a middle-distance precision while yet being wrong or misleading in many details and subscribing to doubtful general ideas about the world. It is clearly of great importance for Christianity that the testimony to Jesus Christ is in the form of realistic narratives which, in their very diversity of detail and modes of generalization, seem to underline the middle-distance identification of Jesus (supremely in his passion, death, and resurrection) as the primary thrust of their witness.

There is a further, wider epistemological implication of the primacy of the middle-distance perspective in that it is a type of reference which tries to mediate both realism and idealism. If the primary emphasis of realism is seen to be on our knowing as receptive—corresponding to reality—and that of idealism on our knowing as constructive—conceiving and structuring the coherence of reality—then middle-distance realism can be seen to affirm both together.[7] A realistic narrative is both a "finding" and a "fashioning," whether it tends more to the historical or more to the fictional. It is a task for fascinating investigation and discussion to explore just how the two may combine and generate tension, contradiction, depth, or illumination in any particular case, but their co-presence is part of what is meant by literary realism, and the masters of the art illustrate the fact that, when it comes to rendering people in middle-distance perspective, the ability to "find" and the ability to "fashion" are both stretched to capacity in an effort to do justice to reality. Solzhenitsyn writes both history and fiction in his effort to convey the truth of Russia before, during, and since the rule of Stalin, and it would be quite a trivial notion of truth that would condemn his fiction as failing to be truthful just because of its inability to meet certain criteria of correspondence.[8] It is partly his mastery of fic-

---

7. Cf. Donald MacKinnon, "Idealism and Realism: An Old Controversy Renewed" and "The Conflict between Realism and Idealism: Remarks on the Significance for the Philosophy of Religion of a Classical Philosophical Controversy Recently Renewed," in *Explorations in Theology* 5 (London: SCM, 1979).

8. On Solzhenitsyn in relation to the Gospels, see Ford, *Barth and God's Story*, pp. 65-71. On "historicity" (which has much in common with Stern's "middle distance") as the crossover point where history and fiction intersect, see Paul Ricoeur, "The Narrative Function," in *Hermeneutics and the Human Sciences*, ed., trans., and introduced by John B. Thompson (Cambridge: At the University Press, 1981), pp. 274-96. Ricoeur's notion of the mode of reference of fiction to reality is one way of showing how "finding" and "fashioning" may be combined. For Stern's way of making a similar point see *On Realism*, pp. 116ff.

tion that enables him to be such an adequate witness. Realism is neither naturalism nor fantasy but an amalgam that may draw on either end of that spectrum to produce a new whole, which may "ring true" in ways that are not verifiable or falsifiable by criteria appropriate to other modes and perspectives.

So far I have implied that realism is a descriptive mode, but in ordinary life "realistic" is more commonly applied to decisions, judgments, evaluations, and assessments. The meaning tends towards the pragmatic and even the cynical, and is mainly concerned with what is conceived to be actually possible in a particular situation. As Stern says,

> "Realistic" is the word that expresses the likelihood of a successful translation of talk and thought into another mode of experience, into the mode of action (which of course does not have to be bereft of talk to be another mode of experience). And it is this translatability, this duality of modes within "life" that distinguishes it from literature. . . . Literature . . . is all one field. It is all medium and knows no translation into another. It may tarry over description to its heart's content, it may play with description and with assessment too.[9]

Stern makes two main points about the realism of assessment, both of them vital to my conception of the role of the Gospels in Christian theology. The first is that, for all the descriptive realism in a particular story, it may be that this is accompanied by an assessment (which may not be at all explicit but may be conveyed by events, juxtapositions, or twists to the story) that qualifies the way in which that reality is understood, even to the point of radical novelty or questioning. Kafka is an extreme example of a writer using meticulously realistic description of apparently ordinary reality, but in the service of a whole which is terrifyingly inhuman, alienating, and destructive. He plays what Stern calls an "endless cat-and-mouse game with realism"[10] in which the familiar, often banal stuff of common life has superimposed upon it a negative transcendental evaluation. The Gospels are also written in the light of a transcendental evaluation, embodied in the climactic events of the crucifixion and resurrection of Jesus. They offer a verdict on Jesus and the story of his life in a way that challenges other claims to reality, expressing in narrative form an ultimate or eschatological message—one that claims primacy for this person in a final way. Because testimony to this person is inseparable from what he said and did and what happened to him, the middle-distance realism of the Gospels is especially appropriate. In literary terms, the role of the resurrection in the story might even be

9. Ibid., p. 139f.
10. Ibid., p. 135.

seen to be an affirmation of the primacy of this perspective. If this man is alive again, raised from the dead by God and rightly called "Lord," then the primary perspective on reality must be one that best helps to identify and recognize him. The most urgent, practical matter will of course be to arrive at the right assessment of him (and here the debate about the titles of Jesus in the early church is relevant), but that in turn is inevitably linked with something more descriptive, the need for which is likely to increase as the message has to be recorded, explained, and justified for a wider audience, including the next generation of Christians. Even Paul, the New Testament writer often seen as least interested in the story of Jesus, draws on the climactic events of last supper, passion, death, and resurrection.[11]

This leads to the second point about the realism of assessment: it pivots between life and literature in a way that helps to translate one mode of experience into another. In terms of my categories, it points to the relationship between "story" and "performance." Paul's letters are obviously oriented mainly to "performance," showing the practical realism of someone facing pressing issues calling for verdicts and decisions, but they include much supporting "realism of description," with a great deal more presupposed. Their overall perspective is undoubtedly that of the middle distance, with the purposes of God linked mainly neither with inner experience of growth nor with general statements of belief or world-view, but with what happens between people living in the worshipping community of the church with a calling in the world that has its principal implications in a way of life that demonstrates faith, hope, and love.

The Gospels, on the other hand, are oriented mainly to telling the story of Jesus and so are predominantly descriptive, but, as a great deal of modern scholarship has shown, they are shot through with evaluations and definite theological positions so that it becomes virtually impossible to separate a descriptive "Jesus of History" from an evaluated "Christ of faith." As Stern analyzes literary realism, the very attempt to do this is doomed to failure or triviality, and what one is most likely to succeed in doing is to replace the middle-distance realism of

---

11. Richard B. Hays illuminates the intrinsic relationship between Paul's letters and the gospel story in *The Faith of Jesus Christ: An Investigation of the Narrative Substructure of Galatians 3:1–4:11* (Chico: Scholars Press, 1983). Hays's conclusions help to support the main argument of the present paper as regards the interrelation of story with doctrine and performance, e.g. "The significant point with regard to Pauline ethics is this: The narrative substructure provides the 'logic' which links the paraenetic section of Galatians to the theological exposition of the central section. Interpreters of Paul have always found it difficult to explain how his ethic is grounded in his theology; this study poses the possibility that both are grounded in his Gospel story" (p. 264).

the Gospels with another genre (perhaps a naturalism that seeks for the "bare facts," perhaps a *Bildungsroman* that tries to reach through to Jesus' individual consciousness and development, perhaps even a form of socialist realism that attempts a materialist account of Jesus in the context of the social, economic, and cultural forces of his time). There is nothing objectionable in the use of more than one genre, but what may be disputed is the attempt to reduce one to another, especially if this violates the genre that was in fact considered most appropriate by the early church. The Gospels must by no means be invulnerable to criticism,[12] but they must be defended against misconstruals that judge them by inadequate criteria. They are, as I construe them, realistic narratives written in the middle-distance perspective in the light of the crucifixion and resurrection of Jesus, and this verdict embodied in the crucified and risen Lord not only is the clue to the distinctive reality rendered by the Gospels but also lies at the heart of Christian "performance" in worship, community, prophecy, and mission.

The temporal dimension of the middle-distance perspective is also important. In the course of living, judgments and decisions are being made continually in relation to the immediate situation, but the imperatives of immediacy have their context in the indicatives of history, horizon, expectation, and key relationships. A mature descriptive realism informed by seasoned assessment is unlikely to be possible except over a period of years, especially if the subject matter is of deep and wide significance. This is the case with the Gospels, and they show the other aspects of the middle-distance perspective, already mentioned, in combination with a temporal perspective that is neither too close to the people and events of which they tell, nor so far distant in time that one loses their realistic particularity and what Dame Helen Gardner, writing of Mark's Gospel, calls "the 'Here and Now' of our daily experience, the 'Then and There' of memory, by which I do not mean detailed precision of testimony, but the deep sense of 'happening.'"[13] As the Christian church developed, it authorized these classic accounts whose perspective both enabled its distinctive message to be communicated and implicitly claimed primacy over other perspectives on the narrative content of Christian faith.

12. See below, Section IV.

13. "The Poetry of St. Mark," in *The Business of Criticism* (Oxford: Oxford University Press, 1959), p. 118. An instructive contemporary example of the temporal distance that seems best suited to the sort of testimony that the Gospels offer is seen in *Mister God, This Is Anna* by Fynn (London: Collins, 1974). The author recounts, thirty years later, a short period of Anna's life focusing on incidents which have, over the years, crystallized into pericope form. There are, of course, many differences from the Gospels, but the relation of temporal distance to the attainment of a classic description informed by matured judgment is instructive.

David F. Ford

One danger facing a theology that gives narrative an important role is that it becomes too exclusively literary and also too exclusively interpersonal in its conception of reality. This could easily be the case with the idea of the middle distance, so that it is worth concluding my introduction of the concept by indicating briefly how it transcends the literary and the constriction to human relationships. One way of showing this is to follow through its implications for a systematic understanding of reality in the general terms of an ontology. The doctrine of the Trinity and its accompanying philosophical elucidations might be seen as the main patristic and medieval attempt to do this. In this there was a determination to try to do justice to the extraordinary belief in a God who becomes man and takes part in this story. That was the explosive, revolutionary conception which helped to transform the understanding of God, cosmos, and human reality together, and is eloquently summed up in the final canto of Dante's *Paradiso*. There Dante's celebration of the Christian medieval cosmology and ontology, in the course of a story that is consistently middle-distance in primary perspective, reaches its climax in the vision of God, at the culmination of which is the human face of Christ, transcending all categories and understanding.

One result of the disintegration of the medieval world-view was the emergence of a plurality of new systems, overarching stories, forms of praxis and of subjectivity. Within the medieval "great chain of being," the Gospel stories, for all their transformative influence, had taken their place in a hierarchical universe. With the end of this, the Gospels were vulnerable to being subsumed into many other frameworks, most of which gave primacy to perspectives other than that of the middle distance. Whereas the medieval system had at least given a firm place to the events of the Gospels, even though the metaphysical framework tended to domesticate them and to inhibit the drawing of certain radical implications (for example, concerning the passibility of God), now there was no such guarantee of their cosmic significance, and many ways of calling it in question. This was part of a wider crisis of the middle distance, which yet remained, of course, the principal perspective in which most ordinary reality was seen.[14] In literature, realistic novels especially tried to affirm its importance, and continue to do so, but their genre has been under great strain (well

14. Hannah Arendt, in *The Human Condition* (Garden City: Doubleday, 1958), makes what could be seen as a sustained and sophisticated plea for the recovery of a true middle-distance perspective in the realm of historical action. She suggests that modern alienation is the result of a "twofold flight from the earth into the universe and from the world into the self" (pp. 6f). Both "earth" and "world" are used in almost technical senses explained elsewhere in the book.

described by Stern) and has often failed to maintain the precarious balance of elements which makes up that middle distance. However the modern situation is construed, it is clearly on the whole far from hospitable to traditional claims for the importance of what is told in the Gospels, and the effort to conceive Christian truth demands the labor of a plausible ontology as part of the testimony to the Gospel from a systematic perspective. That ontology cannot be content with a personalism which ignores the problems of conceiving space, time, creation, and history in a post-Enlightenment, post-Einsteinian way, and it needs to be able to offer an understanding of the proportionality and dynamics of reality such that the Gospel's content and perspective make broad rational sense. As this is attempted by some modern theologians, one can begin to see the liberating, radical possibilities for understanding the Gospel and other reality together in our situation, so that the positive contribution of what is distinctively modern can be appreciated.[15]

Besides the elaboration of an ontology, another way of developing the concept of middle-distance realism beyond the narrowly literary and interpersonal is to concentrate on some aspect of "performance" which includes activities and relationships not exhaustively describable in literary or personalist terms. One such way would be through an ethic that uses central concepts such as responsibility, representation, or suffering. Another would be through the relationship to God in praise, which a co-author and I have attempted recently.[16]

However it is worked out in detail, the middle-distance perspective with content centering on the story of Jesus appears to be vital for the self-description of Christianity. Christian worship is principally neither an affirmation of general truths nor an interior state of communion of the soul with God (or any other relationship which is primarily definable in terms of individual experience, awareness, or consciousness, though these are of course involved), but is rather a social meal- and word-centered communication informed by the key events of the Christian story. Christian initiation is the taking on, in

---

15. For example, Jürgen Moltmann and Thomas Torrance both, though in very different ways, offer an ontology sharply contrasting with medieval systems, highly critical of modern tendencies to retreat into subjectivity or the interpersonal, and completely trinitarian. Moltmann's leading category is "history" (inextricable from "performance"), while Torrance specializes more in "theory," but each maintains, with radical ontological results, the primacy of the gospel story and especially the passion, death, and resurrection of Jesus.

16. Daniel W. Hardy and David F. Ford, *Jubilate: Theology in Praise* (London: Darton, Longman and Todd, 1984); U.S. ed., *Praising and Knowing God* (Philadelphia: Westminster, 1985). Cf. below, Section III.

a particular community, of an identity determined by the death and resurrection of Jesus and the giving of the Holy Spirit. Likewise revelation, reconciliation, and salvation are conceived of "through Jesus Christ" so that revelation, for example, is not first of all a system of truths or an illumination of individual minds and hearts but is "the word made flesh" inseparable from the telling of a particular story. The Christian ethic of love likewise makes the middle-distance perspective primary, in contrast to such possibilities as a system of laws and principles or the attainment of a special state of consciousness or self-development.

The approach to the future too is greatly affected by the perspective and content of the gospel stories. The first Christians lived in an apocalyptic age, with much radical speculation about the future. Might it not be that one important reason why the delay of the Parousia caused no apparent crisis in the community was that the distinctively Christian understanding of the future was increasingly seen to lie not in an ability to date the end of the world but in an affirmation that hope was to be focused through Jesus Christ, as identified by the Gospels, which were written as this belief became clearer? The practical consequence of this was to lead a life that pivoted round faith in Jesus Christ, and, as regards the future, was mainly concerned neither with long-term or comprehensive plans or speculations, nor with the destiny of one's own soul, but rather with the celebration of worship together, the building up of Christian community, and various sorts of prophetic action and communication in the world. The resurrection, as the great sign of hope, acted as a seal on the ultimacy of Jesus Christ as the content of hope, and so established also the primacy of the perspective of the middle distance.

III. Performance

At the cutting edge of history there is the thrust of present speech, action, suffering, and thought, all involved in the many processes that make up the ecology in which we exist. In this, people formed through the whole of their history up to this point take part in carrying it further, as all the elements converge in the present. Here middle-distance realism helps to orient one within what one is actually living, and it is the assessment aspect of evaluations and decisions leading to response and action which is more prominent than the realism of description, and may assume various relationships to it. I call this movement in the historical present "performance," though I am not completely satisfied with the term. It is an attempt to indicate a process in which *lexis* and *praxis* are the main focus and in which dramatic and narrative content is taken seriously.[17]

Performance is a "hot" concept pointing to a concentration and coherence of relationships, levels, and elements in a simultaneity which has its own integrity and is not exhaustively represented in the cooler examination through systematic study of the narrative shaped into some linear sequence. Both "system" and "story" must be used to try to discern the truth of the performance that has been and is taking place and to help in further performance, while recognizing that what happens in true human performance has the characteristic which systems-thinking affirms in its orientation to "the contingent future." The complex co-inherence in performance of past, present, and future, and of thought, feeling, and action, within the web of relationships in the ecology of life as focused at a particular point in time, defies any overview or representation by a single method or genre. What is the best way for theology to grapple with what is involved here? David Tracy's phrase "journey of intensification" is helpful in suggesting a way that differs from the systematic and the narrative modes and that tries to handle the intensity of the concentrated convergence that happens in performance. A journey of intensification, in my usage, follows through one mode of performance in its manifold implications, and things can be learnt and new performance enabled by such a single-minded journey which would not be possible without it. In theology the "hottest" work is often of this sort, such as liberation theologies, various types of spirituality, or other strongly directive and transformative proposals. It is the following through of one type of performance, and this may include consideration of the theoretical and historical dimensions as well as the practical and future-oriented.

In Christian theology I see three dynamics of performance in line with the content and middle-distance realism of the gospel story in its Old Testament and New Testament context. The first is that of active relationship with God most explicit in worship. The second is that of life together in a community of faith and love. The third is that of prophetic speech and action in witness, evangelism and dedication to peace, justice, and goodness.[18] These are all clearly co-inherent, but consideration of them in depth is often best done through a specialist journey

17. Hannah Arendt (*Human Condition*, esp. Chap. V) develops a concept of action within a broader understanding of performance and links it to "story" and "drama." She tries to do justice both to existentialist insights into distinctively human freedom and potential and to the spheres of labor, industry, science, technology, and above all, politics.

18. In the New Testament these dynamics are pervasively present, both explicitly (clearest in Acts, in Paul's Corinthian and Roman correspondence, in John's Gospel, and in Revelation) and also implicitly, as a great deal of scholarship about the worship, com-

of intensification concentrating on one, or one aspect of one, of them. Theology of this type tends to stress the need for self-involvement if one is to understand its message: encouraging one to learn prayer by doing it in certain ways and with a certain understanding; to learn Christian community by living in it and by participating in its thinking, language, and behavior; to learn to witness by engaging in it; and to learn the way to peace and justice by advocating and incarnating them.

In any such theology there will be many issues raised from the direction of thinking in terms of "system" and "story," and much theology can be formally differentiated according to how these issues are handled. Some, such as the existentialists, recommend their "performance" in sharp criticism of the tendency of any system or narrative to exercise the wrong sort of control, inappropriate to the freedom of true Christian living. Others, such as certain liberation theologians and advocates of neo-conservatism, see their *praxis* as the appropriate response to the call of God in a situation which is understood in terms of a clear view of history and where it is heading, often supported by a systematic analysis. But one says very little about these and the many other positions by such formal generalizations. Their intensity, concentration, and practicality are only done justice by an appropriately holistic engagement and response, and the inescapability of the issue of one's own performance invites one into a corresponding journey of intensification.

My position on the interrelation of the other two modes with that of performance is that the systematic questions are unavoidable and need to be thoroughly pursued, and that the story-related questions require a similarly specific attention. The barrenness of that statement indicates that the major need is to do this theology rather than talk about what needs to be done or the method of doing it or the criteria for judging it. *Praising and Knowing God*[19] is an attempt to do this by thinking through the activity of praising God. It is theology done in a middle-distance perspective from the standpoint of the performance of praise, and it relates this to the gospel story, the Old Testament, the history of the Christian tradition, and other history. It discusses the history of theology using the praise of God as a hermeneutical key,[20] and attempts a "system"[21] in line with the rest of the book.

---

munity, and mission of the early church shows. On the relation of the gospel narrative to Paul, and especially to Galatians, see Hays, *Faith*. His conclusion is that "Paul's language *enacts* the ongoing destiny of the foundational story because he sees himself and his churches as agents within the story's final sequence" (p. 266).

19. See n. 16 above.

20. Ibid., Appendix B.

21. Ibid., Appendix A.

IV. System

The system in *Praising and Knowing God* is just one of a large family of systematic enterprises that includes those mentioned in Section I above. They have multiplied in recent centuries, and their rigorous development has profoundly changed theology. Their subject matter has embraced other systems and all that comes under the headings of "story" and "performance." They have been analytic and synthetic, critical and constructive in varying degrees. They have also been controversial, and the obvious dangers of systematizing in theology, such as the tendencies to adopt totalitarian overviews or to reduce the content in the interests of supporting a theory, have led to widespread suspicion and hostility. Of the multifarious aspects and issues in this area I will focus on the relationship of systematic thinking with the realistic gospel narratives.

My opening quotation suggested that "in its multiplicity of functions, its characteristic style, its sensuality and indirectness, the novel is wholly different from the philosophical treatise," and Iris Murdoch's novels were seen as "best equipped to incarnate a philosophy which a treatise could not adequately set down." My discussion of the Gospels' middle-distance realism is in line with a similar conclusion, but just as Iris Murdoch continues to write philosophy as well as novels, so theology needs to relate its systematic thinking to the Gospels. Not only their philosophical implications, their multiplicity of functions, and their style can be investigated but also their structure, historicity, sociology, psychology, culture, economics, linguistics, and much else. There can be no fixing in advance the results of such examinations: each must be carried through in all its specialist particularity, and accusations of manipulation, reductionism, or other forms of insensitivity or inappropriateness need to be considered in detailed argument. Likewise, those consultations which propose fresh understanding or assessment of these stories require the sort of discussion that allows the validity of method, argument, and verdict to be adequately assessed. In short, there is a vast field of intellectual engagement here which has many implications for apologetics. Middle-distance realism, too, needs to be able to argue for its priority in the form in which I have presented it above in Section II, and the thrust of the debate is towards transcending the narrower systematic investigations toward the more comprehensive, especially ontology.

Just as Iris Murdoch supports the relative priority of her novels over her philosophy in rendering what is most important in human life, so I have argued for the primacy of the gospel story's content and perspective in Christianity. Systematic thinking has many roles in rela-

205

tion to this, but crucial issues will concern the way in which it allows itself to be informed by this story, and how far its system, whether critical or constructive, is appropriate to the story's form and content. There can be no general rules for resolving the complex issues raised here, and there is also in the subject matter something deeply resistant to adequate reformulation in systematic terms—perhaps this resistance is best conceived as a combination of what Iris Murdoch says about the realistic novel together with the claim of the Gospels to be testimony. This testimony is of course open to examination by all appropriate systematic means, from logic to archaeology, but it is itself the telling of a story about events which are contingent and particular to one time and place, which can never be re-run, and which therefore are unavoidably entrusted to witnesses whose reliability may be assessed but whose place in history and tradition can never be duplicated. In addition, the criteria of reliability for testimony in a middle-distance perspective can, as mentioned above, never be reduced to accuracy of detail or truth of general statements. It might even be that a testimony to Jesus Christ might be true in its identification of him and its verdict on him while yet containing a great deal of what we would "fictionalized" material.[22]

So far in this section I have been concerned with systematic thinking but not specifically with systematic theology. I take it for granted that systematic theology will take other disciplines seriously and will therefore come to its own task having learnt from them, and open to learning more. My limited focus now is on the relationship of systematic theology to the gospel story, in line with the position I have already developed. How can systematic theology explore and maintain the truth of what is primarily expressed in a very different genre? The main traditional answer has been: through concentration on key *loci*, notably God, election, creation, providence, Jesus Christ, salvation, Holy Spirit, church,

---

22. I have listened to an expert on Soviet history go through point after point in which Solzhenitsyn's *Lenin in Zurich* is inaccurate historically, partly due to the author's bias and partly due to his ignorance of some sources. The fascinating question was raised: At what point does such accumulation of evidence invalidate the overall portrayal of Lenin and his significance? A further question is: Granted the importance of Lenin and his immense continuing influence, and therefore the inevitability of stories, myths, biographies, and "images" of him, might the only adequate response to Solzhenitsyn be the attempt to do better what he has tried to do? He has offered a story that does grapple with the many levels and dimensions of Lenin and has arrived at verdicts which are self-involving and controversial, and it is this whole "icon" to which response is invited. As regards the Gospels, it seems to me that it is in their aspect of testimony to a whole "icon" of Jesus Christ that they are most defensible, and that most critics become less convincing the more they take up the challenge to construct an alternative icon. But of course the very verdict "defensible" is a signal for yet another stage in the endless inquiry into the Gospels' meaning and truth.

and eschatology. The main relationship between these *loci* has not been systematic but has been their ordering in an "overarching story." This meant that the overarching story was the mediation between systematic thinking and my present focus, the gospel story, and this overall narrative framework implied the subordination of the systematic aspect to the narrative.

Yet this subordination accompanied a distinctive development of the systematic that has a parallel in what Stern observed about Thomas Mann's *The Magic Mountain*. Stern noted the interplay of the story-line of events *nacheinander* with the simultaneity of the *nebeneinander* view. In Christian thought the various *loci* display such simultaneity. Each of them involves, explicitly or implicitly, all the others, thus drawing on all parts of the overarching story. For example, to have a doctrine of creation that is developed without regard for its implications for the doctrines of God, salvation, and so on is to have a theology that is inadequate systematically. It is as if each doctrine only reaches its appropriate richness and thoroughness by being led through a series of dialectical encounters with other doctrines. This journey (the equivalent in systematics of the journey of intensification in the mode of performance) should result in a doctrine that has taken account of all the others but still maintains the modesty of being only one among several such doctrines. In this way any totalitarian systematic overview is avoided and there is enabled a systematic particularity of the story — past, present, and future.[23] The doctrine which might seem to have most

23. It is not, of course, necessary to have a traditional understanding of the over-arching story in order to practice such *locus*-centered theology. Recent centuries have seen vast changes in how this can be understood, and the competing secular alternatives (notably the ideological developments of the theory of evolution, the belief in "progress," Marxism's dialectical materialistic theory of history, and fascism's master race destined for world domination) have sharpened the debate that had long been carried on between Judaism, Christianity, and Islam concerning the overarching story. Many recent theologies have been especially concerned with a Christian conception of world history (e.g., Teilhard, Rahner, Pannenberg) but such explicit elaboration is not necessary for a theologian to have a view of the "plot" of history that is deeply influential in his work. It would be instructive to examine the theologians in a similar way to that applied to historians by Hayden White in *Metahistory: The Historical Imagination in Nineteenth Century Europe* (Baltimore: Johns Hopkins, 1973). My conclusion about Karl Barth in this respect is that his avoidance of a conception of world history other than that offered by the Bible, combined with his reluctance to let the biblical accounts compete with others (most noticeable in his doctrine of creation), lead him to displace the effective content of the overarching story in two directions, first into his doctrine of God, especially of election, and second into christology, whose key story, subsuming all others typologically, is that of the Gospel. Since his doctrine of election also pivots around the Gospel, Barth in effect uses the story of Jesus Christ as his overarching story, relating all else in history to that. Not surprisingly this has led to various criticisms. Of these the most powerful offer alternative ways

frequently tried to dominate the others and so escape this essential pluralism is that of the Trinity, but it could be argued that the Trinity represents within itself the irreducible pluralism and anti-totalitarianism of the best Christian thinking, with one of its "persons" after another being emphasized in order to reassert both their distinctiveness and their coinherence in the face of positions that threaten these. Various other doctrines have had their period of hegemony, but the ecology of the system as a whole has tended to qualify and correct this situation.

What are the ontological implications if the best way to understand Christian truth is, as suggested, that it is witnessed to primarily by narrative that informs worship, community, and prophetic speech and action, and that it is capable of endless exploration, most appropriately through distinct yet coinherent *loci?* The very limitation of the scope of certain modes of systematizing by the particularity, contingency, and freedom in Christian faith is itself a major statement about the nature of reality and has long been a focus of reflection and theorizing. This is closely linked to the prominence of "performance" and ultimately concerns the nature of God. The nature of time is also raised acutely by this position, as it is for Stern by *The Magic Mountain.* Much narrative theology suffers from an unexamined notion of time, often playing up its linearity at the expense of its density and of the coinherence of times through memory, causality, anticipation, or faith in God, and very rarely, as Stern does, exploring its relativity. This is an avenue which could lead to more understanding between currently opposed positions, and in particular to a recognition of the complementarity of narrative and *locus*-centered approaches. This also leads to the basic issue of God and his time. A related fundamental aspect of reality suggested by Stern's critique of Mann and also relevant to the Bible, and especially to the understanding of God, is that of the absolute: How can Stern talk of "fictionally achieved absolutes" as the equivalent of the constant speed of light in Einstein's relativity theory? How can a conception of the absolute, or of ultimate constancy, be discerned through biblical narrative and other genres?

One could go on raising in turn all the main matters of ontology and of epistemology within the suggested conception of theology, but, as with the category of performance, the formality of such issue-raising underlines the need to *do* ontology, epistemology, and systematic theol-

---

of handling the problem that can claim to do more justice to creation and science, critical history, the contingency and openness of the future, and the reality of evil. It is as if Barth, for all his sensitivity to the literary realism of the gospel story, was led at times to use it theologically in the interests of an overall doctrinal position in a way that violates its integrity as a realistic story. Cf. Chaps. 5, 6, 8, and 10 in Ford, *Barth and God's Story.*

ogy. I have tried to make the method of Christian theology inseparable from its content, and so the formal principles cannot claim to be neutral *vis-à-vis* any particular theology. There are definite conceptions of God, creation, Jesus Christ, and all the other doctrines implicit in this approach or yet to be discovered through it, and these in turn may lead to considerable revision of the approach. Some of the doctrinal positions will be found in *Praising and Knowing God,* but the main challenge remains the direct handling of the *loci.*

V. Lindbeck's Theory of Religion

George Lindbeck's cultural-linguistic theory of religion is, as suggested above, in many ways congenial to the line I have taken. He sees religion as

> a kind of cultural and/or linguistic framework or medium which shapes the entirety of life and thought. It functions somewhat like a Kantian *a priori* although in this case the *a priori* is a set of acquired skills which could be different. It is not primarily an array of beliefs about the true and the good (though it may involve these), nor a symbolism expressive of basic attitudes, feelings or sentiments (though these will be generated). Rather, it is similar to an idiom which makes possible the description of realities, the formulation of beliefs, and the experiencing of inner attitudes, feelings and sentiments. Like a culture or language, it is a communal phenomenon which shapes the subjectivities of individuals rather than being primarily a manifestation of those subjectivities. It comprises a vocabulary of discursive and non-discursive symbols together with a distinctive logic or grammar in terms of which this vocabulary can be meaningfully deployed. Lastly, just as a language (or "language game" to use Wittgenstein's phrase) is correlated with a form of life, and just as a culture has both cognitive and behavioral dimensions, so also in the case of a religious tradition. Its doctrines, cosmic stories or myths, and ethical directives are integrally related to the rituals it practices, the sentiments or experiences it evokes, the actions it recommends, and the institutional forms it develops.[24]

As he develops his thesis there are several implications which are especially relevant to my position. Firstly, there is the way in which his theory makes primary what I have called a middle-distance realism. He does this partly by his criticism of two alternative theories: the "experiential-expressive," which pivots its understanding of religion around religious interiority and sees the main direction of formative influence being from

24. Lindbeck, *Nature of Doctrine,* p. 33.

David F. Ford

inner to outer; and the "cognitive-propositional," which sees religion as primarily a cognitive system of propositions in a relationship of correspondence or non-correspondence with reality. He does it positively, by claiming that the best way to do justice to the rich particularity of a religion is to engage in "thick description" of the actual behavior, communication, and other exchanges that happen, and in this way to elucidate "the informal logic of actual life."[25] In this way he offers a theory that serves the primacy of the middle-distance perspective, while yet allowing major roles to other types of theory and other disciplines, as well as the fruitfulness of interiorized religion.

In theology Lindbeck recommends a regulative theory of doctrine in which doctrines are not primarily truth-claims or expressive symbols but are "communally authoritative rules of discourse, attitude and action."[26] They are statements of the basic grammar of a religion. This is a narrow definition of doctrine that (like Lonergan's) distinguishes it from systematic theology and particular ways of understanding and developing doctrine in dogmatics. It does not, therefore, rule out cognitive-propositional enterprises or the attempt to do *locus*-centered theology. Rather, it encourages the latter because of its dedication to working through the particularity of a religion, and over against this sort of systematics it plays down the importance both of foundational theology, which proposes a framework transcending such particularity, and of apologetics, which tends, in the linguistic analogy, to translate into other idioms the "language" of a particular religion rather than trying to teach that language itself.

Lindbeck's stress on categorical adequacy and on the enormous importance of the problem of the incommensurability of the primary categories used in various religions and theologies is a more general version of what I have attempted to do within Christianity using the categories of system, story, and performance. He too gives a special primacy to narrative and to literary consideration of it,[27] he even says that "the text . . . absorbs the world rather than the world the text,"[28] and he constantly stresses the intrinsic importance of performance in arriving at conclusions about a religion's identity and truth. The result is an "ecological" view of the meaning and truth of a religion that can take account of the dynamic interaction of system, story, and performance:

> As actually lived, a religion may be pictured as a single gigantic proposition. It is a true proposition to the extent that its objectivities are interi-

25. Ibid., p. 115.
26. Ibid., p. 18.
27. Ibid., e.g., Chap. 2, Chap. 6.
28. Ibid., p. 118.

210

orized and exercised by groups and individuals in such a way as to conform them in some measure in the various dimensions of their existence to the ultimate reality and goodness which lies at the heart of things. It is a false proposition to the extent that this does not happen. . . . A religious utterance, one might say, acquires the propositional truth of ontological correspondence only in so far as it is a performance, an act or deed, which helps create that correspondence.[29]

This paper has not been concerned to propose a theory of religion, but my conclusions, as well as leading to a great deal of agreement with Lindbeck, also prompt some critical questions about his theory. First, I will raise some points under the general heading of system.

With regard to the three ways of understanding religion and doctrine, ought the direction to be more towards a variety of ways of interrelating the cognitive-propositional, experiential-expressive, and cultural-linguistic rather than leaving them somewhat separated and usually contrasted with each other as ideal types? Lindbeck's approach has the virtue of making his polemical points clear, but, that done, there must surely be an attempt at more thorough mutuality and dialogue. Otherwise there is good reason for those who tend towards cognitive or experiential approaches to raise objections of one-sidedness and misinterpretation. In the process of interrelation, one problem might be Lindbeck's insistence that theology is a reflective, second-order activity. This, in line with the linguistic analogy of the second-order status of grammar, plays down its capacity to reach and affirm first-order truth. But this is an analogy that is bound to be inadequate for conceptions of theology which see their task, for example, more in terms of the theories of natural science[30] or the integration of theology and aesthetics.[31] Perhaps most importantly, his somewhat Kantian preference for "rules" and "categories," might need to be corrected in the direction of a more thorough integration of rules, categories, and content.

29. Ibid., pp. 51, 65. Praise, for example, has this logic of performance, creativity, and correspondence, and so has the telling of testimony.

30. Lindbeck understandably mentions Thomas Kuhn's philosophy of science, but that theory's preference for a "softer" conception of knowledge in natural science, thus bringing it nearer to social-scientific theories, is by no means undisputed, and T. F. Torrance, for example, has a theology with a very different conception of science and a theological "knowledge" that is by no means reflective or second-order. Lindbeck would perhaps say that Torrance is excessively "cognitive-propositional," but in fact much of his work is in line with Lindbeck's regulative approach; he differs in relating the regulative and the ontological theoretically rather than practically. Both might be legitimate, but Lindbeck does not allow sufficient scope for Torrance.

31. Cf. Hans Urs von Balthasar, *The Glory of the Lord: A Theological Aesthetics, Vol. 1: Seeing the Form* (Edinburgh: Clark, 1982).

David F. Ford

As regards particular systematic doctrines, this might well result in the categories and Lindbeck's types of religion having different roles to play according to the doctrine being treated. The doctrines may be more pluralist among themselves than can be accommodated under one general account of doctrine. Might it not be that the cultural-linguistic approach is especially helpful in, for example, an ecclesiology, but finds itself inappropriately extended beyond its social scientific background when it attempts to deal with the doctrine of creation, and especially with the contribution to that doctrine of the natural sciences?

In his sensitive discussion of the doctrine of the Trinity, Lindbeck makes a strong case for seeing it as regulative, but his comments make too great a distinction between seeing it as rule and seeing it as ontological proposition. He says about the conflict between Eastern and Western Christian understanding for the economic and immanent trinities that the issue of their ontological truth is

> irrelevant to theological assessment. Which theory is theologically best depends on how well it organizes the data of scripture and tradition with a view to their use in Christian worship and life. In terms of these specifically theological criteria, there may be good or bad theories on both sides of the ontological dispute regarding the economic and immanent aspects of the Trinity. The question of the ontological reference of the theories may often be unimportant for theological evaluation.[32]

The one-sidedness of this lies in its suggested downgrading of the knowledge content in Christian worship and life, and the displacement of the ontological truth question into a practical question as to "how well it organizes the data of scripture and tradition with a view to their use in Christian worship and life."

Under the heading of performance, Lindbeck's bias towards the practical in his conception of the truth of religion (another Kantian tendency) may be one legitimate "journey of intensification," but needs to be able to do justice to other journeys.[33] Uneasiness about the excessive practicality of Lindbeck's conception of knowledge and truth might focus on his final chapter's recommendation of an "intratextuality" in systematics in which the text absorbs the world rather than *vice versa* and might lead—through a recognition of rules and of the creative, demanding nature of redescription of the world in Christian terms—to a higher conception of the locus in theology as an affirmation that may be in a dynamic relationship of truth with its ob-

32. Lindbeck, *Nature of Doctrine*, p. 106.

33. Cf. the discussion of various modern theologies in *Praising and Knowing God*, pp. 196-209, and the criticism of some who "excessively devalue knowledge as such" (p. 204).

ject,[34] and to a reconsideration of apologetics as accompanying systematics.

It is perhaps in relation to story, however, that the most sensitive issues occur. Is the social-anthropological method of "thick description" not essentially biased towards Christianity, with its primacy of a narrative in middle-distance perspective? It may be that cognitive-propositionalism is more in line with the type of revelation represented by the Koran as understood by most Muslims, or that experientialism-expressivism is more congenial to Buddhists or Hindus. This would by no means rule out a cultural-linguistic account of these religions, but it would mean that for a theologian to claim the primacy of the cultural-linguistic in inter-religious dialogue would bias the conversation towards Christianity. In other worlds, if a person and events are crucial to a religion's identity (rather than, say, revealed words or a form of self-transcendence) then it will have an advantage if the primary account is to be in terms of "thick description." Lindbeck might well be willing to grant this, as it would be the logical conclusion of his denial of the possibility of stepping outside one's own idiom for ultimate reality into a position from which various idioms can be neutrally assessed. But it would require his position on the usefulness of his theory in inter-religious relations to be revised.

The last point has to do with the particularity of religions. Within Christianity too there are problems with the way Lindbeck's approach copes with particularity, especially in the form of historical contingency. This is the negative side of the notion of a text that absorbs the world. Lindbeck is aware that the language of inclusiveness is too simple to do justice to the wide variety of ways in which text and world interact. But adequate recognition is needed of the dangers of using the Christian story (for all its irreducible particularity and testimony to contingent events) in the interests of a generalizing "grammar" which may fail to allow other contingent events their proper particularity because it subsumes them too readily as instantiations of the grammar.

The all-inclusive story and its second-order conceptual counterpart, the grammar embodied in doctrines, may also suggest that, as Lindbeck uses it, the cultural-linguistic analogy tends to a conservative bias. It is perhaps right that a Christian theologian in the mainstream should favor "retrieval" over "suspicion," but yet at the heart of the Christian story is an event of radical condemnation and discontinuity, the crucifixion of Jesus. How can one be part of a story with the crucifixion in it? In bap-

---

34. As suggested in *Praising and Knowing God,* Chapters 7 and 8, Appendices A and B. A good test case of the limitations of the conception of "text absorbing world" is the stories of creation. Barth, for example, attempted to let the Genesis stories inform his doctrine of creation in a way that appears unreceptive to scientific and historical knowledge.

tism, identification with it signifies the "death" of the one baptized. In other words, this is a "language" whose learning involves the "death" of the learning self. In the face of the cross and the reality of its appropriation in baptism, is there not implicit a critique of the continuities of meaning represented by the cultural-linguistic theory of religion? It is always possible, of course, to step outside and regard baptism as the internalizing of the message of the Gospel through word and act, but Lindbeck is committed to going the whole way in "thick description" from the inside, and this makes the issue of death, in all its Christian and ontological dimension,[35] inescapable. Instead of tackling the issue of death, Lindbeck in *The Nature of Doctrine* tends to solve important questions, such as the eventual salvation of Christians and the possibility of salvation for non-Christians, by reference to an eschatology in which the nature of death does not seem to be a problem.

VI. Conclusion

This paper's conception of good Christian systematic theology is, therefore, that it aims at the truth of the various *loci* while taking account, in ways appropriate to their content, of narrative, systems, and performance. The best apologetics happens in the course of carrying through this enterprise, as the rigorous pursuit of truth becomes reciprocal with faithful living in a community that worships together and is summoned to service and to sharing its life and truth (including its questions) with others. The apologetics may, as Lindbeck suggests, be *ad hoc*. But that neuter *hoc* hardly does justice to the men and women with whom apologetics is concerned. Christian apologetics is, therefore, also *ad hos* and *ad has,* and in the course of this exchange inevitably becomes involved with its interlocutors' systems and stories. In these relationships, apologetics justifiably elicits, often in highly specialist forms, the best energies of Christian theologians and others. Indeed, Lindbeck's own theory of doctrine could be construed as such apologetics: deeply concerned with the situation of theology in late twentieth-century capitalist societies, offering a plausible alternative to dominant ways of conceiving religion and theology, enlisting other disciplines in the service of his approach with advantage to its academic respectability, and sometimes concealing (if not deliberately) how thoroughly informed by Christianity the whole conception is.

The cultural-linguistic approach, as discussed above, can be taken up into a *locus*-oriented Christian theology involving the coinherence of system, story, and performance, together with an accompanying

---

35. Including the radical problem of sin, not least in theory.

apologetics. In this there would be no neat distinction of first-order from second-order, and no avoiding the challenge of contingent particularity. Death is above all the contingency which is the end of all internalizing and externalizing of language and behavior. When it is further specified as the death of Jesus who rose again from the dead, perhaps one has a non-fictional equivalent of the "fictionally achieved absolutes" discovered by Stern in *The Magic Mountain*. Stern's parallel is with the role of the speed of light in relativity theory. In Christian theology the resurrection of Jesus has a similar role. It informs and transforms systematic conceptions of ontology, of God, and of other doctrines; it establishes and illuminates the primacy of the story witnessing to Jesus; and it liberates an explosion of new worship, community-building, and prophetic speech and action, generating new particularity.

In all of this, the mode of rationality has to be appropriate to the content, and there are few fields which can be more helpfully instructive in this than that with which my opening quotations were concerned. I conclude, as I began, with a quotation from within that British tradition of philosophy whose concern for particularity and reserve, with regard both to systems and to undue concern with the interior of the self, may not be unconnected with a cultural formation in which Shakespeare, George Eliot, and their twentieth-century successors such as Iris Murdoch have played a central role alongside the Bible and the Book of Common Prayer:

> What is said by *King Lear* and *War and Peace* is said through the individuality and particularity of the characters, situations and conversations of which the works consist. Above all it is expressed in different *language* from any that can be used in a short summary or in any paraphrase, and differences of language amount to differences of *meaning*—that is to say, to differences of content . . . these points taken together indicate a degree of overlapping in scope and function between literature and religion that sets in a new light the idea of the Bible "designed to read as literature." . . . When we think about life and conduct, just as when we think about knowledge and its grounds, we must engage in that explanation of the similarities and differences between particulars and particulars on which even the more formal and systematic modes of thought are in the end dependent. In Ezra Pound's words, "Art does not avoid universals, it strikes at them all the harder in that it strikes through particulars" (*Literary Essays*, p. 440). The literary power of accurate and precise portrayal of complexity, individuality, and particularity, is as much as any human power a power of human thought. Literature is one of the functions of the human reason.[36]

36. R. Bambrough, *Reason, Truth and God* (London: Methuen, 1969), pp. 121, 122, 123.

Narrative Emotions:
Beckett's Genealogy of Love

Martha Nussbaum

I

Two voices, immobilized by life, go on telling their stories about emotion. One voice has no name; it says:

> They love each other, marry, in order to love each other better, more conveniently, he goes to the wars, he dies at the wars, she weeps, with emotion, at having loved him, at having lost him, yep, marries again, in order to love again, more conveniently again, they love each other, you love as many times as necessary, as necessary in order to be happy, he comes back, the other comes back, from the wars, he didn't die at the wars after all, she goes to the station, to meet him, he dies in the train, of emotion, at the thought of seeing her again, having her again, she weeps, weeps again, with emotion again, at having lost him again, yep, goes back to the house, he's dead, the other is dead, the mother-in-law takes him down, he hanged himself, with emotion, at the thought of losing her, she weeps, weeps louder, at having loved him, at having lost him, there's a story for you, that was to teach me the nature of emotion, that's called emotion, what emotion can do, given favourable conditions, what love can do, well well, so that's emotion, that's love.[1]

1. Samuel Beckett, *Molloy, Malone Dies, The Unnamable* (New York: Grove Press,

Martha Nussbaum, "Narrative Emotions: Beckett's Genealogy of Love," *Ethics*, 98, 2 (January 1988): 225-254.

The other voice calls itself Malone. It tells a story about one Macmann, who himself tells stories to himself, lying cheek to the ground, soaked by the "heavy, cold, and perpendicular rain":

> The idea of punishment came to his mind, addicted it is true to that chimera and probably impressed by the posture of the body and the fingers clenched as though in torment. And without knowing exactly what his sin was he felt full well that living was not a sufficient atonement for it or that his atonement was in itself a sin, calling for more atonement, and so on, as if there could be anything but life, for the living. And no doubt he would have wondered if it was really necessary to be guilty in order to be punished but for the memory, more and more galling, of his having consented to live in his mother, then to leave her. And this again he could not see as his true sin, but as yet another atonement which had miscarried and, far from cleansing him of his sin, plunged him in it deeper than before. And truth to tell the ideas of guilt and punishment were confused together in his mind, as those of cause and effect so often are in the minds of those who continue to think. And it was often in fear and trembling that he suffered, saying, This will cost me dear. But not knowing how to go about it, in order to think and feel correctly, he would suddenly begin to smile for no reason . . . to smile and give thanks for the teeming rain and the promise it contained of stars a little later, to light his way and enable him to get his bearings, should he wish to do so. (pp. 239-40)

(And that story is a love story too, don't think that it isn't.)

Beckett's voices, here and elsewhere in the *Molloy* trilogy, share an attitude toward emotions like love, fear, guilt, disgust, hope—and to the complex intersection of all of these that is aroused, for the second voice, by the thought of mother's body. It is that emotions are not feelings that well up in some natural and untutored way from our natural selves, that they are, in fact, not personal or natural at all, that they are, instead, contrivances, social constructs. We learn how to feel, and we learn our emotional repertoire. We learn emotions in the same way that we learn our beliefs—from our society. But emotions, unlike many of our beliefs, are not taught to us directly through propositional claims about the world, either abstract or concrete. They are taught, above all, through stories. Stories express their structure and teach us their dynamics. These stories are constructed by others, and then taught and learned. But once internalized, they shape the way life feels and looks. In the first passage, the meaning of love is given in paradigm stories of

1955), p. 406. All references to the trilogy are to this edition, in which the translations of the second and third novels are by the author and that of the first by the author in collaboration with Patrick Bowles. Page numbers will be given in parentheses in the text.

longing, fear, loss, conflict, despair. In the second, the complex scenario that describes Macmann's efforts to reenact a cultural paradigm of guilt, fear, and longing serves the narrating voice, at the same time, as its own paradigm story of the complex interrelationships among all these. Society has given Macmann a story about his guilt and the guiltiness of his very efforts to atone; it has given him, too, standards of "correctness" for his longing for salvation. This complex story, accepted, shapes and expresses the emotional world of the narrating voice. Indeed, it seems right to say, along with the nameless voice, not only that a certain sort of story shows or represents emotion but also that emotion itself is the acceptance of, the assent to live according to, a certain sort of story. Stories, in short, contain and teach forms of feeling, forms of life.

These voices express isolation and despair. They connect their predicament in no uncertain way with the fearful, disgusted, and guilty love that is, because of the stories, the only love they know. So at the same time that they ask us to see the origins of feeling, they invite us to consider critically these contingent structures and the narratives that are their vehicle. Indeed, they themselves make increasingly radical attempts to put an end to the entire project of storytelling and to the forms of life that this practice supports. They ask us to see their forms of feeling as a pattern that can be unraveled, a writing that can be unwritten, a story that can be ended—not by bringing it to the usual happy or unhappy ending but by ending the storytelling life. If stories are learned, they can be unlearned. If emotions are constructs, they can be dismantled. And perhaps the silence onto which this deconstructive project opens is an opening or clearing in which human beings and animals can recognize one another without and apart from the stories and their guilt. And perhaps, too, the longing for that silence is itself an emotion of and inside the stories. Perhaps the negative project is a happy-ending story trapped, itself, inside the very thing that it opposes.

These disturbing thoughts are among the obsessions of Beckett's trilogy, as of much of his work. They are thoughts that need to be confronted by anyone who thinks about the relationship between narrative and human self-understanding or who approaches narrative searching for an understanding of human life and its prospects. But they are especially subversive, dangerous, and necessary for anyone who wishes to claim that fictional narratives play a central and, so to speak, a positive role in self-understanding, a role that is not as adequately played by texts that lack narrative form. There is, in particular, a project that Beckett's voices seem to call into question. This project involves supplementing abstract philosophical attempts at self-understanding with concrete narrative fictions, which are argued by the proponents of the project to contain more of what is relevant to our attempts to imagine and assess possibilities for ourselves, to ask how we might choose to live.

Since this is a project that I believe to be both valuable and viable—not only for professional philosophers but for people who are, in their lives, pursuing questions about life—and since Beckett's voices have been for some time audible to me in the background of this work, speaking their subversive claims, audible even as Henry James praises the moral role of the novelist or as Proust argues for the epistemological value of narrative form, I want to let them speak and to see how much of the work they really do call into question, how their insights about the narrative forms of human desire and emotion would cause us to revise it—or perhaps, even, to end it. In short (already using their words), I want to judge this work with the judgment of Molloy when he writes, "It is in the tranquillity of decomposition that I remember the long confused emotion which was my life, and that I judge it, as it is said that God will judge me, and with no less impertinence" (p. 25). (And perhaps that, and this, act of judgment is itself inside the stories and, therefore, doomed to affirm the stories even as it calls them into question.)

The assessment must begin with a description of the project— just as Moran's search begins with the story of its "quarry" (p. 110). Next we need to describe in more detail the view about emotions that we have heard in Beckett's voices. We shall find that it is not a view peculiar to the voices but one that has a long philosophical-literary history, and one that is recently reemerging as the dominant view of emotion in philosophy and in social anthropology. This means that we cannot evade its challenge by saying to ourselves that Beckett and his voices have a rather peculiar view of life—which, I think, is the way that Beckett is read and refused, more often than not. Then we shall turn again to the *Molloy* trilogy, looking closely at Beckett's particular stories of narrative emotion; not in the trilogy as a whole, which would be too vast a task, but in its first section, *Molloy*, and especially at that novel's stories of love, guilt, and their relatives hope and fear, and the source of all these in a socially taught religious view of life. Moran writes a story whose aim is, increasingly, the frustration of the reader's emotion, the dismantling of narrative structures that both represent emotions and evoke them. We will consider next this project of ending, asking about its relationship to its own critique. And we can then compare this genealogical critique of stories with two other related philosophical enterprises (those of Lucretius and of Nietzsche) and judge its relevance for our own.

Martha Nussbaum

II

I shall speak here of "the project"; and I shall refer to an explicitly organized and theoretically justified enterprise that goes on the borderline (or refuses to acknowledge that there is one) between philosophy and literature.[2] Nonetheless, I do not mean to say that it is only a specific form of more or less philosophical writing that is called into question here. For the project describes itself as an explicit extension of activities that are implicit in the activity of reading and of thinking reflectively about reading. It claims to be a description of a function (not the only function, but an important one) that narrative fiction has traditionally had in human lives, a function that needs to be mentioned in any explanation of the great human importance we ascribe to narrative fiction.[3] The project stands to this human activity as a descriptive grammar to the use of a native speaker.

The project, even in its explicit form, is not new; in its essentials it is as old, even explicitly, as the debate between the Greek tragic poets and their opponent Plato.[4] It is the project of a dialogue between philosophy and literary analysis in pursuit of the human question, "How should one live?" It takes its bearings from Henry James's claim that the

2. My own work in this area will be collected in *Love's Knowledge: Essays on Philosophy and Literature* (Oxford: Oxford University Press, 1988). Among the essays to appear in this collection are: Martha Nussbaum, "Flawed Crystals: James's *The Golden Bowl* and Literature as Moral Philosophy," *New Literary History* 15 (1983): 25-50; "'Finely Aware and Richly Responsible': Moral Attention and the Moral Task of Literature," *Journal of Philosophy* 82 (1985): 516-529, reprinted in expanded form in *Philosophy and the Question of Literature*, ed. A. Cascardi (Baltimore: Johns Hopkins University Press, 1987); "Perceptive Equilibrium: Literary Theory and Ethical Theory," in *Critical Projections*, ed. Ralph Cohen (London: Methuen, 1987); "Fictions of the Soul," *Philosophy and Literature* 7 (1983): 145-161; "Love's Knowledge," in *Self Deception*, ed. A. Rorty and B. McLaughlin (Berkeley: University of California Press, 1987); "Love and the Individual: Romantic Rightness and Platonic Aspiration," in *Reconstructing Individualism*, ed. M. Sosna et al. (Stanford, Calif: Stanford University Press, 1986). See also my *The Fragility of Goodness: Luck and Ethics in Greek Tragedy and Philosophy* (Cambridge: Cambridge University Press, 1986). Other recent work in this area to which my own thought is especially indebted includes the work of Hilary Putnam; see esp. *Meaning and the Moral Sciences* (London: Routledge & Kegan Paul, 1979), pp. 83-96, and his reply to "Flawed Crystals," "Taking Rules Seriously: A Response to Martha Nussbaum," *New Literary History*, vol. 15 (1983); Stanley Cavell, esp. *The Claim of Reason*, pt. 4 (Oxford: Oxford University Press, 1979); Cora Diamond, esp. "Missing the Adventure," a reply to "'Finely Aware and Richly Responsible,'" abstracted in *Journal of Philosophy*, and "Having a Rough Story about What Moral Philosophy Is," *New Literary History* 15 (1983): 155-170; and Arthur Danto, "Philosophy As/And/Of Literature," *Proceedings and Addresses of the American Philosophical Association* 58 (1984): 5-20.

3. For further remarks on this point, see Nussbaum, "Perceptive Equilibrium"; and Danto, "Philosophy As/And/Of Literature." The linguistic analogy is first used (to my knowledge) by Plato's character Protagoras in the dialogue of that name.

4. See Nussbaum, *The Fragility of Goodness*, and "Perceptive Equilibrium."

novelist's art performs a practical task, the task of assisting us in our pursuit of that question by expressing a "projected morality" and an active "sense of life," and also from Proust's claim that it is only in a text having narrative form that certain essential truths about human life can be appropriately expressed and examined.[5] At its core is the claim that literary form and human content are inseparable: that forms themselves express a content and that the content cannot be prized loose, without change, from the form in which it is expressed. The project joins to this claim another: that literary forms call forth certain specific sorts of practical activity in the reader that can be evoked in no other way; that, as Proust insists, a certain sort of self-scrutiny requires a certain sort of text, namely, a narrative text, for its evocation; or, as Henry James would insist, that we need a story of a certain kind, with characters of a certain type in it, if our own sense of life and of value is to be called forth in the way most appropriate for practical reflection.

The project moves on from these claims to a number of more concrete investigations into the relationship between literary form and practical content. One of its primary aims is to criticize much contemporary work in moral philosophy, on the grounds that this work claims, on the one hand, to assess all of the major available conceptions of human personal and social life, while, on the other hand, it confines itself entirely to forms of writing which, in their abstract and emotionless character, are far better suited to investigating some practical conceptions than others and which call up a correspondingly narrow range of responses and activities in the reader. Nor does this work present arguments justifying its implicit assumption that these responses are the only ones relevant to the task of practical assessment.[6] This critical part of the project is especially (or, one might say, obsessively) interested in a certain sort of practical conception: one that, taking its bearings from Aristotle's norm of practical "perception," emphasizes the human importance of a fine-tuned responsiveness to complex particular cases and of a willingness to see them *as* particular and irreducible to general rules. This conception urges a flexible immersion in the "adventure" of living and a process of practical choice based upon perception and improvisation. It insists, as well, that the correct perception of a practical situation requires emotional as well

5. For further discussion of James's conception of the novelist's task, see Nussbaum, "'Finely Aware and Richly Responsible.'" For discussion of Proust on the task of literary art, see Nussbaum, "Love's Knowledge" and "Fictions of the Soul."

6. These criticisms of contemporary moral philosophy are developed in Nussbaum, *The Fragility of Goodness,* chap. 1, in "Perceptive Equilibrium," and in Martha Nussbaum, "The Discernment of Perception: An Aristotelian Conception of Private and Public Rationality," *Proceedings of the Boston Area Colloquium in Ancient Philosophy* 1 (1985): 151-201, to be reprinted in Nussbaum, *Love's Knowledge.*

as intellectual activity, that the emotions have a valuable informational role to play within the ethical life as forms of recognition.[7] The project now argues that for several reasons this practical conception is most adequately expressed—and, therefore, can be most appropriately scrutinized—in texts that have a complex narrative structure; and that those narratives are also the texts best suited to evoke in the reader the moral activities associated with this conception, in particular emotional activities to which the conception ascribes both cognitive and intrinsic ethical value. The argument is that if moral philosophers (and, in general, people pursuing "wisdom" about the practical) wish to assess fairly and duly this and related conceptions of human life, they will need to include in their study texts that have the appropriate form. If philosophy is a search for wisdom about ourselves, philosophy needs to turn to literature.

The project does not wish to claim that this is the only inquiry into narrative that is of literary interest—or, indeed, the only literary inquiry into narrative that is of human interest. But it does urge vigorously the thought that literary study has too frequently failed to speak about the connectedness of narrative to forms of human emotion and human choice.[8] By insisting that narratives embody forms of human life and desire, and by insisting that certain types of human understanding are irreducibly narrative in form, it calls for a literary discourse that studies the connections between narrative forms and forms of life and also between narrative movement and the desiring activity of the reader of narrative. In this way it links itself to various other postformalist currents in the contemporary study of narrative that are urging us once again to regard narrative as a human structure.[9] This does not mean a return to a simple-minded moralizing criticism of literature that extracts a useful practical content while neglecting subtleties of literary form.[10] For the proposed study of content insists on content's inseparability from form. And the project claims, in fact, that a study of literature that attends to form alone, without asking what human content (what desires, projects, choices) the forms themselves express is, while not without great interest, seriously incomplete.

---

7. See Nussbaum, *The Fragility of Goodness*, chap. 10, and "The Discernment of Perception."

8. A similar argument is made by Danto.

9. For example, Peter Brooks, *Reading for the Plot: Design and Intention in Narrative* (New York: Alfred A. Knopf, 1984); Martin Price, *Forms of Life: Character and the Moral Imagination in the Novel* (New Haven, Conn.: Yale University Press, 1983). In "Perceptive Equilibrium," I discuss, in this connection, work of Lionel Trilling and F. R. Leavis (see esp. Trilling, *The Liberal Imagination* [1957; reprint, New York: Harcourt Brace Jovanovich, 1979] and Leavis, *The Great Tradition* [London: Chatto & Windus, 1948]).

10. See esp. Nussbaum, "Perceptive Equilibrium."

III

The project has spoken about emotions and emotional activity. It has praised the novel for representing emotional responses as valuable sources of information about the practical and as of high practical value themselves, even apart from this informational role. It has also insisted on the ability of narrative to evoke emotional activity in the reader; and it has spoken as if this is an activity valuable, again, both for itself and for its epistemological role. In speaking this way, the project has used, and also argued for,[11] a conception of the major human emotions according to which they are not simply blind surges of affect, stirring, or sensations that arise from our animal nature and are identified (and distinguished from one another) by their felt quality alone. Instead, they themselves have a cognitive content; they are intimately related to beliefs or judgments about the world in such a way that the removal of the relevant belief will remove not only the reason for the emotion but also the emotion itself. The belief is the necessary basis and "ground" of the emotion. It might even be said to be a constituent part of the emotion itself. Anger, for example, is defined by Aristotle, the first great proponent of this view, as a composite of painful feeling with the belief that I have been wronged. This implies (as seems correct) that if I discover that my belief is false — that the apparent wrong did not in fact take place — I will, discarding my false belief, cease to be angry. If some residual painful feeling does persist, it will not be considered anger any longer but, rather, as residual irrational irritation or excitation.[12]

Within this general cognitive picture of emotion, several different accounts are given about the precise relationship between emotion and belief. Some versions make the belief a necessary cause of the emotion but no part of what the emotion is. Some, for example Aristotle's, make the belief one component part of the emotion but hold that it is not, by itself, sufficient for the emotion. (I can believe that I am wronged and yet not be angry.) Some hold that the belief is (whether as external cause or as component part) sufficient for the emotion: if I do not get angry, then I do not really truly accept or believe that I have been wronged. Some, in particular the view of the great Greek Stoic philosopher Chrysippus, who is in my view the most profound thinker on emotion in the entire philosophical tradition, insist that the emotion is itself identical with the full acceptance of, or recognition of, a belief. I

11. Especially in Nussbaum, *The Fragility of Goodness*, chap. 10 and Interlude 2, and "The Discernment of Perception." But this account is developed in more detail in Martha Nussbaum, *The Therapy of Desire*, Martin Classical Lectures (in press).

12. See Nussbaum, *The Fragility of Goodness*, Interlude 2, and *The Therapy of Desire* for extended discussion of this passage.

myself defend this last and strongest cognitive view.[13] But since it is at first sight a rather strange view, it takes detailed argument—in particular, it requires careful unpacking of Chrysippus's notions of recognition and acceptance, or "assent" to a belief—to make it plausible. So I shall not insist upon it here.

What we find in this entire family of cognitive conceptions, however, is a common idea: the idea of the criticism and assessment of emotion. If emotions are not natural stirrings but constructs, if they rest upon beliefs, then they can be modified by a modification of belief. And they can be assessed in the way that beliefs are assessed—as rational or irrational (in respect of their manner of acquisition), as helpful and noxious, even as true and false. If I hastily and uncritically believe a false story that I have been wronged, my anger may be criticized as both irrational and false. And argument can change it, by removing the belief that was both false and irrationally formed.[14]

This idea can be applied at several different levels of specificity: for I might hold on to the very general belief that there are some wrongs that I can suffer through another's agency that would, if they did occur, be grounds for anger, while criticizing particular cases in which my beliefs about wrongs had been false: X did not, in fact, wrong me in that way just now. Moving toward a more general criticism, I might judge that a whole range of cases that I had previously taken to be serious wrongs, and therefore grounds for anger, were not of serious importance after all. For example, by changing my views about the importance of public reputation, I would alter my experience of anger with respect to that class of situations involving slights to reputation. Finally, at a still higher level of generality, I might decide that the whole structure of belief that made that emotion possible was false and/or irrational: for example, I might come to feel that there are in fact no damages that anyone could do to me that would be sufficiently important to be grounds for anger. And the claim of the cognitive view is that if I really truly believe that, I will no longer be angry.

What this picture is claiming is, then, not only an intimate connection between emotion and belief but also, in particular, a connection between the emotions and a certain *sort* of belief, namely beliefs about what is valuable and important.[15] Anger requires the thought that I have

---

13. Nussbaum, "The Stoics on the Extirpation of the Passions," in *The Therapy of Desire*.

14. This is the central theme of Nussbaum, *The Therapy of Desire*, developed in connection with Epicurean, Skeptic, and Stoic therapies.

15. See Nussbaum, *The Fragility of Goodness*, Interlude 2, and *The Therapy of Desire* on the Stoics. This aspect of the cognitive conception of emotion is not, so far as I know, stressed in any of the modern defenses of it.

suffered not trivial but important damages at another's hand. Fear requires the thought that I may possibly suffer serious damages in ways that lie beyond my control. Love requires a high evaluation of its object, grief the thought that what is lost is of serious value. And, we notice, these emotions all require not only beliefs about value but also beliefs about a certain sort of thing: beliefs that things outside of us, things not fully under our own control, have value or importance. Thus if we imagine a person who cares nothing at all for the world outside of him or her, who attaches no importance at all to that which he or she does not fully control, we see that nothing that happens to that person could ever have the power to grieve, or to anger, or to frighten, or to delight. And here we arrive at the most general level of emotion criticism. For now we see that if we really get someone to hold the Stoic belief that no external or uncontrolled item was of any value at all, that person would have (as, indeed, the Stoics insisted) no emotional life at all. We would not want to teach a person this if we think their emotion beliefs are either true or helpful. But if we should believe, with the Stoics, that they are both false and in other ways pernicious, if we believe that a life with emotion beliefs in it is bound to be in certain specifiable ways a life in which we both suffer agony ourselves and do harm to others, then we would have good reason to set about undoing those beliefs. This project of undoing would take different forms in different societies, for each society structures emotion beliefs in certain highly specific ways, and the undoing will have to be correspondingly specific in order to counter the very thoughts that grip us. It is my suggestion that Beckett's voices are engaged in one form of this project of radical undoing.

The criticism of emotion cannot proceed in the same way in which the criticism of, for example, scientific or mathematical beliefs proceeds—by giving the person a logical argument, or fresh perceptual evidence. For the evaluative beliefs that ground our emotional life are not learned in logical arguments either. They are learned through exposure—usually very early and very habitual—to complex social forms of life, in which these beliefs and the related emotions are housed, so to speak, and by which, for the individuals who learn them, they are constructed. A child does not learn its society's conception of love, or of anger, by sitting in an ethics class. It learns them long before any classes, in complex interactions with parents and society. These interactions provide paradigms of emotion and teach the cognitive categories that underlie the experience of emotion. And, since we are all tellers of stories, and since one of the child's most pervasive and powerful ways of learning its society's values and structures is through the stories it hears and learns to tell, stories will be a major source of any culture's emotional life. What fear, or love, *is* will be, for a child—as for Beckett's

225

voices—a construct out of stories, the intersection, the somewhat confused amalgam of those stories. Stories first construct and then evoke (and strengthen) the experience of feeling. So a criticism of emotion must be, prominently, an unwriting of stories.

So much, roughly speaking, is common ground among the major cognitive theories of emotion, from the ancient Greek thinkers through to today's philosophy of psychology and cognitive psychology, the more cognitive parts of psychoanalytic thought, and the various forms of "social construction" theory about emotion that prevail in social anthropology and also in radical social history.[16] (In the case of the last group I am thinking of Foucault, but also of more objectively critical historians of desire, who write, frequently, from a left-wing perspective and stress the possibility of criticism and change in our socially taught distinctions of feelings.)[17] Views vary at this point in many ways: in the degree to which they find the origin of the emotions in early infancy and in the family, as opposed to later social interactions; in the degree to which they find a common cognitive structure across societies or, on the other hand, stress the relativity of emotion to particular social forms; and, finally, in the degree to which they hold that there is available any possibility of change in the structures with which our past has presented us. (For the cognitive conception makes change a logical possibility; but the real availability of change depends on further beliefs about how structures of this sort can be challenged.)

There is a great deal of territory here that needs further exploration; and it is unfortunate that there is very little contact among the different groups who hold views of this type, therefore little synthetic working out of these issues. I cannot even begin to sort them out here in an adequate way, so I shall simply assert what I myself take the status of the current debate (and nondebate) to be, what I myself would be prepared to argue for. It is, that emotions are taught to us by our culture from early infancy, in patterns of interaction between the child and

16. For examples of these different approaches, with extensive bibliography, see Amelie Rorty, ed., *Explaining Emotions* (Berkeley: University of California Press, 1980); for an excellent recent collection of articles on anthropological social-construction views, see R. Harré, ed., The *Social Construction of Emotion* (Oxford: Basil Blackwell, 1986), especially articles by Harré, Armon-Jones, and Averill. In psychoanalytic thought I have been particularly influenced by the work of Melanie Klein: see esp. *Love, Guilt, and Reparation and Other Works, 1921-1945* (London: Hogarth Press, 1985).

17. M. Foucault, *Histoire de la sexualité*, vols. 2 and 3 (Paris: Gallimard, 1984). For an especially lucid presentation of the latter group of views I am indebted to Henry Abelove, "Is Gay History Possible?" (paper delivered at the Brown University Conference on Homosexuality in History and Culture, Providence, R.I.); but there are numerous other historians of desire writing from a similar perspective, e.g., Jeffrey Weeks, *Sex, Politics, and Society: The Regulation of Sexuality since 1800* (London and New York: Longman, 1987).

others, prominently including parents, and later including the wider community. (But parents, as psychoanalytic thought too frequently forgets, already embody and teach the social conception of which they are a part.)[18] This teaching takes highly specific forms in specific cultures. Prominent among the structures that embody and teach these specific forms are a culture's stories. There will be many family resemblances among cultures, since most societies teach schemes of value that support some form of anger, fear, love, grief, and so on by supporting the beliefs about importance, on which, as we argued, these emotions depend. But the ways in which emotions are demarcated, related to one another, and connected with other aspects of life will vary greatly among societies, as will, then, the narrative structures in which they are housed. This concrete social shaping is an essential part of what it is to have an emotion in each case. We could not sufficiently define the emotion in terms of the acceptance of a certain sort of abstract proposition. And if stories are, as Beckett's voices claim, primary vehicles of emotion teaching, then we might say that to have an emotion will be (or will centrally involve) the acceptance of a certain sort of story. This implies that to grasp the full story of the emotional life of an individual or group will require examining the stories it tells itself and the connections among these: understanding, for example, why love, in our first story, is connected in that particular way with frantic anxiety and with the expectation of death; why, in the second, love of a mother is associated with guilt, with a need for atonement that is unsatisfiable, with a feeling of sinfulness and a fear of judgment, with, finally, a certain sort of impossible hope. And if it should be seen that this complex emotional fabric is, in its specific cultural manifestation, in some ways an obstacle to human life, then its criticism will require the criticism not only of abstract propositions but also, above all, of stories (including those stories that dwell in us at an unconscious level), and also of our love of stories, of the patterns of desire, hope, and expectation that are formed and called forth by our experience of reading.

Acceptance of a social constructionist account of the origins and the nature of emotion do not seem to me to imply that we are simply stuck with what we have got, with no possibility for active criticism and change. The depth at which these stories dwell in us is sufficiently great that change is going to be a matter of prolonged therapy, not of one-shot argument. But I see no reason to suppose that we cannot devise

18. But as Melanie Klein insists, anthropologists too frequently ignore similarities in the structure of infantile object-relations across societies (see Melanie Klein, "Postscript" to "Our Adult World and Its Roots in Infancy," in her *Envy, Gratitude, and Other Works, 1946-1963* [London: Hogarth Press, 1984], pp. 247-263).

Martha Nussbaum

therapies capable of altering us, even at the unconscious level. Nor does the view imply that there is no account of human flourishing available to us, as we ask the question of how we ought to live, with reference to which we may appropriately criticize our own social stories. Although this is not often seen by proponents of social constructionist views (especially in anthropology), the diversity of cultural emotion stories in no way implies a complete cultural relativism about the normative values involved in the emotions, any more than in any other case a conflict of beliefs implies the subjectivity of belief. Social constructionist theory makes us face the question of relativism; it does not, by itself, answer it. I think it is plain that individuals are critical and active, as well as passive, in the process of social construction and that frequently they criticize and act out of a view about what is good for the flourishing of human life—either a view that they have found within that society itself narrowly understood, or one that they have discovered elsewhere and made comprehensible to themselves. Marxist versions of social-construction theory insist that we must conduct a criticism of desire with reference to some such notion of human flourishing. I see no reason to suppose that this general approach is doomed and that all such critical projects are merely uncomprehending intrusions upon each culture's own autonomous self-constructive activity.[19]

IV

In one way, the acceptance of this view of emotion gives great support to the philosophical/literary project we have described. For the view makes clear exactly why, and on what basis, we wish to say that the emotions are cognitive and that a process of practical deliberation that omits them leaves out material of rich informational value. It shows us, too, a deeper reason than the project has so far given why *narratives* are essential to the process of practical reflection: not just because they happen to represent and also to evoke emotional activity, but also because their very forms are themselves the sources of emotional structure, the paradigms of what, for us, emotion *is*. This gives us additional reason to say that we could not acquire the rich information we seek by simply adding to abstract theoretical treatises a few examples of emotion and a few emotive appeals: for the whole story of an emotion, in its connections with other emotions and forms of life, requires narrative form for its full development.

19. The issue of the rational "internal" criticism of a culture is discussed in M. Nussbaum and A. K. Sen, "Internal Criticism and Cultural Rationality," in *Relativism*, ed. M. Kraus (Notre Dame: University of Notre Dame Press, 1988).

But in another evident way the acceptance of this view of emotion calls the project into question. For the project has in common with a good deal of work in contemporary moral philosophy a reliance upon intuitive responses to the concrete, prominently including emotional responses, as data of special importance and, so to speak, veracity in giving us a sense of life.[20] It insists with Aristotle that "the discrimination rests with perception" and that "among statements about conduct, those that are universal are more general, but the particular ones are more true—for action is concerned with particulars, and statements must harmonize with these."[21] Its case for the practical ineliminability of stories rests on an idea that the concrete judgments and responses embodied in stories are less likely to lead us astray, in the sense that they will contain what is deepest for us, most truly expressive of our moral sense, and most pertinent to action, by comparison with the abstractness of theory. But once we are reminded that intuitions do not come from nature, or indeed from any special part of ourselves that is more "pure" and more accurate than the place from which our theories and principles emerge, that, indeed, they are learned in a society in much the same way as our other beliefs, we can no longer leave the intuitions, emotions, and stories unsuspected and unquestioned.[22] And indeed, when we reflect that we learn emotion stories when we are less critical and less rationally adept, on the whole, than when we learn our theories, when we reflect that these stories from then on constrain, in many ways of which we are not even aware, our new perceptions and responses—then we see that it would be foolhardy indeed to rely uncritically on the data drawn from our experience of stories and, also, that it will be extremely difficult to find a criticism that is not itself shaped by and expressed in terms of the structures that it purports to criticize. This does not exactly undermine the project, as we shall see, but it tells us not to expect to find in stories a golden age of unsullied ethical purity.

V

"It is in the tranquillity of decomposition that I recall the long confused emotion which was my life, and that I judge it, as it is said that God will

20. See esp. Thomas Nagel, *Mortal Questions* (Cambridge: Cambridge University Press, 1979); and Bernard Williams, *Problems of the Self* (Cambridge: Cambridge University Press, 1973), and *Moral Luck* (Cambridge: Cambridge University Press, 1981).

21. Aristotle, *Nicomachean Ethics* 1107a29-32.

22. Nagel's criticism of Epicurus's position on death seems to me to miss this dimension of Epicurus's critical argument, simply assuming that we can use uncriticized intuition to object to Epicurus's position (see Thomas Nagel, "Death," in *Mortal Questions*).

judge me, and with no less impertinence" (p. 25). Molloy suggests that the emotions are not a discrete episode inside his life story but, rather, the living out of a story that has a certain shape. And in fact his story shares with the story of his double Moran a complex emotional structure in which guilt, fear, disgust, hope, and love do not pop up in isolation from one another, identifiable separately and singly defined. Instead, they emerge as interwoven aspects of a single narrative. The two passages with which we began, and especially the second, give a part of the recipe for this emotional concoction, showing that love does not occur without guilt, the fear of judgment, and the longing for reparation and salvation—and that all attempts to love are watched and judged, as Molloy now judges himself, as God will judge him.

The life story that is Molloy's "long confused emotion" is the story of two journeys: of Molloy's journey back from the outer world to the inside of his mother's room and of agent and detective Moran's journey to find and judge Molloy. Both are stories of progressive disintegration, as the crisp orderly Moran becomes indistinguishable from the prey he quarries and as the bodies of both give way, increasingly, to ludicrous and somewhat revolting weaknesses. This search, which Moran explicitly describes as a search for and through his own insides (p. 113), so that is is more than usually apparent that the story of this novel is the story of emotions, has a geography that informs us about the structure of those insides. Molloy's native country is called Bally. It is the hub of the region of Ballyba (p. 134). Moran, on the other hand, is a native of Turdy, home of the Turdy Madonna, goddess of pregnant married women (p. 173). Another town in the vicinity is Hole. And Moran's son "was capable of hanging about Hole, under God knows what conditions" (p. 143). So Moran travels from Turdy to Ballyba (he never quite reaches Bally) and camps out in the vicinity of Hole. And Molloy, having departed from Bally, ends up inside his mother's room (p. 7)—"her who brought me into the world, through the hole in her arse if my memory is correct. First taste of the shit" (p. 15). So the basic fact in this world, the fact that structures all of its geography, is the fact of the filthiness of conception, the fact that the pregnant married woman is by her act wrapped in shit, and that the new baby, even before it acts or feels, is born into the world through the shit. His entire life is lived, from then on, in shameful proximity to vagina, anus, and balls. Inasmuch as the child is a child born of a woman, he is covered in her filth. Inasmuch as he is a man who feels sexual desire (a resident of Bally), he compounds the transgression. His desire is filthy because of the original filth and also because it is a desire for the mother, who is already seen as covered, herself, in filth. The journey back to the mother's room or womb, which might in one way be a project of atonement, an attempt to cancel the sin of his birth by returning to a fetal condition, is, in the light of the sexual desire that motivates it, a guilty desire for filthy penetration and a compounding of original guilt (". . . that this atonement was in itself a sin, calling for more atonement, and so on, as if there could be anything else but life for the living"). "What business has innocence here?" asks Molloy as he sets out. "What relation to the innumerable spirits of darkness?" (p. 10). Guiltily placed between balls and hole, born through the anus and doomed to return through it, sinning further.

And there is one further fact about the geography of this place. It is all watched—watched by the chief of a vast organization, whose home is at a distance but who gives all journeys their purpose and meaning and who judges them all with an arbitrary and unpredictable (p. 115) combination of paternal care, anger, and furious judgment (p. 162). He likes to use the "prophetic present" tense of actions that the beings under his command will perform (e.g., "Your son goes with you"). And his name is just such a prophetic present: "Youdi," or "You die." Morality is the punishment meted out for universal original transgression. Youdi has a messenger named Gaber (a relative of angel Gabriel), who visits Youdi's "agents" to convey his commands; and even this messenger is watched, not permitted to perform a sexual act without disturbance (p. 94). Youdi's role of judge and assessor is imitated by his agents in their own lives, as they play the role of judge to their women, their children, their own guilty thoughts and desires. The paradigm of Youdi infuses their journeys with purpose; and through membership in the Youdi organization all their movements and actions take on a significance beyond themselves.

We could summarize the emotion story that is Molloy's life by saying that it is the story of original sin, of the fear of God's judgment, and of the vain longing for salvation.[23] This would begin to show us how these voices' experience of fear and love differs from the experience of those emotions in a non-Christian culture; but it would not, being a summary, contain the particular and highly specific learned tonality that makes the Christian world of these people a world of highly concrete and distinct form and feeling, in which the ubiquity of guilt and an anal form of disgust (and humour) color every emotion and perception. We want not only to say that these people feel guilt at original sin; we want to say also that it is guilt at a parental sexual act that is seen as immersing the mother in excrement and causing the birth of

23. A marvelous discussion of these aspects of Beckett's work is in Stanley Cavell, "Ending the Waiting Game," in his *Must We Mean What We Say?* (1969; reprint, Cambridge: Cambridge University Press, 1976).

the child through excrement. Not only that they feel disgust and loathing, but also that their disgust has as its object, above all, the female
body—and their own bodies seen in the aspect of virility and desire,
seen, by extension, as mortal, since mortality is seen itself as the punishment for sexual guilt. Not only that they feel fear, but that it is a fear of
being punished by a supreme being who watches their every feeling,
and a punishment that they more than deserve simply in virtue of existing. Not only that they feel hope, but that it is hope for "succour"
(p. 71) and for a merciful waiving of just punishment (p. 162). And even
this is so far too abstract. What they feel is best given in the concreteness of the sentences of the story.

And love? We cannot tell the story of their love without making
all of these connections and still others. For erotic love, here, lived
around the paradigm scenario of the child's reparative but guilty attempt
to enter his mother's womb, becomes a peculiar, highly specific mixture
of longing for bliss with loathing and disgust, both toward the object
and toward oneself, suffused, always, with the premonition of disaster.
When Molloy recalls his experience of "true love," he thinks first, guiltily, of his mother: "Could a woman have stopped me as I swept towards
mother? Probably. . . . Now men, I have rubbed up against a few men
in my time, but women? Oh well, I may as well confess it now, yes, I
once rubbed up against one. I don't mean my mother, I did more than
rub up against her" (p. 56). The woman met him, he goes on, in a rub-
bish dump, as he was "limply poking about in the garbage saying probably, for at that age I must still have been capable of general ideas, This
is life" (p. 57). Her invitation to him to "know what love was" (p. 57)
is greeted with eagerness, as a salvation. She even at first appears to
have an aperture for lovemaking that is "not the bunghole I had always
imagined, but a slit." But after the act—made pleasureless (or remembered as pleasureless) on account of her ugliness and the "doglike" position she assumed, Molloy is not certain after all that their intercourse
was not anal: "Perhaps after all she put me in her rectum. A matter of
complete indifference to me, I needn't tell you" (p. 57). It is of indifference because genitality is covered in shit, and the vagina, as birth
canal, is just a rectum.

All of this, and more, is a view of love, a view taught by a certain concrete society at a certain point in history. The view forms a seam-
less unity with the society's other views or stories of emotion, with its
cosmology, its shared forms of life. Molloy feels always, in this world,
that he dwells in an "atmosphere of finality without end" (p. 111) and
that he is a "contrivance" of this world, a role-player "playing my parts
through the bitter end" (pp. 114, 122). The substitution of "through the
bitter end" for the expected "through to the bitter end" expresses his

sense that all social parts are played out through filth. All utterance, like birth, is anal.

We have said that this story is a structure of feeling. But we could equally well say that these forms of feeling act themselves out in forms of life, as the characters play out with doomed repetitiveness the paradigm scenarios that their culture and its stories have taught them. The central drama of these two narratives (interweaving with the drama of the search for mother's room) is the plot of the hunt for the guilty one, who is at the same time oneself. For the human being internalizes, as we said, the role of judge and punisher, even as he is aware that his own desires are the object of the punishment. Moran, agent of Youdi, imagines his task:

> There somewhere man is too, vast conglomerate of nature's kingdoms, as lonely and as bound. And in that block the prey is lodged and thinks himself a being apart. Anyone would serve. But I am paid to seek. I arrive, he comes away. His life has been nothing but a waiting for this, to see himself preferred, to fancy himself damned, blessed, to fancy himself everyman, above all others. (Pp. 110-111)

This drama, a detective-adventure story in which the guilty party is "man" and any individual man would do as well as any other, displays the strange mingling of damnation and salvation, fear and hope, that are intrinsic to Moran's story.[24] The story is an expressive structure and, at the same time, a source or paradigm for emotions. And it shows us how our most loved story patterns, prominently including the detective story, express and further nourish the emotions of this world, teaching us to imagine ourselves as hunters after guilt and to long for a final judgment.

In other parts of life the same story is played. "I knew how difficult it was not to do again what you have done before," says Molloy (p. 85). And both he and Moran re-enact, compulsively, their cultural habits, in every relationship. It should be no surprise by now that all relations with women are colored by the longing and loathing that makes Molloy add to the syllable "Ma" the phoneme "-g":

> because for me, without my knowing why, the letter g abolished the syllable Ma, and as it were spat on it, better than any other letter would have done. And at the same time I satisfied a deep and doubtless unacknowledged need, the need to have a Ma, that is a mother, and to proclaim it, audibly. For before you say mag you say ma, inevitably. . . . Besides for me the question did not arise, at the period I'm worming into now, I mean the question of whether to call her Ma, Mag or the Countess Caca. (p. 17)

24. On the plot of the detective story, see Brooks, *Reading for the Plot.*

Nor should it be a surprise that Moran is reminded, in his journey, of "the old joke about the female soul. Question, Have women a soul? Answer, Yes. Question, Why? Answer, In order that they may be damned" (p. 137). Nor is it surprising that the world of nature is itself, in many perceptions, infused with Christian significances: that plants offer Moran "a superfetatory proof of the existence of God" (p. 99), that the earth, in his eyes, is "the earth that lifts itself up, to be approved, before it sets out" (p. 140).

But it is in the most fully developed fictional relationship in the trilogy that the consequences of these repetitions are most vividly seen —namely in Moran's relationship with his son. We first meet the boy as he passes by, "caught up," his father hypothesizes, "in I know not what fantasy of flight and pursuit. I called to him not to dirty himself" (p. 93). From this point on, the relationship plays out the Youdi roles: parental punishment strangely mixed with parental care, love blocked by the need to discipline. Moran's own feeling that "I myself had never been sufficiently chastened" causes him to "go too far when I reprimanded my son, who was consequently a little afraid of me" (p. 95). In consequence, each instinct of affection must be checked by guilty moral resolve: "This sight went straight to my heart, but nevertheless I did my duty" (p. 109; cf. p. 121). Moran's conception of the proper job of father is that it requires, above all, teaching the young human a proper degree of guilt: "I inclined his young mind towards that most fruitful of dispositions, horror of the body and its functions" (p. 118); "I brought him unerringly to a proper sense of his iniquities" (p. 160). And it requires, as well, a vivid disgust at the child, seen as a being similar to oneself: "Did he love me then as much as I loved him? You could never be sure with that little hypocrite" (p. 120). The human communication of the pair is never personal, never direct or directly tender, mediated as it always is by the structures of religion: "And the only walk we regularly took together was that which led us, every Sunday, from home to church, and, mass over, from church to home. Caught up in the slow tide of the faithful my son was not alone with me. But he was part of that docile herd going yet again to thank God for his goodness and to implore his mercy and forgiveness, and then returning, their souls made easy, to other gratifications" (p. 129). That's parental love, and the narrative language it uses, reproducing itself from generation to generation.

VI

Moran's journey is a journey of disintegration and of ending. The Molloy who was seen as a quarry outside him proves to be the disorder and unseemliness within (pp. 113, 115). And his "pilgrimage," which takes him out as far as Ballyba (though not to Bally itself, nor yet to Hole)[25] proves to be, finally, a journey back home to Turdy—a pilgrimage, as he lies, to the Turdy Madonna, goddess of pregnant married women (p. 173). In short, it becomes, increasingly, indistinguishable from Molloy's journey to his own mother's room or womb, his desirous and therefore guilty attempt to pre-exist the sin of his own conception. From the straight, crisp, orderly life that was his at the story's opening, Moran moves increasingly into Molloy's life of inertia and decomposition. He speaks of the "change" from what he was, of a "crumbling, a frenzied collapsing of all that had always protected me from all I was always condemned to be" (p. 148), of his "growing resignation to being dispossessed of self" (p. 149).

In one way, this journey is simply a discovery, within him, of the other side of the social emotions that Moran already inhabited and a working out of their inner logic. For wherever there is a hunter there is a prey. And if the hunter is born and dwells in Turdy he must himself be at the same time the prey; and Youdi's purpose must surely be to judge and punish him (cf. pp. 154, 162) as he judges and punishes the prey; and so, inasmuch as he imitates Youdi's judging activity, this must be his own purpose toward himself. And so the discovery of self as prey and filth and disorder is simply the discovery of self as "man." But man is what he always was, so guilt and fear and the role of prey were always his also.

There is, however, another and more radical collapsing in this story. It appears to be the collapsing of the emotional structure itself, as Moran increasingly distances himself from the entire armature of love, disgust, guilt, and longing, by distancing himself from the religious meanings that have constituted them and the stories that are their primary vehicle. At first the "crumbling" looks just like the reverse side of the earlier judging and seeking. But as Moran goes further on, his project of ending seems to become the project of ending the whole game, of cutting himself off from both of its sides, even at the cost of losing the order on which he has based his life and a great part of himself.[26] When he finds in his thought the "hopes that spring eternal, childish hopes"—hopes of a reconciliation with his son, of a reconciliation with Molloy in the role of father, of a reconciliation, at last, with a Youdi who ceases to be angry and to punish—he does not indulge or nourish the hopes but rejects them in an attempt to empty out his entire spiritual being, cleansing it of these conceptions: "Yes, I let them spring within

25. This may suggest that he is impotent as well as guilty.
26. See Cavell, "Ending the Waiting Game."

me and grow in strength, brighten and charm me with a thousand fancies, and then I swept them away, with a great disgusted sweep of all my being, I swept myself clean of them and surveyed with satisfaction the void they polluted" (p. 162). And now, thinking of his possible punishment at Youdi's hands, Moran simply laughs, shakes with "a mighty fit of laughter" (p. 162).

It is at this point that Moran hears the report of Youdi's words to Gaber, that life is "a thing of beauty . . . and a joy forever" (p. 164); and instead of embracing the sentiment with longing and desire, he asks, with what seems to be a new detachment, a skeptical question: "Do you think he meant human life? . . . Perhaps he didn't mean human life" (p. 165). It is at this point, too, that he speaks a few words to himself "to prepare my soul to make an end" (p. 166). These words include sixteen absurd and abstruse theological questions, whose grim and outrageous humor serves to distance us (Moran and the reader both) from the serious life of the religious view. (Christ never laughed [p. 101].) They also include a prayer that displays, even more vividly, Moran's new distance from religious emotions: "And I recited the pretty quietist Pater, Our Father who art no more in heaven than on earth or in hell, I neither want nor desire that thy name be hallowed, thou knowest best what suits thee. Etc. The middle and the end are very pretty" (p. 167). The narrative is progressing in the direction not of any conventional happy or unhappy ending but of a more radical breaking down of religious significances and religious desire.

Increasingly at this period Moran's thoughts turn to his bees, as to creatures whose lives are not "polluted" by religious meanings. Their dances seem to him to display a "different way" from human communication, for they have a complex and discernible form, they can be studied, and yet (unlike human agency under God's eye) they have no significance—or, if a significance, then an alien one, "too noble ever to be sullied by the cogitations of a man like me, exiled in his manhood" (p. 169). He considers the life of the bees to be a life apart from the life of emotions and his own relation to the bees to be the one relation in his life that is not mediated by emotion and the other infirmities of the flesh: "And I would never do my bees the wrong I had done my God, to whom I had been taught to ascribe my angers, fears, desires, and even my body" (p. 169).

And increasingly Moran gives indications that this new and radical attitude to religious emotion requires a new attitude to literature and the writing of literature and a new attitude to the relationship between writer and reader. We might say that in the old narratorial relationship the writer is, for the reader, God the father: the one who makes things mean, the one who makes the world, the one who evokes and structures the reader's emotions of delight and longing and guilt and fear. In Moran's detective story, the writer is the one who manipulates the reader's desire to seek and condemn, to track and judge the guilty prey. So increasingly, as he distances himself from Youdi and from that fear and longing, Moran refuses the task of the narrator and refuses us the emotions of the reader. He calls his life an "inenarable contraption" (p. 114), reminding us of the simplifications and refusals imposed by narration. Shortly after this, he identifies himself as the author of this entire novel and of Beckett's other novels—but he tells us that, this time, novel writing will not take place: "Oh the stories I could tell you, if I were easy. What a rabble in my head, what a gallery of moribunds. Murphy, Watt, Yerk, Mercier and all the others. . . . Stories, stories. I have not been able to tell them. I shall not be able to tell this one" (p. 137). In such moments he seems to echo Molloy's expression of frustration with the ongoing and unending character of the stories: "For if you set out to mention everything you would never be done, and that's what counts, to be done, to have done" (p. 41). But whereas Molloy considered that goal unachievable and hoped, at most, for a "change of muck, to move from one heap to another a little further on" (p. 41), Moran seems to believe that narration will not take place any more, that it is all ending, that he is ending it all.

And often he finds himself on the verge of the old literary games, writing so as to arouse our narratological desire—and he turns away from that activity with firm resolve. "I'll tell you. No, I'll tell you nothing. Nothing" (p. 134). Introducing a new character, he balks at the narrator's task of rich description, one of the primary strategies used by an author to summon up our interest in a character who will then hunt, or be hunted, or love, or be filthy, or all of these. "I shall have to describe him briefly, though such a thing is contrary to my principles" (p. 150). Twice he politely refuses us what we would have wanted from his story, as if literature would be his, and our, weakness, and the time is now too late for backward movement: "I am sorry I cannot indicate more clearly how this result was obtained, it would have been something worth reading. But it is not at this late stage of my relation that I intend to give way to literature" (p. 151). "I would have described them once, not now, I am sorry, it would have been worth reading" (p. 166). And even as he frustrates and destructures our desire, he achieves an ending to his own narrative longing. Refusing the opportunity to tell of adventures (obstacles, fiends, misdemeanors, disintegrations) on the road to Ballyba, he comments: "It was my intention, almost my desire, to tell of all these things, I rejoiced at the thought that the moment would come when I might do so. Now the intention is dead, the moment is come and the desire is gone" (p. 159). He even wonders whether he is beyond thinking and conceiving altogether (p. 165). But whatever awaits him, what is "certain" is that it will not "be known," will not be in any story (p. 172). His talk of preparing his "soul to make an end" (p. 166) and his announcement, "Now I may make an end" (p. 174) refer, perhaps, to the end of this written story. But, beyond this, they point to the end of storying, the end of the forms of life taught and lived in stories.

Moran's narrative ends where it began, in the garden of his home. But this ending seems to confirm our view that a great change has taken place and that a new life is beginning:

> My birds had not been killed. They were wild birds. And yet quite trusting. I recognized them and they seemed to recognize me. But one never knows. Some were missing and some were new. I tried to understand their language better. Without having recourse to mine. They were the longest, loveliest days of all the year. I lived in the garden. I have spoken of a voice telling me things. I was getting to know it better now, to understand what it wanted. I did not use the words that Moran had been taught when he was little and that he in his turn had taught to his little one. So that at first I did not know what it wanted. But in the end I understood this language. I understood it, I understood it all wrong perhaps. That is not what matters. It told me to write the report. Does this mean I am freer now than I was? I do not know. I shall learn. Then I went back into the house and wrote, It is midnight. The rain is beating on the windows. It was not midnight. It was not raining. (Pp. 175-76)

We seem to see here a clearing beyond disgust and guilt, an acceptance of nature and body that does not ask them to be redeemed by any beyond, a relation with living beings that no longer requires to be mediated by religious emotions or even by the language in which they are constructed. With the refusal of human language we seem to have broken the chain by which the "long confused emotion" perpetuates itself, father to son. Even Moran's indifference to questions of meaning and understanding seems to be the happy discovery that the world does not need to be interpreted, it can simply be lived in, accepted, trusted as the birds trust. He lives in the garden, a part of nature, no longer hunting, no longer hunted.

Beckett alludes, in this ending, to two powerful stories of anti-religious salvation; and these allusions strengthen our conviction that the constraints of religious emotion really have been transcended. The ending in the garden refers, most obviously, to the conclusion of Voltaire's *Candide,* in which the return home to one's own and the choice *cultiver son jardin* represents the overthrow of the Leibnizian search for a religious meaning in all events, and a decision to live in the world as in a chancy arbitrary place made partially habitable by the decency of friendship. But Beckett's and Voltaire's gardens have, as well, an earlier reference: to the Garden of Epicurus, in which pupils learned, by a patient therapeutic criticism of the emotions that society had taught them, to live a life free from religious fear and longing, and the love that is based upon these.[27] Epicurus's doctrine that the root cause of human unhappiness lies in our desires and emotions and that these bad desires are "empty" social constructs, erected by convention and capable of being dismantled by opposite habits, is the doctrine about emotion that is being worked out in this book as a whole; so it is not really surprising that the ending to Moran's story should have this Epicurean setting. Even Beckett's interest in animals parallels that of Epicurus (and Lucretius): animals have forms of life apart from the pollution of religion; they show us what it could be to be alive without hope or fear or disgust or even love.

But for Epicurus, Lucretius, and Voltaire, the garden really is a place of happiness, an oasis of human acceptance in a casual and violent universe. Does Moran's story have a similarly happy ending, even to this limited extent? And if it did have one, if in this way it did fulfill our readerly longing, wouldn't that itself imply that what we have just been saying about the end of storytelling has been in part false? A happy end state is precisely what the reader's old emotions deeply desire: a salvation, a redemption. So if this is what we are getting here, then, ironically, it really is not what we are getting. We can be redeemed only by ending the demand for redemption, by ceasing to use the concept of redemption. Beckett's anti-narrative is too many-sided, too ironic, to leave us with any simple comfort. He makes us call the new turn into question from its inception, making us ask ourselves whether this project of bringing hope and the other emotions to an end is not itself a project that lies securely in the grip of the old emotions, a project born of disgust, straining toward salvation. Remember that when Moran swept away his hopes, he did so "with a great disgusted sweep of all my being" (p. 162). His ensuing laughter at Youdi is indistinguishable, in its violent shaking, from fear: "strange laughter truly, and no doubt misnamed" (p. 162). The list of mocking theological questions is followed by a list of personal questions that ask about the salvation, in heaven, not only of Moran and his family but also of the author's other characters in other novels (pp. 1567- 68). It begins to look as if the new movement of ending is motivated, like the old, by guilt. The only difference is that previously the disgust was directed at only a certain aspect of the self—the

---

27. See Nussbaum, *The Therapy of Desire,* and also Martha Nussbaum, "Therapeutic Arguments: Epicurus and Aristotle," in *The Norms of Nature,* ed. M. Schofield and G. Striker (Cambridge: Cambridge University Press, 1986), pp. 31-74.

bodily, born-of-woman aspect—whereas now it moves, so to speak, one level up and takes as its target Moran's whole being as a social "contrivance," including, and especially, his emotions of guilt and disgust. This second-order disgust, and the corresponding second-order longing (for a redemption from the longing for redemption) are the structures that organize Moran's homeward journey. Even his search for ending is a preparation of the soul (p. 166), a preparation, presumably, for final judgment.

We are forbidden by such indications to have the comfortable thought that something happy and liberating and conclusive is happening here. And when we notice that things are not happy and conclusive, we notice in ourselves yet a third level of disgust: disgust at the disgust with human disgust that motivates Moran's search for ending and keeps him always within the constraints that this search opposes. But then, of course, we are likely to notice that that reaction is, as well, a part of the same old trap: for it sets our desires rushing off to imagine what would be a *real* happy ending. And that's itself a defect calling for more judgment. "Atonement was in itself a sin, calling for more atonement, and so on, as if there could be anything but life for the living."

And Moran's writing? The fiction that he is putting an end to fictions is, we are informed in the end, an artfully constructed fiction of his own, commanded as a penance (p. 133), executed under orders from a strange voice (p. 131). So—once again—it is encased within the very structures it opposes, and it announces as much with relish, confessing, in the end, to its own fictionality and making us see that this assault on stories is just another story. Only, perhaps, one in which the prey is stories themselves and their structures of desire, the hunter our readerly judgment upon the lying character of stories, and the judgment our aggressive and disgusted lashing out at the disgust and guilt that hold us. Its acts of confessing and judging, though directed at the whole apparatus of confession and judgment, are nonetheless the same old religious acts and are no less violent, no less constraining, than the original first-order confession concerning the filth of the body. More damning, really, since we might have thought that it was the word that was going to be our salvation.

What it comes to is that you can't go beyond writing, if writing is what you are in fact doing. You are, apparently, stuck with "the convention that demands you either lie or hold your peace" (p. 88). Perhaps a bee dance, or Moran's birds, would be truly beyond disgust and guilt—*but*—that song and dance are not what we readers of literature desire, for they would not express *us*, as we have been contrived. We have learned our lesson so thoroughly that we cannot depart from it, even to end it. We go on telling stories in the only way we know; and on the other side, if anything, is only a silence. But we feel that if our death and its silence did come at last, they would probably come, like Malone's, inside a story of our own telling. And the weapon of aggression might be, indifferently, a hammer, a stick, a fist, a thought, a dream, or a pencil (p. 288).

VII

This attack on religious desire has ancestors. Two of them are Lucretius and Nietzsche. For both Epicurus's great poet-pupil and the evangelist of God's death believed that a religious view of the world had deeply poisoned human desires in their time, constructing deformed patterns of fear and longing. Both believed, too, that certain influential art forms were powerful accomplices of religious longing and that a successful attack on religion required the undoing of these forms. And yet neither ended by embracing silence. Both, indeed, imagined a fruitful life for human beings beyond religious expectation, and both constructed forms of writing that seemed to them appropriate for that more fruitful life, or at least for the movement toward it. Perhaps the pursuit of this difference of ending, so to speak, will help us to see where we have been and whether we had to go there.

Lucretius, following Epicurus's teaching, held that a great part of human desire and emotion is "empty": built upon beliefs that are both socially taught and false, beliefs that express, for the most part, the aim of a religious elite to gain power over humans by making them unhappy and disgusted with the merely human in life. Central to this religious project is a teaching about death that engenders fear and loathing, along with the passionate longing for immortal life. And it was Lucretius's view that most of our other emotions—including the anger that motivates war and the erotic love that seeks personal salvation through fusion with a "goddess"—were disguised forms of this religious fear and longing. These forms of feeling are perpetuated in poetry, especially in the poetry of mourning and in erotic love poetry. So an attack on these socially constructed emotions requires an attack on those poetic forms. In his own poetry, Lucretius pursues the attack, through satire and scathing negative argument.[28]

Yet Lucretius believed that there were many human desires and motivations that were not pernicious in this way. There were the natural desires of the body; there was a human being's natural love of the use

---

28. This account of Lucretius is developed in detail in Nussbaum, *The Therapy of Desire.*

of reason; and, finally, there were some learned but still fruitful desires, such as the desire for friendship and the sense of justice—all of which could be tapped in order to construct a fruitful human life on the other side of religion. He believed that one could imagine this life and even describe it in writing. And he seems to have believed that even though some of the desires that motivate writing are the same ones that his argument attacks—longing for immortality, erotic love, anger at one's finitude—still, this was not true of all writerly motivations. For example, there is a "pure" desire to give and receive pleasure that stands apart; a desire, as well, for social justice and peace, a desire for fruitfulness. So even though his writing had to attack many of the forms of writing common in his time, including most actual poetry, still it did not have to tear all writing down, and it did not need to subvert itself. There is a therapeutic discourse that can be housed in verse, albeit very unusual verse, that will give pleasure to the reader without falling under its own critique. Perhaps even on the other side of therapy—though this is less clear—there is something for writing to do and to be: a source of pleasure, a bond of friendship.

Nietzsche had a still more pessimistic view about the extent to which existing patterns of feeling in his time were the product of religious teaching. Nineteen hundred years of Christianity have, he believes, made a tremendous difference in human self-conceptions. Now the human being is so radically alienated from natural bodily humanity, so thoroughly immersed in longing for a happy ending in another world, by contrast to which this one is seen as poor and loathsome, that the removal of religious hope creates a crisis of nihilism. Religious teleological patterns of desire are so deep in us, the horror of the body is so deep in us, that it is not clear that there is any vivid life in us that is not made in religion's image, nothing, therefore, to motivate us to construct a new life after its demise.[29] The threat of nihilism is the prospect of the collapse of the will, the refusal to continue ordering and valuing.

And yet Nietzsche did hold out hope for a human life beyond nihilism. And he believed his task as a writer to be the creation of that hope as a vivid possibility. The first step in the creative task must be negative: the thorough, detailed dismantling of religious beliefs and teleological desires through the techniques of debunking genealogy, mordant satire, horrific projection. But even this negative movement in Nietzsche's writing contains, already, a positive side: images of human strength and "virtue," and, in its portrait of the ancient Greeks, the image

---

29. A fine discussion of this element in Nietzsche's work is in Henri Birault, "Beatitude in Nietzsche," in *The New Nietzsche*, ed. David Allison (Cambridge, Mass.: MIT Press, 1985).

of an entire people who lived, and felt, without fear. And beyond the "nay-saying" stage of the spirit, Nietzsche foresaw, and held out as a possibility, a joyful affirmative life for the spirit and the body together, a life truly beyond the constraining oppositions of disgust and awe, loathing and longing. And although most actual poets and artists are criticized as valets of conventional religion—even Goethe is in the end found lacking, a captive of the quest for beatitude—Nietzsche clearly believed, as well, that art, including music and dance and including as well the art of the philosopher-poet, had a central positive role to play in restoring man to himself and to the earth. This writing has to struggle against being inspired, and limited, by the desires of its own time; even Zarathustra longs for a contented end-state and yearns to throw off his burdens. But this temptation is one that the writer can overcome in himself and still find speech and creation. "Do I aspire to *happiness?*" says Zarathustra joyfully at last. "I aspire to *works.*" [30]

VIII

Beckett is a member of this therapeutic company. But his pessimism (or that of his voices) denies a possibility that they hold open. We need to understand this denial more deeply if we are to see, finally, where we are. One thing that becomes very clear, as we read these novels, is that we are hearing, in the end, but a single human voice, not the conversation of diverse human voices with diverse structures of feeling. Beckett emphasizes this fact, by identifying Moran with the author of his other novels.[31] And the solipsism of this voice's sense of life is so total that we get no sense of the distinctive shape of any other lives in this world. An implicit claim is made by these voices to be the whole world, to be telling the way the world is as they tell about themselves. But is there any reason to suppose that this one life is, in that way, representative? To speak rather bluntly, even if Christian emotion of this particularly sterile form does so deeply infuse *some* lives in some parts of the world, that for those people there is no emotion and no writing beyond it, have we any reason to think this true for us all, or an undermining of the emotional lives of us all? This question arises naturally if one reads Beckett side by side with one of his own great heroes, Proust,

30. Friedrich Nietzsche, *Thus Spoke Zarathustra*, pt. 4, "The Sign," my translation. (W. Kaufmann's version uses "work" for *Werke,* which does not adequately convey Zarathustra's emphasis on creation. See Kaufmann, *Nietzsche: Philosopher, Psychologist, Antichrist,* 4th ed. [Princeton, N.J.: Princeton University Press, 1975].)

31. See also p. 412, where the unnamed voice proves to be the author of all the trilogy's stories.

and even more so if one at the same time reads other great novelists whose work Beckett would, in his youth, have read, such as Henry James or Virginia Woolf. For in none of these writers does one find that religion plays a role of paramount importance; nor is religion's disgust with the body a major source of emotional life. Whatever problems they find with our emotions and their social construction, these problems do not generate Beckett's nihilism and his search for silence. Is this simply because they have failed to see something about our society that Beckett sees more clearly? Or isn't it, instead, because in the lives they depict and the sense of life they express, these problems really are not central? Not all persuasive voices speak Moran's language.

Along with an absence of human diversity, we find in Beckett, as well, an absence of human *activity* that seems foreign to our experience of emotional development, even at the cultural and social level. Beckett's people are heirs of a legacy of feeling that shapes them inexorably. They cannot help being shaped in this way, and they feel like "contrivances," like machines programmed entirely from without: "You think you are inventing, and all you do is stammer out your lesson, the remnants of a pensum one day got by heart and long forgotten" (p. 31). They are made, and the only thing they make is a child in their own image. This is not a convincing picture either of an individual child's development or of a society's evolution. Children actively select and interpret; and the society around them contains a plurality of active voices, striving to persuade us in new directions. And persuasion, not just manipulation, is at least a part of what explains those changes. The point about diversity and the point about activity seem connected: for it is in part because Beckett sees society as single and monolithic that he is able to omit the presence of argument, criticism, and change. In all this we sense, I believe, a deeply religious sensibility at work; for we have at all times the sense that mere human beings are powerless to make, on account of the fact that there is something very much more powerful in this universe that does all the making. We are at best its *agents;* and that is why we cannot *act.*

Beckett has shown us how the desires engendered by narrative are responses to our sense of finitude, our powerlessness. Hope, fear, passionate longing, all are bound up with our feeling that the world eludes our control and that cherished things out in the world are not governed by our will. But we could agree with this general analysis of the relationship between emotion and finitude—indeed, we did agree with this in our general account of emotion (Sec. III above)—without conceding that this sense of finitude, and our emotional responses to it, are themselves necessarily suffused with a sense of *guilt* and of *disgust.* There is a peculiar movement in Beckett's talk of emotions—which we notice even in our first two passages—from a perception of human limits to a loathing of the limited, from grief to disgust and hatred, from the tragedy and comedy of the frail body to rage at the body, seen as covered in excrement. It is as if Beckett believes that the finite and frail can only inspire our disgust and loathing—that life (in the word of Youdi) can be "a thing of beauty and joy" only if it is "forever." And this is because, as we said, mortality in Beckett's world is seen not as our neutral and natural condition but as our punishment for original sin.[32] The complete absence in this writing of any joy in the limited and finite indicates to us that the narrative as a whole is an expression of a religious view of life. Lucretius and Nietzsche stand apart from what they condemn. They have a separate and uncorrupted sense of pleasure and of value; and because of this they can see how a finite life can have its own peculiar splendor. Beckett's narrative does not see this. But then his assault on narrative does not remove from us the possibility of another sort of narrative: one whose structures express the beauty of that which is human and fragile and call forth in us a love of that beauty and the limits that constitute it.

Finally, we notice in this narrative one further religious prejudice: the prejudice against that which is made in society and in favor of the pure soul, the soul before and apart from all social constructing. For it is not only the specific forms of socially constructed desire that inspire loathing in Beckett's voices. It is also the whole idea of social construction itself, the whole idea that a group can tell me who and what I am to be and to feel. These reflections are most fully developed in *The Unnamable*, with its attacks on the "pupil Mahood," who thinks and feels as he has been taught to do and who has, therefore, only a species language, only species feelings, who can never, in virtue of this, say or even think *himself*. But this line of reflection is present throughout the trilogy, beneath its loathing of specific social forms, and it contributes powerfully to the novels' despairing message.

But, we might ask, why is it that these voices are so intolerant of society and of shared forms of thought and feeling? Why aren't they willing to allow that the common to all might be and say themselves? Isn't it, really, because they are in the grip of a longing for pure soul, hard as a diamond, individual and indivisible, coming forth from its maker's hand with its identity already stamped upon it? Don't they reject shared language because they long for a pure language of the soul itself by itself and for pure relationships among souls that will be in no

32. Compare the illuminating remarks about the difference between Lucretius and Dante in George Santayana, *Three Philosophical Poets* (Cambridge, Mass.: Harvard University Press, 1910).

way mediated by the contingent structures of human social life? Everywhere the voices turn, they find the group and its history. They cannot go beyond that. But this is a tragedy for them only because they are gripped by the conviction that nothing man-made and contingent could ever stand for them. Their very despair gives evidence of their deep religiosity. They have not been able to go far enough outside the Christian picture to see how to pose the problem of self-expression in a way that is not shaped by that picture. If they could get that far outside, they might discover that it is no disgrace to be a political animal, that the fact that human language is not available either to beasts or to gods is no point against it.

IX

The project, and related projects, have several important lessons to learn from Beckett's voices, despite these criticisms. First, it must always bear in mind that the emotions, if they are cognitive and therefore useful sources of information concerning human values, are also, by the same token, subject to social manipulation. This, as I said, does not imply a relativism in which no construct is better than any other, any more than the fact that different societies teach different beliefs implies that they are all equally true. But it does mean that the issue of social origin must be squarely faced with emotions as with beliefs, that emotions do not give us a bedrock of reliable "natural" evidence that stands apart from what society makes. It means that with emotions as well as with beliefs, the social and also psychogenetic origins must be carefully investigated, before we are entitled to draw any conclusions about their role in human life. And before any normative conclusions can be drawn about what is or is not conducive to human flourishing, the issue of relativism must be confronted. The project, in short, must look at social history, and not without a critical eye.

We need to bear in mind, as well, that narratives contain emotions in their very structure; so their form stands in need of the same sort of scrutiny that we give to emotions represented within it. Narrative is not unshaped human life; indeed, human life is not either. Narratives are constructs that respond to certain patterns of living and shape them in their turn. So we must always ask what content the literary forms themselves express, what structures of desire they represent and evoke.

This means, where the assessment of abstract principles and theories is concerned, that we must not treat the literary "evidence" as Baconian observation data that any good theory must fit. Instead, we will see both principles and stories as different sorts of theories or views about life; and in the case of a discrepancy we would not always give priority to the story and its emotions. The whole enterprise of examining our sense of life should be holistic: frequently we will reject an abstract theoretical account for being at odds with the concrete perceptions of life and feeling embodied in literary forms; but sometimes, too, we may criticize a story by setting it beside a theoretical account—if we decide that the latter includes more of what we want to preserve. There is no Archimedean point that we can occupy as we do this; and there is no hard-and-fast rule as to how this will be done.[33] But our reflection about the depth of Christian feeling in the construction of our narrative forms suggests, at the least, that we should keep strongly alive the theoretical and critical side of the enterprise and subject the emotions to rational scrutiny.

Finally, we need to consider, as Beckett forces us to consider, that the choice to write at all expresses, itself, a content, that, therefore, if we really wish to examine all the attitudes toward human life and its value, we cannot simply examine the contrasting forms of writing. We must ask as well, if we can, along with Beckett's voices, exactly what writing itself *is* in human life; how it is related to the ambition to control and order, and also therefore, perhaps, to a certain discontent with or even a hatred of human life as it is lived; how it might displace both writer and reader from a loving acceptance of the world. We have so far spoken as if writing could express all the human forms of feeling, in its own many forms. But writing is itself a choice, an act, and not a neutral act either. It is opposed to other forms of action or passion: to listening, to waiting, to keeping silent.[34] And so its forms of feeling may be similarly confined, opposed to other forms. In *The Unnamable,* the voice perceives itself as "shut up" inside a wall of words, constrained by its own speaking. And "the silence is outside, outside . . . nothing but this voice and the silence all round." And the thought of silence is linked with the thought of freedom (p. 409); a freedom, perhaps, from both making and being made.

And even that thought, the voice realizes, is uttered in the old language, the language of stories, of progress, of hope and happy endings. It is not silent enough to accept being as it is. In the end, he imagines that he might live a different story and that words have taken him only to the "threshold of my story, before the door that opens on

---

33. On this (with reference to Rawls), see Nussbaum, "Perceptive Equilibrium."

34. It is opposed, as well, of course, to speaking orally; but Beckett's voices do not seem to make a significant distinction between storytelling and story writing. In any more extended treatment of this matter, however, the difference between writing and speaking would have to be considered.

my story" (p. 414). And if that door opens, "it will be the silence" (p. 414), and the end of knowing and conceiving, and the end of writing and speaking; and that silence would be the only exit from a life of writing, the only story that ends stories. (And isn't that thought of ending itself an ending, in the old style?) These things, too, we must consider as we go on (as we must, as he must) using the words that are all we have to say ourselves.

And what emotion, if any, does the silence itself express? Could there be a form of love in the silence, in the act of not structuring, not writing? Or perhaps an absence of emotion, of story construction, that is itself more loving still than love has ever been? This, too, must be considered in any writing on this topic, although the act of writing obscures it as a possibility.

III: NARRATIVE'S THEOLOGICAL SIGNIFICANCE

A Short Apology of Narrative

Johann Baptist Metz

Translated by David Smith

Contemporary theological dictionaries are in some ways unreliable because they leave out so much—for example, the word "story" or "narrative." Harald Weinrich has shown in his contribution to this number of *Concilium* what a serious gap in theological understanding is revealed by this absence. I should like, in this article, to write a short apology of narrative, especially since the category of "dangerous memory," which I used in a previous article in *Concilium*[1] to throw light on the understanding of Christian faith in our present situation, clearly has a narrative structure.[2]

I cannot hope to deal systematically or fully here with the theological theme of narrative, but can only mention a number of different and significant points.[3] I have not attempted a linguistic analysis, partly be-

---

1. "The Future in the Memory of Suffering," *Concilium*, American ed., 76 (June 1972).

2. I have discussed this in greater detail in my article "Erinnerung," in H. Krings, H. M. Baumgartner and C. Wild, eds., *Handbüch Philosophischer Grundebegriffe*, vol. I (Munich, 1973).

3. I have dealt with the significance of a memorative and narrative soteriology for the central theme of the history of redemption and freedom in "Erlösung und Emanzipation," *Stimmen der Zeit*, 98 (1973).

Johann Baptist Metz, "A Short Apology of Narrative," *Concilium*, 85 (1973): 84-96.

cause I am simply not competent to do so, and also because it is not theologically relevant to incorporate the narrative potential of Christianity into a linguistic theory (in order to close it as a form of pre-scientific communication). An even more important reason is that narrative processes have to be protected, interrupted in order to justify them critically and even guided in the direction of a competent narrative without allowing the experience of faith to be silenced like every original experience.

I. Narrative and Experience

"However familiar we may be with the name, the narrator is not present for us, alive and active. Not only is he remote from us—he is always becoming more remote. It is as though an apparently inalienable and assured ability had been taken away from us. This is the ability to exchange experiences."[4] The atrophy of narrative is particularly dangerous in theology. If the category of narrative is lost or outlawed by theology as pre-critical, then real or original experiences of faith may come to lack objectivity and become silenced, and all linguistic expressions of faith may therefore be seen as categorical objectivizations or as changing symbols of what cannot be said. In this way, the experience of faith will become vague and its content will be preserved only in ritual and dogmatic language, without the narrative form showing any power to exchange experience.

Theology is above all concerned with direct experiences expressed in narrative language. This is clear throughout Scripture, from the beginning, the story of creation, to the end, where a vision of the new heaven and the new earth is revealed. All this is disclosed in narrative. The world created from nothing, man made from the dust, the new kingdom proclaimed by Jesus, himself the new man, resurrection as a passage through death to life, the end as a new beginning, the life of future glory—all these show that reasoning is not the original form of theological expression, which is above all that of narrative. The Logos of theology, so long as it conceals its own narrative form, is as embarrassed by them as reason is by questions concerning the beginning and the end and the destiny of what is new and has never yet been. The question about the beginning, the *arche*, which enabled the Greeks with their Logos to break the spell of pure narrative in myth, leads thought straight back to narrative. The beginning and the end can only be discussed in narrative form—Kant was aware of this when he spoke of the "rhapsodic beginning of thought" which was not open to argumenta-

---

4. W. Benjamin, "Der Erzähler," *Illuminationen* (Frankfurt, 1961), p. 409.

tive reconstruction. Above all, what is new and has never yet been can only be introduced in narrative. As Adorno has observed in the closing passages of his *Minima Moralia,* if reason is closed to the narrative exchange of experiences of what is new and completely breaks off that exchange for the sake of its own critical nature and its autonomy, it will inevitably exhaust itself in reconstructions and become no more than a technique. This question will be discussed more fully in Sections IV and V below.

II. The Practical and Performative Aspect of Narrative

There are examples of narrative traditions which resist the influence of our supposedly post-narrative age — for instance, the Hassidic stories, Johann Peter Hebel's or Bertolt Brecht's "calendar" stories, or the "traces," or Ernst Bloch, whose main work, *Das Prinzip Hoffnung,* reads like a great encyclopedia of "hope" stories. They all illustrate the practical character of such narratives, their communication of an experience, and the close involvement of the narrator and the listener in the experience narrated. "Most story-tellers pursue a practical interest. . . . This is indicative of the distinctive nature of all true stories, all of which have an overt or hidden use—a moral, a practical instruction, a rule of life. In every case, the story-teller is a man who knows what to do with the listener. . . . His stories are based on experience, either his own or other people's which he transforms into the experience of those who listen to his stories."[5]

Martin Buber has reaffirmed this characteristic in his introduction to the Hassidic stories and has also drawn attention to other important features of narrative form: "The story is itself an event and has the quality of a sacred action. . . . It is more than a reflection—the sacred essence to which it bears witness continues to live in it. The wonder that is narrated becomes powerful once more. . . . A rabbi, whose grandfather had been a pupil of Baal Shem Tov, was once asked to tell a story. 'A story ought to be told,' he said, 'so that it is itself a help,' and his story was this. 'My grandfather was paralysed. Once he was asked to tell a story about his teacher and he told how the holy Baal Shem Tov used to jump and dance when he was praying. My grandfather stood up while he was telling the story and the story carried him away so much that he had to jump and dance to show how the master had done it. From that moment, he was healed. This is how stories ought to be told.'"[6]

5. W. Benjamin, *op. cit.,* pp. 412ff.
6. M. Buber, *Werke III* (Munich, 1963), p. 71.

This text is remarkable for two reasons. In the first place, it is a successful example in a critical, post-narrative age of how narrative teaching can be linked with narrative self-enlightenment about the very interest which underlies the narrative process. In this case, the story is not ideologically unconscious of the interest that governs it. It presents this interest and "tries it out" in the narrative process. It verifies or falsifies itself and does not simply leave this to discussion about the story, which lies outside the narrative process. This is, in my opinion, a very important aspect of the narrative form which cannot, unfortunately, be pursued further here.

In the second place, Buber's text points to an inner relationship between story and sacrament, in other words, to the story as an effective sign and to the narrative aspect of the sacrament as a sign. The sacramental sign can easily be characterized as a "linguistic action" in which the unity of the story as an effective word and as practical effect is expressed in the same process. The aspect of ceremony and ritual may perhaps mean that the sacrament is not clearly recognized as a saving narrative. On closer inspection, however, it is evident firstly that the linguistic formulae used in the administration of the sacraments are typical examples of what are known as "performative" expressions,[7] and secondly that they narrate something. The story form occurs, for instance, in the eucharistic prayer ("on the night that he was betrayed . . ."), and the formula of the sacrament of penance is incorporated within the framework of a narrative action.

I am convinced that it is very important to bring out this narrative aspect of the sacrament more clearly. If this is done, the relationship between word and sacrament may be more fully elaborated theologically. Above all, it should also be possible to relate the sacramental action more closely to stories of life and suffering and to reveal it as a saving narrative.

III. The Pastoral and Social Aspect of Narrative

Marginal groups and religious sects are always active in society and it would be wrong for the churches *a priori* to silence or reject their disturbing message. Although the underlying ambiguity of the Jesus People, for example, prevents us from accepting them uncritically as providing the best chance of Christian renewal, they have one very positive merit—they and others employ, not argument and reasoning, but narrative. They tell the story of their conversion and retell

---

7. See J. L. Austin, *How to Do Things with Words* (Cambridge, Mass., 1962).

biblical stories, sometimes in a patently helpless way that is open to manipulation. Is this simply a sign of spiritual regression, of the danger of archaism or infantilism in the religious life, or emotional, pseudo-religious enthusiasm, or of an arbitrary and contemptuous rejection of serious theological reasoning? Or is it rather the visible appearance of something that is usually repressed in the public and official life of the churches? Are these marginal groups not in fact drawing on something that has for too long been hidden and neglected in Christianity, its narrative potential? Are they not remembering that Christians do not primarily form an argumentative and reasoning community, but a story-telling community, and that the exchange of experiences of faith, like that of any "new" experience, takes a narrative form? Finally, does this not apply above all to the marginal groups which, in their refusal to speak the language of ritual and theology, are almost silent?

This is important in the question of pastoral care and the proclamation of faith, which are, I believe, in a critical situation because we are no longer able to narrate with a practical and socially critical effect and with a dangerous and liberating intention. For too long, we have tried to suppress the narrative potential of Christianity and have confined it to credulous children and old people, although it is these who are especially sensitive to false or substitute stories or to an illusory exchange of experiences. This is why, in giving renewed emphasis to narrative, it is important to avoid the possible misunderstanding that "story-telling" preachers and teachers will be justified in their narration of anecdotes, when what is required are arguments and reasoning. After all, there is a time for story-telling and a time for argument. There is a difference between the two which has to be recognized.

A second misunderstanding has also to be avoided, that of believing that to stress the narrative element in pastoral care, preaching and teaching are to withdraw into the purely private sphere or the aesthetic sphere of good taste. If they give this impression, our stories will only reveal the extent to which we have forgotten how to tell them. It is true that there are many different kinds of narrative: stories which pacify, those which relieve feelings—like political jokes made under a dictatorship—and those which conceal a quest for freedom and stir the listener to imitation. Stories are told by very wise men, who have, as Heinrich von Kleist observed, "eaten a second time of the tree of knowledge," and by little people who are oppressed or have not yet come of age. These, however, tell not only stories which tempt them to celebrate their immature dependence or their oppressed state, but also stories which are dangerous and which seek freedom. Freedom and enlightenment, the transition from dependence to coming of age, are not achieved simply by giving up narrative language in favour of the art of reasoning possessed by those who are enlightened and those who claim it as their privilege. (The old problem of the relationship between intellectuals and the working classes has, I believe, its origins primarily in a misunderstanding among intellectuals of the emancipatory character of narrative language, just as the value of the narrative form which is at the basis of Christianity is so often underestimated by theologians.)

There can, of course, be no *a priori* proof of the critical and liberating effect of such stories, which have to be encountered, listened to, and told again. But surely there are, in our post-narrative age, story-tellers who can demonstrate what "stories" might be today—not just artificial, private constructions, but narratives with a stimulating effect and aiming at social criticism, "dangerous" stories in other words. Can we perhaps retell the Jesus stories nowadays in this way?

IV. The Theological Aspect of Narrative—Narrative as the Medium of Salvation and History

The emphasis given in the preceding section to the pastoral aspect of the story form might give the impression that narrative is above all useful in teaching, and catechesis as an indispensable aid to applied theology, but that it does not affect the structure of theology itself in any way. This is, of course, not the intention at all. To say that the narrative form characterizes the proclamation of faith and rational argument theology is too superficial a distinction, suppressing the underlying structure of theology itself. In this section, then, the theological aspect of narrative and the inseparable connection between narrative and argument (explanation, analysis, and so on) will be discussed. In Section V, the categories used in this section, including that of a narrative history of suffering, will be discussed in greater detail.

The question as to how history and salvation can be related without either being diminished may be regarded as of central importance in contemporary theology. History is the experience of reality in conflict and contradiction, whereas salvation is, theologically speaking, their reconciliation by the act of God in Jesus Christ. An integral part of history is the suffering experience of non-identity through violence and oppression, injustice and inequality, guilt, finiteness, and death. In this sense, history is always a history of suffering. (When all men enjoy, as they do now, equal opportunities in a classless society, it should not be difficult to regard history as a history of suffering, since it is precisely in such a period that man's self-destructive nihilism, his despair and boredom—what Ernst Bloch has called the "melancholy of fulfillment" —often become so apparent.)

Can the theology of salvation and of man's redemption and reconciliation through Jesus Christ really hold its own against this history of suffering and the non-identity of history? Does it not *a priori* avoid the suffering of historical non-identity and lead an unhistorical and therefore mythological existence above the heads of men who are humiliated and even destroyed by the burden of their own history of suffering? Does the accumulated suffering of history not result in theology becoming cynical towards history? Is there perhaps a theological mediation between salvation and history which has only been taken seriously as a history of suffering? Can this theological mediation exist without becoming reconciled in too ambitious and ultimately too speculative and too self-deceiving a way with this history of suffering, or without salvation-history being suspended in view of this history of suffering? With variants, this is the central question of systematic theology today, and I believe that purely rational theological arguments cannot provide an answer to it. I should like at this point to clarify this statement by referring to the solutions to this problem which have been suggested by modern theology.[8]

The first of these solutions can be described as the existential and transcendental interpretation of the relationship between salvation and history. The question here is whether salvation and history are not reconciled by an existential or transcendental reduction of history to "historicity" and by a withdrawal from the non-identity of history to a mysterious identity of existence or of the subject which cannot be expressed.

A second solution suggests that salvation is conditioned by the history of suffering, projected into the future and, out of respect for the non-identity of history as a history of suffering, kept—so to speak—at stake. One question which arises again and again in connection with this solution, however, is whether a salvation which is always at stake is in any way different from a saving utopia, of which only heuristic use can be made in the history of human freedom.

A third solution has been received with interest in the German-speaking countries especially, and merits rather more detailed discussion. A connection between the history of salvation and that of suffering is to be found in referring this question back to the central question of the specifically Christian understanding of God, in other words, by reference to the theme of the Trinity. The non-identity of the history of

8. I have considered the relationship between salvation and history in some detail in the medium of man's history of suffering in my article mentioned in note 3 above.

suffering can therefore, with God's *kenosis* in Jesus' crucifixion in mind, be included in the trinitarian history of God, so that, as Moltmann has observed, suffering becomes "suffering between God and God."

This solution has been suggested by certain Protestant theologians following Karl Barth, especially Eberhard Jüngel and Jürgen Moltmann in his book on the crucified God, and by Catholics following Karl Rahner's proposals regarding the unity of the immanent Trinity. Among the latter, Hans Küng has touched on this question of the historicity of God in his interpretation of Hegel's christology, and Hans Urs von Balthasar has dealt with it penetratingly in his interpretation of the paschal mystery within the sphere of God's *kenosis* history understood in the trinitarian sense.

In view of these attempts to solve the problem, I should like to express a fundamental consideration here. The non-identity of the history of suffering cannot be cancelled out in a dialectical process of the trinitarian history of salvation in such a way that it preserves its historical character. This is because this non-identity is not the same as the negativity of the dialectical process. In any attempt to interpret the division in the history of man's suffering within this dialectical process, an exchange will take place between the negativity of suffering and the negativity of the dialectical concept of suffering. A purely conceptual reconciliation between the history of salvation, as the expression of the history of the redemption accomplished in Jesus Christ, and the history of man's suffering is, in my opinion, not possible because it can lead either to a dualistic gnostic perpetuation of suffering in God or to a reduction of suffering to the level of a concept. This dilemma cannot be resolved by any more subtle speculative reasoning. It can only be resolved if salvation and redemption in the non-identity of the history of suffering are approached in a different way.

This brings me to the formulation of the following thesis. A theology of salvation which neither conditions nor suspends the history of salvation nor ignores the non-identity of the history of suffering cannot be purely argumentative. It must also be narrative. It is fundamentally a memorative and narrative theology. A narrative memory of salvation would in no sense lead to a regressive confusion of the distinction that dominates our problem. On the contrary, it would enable salvation in history, which is, of course, a history of suffering, to be expressed without either salvation or history being diminished. The category of narrative memory both prevents salvation and redemption from becoming paradoxically unhistorical and subordinates them to the logical identity of dialectical mediation.

Narrative is unpretentious in its effect. It does not have, even from God, the dialectical key which will open every door and throw light on the dark passages of history before they have been trodden. It is not, however, without light itself. Pascal drew attention to this light in distinguishing, in his *Memorial*, between the narrated "God of Abraham, Isaac, and Jacob" and the God of rational argument, the "God of the philosophers."

This narrative memory of salvation is above all not a purely *ad hoc* construction designed to solve our problem. It goes much deeper than this, making present the mediation of the history both of salvation and of man's suffering as encountered in the testaments of our faith. If this narrative memory is reduced by theology to a preliminary mythological stage in the Christian Logos, then theology is clearly functioning uncritically with regard to the possibilities and the limits of expressing the Christian message positively in the experience of the non-identity of history.

It is often forgotten, in the theological criticism of mythology, that the narration of critical argument is inherent in theology as a mediating aspect of its content. This also has to be borne in mind in connection with historical criticism in theology. Without anticipating the content of the following section too much, it is important to point out here that there is a difference between regarding the historical question and the historical truth that is related to it as a problem that has been forced on Christianity in modern times and is therefore in this sense inevitable and as a medium in which the truth of Christianity and its saving message are originally expressed and identified. A purely argumentative theology which conceals its origin and does not make this present again and again in narrative memory inevitably leads, in the history of human suffering, to those many modifications in reasoning which result in the extinction of the identifiable content of Christian salvation. I do not intend this to be regarded as a reason for excluding argument from theology. There is no question of regressively obscuring the distinction between narrative memory and theological argument. It is much more a question of acknowledging the relative value of rational argument, the primary function of which is to protect the narrative memory of salvation in a scientific world, to allow it to be at stake and to prepare the way for a renewal of this narrative, without which the experience of salvation is silenced.

V. The Narrative Structure of Critical Reason

Does what I have suggested so far in this article not amount ultimately to an uncritical blurring of differences in view of the modern emphasis on critical reason? Is the idea of a history of human suffering not made arbitrary and unsuitable by modern historical criticism? How can narrative and criticism be reconciled with each other?

As a result of the triumph of historicism, all tradition, including the narrative and memorative tradition of Christianity, has been transformed into history—that is, into the object of a critical reconstruction of historical reason. As Gustav Krüger pointed out, the relationship between historical criticism and the past "not only presupposes that this past is past, but also clearly aims to strengthen and affirm this absence of present reality in what was in the past. History has taken the place of tradition and this means that it occupies that place."[9] Since this statement was written, a criticism of this historical reasoning has been developed, which does not accept without question the absence of memory and tradition in the scientific world of today, the absence which has resulted from our preoccupation with historicism. This criticism has above all been developed in the context of modern hermeneutics and also in the context of a practical and critical philosophy of history and society which is especially indebted to the practical philosophy of Kant and his successors and to the modern criticism of ideology, including the neo-Marxist and the psycho-analytical varieties.[10]

This criticism, which is based on the distinction between Moltmann's "knowledge and interest," is concerned with the fundamental themes of historical reason, with the "criticism of criticism," and with the need to expose the abstract will to criticisms as an ideology which unquestioningly gives way to a supposed progress in the critical consciousness. This "criticism of criticism" is not a purely formal meta-criticism which transposes the problem onto a purely theoretical plane. Rather, it deals with the problem as one of practical reason which occurs within certain historical memorative and narrative traditions. In this sense, history is—not as reconstructed history, but as memorative and narrative traditions—immanent in reason, which, in this criticism, becomes practical reason. The theme of narrative memory inevitably occurs again and again in this context and, what is more, it is in this case critical with regard to historical reason, which itself becomes more and more a technology looking back at the past and finally a "history" processed into a data bank, a computer memory without narrative and unable either to remember or to forget.

As Theodor Adorno observed, "Forgetting is inhuman because man's accumulated suffering is forgotten—the historical trace of things,

---

9. G. Krüger, "Die Bedeutung der Tradition für die philosophische Forschung," *Studium Generale*, 4 (1951), pp. 322ff.

10. A detailed discussion of the whole question outlined in this section will be found in my article "Erinnerung," cited in note 2 above.

words, colours and sounds is always the trace of past suffering. This is why tradition is nowadays confronted with an insoluble contradiction. It is not present and cannot be evoked, but as soon as all tradition is extinguished, inhumanity begins."[11]

Anyone who does not accept this almost insoluble difficulty will inevitably insist that there must be renewed respect for the history of man's suffering in our critical consciousness. This intention will only strike critical reason as obsolete if this respect for the history of suffering is denied because of a fear of heteronomy, and if the authority of those who suffer is consequently destroyed in the interest of an abstract autonomy of reason. Whenever this respect is preserved, however, then reason becomes in a sense "perceptive" in a way that cannot be expressed in the usual contrast which is made between authority and knowledge and which forms the most common framework for any discussion of the problem of the autonomy of reason. In this perception, history, as a remembered history of suffering, acquires for reason the form of a "dangerous tradition," which is passed on not in a purely argumentative manner, but as narrative—that is, in "dangerous stories."

These dangerous stories break through the spell of a historical reconstruction based on abstract reason and repudiate any attempt to reconstruct man's consciousness from the abstract unity of "I think." Above all, they show that man's consciousness is a consciousness which is "entwined in stories," which always has to rely on narrative identification and which, when the relative importance of the magisterium of history has been recognized, cannot entirely do without the magisterium of stories. In his film *Fahrenheit 451*, Francois Truffault presented in a most vivid form this "consciousness in stories," which is nourished by the accumulated narrative potential that is derived from books, as a refuge of resistance: the only alternative to a world of total manipulation and absence of freedom.

VI. Some Questions in Conclusion

I should like to conclude by asking a number of questions that arise in connection with this short apology of narrative. How, for example, can the term narrative or story be defined more precisely? It cannot, after all, be regarded as synonymous with the term "historical account," since non-historical forms of knowledge or communication, such as the saga, fairy-tale, or legend, have a narrative structure. What is the relationship

11. T. W. Adorno, "Thesen über Tradition," *Ohne Leitbild* (Frankfurt, 1967), pp. 34ff.

Johann Baptist Metz

between fiction and authenticity in narrative texts? What does it mean when we say that a story is "true" and in what sense can we speak of a narrative disclosure of truth? What relationship is there between narrated time and physical time? How are the story and the story-teller related to each other and how does the difference between the story and the story-teller prevent us from regarding narration as a pure textual problem?

In connection with the undoubted presence of narrative aspects in the individual sciences, we are bound to ask whether these are of merely secondary importance and of purely heuristic value. Do change, continuity, and discontinuity in the sciences and in examples of narrative form have to be made explicit in logic? Does our insistence on the narrative structure of theology not give rise to renewed questions about the scientific nature of theology and the cognitive character and the binding force of theological propositions?

Finally, among other questions, there is that of the historical Jesus —how are the history of Jesus and the stories of Jesus related? Has the canon of the Old and New Testaments not caused a "ban" to be imposed on narrative, preventing a retelling or further telling of stories in accordance with the contemporary situation? And should the meaning of the distinction between canonical and apocryphal stories not be reexamined?

The Narrative Structure of Soteriology

Michael Root

The narrative form of the Christian message has been celebrated with great enthusiasm over the last fifteen years. Books proclaim "narrative theology" as their subject matter, professional meetings have sessions on narrative, and theologians are expected to know the rudiments of contemporary trends in literary criticism. But the question in the back of the mind cannot be silenced: So what? What difference for the actual process of theological reflection follows from the recognition that the Christian message is a narrative? What can be understood in light of this recognition that could not be understood before?

In this essay I will present a partial answer to these questions. I will look at an important topic within Christian theology, soteriology, and argue that its structure and explanatory power is a function of its narrative form. Narrative is not merely ornamental in soteriology, but constitutive. Within soteriology, theologians for centuries have been drawing on narrative skills to explain how Jesus is redemptive.

My choice of soteriology is not arbitrary. Soteriology is the moment within theological reflection at which the narrative form of the Christian message cannot be avoided. Soteriology presumes two states of human existence, a state of deprivation (sin, corruption) and a state of release from that deprivation (salvation, liberation), and an event that produces a change from the first state to the second. It presumes then the sufficient conditions of a narrative: two states and an event that trans-

Michael Root, "The Narrative Structure of Soteriology," *Modern Theology*, 2, 2 (January 1986), pp. 145-157.

Michael Root

forms the first into the second.[1] In soteriology, theologians cannot completely abstract themselves from the movement of the narrative. If the narrative character of the Christian message makes no difference here, then the recent enthusiasm for narrative as a category of theological analysis is called into question.

Soteriology has occupied an odd place in the history of doctrine and theology. While soteriology may have been a deciding factor in the christological controversies of the early church, no soteriological dogmas were explicitly promulgated. While talk about the person of Christ was being hedged with restrictions, talk about the work of Christ remained free and undefined. This freedom has been exercised throughout the history of theology. The student of soteriology faces a bewildering variety of explanations of just what it means to say Jesus saves. It is no wonder that modern scholarship has abounded in classifications and typologies of "atonement theories." Simply to organize the material seems to be a major achievement.

Yet in the midst of this variety, some common organizational and explanatory processes are at work. Different conclusions are reached in similar ways. What I will do in this essay is lay bare these similar processes and show their dependence on narrative. The analysis will focus on what the theologian must do with the Christian message in presenting a soteriology. In a single essay I unfortunately cannot supplement this analysis with extended illustrations. I do think the analysis presented makes much clearer what is going on in texts such as Anselm's *Cur Deus Homo,* Gregory of Nyssa's *Catechetical Orations,* or the soteriological sections of Schleiermacher's *The Christian Faith.* In this essay, however, I can only hint at such applications. I am confident that these applications can be fully developed and that they will further validate the analysis here presented.

I. The Task of Soteriology

Soteriology is concerned with how humanity has moved or can move from a state of deprivation (however understood) to a state of release from deprivation. A necessary condition of a *Christian* soteriology is that the story of *Jesus* is seen as decisive in that movement.[2] Buddhism also speaks of a release from a state of deprivation, and thus there is

1. On the minimal requirements of narrative, see Arthur C. Danto, *Analytical Philosophy of History* (Cambridge: Cambridge University Press, 1965), p. 233f.

2. I use the vague term "decisive" here deliberately. At this point, I do not wish to exclude soteriologies such as that implied within the work of Schubert Ogden (e.g. *Christ Without Myth: A Study Based on the Theology of Rudolf Bultmann* [New York: Harper & Row, 1961], pp. 142-145, 153-164; *The Point of Christology* [San Francisco: Harper &

a Buddhist soteriology. Buddhist soteriology, however, ascribes no decisive role to the story of Jesus. A Christian soteriology must show how this release occurs and what the role of the story of Jesus is in this release.

An ambiguity is built into the phrase "the story of Jesus." It might refer to the event depicted by the story. To speak of the redemptive significance of the story is then to speak of the redemptive significance of events to which the story refers. Or it might refer to the story itself, to the narrative of the events and not to the events independent of their narration. In that case, to speak of the redemptive significance of the story is to speak of the redemptive significance of a contemporary event, the telling of the story of Jesus. Most soteriologies utilize both sides of the ambiguity. Neither simply the events nor simply their narrations redeems. The events are redemptive as they grasp peoples and individuals through their depiction in narrative and ritual, Word and Sacrament.

The soteriology task within Christian theology is, then, to show how the Christian story is the story of human redemption.[3] What soteriology must make evident is a specific form of what Robert Scholes and Robert Kellogg call the meaning of a narrative, but which I will call the story's significance.[4] Significance is a function of the relation between the story and the world or life of the reader. An insignificant story would be the one that did not illumine or transform the world or life of the reader.[5] A profoundly significant story would be one that in penetrating and thoroughgoing ways illumined and transformed that world and life. Within soteriology, the theologian attempts to show how the Christian story has a particular kind of relation to the reader's life and world. This story is the story of the reader's redemption. The task within soteriology is to explicate that highly significant relation.

What might a redemptive relation between the Christian story and the life and world of the reader look like? At least two sorts of rela-

Row, 1982], pp. 83f.) which ascribe decisive but not unique redemptive significance to the story of Jesus. While I do not think such soteriologies are adequate, I do not wish simply to assume their inadequacy within a definition.

3. Throughout the essay I will refer to "the Christian story." By this I mean the stories that make up the Christian Bible read as constituting a single comprehensive narrative.

4. Robert Scholes and Robert Kellogg, *The Nature of Narrative* (New York: Oxford University Press, 1966), p. 82. I will use the term "significance" to avoid pointless arguments over what constitutes *the* meaning of the text.

5. I will use the word "reader" to refer to the recipient of the narrative. Of course, the narrative may be received through written texts, oral recitals, comic books, films, and so on.

tions are possible.[6] The story can bear an *illustrative* relation to the reader's life and world. The story illustrates certain redemptive truths about self, world, and God. The soteriological task is to bring out the truths the story illustrates and show how they are redemptive. Only when the narrative is transcended does the redemptive relation become clear. The tendency within such an interpretation is to make the story of Jesus only pedagogically necessary and ultimately dispensable to redemption. As a result, rightly or wrongly, few theologians have sought to interpret the redemptive relation along strictly illustrative lines.

The Christian narrative can also bear a *storied* relation to the reader. The Christian story and the life and world of the reader do not exist in isolation, but constitute one world and one story. The reader is included in the Christian story. The relation of story to reader becomes internal to the story. As a result, the relations between the story and the reader become storied relations, the sort of relations that are depicted in narratives. The stories of Jesus and of the reader are related by the narrative connections that make them two sequences within a single larger story. These storied relations, rather than general truths the story illustrates, mediate between story and reader. The story is good news because redemption follows from the primary form of inclusion in the story. The task of soteriology is, then, to show how the reader is included in the story and how the story then is or can be the story of that reader's redemption.

Hans Frei has shown how for most of Christian history such inclusion has been the dominant way the Christian story and the world of its reader have been brought together.[7] As a result, the second, storied approach to soteriology has been dominant within Christian theology. As indicated in the last sentence of the previous paragraph, this approach to soteriology includes a twofold task. How the Christian is effectively included in the story needs to be elucidated. Historically, this issue has usually been addressed in discussions of baptism or conversion. But one also needs to discuss how the story redeems those who are thus included within it. It is not obvious how bearing a special relation to a story of the life, death, or even resurrection of a first-century Palestinian preacher means that someone centuries later and continents away is released from the most important deprivations that plague human existence. Why inclusion into this story is redemptive has often

---

6. These two sorts of relation are suggested by Scholes and Kellogg's discussion of illustrative and representational relations between text and world (*The Nature of Narrative*, pp. 84, 138). I have put their distinction to such a different use, however, that it is no longer the same distinction.

7. Hans W. Frei, *The Eclipse of Biblical Narrative: A Study in Eighteenth and Nineteenth Century Hermeneutics* (New Haven: Yale University Press, 1974), pp. 3, 24, 27, 36.

been discussed under the heading, "the world of Christ." What have come to be called "atonement theories" are explications of this redemptive relation. It is on this second aspect of soteriology that I will focus and in which the narrative form of the Christian message makes a decisive impact.

The problem that an "atonement theory" seeks to solve is how the story of Jesus is the story of redemption, at least for those who bear a certain relation to it. If this special relation is understood as a kind of inclusion, then the task is to elucidate the relation between one sequence in the story, the life, death, and resurrection of Jesus, and another sequence now included in the story, the life and redemption of the Christian. Again, we have a task of narrative interpretation, of the explication of the relation between two sequences within an allegedly unitary story.

How is this task carried out? Frank Kermode has noted that prior to canonization, interpretation of a biblical story took the form of a retelling of the story. The story was retold in an augmented form that brought out a particular interpretation.[8] Once particular versions of the story became canonical, interpretation through revision or redaction was replaced by interpretation through exegesis. Kermode is not quite right, however, that interpretation by narrative augmentation has disappeared from the Christian tradition. Hans Frei has described the theology of Karl Barth as a conceptual redescription of the biblical story. Barth took "the classical themes of communal Christian language . . . and he restated or redescribed them, rather than evolving arguments on their behalf."[9] What are called atonement theories can be understood analogously as narrative redescriptions of the story of Jesus. Atonement theories imply augmented, expanded forms of the story of Jesus that make clear how it is the story of redemption. *It is by the construction of such augmented forms of the story of Jesus that the soteriological task is carried out.*

This last statement is the central assertion of this essay. The construction of augmented narratives is not merely illustrative or incidental to the work of soteriology. Rather, it is the construction of such narratives that accomplishes the task of soteriology. The constructed narrative explains how the story of Jesus is the story of redemption. The explanatory work of any Christian soteriology that does not take a strictly illustrative approach is done by the construction of an augmented version of the Christian narrative that makes clear the redemptive rela-

8. Frank Kermode, *The Genesis of Secrecy: On the Interpretation of Narrative* (Cambridge: Harvard University Press, 1979), pp. 81, 98.

9. Hans W. Frei, "An Afterword: Eberhard Busch Biography of Karl Barth," in *Karl Barth in Review: Posthumous Works Reviewed and Assessed,* ed. H. Martin Rumscheidt, Pittsburgh Theological Monograph Series 30 (Pittsburgh: Pickwick Press, 1981), p. 110.

tion between Jesus and the Christian. This assertion is elaborated and defended in the following three sections of this essay.

II. Soteriology and Comprehensive Narrative Structures

Explanatory interpretation through narrative augmentation operates both on the level of the organization of the narrative as a whole and on the level of detailed elements within the narrative. Only as we see how soteriology works at both levels can we see how it carries out its task.

Any Christian use of the Bible must involve what Charles Wood has called a "canonical construal."[10] Somehow the Bible must be read as a whole with some kind of unity. If the Bible is read as it has been most often read, as a single overarching story, then it will have the sort of unity stories have. Stories have various aspects (e.g., character, plot), and a story can be unified in different ways in relation to its different aspects. Most often, however, we look to the plot to find the unity that makes one story out of a set of episodes. But how does plot create unity? Scholes and Kellogg contend that "All plots depend on tension and resolution."[11] Some sort of tension, problem, or complication sets the unifying movement of the plot. The end of the story is constituted by the resolution of the initiating tension. Episodes are or are not germane to the plot in terms of their relation to the movement from tension to resolution. This movement constitutes the organizing axis of the plot.[12]

What sort of complication/resolution axis might unify the scriptural narratives read as a single, overarching story? Christian theologians have tended toward two basic schemes. On the one hand, the initial tension can be seen within the creation of humanity. Humanity is created for a destiny that it does not possess at the beginning of the narrative, e.g., deification or participation in the divine nature. The resolution of this tension comes when that destiny is realized. For this scheme, sin and release from sin constitute a massive delaying parenthesis within a larger narrative movement not itself defined by the problem of sin. The initial complication is not so depicted that release from sin is a necessary part of its resolution. The necessity of a release from sin is contingent upon an event (humanity's fall) logically distinct from the

---

10. Charles M. Wood, *The Formation of Christian Understanding: An Essay in Theological Hermeneutics* (Philadelphia: Westminster Press, 1981), pp. 93f., 99-105.

11. Scholes and Kellogg, *The Nature of Narrative*, p. 212.

12. The idea that the unity of plot is set by a dynamic of tension/release or problem/resolution is not unique or new with Scholes and Kellogg. The importance of complication/resolution for plot is also described in T. A. Van Dijk, "Action, Action Description, and Narrative," *New Literary History*, 6 (1975): 289ff.

initial complication. Once this twist of sin is added to the initial complication, however, release from sin and attainment of the destiny implicit within creation are usually seen as realized in a single redeeming, fulfilling event of narrative resolution. Such a scheme can often be found in patristic and medieval theology.

On the other hand, the initial complication or tension can be seen precisely as sin. The fall, of course, is not the first event in the Bible. But only the entrance of sin into the created world is seen as initiating narrative movement. The fall is then analogous to the murder in a stereotyped mystery novel. It may not occur on page 1, but it sets the narrative tension that impels the plot's movement and whose resolution constitutes the story's end. For this second scheme, release from sin is intrinsic to any possible narrative resolution. Sin/release from sin is not a massive delaying parenthesis within a larger narrative movement. Rather, it is itself the encompassing plot structure that unifies the story. Such a scheme can be found particularly in modern Protestant theology.[13]

Any canonical construal of the Bible as a single comprehensive narrative unified by its plot will need to imply some comprehensive tension/resolution scheme. What must be noted is that the construction of such a scheme along either of the lines laid out above will also imply a soteriology. The depiction of fall or creation/fall as the initial tension of the narrative will depict the human deprivation from which one seeks release. As the story of Jesus is convincingly depicted within the narrative as the resolution of this initial tension, how Jesus redeems is also explained. That which revolves the initial tension must also be that which redeems. To show in a narrative how the life, death, and resurrection of Jesus bring about plot resolution is to show simultaneously how they bring about redemption. The construction of a coherent plot out of the biblical materials is then at the same time the construction of a soteriology.

Soteriology as narrative augmentation, then, operates at the level of the organization of the total narrative. This organization, however, must be realized in the details of the story. We need to see how soteriology is worked out within the details of narrative structure. This investigation will force a detour into the vexed issue of the sort of understanding of events that is provided by narrative. This detour will help us see how soteriology depends on its narrative form for its explanatory power.

13. I have gone to the trouble of outlining these differing schemes because they seem to explain why some patristic theology looks so odd to a certain modern outlook. A theological scheme will look very odd, perhaps even marginally Christian, if what one takes to be *the* dynamic that unifies the Christian story (sin/release from sin) is seen only as a parenthesis within a larger dynamic foreign to one's religious sensibilities (deification).

III. Soteriology and Narrative Patterns

An important guidepost for this detour is Louis Mink's analysis of the different kinds of understanding achieved through theory and narrative: "Theory makes possible the explanation of an occurrence only by describing it in such a way that the description is logically related to a systematic set of generalizations or laws. One understands the power of a spring-powered watch, for example, only insofar as one understands the principles of mechanics, and this requires describing the mechanism of the watch in terms, and only in terms, appropriate to those principles. . . . [A]n ideally theoretical understanding of those occurrences . . . would treat each as nothing other than a replicable instance of a systematically interconnected set of generalizations."[14]

In contrast, the sort of understanding gained from narrative does not abstract from the concrete individuality of that which is understood. Narratives depict events ". . . as elements in a single and concrete complex of relationships. Thus a letter I burn may be understood not only as oxidizable substance but as a link with an old friend. It may have relieved a misunderstanding, raised a question, or changed my plans at a crucial moment. As a letter, it belongs to a kind of story, a narrative of events which would be unintelligible without reference to it. But to explain this, I would not construct a theory of letters or of friendships but would, rather, show how it belongs to a particular configuration of events like a part in a jig-saw puzzle."[15] Narratives help us to understand events by locating them within larger meaningful patterns.[16] Thus, Mink calls this form of understanding configuration. Configurational understanding is the sort of understanding provided by a narrative. Within a narrative, an event ceases to be an isolated monad and becomes a part of a larger whole. It is this relation of part to meaningful whole that is the key to the sort of explanation narrative provides.[17]

14. Louis O. Mink, "Narrative Form as Cognitive Instrument," in *The Writing of History: Literary Form and Historical Understanding,* ed. Robert H. Canary and Henry Kozicki (Madison: University of Wisconsin Press, 1978), pp. 131f.

15. Louis O. Mink, "History and Fiction as Modes of Comprehension," *New Literary History,* 1 (1970): 551.

16. The importance of such organizing patterns to narrative meaning, explanation, or interpretation is also recognized by Danto, *Analytical Philosophy of History,* p. 140; A. J. Greimas and J. Courtes, "The Cognitive Dimension of Narrative Discourse," *New Literary History,* 7 (1976): 436; A. R. Louch, "History As Narrative," *History and Theory* 8 (1969): 69; and investigated in detail in Paul Ricoeur, *Time and Narrative,* Vol. I, trans. by Kathleen McLaughlin and David Pellauer (Chicago: University of Chicago Press, 1984), pp. 40ff.

17. The importance of the part/whole relation in the explanation provided by narrative has been particularly stressed by historiographers; Mink, "History and Fiction,"

We have already seen one narrative pattern, the complication/ resolution pattern which forms the unifying axis of a plot. At a more detailed level, this overarching pattern is realized in a web of interlocking patterns of, e.g., problem/solution, project/completion, or desire/fulfillment. Three important aspects of these interlocking patterns need to be discussed. Each has important implications for soteriology.

First, the tension/resolution pattern already points to a general feature of the meaningful patterns within narratives. They both derive from and creatively transform structures and patterns of everyday life. The patterns of tension/release and complication/resolution, for example, are patterns ingredient in human existence. We bring these patterns with us to our reading, and the narrative plays off these patterns in the organization of episodes in a coherent whole. In any narrative beyond the most simple, a variety of such patterns are simultaneously being worked out, interweaving the characters and events into a whole. In any narrative beyond the most predictable, the patterns we bring to the narrative are transformed, reorganized, and extended. In the process, the task of portraying the significance of the story, in the sense described above, is accomplished.

A second important aspect of these patterns was mentioned in a quotation from Mink given above. Configurational understanding is not achieved by subsuming that which is understood under strictly general laws. Generalization does play a role in configurational understanding. We are able to relate patterns from daily experience to patterns within narratives because of similarities between them. If a pattern within a narrative does not bear some similarity to patterns in daily life, I will not be able to recognize it as a pattern. I do not know anyone who bears close, extensive, statistically formulable similarities to Captain Ahab (thank goodness!), but I do know of persons who in this way and that bear a variety of similarities to him. If Ahab's obsessive quest for the white whale did not in some way resemble more widely shared human quests, it would be simply opaque. Configurational understanding relies on such similarities between patterns, i.e., on a particular sort of generalization. At least in this sense, Aristotle is right that poetry is concerned with the universal.[18]

---

pp. 547-549; and also "The Autonomy of Historical Understanding," in *Philosophical Analysis and History*, ed. William H. Dray (New York: Harper & Row, 1966), p. 184; Maurice Mandelbaum, "A Note on History as Narrative," *History and Theory*, 6 (1967): 418; William H. Dray, "On the Nature and Role of Narrative in Historiography," *History and Theory*, 10 (1971): 169f.; see also Paul Riceour, "Narrative Time," in *On Narrative*, ed. W. J. T. Mitchell (Chicago: University of Chicago Press, 1981), pp. 174f.

18. Aristotle, *Poetics*, 1451b5-11.

Nevertheless, configurational understanding organizes episode, event, and character into meaningful patterns without systematically abstracting from their individuality in the way that general laws do. While the organizing pattern inevitably shapes the description of that which it organizes, it does not require a redescription of an event "as nothing other than a replicable instance of a systematically interconnected set of generalizations." The understood Ahab is still irreducibly Ahab. In a well told narrative the patterns which constitute generality and intelligibility arise out of the arrangement of the particular details narrated and no others. Except for extreme examples of fable and allegory, that which is understood in a narrative is inseparable from the narrative itself.[19] The complex web of interconnections and patterns that holds a narrative together bears similarities to other patterns in other stories and in life, but this particular complex is a complete instantiation of nothing but itself. Eberhard Jüngel aptly states: ". . . in narrative the unique and individual are mediated through language into generality without losing their uniqueness and individuality."[20] This mediation is carried out by the sorts of narrative patterns I have been discussing.

Closely related to this preservation of individuality is a third aspect of narrative patterns. The connections that hold a narrative together are not necessary connections. One has grasped a theoretical explanation when one has grasped that, in light of X, Y, and Z, A *must* follow. Grasping or following a narrative does involve seeing how one episode fittingly relates to another.[21] But such a grasp does not involve a perception that this and nothing else *could* have followed. In fact, an aspect of a relatively complete grasp of a narrative is often a perception of just how easily something else might appropriately or fittingly have occurred. The contrafactual "what if" question cannot be eliminated from

---

19. The description I give here of narrative meaning applies more completely to some narratives than to others. It applies most fully to what Erich Auerbach, in *Mimesis: The Representation of Reality in Western Literature,* tr. W. Trask (Princeton: Princeton University Press, 1953), describes as realistic narrative. Nevertheless, I would contend that it applies to some degree to most narrative forms.

20. Eberhard Jüngel, *God as the Mystery of the World: On the Foundation of the Theology of the Crucified One in the Dispute between Theism and Atheism,* tr. Darrel L. Guder (Grand Rapids: Eerdmans, 1983), p. 303 n. 13.

21. This aspect of narrative relations has been often noted. See, for example, Wood, *The Formation of Christian Understanding,* pp. 78f.; Jüngel, *God as the Mystery of the World,* p. 306; Claude Bremond, "The Logic of Narrative Possibilities," tr. Elaine D. Cancalon, *New Literary History,* 11 (1980): 406; Hans W. Frei, *The Identity of Jesus Christ: The Hermeneutical Bases of Dogmatic Theology* (Philadelphia: Fortress Press, 1975), p. 57. There are critics of this position who maintain that explanation occurs only when one has laid bare necessary connections of the sort that could provide the basis for prediction; see, e.g., C. B. McCullagh, "Narrative and Explanation in History," *Mind,* 78 (1969): 256-261. Such a position assumes, however, that all explanation is crypto-theoretical.

a lively understanding of narrative. As Barthes commented, within narrative every sequence is a threatened unit, for alternative paths are always being presented.[22]

Such a celebration of narrative as preserver of individuality and contingency should not blind us, however, to the tendency of narrative patterns to overpower their components. Scholes and Kellogg discuss the tension between plot and mimesis;[23] Ricoeur refers to the tension between the episodic and the configurational.[24] When pattern arises out of its components, there one finds the "union of contingency and consecution, of chronology and configuration, of sequence and consequence."[25] When pattern seems to dictate the shape of its components, however, one feels what Harold Toliver has called "the fatality of narrative logic."[26] Detail becomes mere instance of pattern; plot becomes a fourth Fate. The role of generalization within configurational understanding can represent a threat to that which we value in narrative.

In summary, the detailed organization of a narrative is achieved by means of interconnected patterns. These patterns relate in varying ways to expectations we bring to the text. These patterns do not organize their components through a redescription that makes them only examples of strictly general laws. Rather, their specificity is preserved. Similarly, the narrative connections are not depicted as instances of general laws, and thus are not depicted as necessary connections. Narrative patterns seek to convey the fittingness of what occurs without implying its necessity.

What is the relation between soteriology and such narrative patterns? First, what any soteriology must do is bring to light patterns in

22. Roland Barthes, "Introduction to the Structural Analysis of Narratives," in his *Image-Music-Text*, tr. Stephen Heath (New York: Hill & Wang, 1977), p. 102. The nature of these connections is explored in Ricoeur's argument (against Mink) that contingency is not destroyed but preserved within configurational understanding. See Ricoeur, *Time and Narrative*, I, p. 158.

23. Scholes and Kellogg, *The Nature of Narrative*, p. 232.

24. Ricoeur, "The Narrative Function," in his *Hermeneutics and the Human Sciences: Essays on Language, Action and Interpretation*, ed. and trans. by John B. Thompson (Cambridge: Cambridge University Press, 1981), p. 279.

25. Ibid., p. 292; compare Ricoeur, *Time and Narrative*, I, p. 208. A strength of Ricoeur's analysis is that he illuminates how narrative organizes the episodic without destroying its chronological character. His analysis thus better illuminates the logic of narrative than the chronology-destroying analyses of structuralism.

26. Harold Toliver, *Animate Illusions: Explorations of Narrative Structure* (Lincoln: University of Nebraska Press, 1974), p. 284. About the tension between generalizable pattern and unique event, Toliver states: "In effect, then, any narrative pattern salvages potentially random, errant, and unique moments of unredeemed characters by incorporating them into a repeatable logic, a disciplining stamp of form that regiments their wildness . . ." (p. 128).

the Christian story which will make clear that story's redemptive character. Soteriological interpretation of the Christian story must play off, both utilize and shape, patterns that do or can exist in the reader's life that are like redemption. Typically these will be patterns of deprivation/release from deprivation. For example, the story of Jesus can be interpreted as the repayment of a debt, or as the liberation of captives, or as the achievement and evocation of a desired form of consciousness. In each case, a pattern in the story is highlighted that will bring out the story's redemptive character. Through similarities between this pattern and patterns that exist or can exist within the life and world of the Christian, the story can be seen as redemptive.

Second, the highlighting of such redemptive patterns need not compromise a unique redemptive significance of Jesus. The pattern a soteriology highlights will usually be different in important ways from patterns with which it is similar. The debt Jesus pays, the consciousness he realizes and evokes, the captivity he overcomes will be seen as significantly different from all other debt, consciousness, and captivity. He repays an infinite debt owed to God's honor; he achieves and evokes perfect God-consciousness; he releases us from captivity to Death and the Devil.

More importantly, one can still claim that redemption lies only in Jesus' unique instantiation of this unique pattern. The pattern that soteriological interpretation finds in the story of Jesus will bear similarities to other patterns, but some highlighted patterns may be inseparable from this particular story. Soteriological significance may be found in a web of patterns which only this one story can fully instantiate. In *The Identity of Jesus Christ,* Hans Frei makes just such an argument: in the passion narratives soteriological pattern is inseparable from the story of Jesus. The pattern is not one that can be fully repeated in the stories of other "Christ figures."[27] The generality that soteriological interpretation requires need not reduce Jesus to an illustration of a general truth or one realization of a repeatable pattern. The interplay of generality and specificity in narrative allows the Story of Jesus in its uniqueness to have soteriological significance.

Finally, the contingency of narrative connections means that soteriology can focus on the concrete narrative patterns. The connections among events in the story and between the story and the reader will not be fully explicable in terms of theoretical generalizations. However much theoretical explanations may play a role in achieving configurational understanding, the particular storied connections remain the structures that bear the final explanatory weight. The web of storied

27. Frei, *Identity of Jesus Christ,* pp. 45-84.

connections themselves accounts for this and not that occurring. Precisely how this is so will be developed in the next section.

Soteriology is thus a particular form of configurational understanding. Within soteriology, the Christian story is understood as a unique, patterned whole. In grasping the story in this way, the story is understood as the story of redemption.

IV. Soteriology as Narrative Redescription

Soteriology carries out its task by an interpretation of the story of Jesus that highlights those patterns which bring together Jesus and the Christian in a single story within which is realized the redemption of the Christian. That this interpretation operates by a redescription, expansion, or augmentation of the story can be seen by asking what is the relation between the soteriological interpretation and the story it interprets.

One must avoid the picture of the story as interpreted data upon which an interpretation needs to be imposed. The truism of recent philosophy that all data are "theory-laden" is particularly true in the case of narratives. As I have noted, narratives are themselves held together by interwoven patterns. These patterns are not external to statements of "what happened" but ingredient in them. When I say "he repaid the debt," I have made what Mink calls a story-statement.[28] The statement of what occurred implies a relation between this event and other events (e.g., a loan.) A pattern is ingredient in the statement of what occurred; interpretation has already begun.

The theologian seeking to interpret the Christian story does not then face uninterpreted data, but a story that already contains at least the seeds of interpretations in its descriptions of events and patterns that organize those events into a narrative. What relation there should be between these interpretive patterns already within the text and the soteriology proposed by a theologian is a question for hermeneutics and the doctrine of biblical authority. I need only note that, while the patterns in the text may be able to place limits on soteriological construction, they are not sufficiently specific to dictate a particular soteriology and thus eliminate the need for contemporary soteriological construction.[29]

The inseparability of story and interpretation, however, has fur-

---

28. Mink, "History and Fiction," p. 556.

29. I have shown the way biblical patterns place limits on soteriology in "Dying He Lives: Biblical Image, Biblical Narrative, and the Redemptive Jesus," *Semeia*, 30, *Christology and Exegesis: New Approaches*, ed. Robert Jewett, pp. 155-169.

ther consequences more directly related to my concerns. Just as interpretations are ingredient within the story, so newly constructed interpretations do not remain simply external to the story interpreted. Rather, they at least imply and at most embody new versions of the story. Not only are the existing patterns interpreted, but also in the process of interpretation patterns are rearranged and new patterns created. This reconstitution is a necessary moment in the canonical construal of the Bible as a single comprehensive narrative. More radically, as the organizing patterns within the story are put into new relations and subtly changed, the components of the story, the events themselves, are redescribed and thus reconstituted. The interrelation through story-statements of event and organizing pattern means that changes in organizing patterns involve changes in that which is organized. There is a sense in which Anselm's *Cur Deus Homo* and Gregory of Nyssa's *Catechetical Orations* contain descriptions of the same event, the death of Christ. Nevertheless, they find redemptive meaning in that death only by redescribing it as the voluntary payment of a debt owed to the honor of God or as the deceptive surrender to the Devil in exchange for the souls of humanity. The redescription is the soteriological explanation. The explanation succeeds only when it convincingly reconstitutes in its own image that which it explains. If I accept and understand the redescription of the story of Jesus' death as the story of the repayment of an infinite debt, then I have had the soteriological significance of that death shown to me.

I stress this reconstitution of the narrative by soteriological interpretation, for it is precisely in this creation of a new version of the story that the soteriological task is carried out. The soteriological task cannot be completed without the creation of such a new version of the story. If the relations that significantly connect the story with its reader are not merely illustrative but storied, then soteriology can only succeed by developing a redemptive pattern within these connections. And developing such a redemptive pattern involves recasting the story.

Soteriology is thus inseparable from what I have called narrative redescription or augmentation. Soteriology involves the recasting of the overall shape of the Christian story and of the internal patterns that both hold it together and form the matrix of its descriptions of particular events. This narrative redescription is not incidental to the task of soteriology, but constitutes the necessary means of achieving its goals. To speak of "atonement theories" is thus a mistake, for explanations of soteriology are not theoretical. Within soteriology, at least, the categories of narrative have the decisive significance that have been claimed for them in recent years.

V. Conclusion

What are the results of a recognition of the narrative structure of soteriology? Most importantly, a program is suggested for the analysis both of the history of soteriology and of the contemporary possibilities of soteriological construction. Unfortunately, in this essay I can do little more than suggest some implications of the preceding analysis.

Most directly, the preceding analysis should provide some guidance for the study of texts concerned with soteriology. The question to be asked in such study is what explanatory narrative structure is being created. At the level of comprehensive organization, one must ask what tension/resolution pattern is the organizing axis of the plot. At the level of more detailed organization one must look for the interpretive patterns that highlight the redemptive character of the story.

The nature of these patterns may be illustrated by the aspects noted above. First, the augmented narrative must relate to patterns that either already exist or can be brought to exist in the life and world of the Christian. Anselm's discussion of Jesus repaying the debt owed to honor, Grotius's discussion of the requirements of governance, or Schleiermacher's discussion of the impact of personality each seeks to point out patterns by which the Christian can readily recognize the redemptive significance of the story of Jesus.

Second, there is a constant play in soteriology between the alleged uniqueness of what occurred in Jesus and the need for more general patterns that make clear the significance of this event. As discussed, the configurational understanding provided through narrative does not require the redescription of events in strictly general terms. Individuality need not be eliminated in the process of explanation. Nevertheless, the tension between pattern and event is not eliminated. Pattern can illegitimately dictate the descriptions of what it patterns. How this tension is handled is a question to be addressed to any soteriological text.

Third, the connections created within soteriology are only fitting or appropriate, not necessary. The evaluation of such connections is a difficult matter, more aesthetic perhaps than logical. Questions of the success of soteriological construction will more often be matters of persuasion than demonstration.

More broadly, the analysis given above lays bare the close relation between soteriology and the way the Christian message is understood to form a coherent whole. In investigating the narrative structure within a soteriology one must also investigate the comprehensive narrative construal by which a single narrative is formed out of the diversity of biblical material.

With this final comment, we can return to my initial question. What difference follows from the recognition of the narrative form of the Christian message? The recognition of this narrative form illuminates the structures and forms of explanation that have shaped theology in the past. In addition, it clarifies the systematic and explanatory tasks that lie ahead of us. If theology concerned with narrative turns out to be a passing fad, it will not be because there is not enough for it to do.

Theological Investments in Story: Some Comments on Recent Developments and Some Proposals

Julian Hartt

This paper is a treatment of claims recently made concerning the priorities of story in Christian experience and therefore in theology as a reflective enterprise. These claims are made by Stephen Crites in his article, "Unfinished Figure: On Theology and Imagination,"[1] and by Stanley Hauerwas in his book, *A Community of Character.*[2] My comments on their claims are not intended to be taken as a systematic exposition of these substantial and provocative ventures. The issues I propose to deal with are: (1) cognitive powers and successes credited to imagination; (2) historical knowledge as a specialization of imaginational cognitivity; (3) theories about historical reality; (4) truth versus truthfulness in relation to story.[3]

This is a formidable array of topics. I hope that this paper will not inflict permanent damage on any of them.

I begin with Crites. Hauerwas appears at IV.

---

1. In *Unfinished . . . : Essays in Honor of Ray Hart*, JAAR Thematic Studies, ed. Mark C. Taylor (Chico, Ca.: Scholars Press, 1981), pp. 155-184.
2. *A Community of Character* (Notre Dame: University of Notre Dame Press, 1981).
3. "Story" signifies Christian/biblical narratives throughout.

Julian Hartt, "Theological Investments in Story: Some Comments on Recent Developments and Some Proposals," *Journal of the American Academy of Religion*, LII, 1 (March 1984): 117-130.

Julian Hartt

I. Cognitive Powers and Successes
Credited to Imagination

Crites is a persistent,[4] and in this piece eloquent, spokesman for the imagination as the primary instrument for the attainment of religious meaning and truth. He works persuasively with a familiar distinction between *image (figura)* and *concept.* Applying the distinction to traditional (here Patristic) theology, he says:

> I have insisted on the figural *imagination* [emphasis his] as the primary faculty of traditional theology, because however abstracted theology became in its attempt to understand what faith believed, its starting point and the locus in experience to which it steadily returned was that proper object of the imagination: the concrete *image,* in particular, the personal image forthcoming in biblical narrative. The Gospel in particular is essentially and necessarily a story, for its central figure is a man of flesh and blood.[5]

I assume that the intended force of "for" in the last sentence is *because.* And I think we are entitled to wonder a bit about that. One of the very few lasting virtues of Carlyle's *French Revolution* is to be attributed to his success in conjuring the presence of such persons as Mirabeau and Charlotte Corday and Danton. I have deliberately said "conjure": some sort of evocational magic seems to be involved in effecting a conflation of imagination in writer and reader.[6] For the historian the conjuration is intended to serve the interests of historical truth; in Carlyle's case it is drenched, no doubt, with high moral sentiments. The historical-truth question is on the agenda. Here I simply file a demurrer in passing: it is not clear—so far—in Crites's paper, why the representation, vivid and putatively authentic, of an historical person calls for *story.* Is this entailed by assimilating narrative to story? But perhaps Crites means "essentially and necessarily" to hold only for the Gospel. We shall wait and hope to see.

Crites moves along to formulating a general (that is, not specifically religious) theory of the imagination. He says:

---

4. His earlier piece, "The Narrative Quality of Experience" (pp. 65-88 in this volume), is commonly regarded as a landmark statement.

5. Crites, "Unfinished Figure," p. 163.

6. "On this same evening therefore, about half-past seven o'clock, from the gate of the Conciergerie, to a City all on tiptoe, the fatal cart issues; seated on it a fair young creature, sheeted in red smock of Murderess; so beautiful, serene, so full of life; journeying towards death—alone amid the World. . . . As the last act, all being now ready, they take the neckerchief from her neck; the cheeks were still tinged with it when the executioner lifted the severed head, to show it to the people." Thomas Carlyle, *The French Revolution* (New York: Random House, 1934), pp. 608-609.

Imagination is not a distinct faculty or quasibiological organ, but it is a distinct activity of the psyche as a whole. The term signifies the activity of holistic formation, forming the sorts of mutidimensional images, associated and presented against a complex visual, aural, narrative background, that make up immediate experience. Indeed, imagination is a synthesizing activity in the formation of experience, but it engages as well in a free play of such experienceable forms.[7]

This is a striking claim. I do not know what sorts of evidencing would go to support it. Crites supplies none. Moreover, "holistic" begs the question, if it is intended to say more than that part of the furniture of the mind is master-mastering images: imperial representational-expressive forms charged with prosecuting large and urgent business with reality. But Crites is proposing more than that. In his view imagination is the primary integrating power of experience and mind. He says:

As an activity of the psyche as a whole, it [imagination] returns constantly to that fluidity in which the psyche itself dissolves to mingle with the environing potencies of things, and out of which, individually and collectively, it is reborn. *Consciousness itself takes form out of the imagination, rather than the reverse* . . . [emphasis mine]. Imagination not only parallels but participates in the life of nature, with its rhythm of negation and formation. They are one life. Furthermore, if I may add a theological gloss, when this one life of nature and imagination is animated by the breath of the spirit, it joins our experience at its divine source. [8]

These are large and strong claims, attributing both cognitive and ontotheological successes to the imagination. The cognitive claim is our present concern. I think Crites would have at least as much trouble showing it to be the case as Kant did in bringing off the schematism in the First Critique ("The Schematism of the Pure Concepts of the Understanding"). The juxtaposition with Kant is not whimsical. Kant says:

The schema is in itself always a product of the imagination. Since, however, the synthesis of imagination aims at no special intuition, but only at unity in the determination of sensibility, the schema has to be distinguished from the image. . . . This representation of a universal procedure of imagination in providing an image for a concept, I entitle the schema of this concept. . . . This schematism of our understanding, in its application to appearances and their mere form, is an art concealed in the depths of the human soul, whose real modes of activity nature is hardly likely ever to allow us to discover, and to have open to our gaze.[9]

7. Crites, "Unfinished Figure," p. 172.
8. Ibid., p. 173.
9. Immanuel Kant, *The Critique of Pure Reason*, trans. by Norman Kemp Smith (New York: Macmillan, 1965), pp. 182-183.

Kant, I suppose, is at the antipode of what Crites is after, despite what Kant proposes for the role of imagination in the cognitive enterprise. Kant is too much a man of Enlightenment mentality to put imagination in the driver's seat when the game is our knowledge of nature. But he was, of course, in the cognitive game in as large a way as one could wish, or endure.[10] He would not have expected imagination to affect the unity of human beings with/in nature or with God. Kant, or at any rate someone imbued with the Kantian spirit, would find Crites's views finely poetical, but indemonstrable.

Be that as it may, I want to reduce the epistemological issue to more manageable proportions, that is, to the question of historical knowledge.

II. Historical Knowledge as a Specialization of Imaginational Cognitivity

Crites has very little to say on this topic—directly, that is; by indirection (more properly, by inference), a good deal. Consider this:

> What is properly christological is this story, and not a God-man as such, mythic or otherwise. . . . To say that it is the gospel of incarnation is to say that God is fully present in this story, in its enactment and wherever it is told, sung, sacramentally celebrated. The Word becomes flesh in this story and its figurations. It is living flesh, in movement: he lives, he dies, and behold he lives again.
>
> What is redemptive about the Gospel story is precisely that in it God shares our human lot and identifies his own existence with it, full of possibility.[11]

Does this mean that God becomes an object-subject of knowledge in the telling of the Story, both in its original (first-century) telling and forever thereafter in its *authentic* telling?[12] Grant Crites that in his view *telling* is an inclusive metaphor: "told, sung, sacramentally celebrated."

10. According to the standard view, the game's outcome is pitifully thin for religion. This paper has no stake either in challenging or in accepting that understanding of Kant.

11. Crites, "Unfinished Figure," pp. 178-179.

12. What are the criteria of the authenticity thus engaged? Properly, this trips the truth-truthfulness again. Here I anticipate results by noting that for Crites (this holds also for Hauerwas) the criteria and definition of authenticity cannot be primarily or essentially historiographical. That is, the truth of/about Jesus Christ cannot be *reconstructed*. It has to be existentially replicated.

This concession compounds the confusion of diverse modes of presumptive cognitivity:[13]

    a. the expressive;
    b. the fact-assertive (assertoric).

This distinction, a-b, ought not to be construed as subjective-objective. It is not drawn, in other words, to activate modern philosophic prejudices. Expressive (a) modes of discourse ("discourse" = every kind of "voice") may well have a superior—relative to (b)—purchase on the richest modes of *experience*. It does not follow, and it is not *prima facie* the case, that the expressive mode in any "voice" has a superior cognitive purchase on the modes of *being*.

So rough-and-ready (no doubt more rough than ready) a distinction between modes of experience and modes of being threatens to throw us prematurely into metaphysics. Let us try to diminish, or at least contain, so dire a threat by keeping our eyes fixed for the moment on the issues of historical knowledge and thereafter of historical reality, as follows.

When we are seriously and affirmatively engaged with the Christian faith we not only *believe* the Gospel is true, we *claim* it is true, and we assert its truth. This means *first*: there are items in the New Testament-grounded faith that are historically true. Item: Jesus Christ did indeed and in fact rise (was raised: Acts 2:24; 13:30) from the dead. We know of course that Resurrection eventually becomes a symbol. No one in the Story claims that God created a symbol in raising Jesus from the dead. Using Acts 13 as a model we should say that the point and climax of the narrative is an assertion of the resurrection of Jesus as an actual event.

Secondly, the New Testament faith is ontologically true: what it says about God, and about human existence and its good and its destiny, is the case. If it is not the case, then "we are of all men the most to be pitied" (I Cor. 15:19). How so? What sort of failure would be involved? Not a failure of imagination; it would not be a failure rightly to appropriate a symbol in which the heights and depths of existence are expressed. If the ontological truth-claims of the New Testament are false, then the Christian religious life, understood and pursued as the knowledge and service of God in Jesus Christ, is founded on an illusion. The effects of entertaining such an illusion might be benign; so is Santa

---

13. The particular point at issue is historical knowledge, i.e., knowledge of the past. I think the diverse modes can be tracked into other cognitional fields, but this is not ventured in this paper.

Claus. Santa is a gloss, a purfle, on societal and individual life-patterns, adopted and adapted without significant recourse to Jolly St. Nick. For the coherence, value, and durability of those structures, it does not matter that Santa Claus is an illusion, or, if you prefer, a myth. But if we are not in fact and truth covenanted with God in Christ, from whom nothing in life or death can separate us, then we are fatefully positioned to be religious freebooters and exploiters, carpetbaggers; or, alternatively, their victims. Our Christianity might still retain some functional value: an instrument for social control (Marx), a screen for self-aggrandizement (Nietzsche). But there would be no truth to it; and actuality would be lost on its adherents.

I do not mean to question that New Testament faith has a "narrative structure." If for the moment we look again at Acts 13, we ought to see that the narrative is focused absolutely on what God has done in (then recent) history. The narrative altogether is intended to furnish the authentic and indispensable clues for the recognition of God's agency in "the course of human events" (to pilfer a phrase from a semireligious proclamation).

Nothing is gained by denying that many biblical stories are full of imaginational-expressive content. But how many of these are in the New Testament? How many of the ones in the New Testament are parables told by, or attributed to, Jesus? Crites's construal of the infancy stories is richly suggestive.[14] As we all know, these charming stories do not appear in the Pauline preaching; nor in Mark or John. The best we can attribute to them is *verisimilitude* (see below, p. 288). But what is the *truth* of which they are a seeming, a simulation? A spiritual value, an ideality susceptible of incorporation in an actual infinity of societal and personal life-patterns? Or are they imaginational elaborations of b-mode truth? And as such do they not have a *nisus* against which the church fathers had, early on, to set the brakes?

It is also a fact of history that theologians have sometimes misappropriated b-mode truth items, assimilating them to categorial systems whose provenance is anything but scriptural. But, surely, very few of the monumental systems of Christian doctrine thus fashioned have substituted a theory of rational-conceptual cognitivity for a historically situated acknowledgment of God as that "truthing" Presence "full of grace and truth" in whom all things are constituted.[15]

14. Crites, "Unfinished Figure," pp. 167-168.
15. See David Burrell's criticism of rationalistic-metaphysical interpretations of Aquinas's analogical theories in his *Aquinas: God and Action* (Notre Dame: University of Notre Dame Press, 1979).

III. Metaphysical Theories of History

I intend to make comparatively short work of the third topic, metaphysical theories of history. Neither Crites nor Hauerwas has much to say directly on it. Some things can be legitimately inferred.

Let us begin with a conventional distinction: *linear* versus *cyclical*. There are good reasons for being unhappy with this conventionality. For one, both concepts (though perhaps we should say *metaphors)* are vague. Another reason: both concepts/metaphors have often been captured and reduced to unnatural servitude in a variety of metaphysical-theological systems. Consider linearity. In much of modern historiography, linearity has been understood as the causal nexus linking temporally successive events in unbroken and unbreakable necessity, either rational or mechanical; or, as for Spinoza, both rational and mechanical.

The model for this modern historiographical version of linearity was Newtonian mechanics. Uniformitarian doctrines of causality are still around, but their courts are filled with tumult.

Another version of linear history is rooted in biblical faith: historical time (the time of human being) is phasic. Its phases describe the life-process, so to speak, both of history and the space-time world as a whole. That life-process is irreversible. It includes the cycles of empirical nature and the rhythms of human empire. But the whole of space-time creation is moving—rather, is being moved—to an unutterably grand denouement.

Now how does a typological interpretation of scripture-history (in which Crites expresses a lively and instructive interest) relate to this linearity? Jesus Christ does not *repeat* the Adam-figure. The first Adam is—forgive the sober pun—an adumbration, in some essential aspects, of Jesus Christ. Mary is not a *recurrence* of Eve. Eve is an anticipation, pledge, and promise, of Mary. Eve is an envisagement of the fulfillment of human-as-woman in Mary.

Seen from such a perspective, biblically grounded history is structured; it is a divinely orchestrated progression of patterns. If Barth is right, the pattern-imperator is Covenant. Covenant, however, is hard pressed by another: the Lord-in-his-kingdom. It says something about our political sensibilities, and about the softening of Barth's theological fiber, that we should like to play down that competitor to Covenant; and that Barth comes nearly all the way to confessing that God has no other business, perhaps no other life worth mentioning, than Humanity.

The expansion of the second commanding metaphor (the Lord-in-his-kingdom) inspires and sustains an analogy. Just as God's will grounds and binds all time-events together with all created powers, so there is an immanent monarchical power-center in human beings, and it is a triumvirate. The triumvirate consists of: memory, by which human time is bound; understanding, by which the empirical-sensory manifold is united; will, the prime agent in human action.

Hence to a conclusion on topic 3. We must look for *agency* as well as *pattern* in a theory of historical reality. Some parts of the Story are largely concerned with what we (= the human subjects-objects of God's actions) make of what God has done in/as revelation: Have we been "obedient to the heavenly vision" (Acts 26:19), that transaction in which a categorical command-mission is conveyed? These parts of the Story are unintelligible, except perhaps as scraps of biography or autobiography, without the great grounding-framing of truth-assertions: "God was in Christ"; "and he dwelt among us, full of grace and truth . . . and from his fullness have we all received, grace upon grace." In such matchless, all but unutterably glorious displays of creative process and providential ordering and redeeming Presence, God is the agent, God alone.

I suggested above that such historical-ontological claims inescapably involve *criteria of recognition*. God is as God does: true; but insufficient for the purpose just identified. The Gospel Story sets forth the criteria of recognition both of God's action and of the authentic human response. But I do not intend to develop this thesis until the fourth item on the agenda has been considered.

IV. Tensions Between Truth and Truthfulness: The Case of the Gospel and the Christian Story

My treatment of this topic is centered at the outset on proposals Hauerwas has made in *A Community of Character*.

First of all, Hauerwas puts "narrative structure" in a fundamental and commanding position. Here are some samples of that:

> The social significance of the Gospel requires the recognition of the narrative structure of Christian convictions for the life of the church.[16]

> Communities formed by a truthful narrative must provide the skills to transform fate into destiny so that the unexpected, especially as it comes in the form of strangers, can be welcomed as gift. (Emphasis his, all the way.)[17]

> . . . descriptively the self is best understood as a narrative, and normatively we require a narrative that will provide the skills appropriate to

16. Hauerwas, *A Community of Character*, p. 9.
17. Ibid., p. 10.

the conflicting loyalties and roles we necessarily confront in our existence. The unity of the self is therefore more like the unity that is exhibited in a good novel.[18]

Thus the issue of truthfulness is already heavily engaged. What follows makes this even clearer: "A truthful telling of the story cannot
be guaranteed by historical investigation (though that investigation
certainly can be in service to the truth), but by being the kind of people
who can bear the burden of that story with joy. We, not less than the
first Christians, are the continuation of the truth made possible by
God's rule."[19]
What is it that makes narrative truthful?

> The necessary interrelation of narrative and character provides the
> means to test the truthfulness of narratives. . . . Just as scientific theories
> are partially judged by the fruitfulness of the activities they generate, so
> narratives can and should be judged by the richness of moral character
> and activity they generate . . . so significant narratives are at once the
> result of and continuation of moral communities and character that form
> nothing less than a tradition. And without tradition we have no means
> to ask questions of truth and falsity.[20]

Does Hauerwas mean that tradition is a necessary but not a sufficient
condition for the determination of the truthfulness of Christian life
and thought? Surely, it makes some kind of sense to ask of *any* tradition whether its truth-claims are in fact true. Perhaps this is conceded
by the following: "What we require is not no story but a true story."
But perhaps not: "What is crucial is not that Christians know the truth,
but that they be the truth."[21] Such a claim is an all but irresistible
temptation to beg Hauerwas to distinguish one kind of truth (cognitional) from another kind (moral: integrity, existential authenticity,
and the like). But I manage to fend off this temptation in order to
pursue a different though related interest. That is to test the differ-
ence(s) between truth and truthfulness in/of story. This interest is deployed in the following questions:

> A. What is the relation of aesthetic truthfulness to historical-his-
> toriographical truth?
> B. Is aesthetic truthfulness the strongest and most reliable bridge to
> actuality? If we grant that metaphor is the indispensable speciality of im-

18. Ibid., p. 144.
19. Ibid., p. 52.
20. Ibid., p. 95.
21. Ibid., pp. 149, 150.

agination in story, what enables us to discern the "fit" of a metaphor with actuality?[22]

C. Parts of the Story (Gospel) are clearly experiential-confessional. Other parts are as clearly apodictical: they purport to demonstrate where and even how God's action and character dominate and dictate the structure and the vectors of experience as well as the shape and movement of actuality more generally.

(A.) Truthfulness in the aesthetic mode, in respect to story, is verisimilitude: likeness to truth.[23] We judge a fictional story, say Faulkner's "The Bear" or *Absalom Absalom!* to be authentic, true to life. Natives of Oxford, Mississippi might say, "I knew the man from whom Thomas Sutpen, in *Absalom Absalom!* is drawn," or Ike McCaslin in "The Bear." True or not, that is a biographical claim. As such, it does not bear on the truthfulness of the story. Faulkner created a possible world, an imaginational state of affairs with a veridical consistency (= texture) and a coherence (= intelligible connectedness). Yoknapatawtha County hangs together; not of course, like a conceptual system, but as an imaginational narrative history, its phases, characters, and components altogether coinhering. The world thus created is not a *copy* of the south across one hundred and fifty years, more or less. It is an alternative historical world. Granted, cross-referencing to/with the "real" historical world is inevitable. Properly disciplined, such cross-referencing may be appropriate and even fruitful. Faulkner's fictional world tells us something about the human condition that we need to know. I do not linger to specify that, except to note that what we properly learn is not in the modality of: "the real historical world *might* have turned out this way." What we learn (or ought to) is more like this: "That is the way, it really is the way, community and character interact under the historical givens Faulkner specifies."

So much, for the present, for the truthfulness of fictive historical worlds. What should we say about historiographical reconstructions of the putatively real past? First: Hauerwas was well advised to take on historical-moral relativism.[24] It is a serious problem for his thesis: "Through the church, therefore, the world is given a history. Indeed the

---

22. Brian Wicker draws and employs systematically a distinction between metaphor and analogy. "In analogical talk about God, we do not have to deny before we can affirm; we simply affirm that the statement is only true as long as we remember that it is no more than analogical. When we say that God is the cause of the existence of the world, the word *cause* is being used analogically. But this does not mean that (as with metaphor) we want to deny the literal truth of the statement." *The Story-Shaped World* (London: Athlone Press, 1975), p. 26.

23. From the Latin, meaning *probability*.

24. Hauerwas, *A Community of Character*, pp. 101-108.

term 'world' derives its intelligibility from there being a people who can supply a history for the world. Of course such a history cannot ignore the fact that the world involves many separate stories that cannot be easily reconciled or even related."[25] Second: The heart of the problem for historiographical cognitivity is not the sheer multiplicity of story-ordered worlds. Some of these stories themselves claim (= inwardly purport) to be true accounts of the dealings of God(s) with human beings. Those claims, as well as claims made for such stories, require cross-referencing. This demand is not primarily for true-false correlations with other stories but with imperious engagements with actuality. *Hence with a world imposed, not a world humanely created.*

Third: On Hauerwas's terms, and Crites's, what is the truth-bridge from tradition-community-history to actuality? For neither Hauerwas nor Crites is the truth-correlational route to be found in the latest update of putatively scientific historiography, neither in its methods nor in its specific cognitive yields. The time-modes (not just the past) that matter most for human existence are misshapen, deformed, by scientific "rationality." So some other ontological-cognitional warranties must be found with their own kinds of universals, and their own kinds of predictabilities.

If the New Testament Story is true, it is God in Christ who sponsors,[26] in one mode or another, all our transactions with actuality. "In one mode or another" is inescapable. Can this be translated into the terms preferred by Crites and Hauerwas, that is, into one kind or another of narrative? Not unless "narrative" can be properly inflated to include every kind of recounting and relating, except sheer mathematical computation. More specifically, the recounting, the laying out, of the transactional relations between God, world, and human being must be capable of diagrammatic elucidation.

I have intentionally put the issue in a way that appears to drain off the aesthetic (affectional-conational) densities of the Christian life. But I do not assume that any kind of conceptual schematism is divinely or rationally appointed to lord it over the figural imagination. The issue is put, as I just have, to bring again to the fore the (B) question: "Is aesthetic truthfulness the strongest and most reliable bridge to actuality? If we grant that metaphor is the indispensable speciality of imagination in story, what enables us to discern the 'fit' of a metaphor with actuality?"

My answer has the following parts. (i) Aesthetic truthfulness gives place to truth in the ontological mode when the world-action im-

25. Ibid., p. 91.
26. From the Latin, meaning *guarantor;* or from *spondere,* to promise solemnly.

peratives of faith are directly engaged. (ii) Hence, the "fit" of metaphor is not determined by appeal to tradition-narrative, either scriptural or secular. In the Story the man asks, "What must I do to be saved?" The actuality-determination displayed in Jesus' response goes beyond the received tradition (Law): liquidate all your holdings; and sign on for the duration. Which being translated means: "You must be aware that a new vectoring presence-power confronts you. Embrace it and engage it. For you are already beyond salvation from Tradition. Do this, or else. . . ." (iii) In the engagement with God, whatever metaphoric imagination can, and does, contribute to situational discernment and existential resolution, it cannot, and does not, move the will. The engagement with God is always on the time-frontier. Hence: "What must I do . . . ?" must be answered in perceived and understood disjunctive consequential alternatives running into the future.

We come now to (C): Parts of the Story are clearly experiential-confessional. Other parts are as clearly apodictical. . . . The confessional mode (a—on p. 283) specializes in the effects of putatively divine activity. Balaam's question (Numbers 23:23), "What has God wrought?" comes after: "God brings them [Israel and Jacob] out of Egypt; they have as it were the horns of the wild ox. . . . Behold, a people! As a lioness it raises up and as a lion lifts itself" (Numbers 23:22-24; RSV). And goes about a bloody business.

Here is a tumult, a riot, of metaphors. They celebrate the potency of the religious community. But they also identify the source of its power and integrity: What has *God* wrought?

Does this mean that the effect is such that only God could have brought it off? Have we isolated here the germ of an *argumentum a contingentia mundi (historiae)*? Hardly. The religious roots of that classical metaphysical argument are not to be despised, but that is another question. A very different phenomenon is presented here. *The vectorial structure of a historical situation* (a community = the impacting environment, natural and societal) *is such that God is its ground, its providence, and its end.*

To come to terms with this we must set aside any monolithic modern causality doctrines. Causal efficacy is indeed involved: that of God, and that of created agents, notably, of course, persons. Notably persons because such is the agency we know intimately, though not always—God knows—perspicuously. To be a person is to be "a vectorial structure" in a historical situation. Dark sayings, barbaric metaphors. Let us seek to enlighten them, dream of civilizing them.

(i) "Vectorial structure": one which can be defined only in relation to a direction. If it is the case that the self is a narrative (Hauerwas), it is so because self-agency has a *trajectory:* (a) it is phasic in/across time;

(b) it is end-(good)-oriented. So also for societal-communal life.[27] Social reality is described by a complex trajectory. The trajectory can be cross-sectioned; but social actuality is not a composite of cross-sections.[28]

(ii) Personal and societal trajectories can be "mapped" in relation to categorical obligations: goods that are differentially necessary and sufficient for right relations with the primordial and ultimate powers of being.

(iii) God's being is not teleologically organized. It is teleologically displayed (revealed). God does not have to act in/across time to be one with himself, either in power or satisfaction. Nevertheless God wills, sustains, and redeems a world. This is congruent with his goodness. It is not necessitated by his goodness.

As persons we are teleologically synthesized and teleologically displayed (expressed): vectorial structures. But a human being is persistently deficient both in self-unity and societal unity. The great historic religions acknowledge this. They display paradigmatic persons, historical figures, in whom that persistent historical-ontological deficiency is overcome. In each of these religions many stories are told about the paradigm. And each of these great traditions provides a variety of guides, directives, clues, keys for the existential-practical appropriation of the truth of the stories.[29] Each of them provides a bridge to link the story and its imperial paradigm to worlds external, if not hostile, to the story. For this weighty purpose the core Story and its primitive community have to be construed as a metaphor for humanity as such and altogether.

I suggest that the indispensable pattern for the bridging is the character-action structure (= the normative self) accepted in the historical community as the necessary response to the comprehensive divine imperative: the proper service of God. I invite you to consider St. Paul's formulation of this principle in Romans: "Do not be conformed to this world but be transformed by the renewal of your mind, that you may prove what is the will of God, what is good and acceptable and perfect" (Romans 12:2). And again in Philippians: "Have this mind among yourselves, which is yours in Christ Jesus, who, though he was in the form of God, did not count equality with God a thing to be grasped, but

---

27. Modern-classical distinctions between statics and dynamics are very like "an unearthly ballet of bloodless categories" (Bradley).

28. There is good reason why a rigidly class-hierarchized society might in its metaphysical pieties treat time as an illusion. If there is no movement through the structures, no alternative futures anywhere in the social system, existential time is frozen. Hence the infinite wisdom of the Hinduism-Buddhism axis: the gap between desire and its fulfilling object-time must be closed — by extinguishing desire.

29. See David Little and Sumner B. Twiss, *Comparative Religious Ethics* (San Francisco: Harper & Row, 1978), on action-guides, both moral and religious.

emptied himself, taking the form of a servant, being born in the likeness of men. And being found in human form he humbled himself and became obedient unto death, even death on a cross" (Philippians 2:5-8; RSV).[30] Jesus Christ has "the form of God." He assumes "the form of a servant." He is found in human likeness. And he becomes obedient even unto death on a cross. So he is the example, the paradigm supreme: he is the decisive and ultimate clue to the nature—the being and disposition—of God.

The ethic straightway follows. The mandated response to the recreative love of God in Christ is love for all God's children: doing good to all.

Thence a swift and sure return to the metaphysical-theological dimension: the acquisition of Christian (= Christlike) virtues (moral attributes) is the work of God's power-presence in us. This is the true *pietas*[31] of faith: not what we mean habitually by pious feelings or sentiments, but responsibility, loyalty, sense of duty. So disposition is the clue, not sentiment or feeling.

In sum, then, the (Gospel) Story displayed, enacted, in the confessional mode expresses (such is its intentionality) the self-identity of the Christian community in/across time and space. In its assertoric-apodictical mode the Story is told *apologia pro vita sua:* it is the reason why we act (again, the intentionality is decisive) "Christianly." It is the background of the "vectorial structure" of Christian existence. Not that one is thus positioned and empowered to predict where the "project" will land, the point at which the trajectory will be completed. (Steadfastness, faith-keeping, is not the name of a policy; courage is not a label for a program; love is not a strategy; hope is not a dream of Utopia.) In us all strength finally and surely diminishes, and then fails us altogether: a fact of life.

The metaphysical import of the Story is that the real and final sense of the trajectory lies absolutely in the life of God. In the covenant of creation we are not aimed at becoming God, or gods. Communion, identity of will: that is the divine appointment. In ancient language God comes to earth so that such earthlings as ourselves might rise to God. And that during all the earthbound time we might in good cheer give God the glory.

30. C. H. Dodd translates: "Have the same thoughts among yourselves as you have in communion with Christ Jesus," *The Apostolic Preaching,* cited in William F. Arndt and F. Wilbur Gingrich, *A Greek-English Lexicon of the New Testament* (Chicago: University of Chicago Press, 1957), p. 874.

31. I remember with great fondness how Miss Jones struggled in her class in Virgil's *Aeneid* to show us how his *pietas* was very different from what we understood by *piety.* Not that she wasn't a good Methodist. . . .

A Respectful Reply to the Assertorical Theologian

Stephen Crites

To find myself on the business end of Julian Hartt's cudgel is no new experience. Having been Professor Hartt's student during the fabled fifties, I am put into a nostalgic state of masochistic ecstasy as his blows rain on my cranium, delivered with that unmistakable rhetorical flourish and logical thump. There are few teachers, and few colleagues in the years since, whom I honor so cordially. He will perhaps prefer that I do not say he taught me everything I know. But his critique does remind me to whom I am indebted for my model of restraint in making large claims.

Actually my claims are not so sweeping as Hartt suggests in Part I of his article. I will not presume to speak for Stanley Hauerwas, who is more than capable of speaking for himself. Nor will I repeat here the analysis I offered in the article to which Hartt refers. But the article does not treat narrative as the only imaginative form, nor does it imply that all discourse short of pure mathematics is imaginative. Theology, for instance, is not a work of imagination but a hermeneutical discipline, a *Wissenschaft* charged with the critical interpretation of expressions that do take imaginative form, such as biblical narrative or personal vision.

Still, I do not plead to be let off on grounds that I have been

Stephen Crites, "A Respectful Reply to the Assertorical Theologian," *Journal of the American Academy of Religion*, LII, 1 (March 1984): 131-139.

grossly misinterpreted. I am basically guilty as charged, your honor; but before you pass the hemlock, let me see what I have to say for myself.

I surely agree that a merely expressive act cannot entitle anyone to assert a fact. But Hartt's central distinction between the expressive and the fact-assertive is much less theologically useful than he thinks. On the one hand, the category of "fact," in any strait-laced sense of the term, has a rather minor theological role. On the other hand, imagination is not merely expressive. Its expressive function, indeed, is founded on its more basic role in the formation of experience and the envisioning of possibility. Otherwise there wouldn't be much to express. Experience is our access to what-is, and imagination gives experience its aesthetic coherence.

Spelling out these counterassertions and some related theological points will furnish my agenda in the following remarks.

I. Izzata Fact?

Professor Hartt is not to be put off by lyrical effusions and *Schwärmerei*. Like a theological Sgt. Friday he confronts rapture with an impassive demand for facts. He does at one point (p. 289) seem a little apologetic about draining theological claims of their vital religious juices, but he has driven his distinction between the expressive and the fact-assertive so hard that everything but the latter seems largely decorative.

I should think that it might be assertive enough simply to recite the creed, tinctured though it plainly is by narrative form. But Hartt is having none of that either: we must assert not only *belief* in the gospel, but its *truth* (Part II). Let us ponder this distinction a little. The former, I take it, is a statement about the believer, the latter about a putative fact. But I should have thought that a statement of belief refers both to the subject and to the object of belief. If indeed it can be said to unite the two, that is just what is wanted. It is at least what I should want. For a Christian who recites his creed in good conscience, what is problematic is not whether Jesus Christ was resurrected or whether it was God who raised him, but what the believer means when he asserts those beliefs. Where in the topography of human discourse are such assertions located? But here again Hartt offers us a stark choice: Is the statement true in a merely symbolic sense, as the content of a purely expressive act on the believer's part, or is it a fact? Now my article nowhere appeals to the shifty notion of symbolic truth, and Hartt's alternatives put me in the position of a man who is asked whether he would prefer to be shot or garroted. Aren't there some other options? Something less deadly perhaps?

Posing these stark alternatives makes Hartt's own choice seem clearer than it is. Does a statement become factual by being asserted? Perhaps, but only in its grammatical form, which precisely cannot distinguish veracity from verisimilitude, or from wishful thinking. In order to state a fact some material criteria have to be met. Its correctness must be open to any investigator who examines available evidence, i.e., it must be verifiable. The positivists were not wrong about that. They were wrong in making such facticity the measure of the meaning of referential statements. There is no reason to doubt, in general, that the class of actual events is much larger than the class of verifiable facts. But there is always reason to doubt, in any particular case, whether something has transpired that cannot be empirically verified.

Now, the New Testament is not particularly rich in verifiable facts. The residue left by two centuries of historical criticism, in particular, is not impressive at all. More important: even among the facts that an impartial investigator might be able to determine with more ample documentary or physical evidence, one could not in principle find confirmation for any of the paramount claims of the New Testament. For the prime sticking point concerns precisely the assumption of divine agency that, as Hartt rightly asserts, informs the entire New Testament message. Not one to make things easy for himself, Hartt boldly chooses the resurrection of Jesus as an example. It does seem to be a fact that Jesus was crucified. That this certifiably dead man was resuscitated might at a pinch count as a putative fact, though the prospects of verifying it are not promising. But that God raised him from the dead is not a factual statement at all. It is either much more or much less. It is not possible, in the very nature of the claim, to provide evidence for it. So elusive is divine agency, from any empirical standpoint, that it is always subject to doubt. Whether I assert it, or whether I assert my belief in it, is from a factual point of view a distinction without a difference. It does suit the nature of the claim, on the other hand, that if I am to assert belief in this story I must undertake a moral responsibility for the assertion that is never required merely to acknowledge a fact: a convergence of this story with my own story, at once a hermeneutical and a moral task.

Still, the assertion does not make it a fact. Hartt is entitled to the language of fact only if he is willing to submit his claims about divine agency to the normal procedures by which critical historians settle other matters of sober historical fact. Of this he gives no sign. I suspect that like other theologians of assertorical disposition he wants to have it both ways: to assert his claims as facts while denying the applicability of the usual fact-testing procedures. But that seems a textbook case of a category mistake.

II. Royal Metaphysics

Without yielding on this point, however, Hartt hastens to higher ground. The New Testament not only lays out the facts, but discloses metaphysical truth. "If the New Testament Story is true, it is God in Christ who sponsors, in one mode or another, all our transactions with actuality" (p. 289). Now there is an assertion so stout and so comprehensive that it might have been translated from the German. "In one mode or another," perhaps, but surely Professor Hartt would agree with Miss Jones and me, pious Methodists all, that you do have to make distinctions.

For here again I find, if not precisely a category mistake, at any rate a confusion in forms of discourse. The Gospel is a narrative, and from the language of narrative one cannot legitimately derive universally inclusive statements about actuality. However one judges the viability of metaphysics, its appropriate language is abstract, its method dialectical argument. Honest metaphysicians have undertaken through rigorous argument to penetrate the veil of appearance and to descry the true nature of things. The job is not done through evangelical assertion, as though that provided some privileged access. A Christian metaphysics is in a class with such current absurdities as Christian geology or Christian economics. You either pay the price of admission, in the slow cultivation of a discipline, or you are not entitled to a seat. There have certainly been Christian thinkers, including Professor Hartt, who have amply paid that price, but there is always a significant logical hiatus between their Christianity and their metaphysics. The hiatus creates no problem so long as it is acknowledged, but if the authority of the Gospel is invoked in support of a metaphysics (or a geological or economic theory) the resulting confusion infects both the discipline and the meaning of the Gospel.

The effort, on the other hand, to make the Gospel meet an independent criterion of historicity, facticity, or metaphysical truth is, as Hans Frei has shown (in *The Eclipse of Biblical Narrative,* [New Haven, Conn.: Yale University Press, 1974]), what has driven Protestant theology into that cul de sac in which it has been languishing since the Enlightenment. For this move does violence to the form in which the Gospel itself expresses its meaning.

It seems innocent enough, for instance, to attribute personal agency to God. There is certainly nothing impersonal about the biblical God, if that were the issue. But for Hartt this quality of personal agency appears to express a general truth. Again, the issue concerns language. What Hartt calls the personal agency of the biblical God consists formally in the fact that he appears in the text in a series of stories, or is addressed in psalms and prayers. There are of course other biblical contexts, but to the extent that the narrative or lyric form of the language fades, so does the vivid sense of personal agency. But in the narrative God heads a cast of characters including men and women, angels, demons, and the like. He speaks, hears and answers, acts, he threatens Nineveh and then thinks better of it, and he teases Jonah when his prophet can't stand this change of heart. "Aha!" says the skeptic, "this God is anthropomorphic, or andromorphic, patriarchal." "Aha!" says Professor Hartt, doughty defender of the faith, "This God is a personal agent." I think both of them are jumping to conclusions, confusing the exigencies of narrative locution with the generalized language of metaphysical definition. No doubt the story requires critical interpretation, but a hermeneutical theology will not be quick to dogmatize, either with the story or against it, about what God is everywhere and always. For now we see in a glass darkly, see something like our own faces looking back at us, though further enlightenment will disclose that we are not even seeing our faces all that clearly (I Cor 13:12).

But beyond this formal problem there is a more serious difficulty in a metaphysical reduction of the narrative, a difficulty deriving from the actual content of gospel narrative in particular. He is born among cattle, he grows up in a carpenter's shop, he recruits a band of simple working folk and goes about preaching and telling stories in the open air, he runs afoul of the authorities and is consigned to a miserable death at an early age. Now, this is the messiah, a king Davidic and in some sense divine. As if that claim were not bizarre enough, Paul says he is the image of the invisible God, John that he is the enfleshed Logos through whom all things were made. King, Lord, Son of God, this crucified spinner of parables: make a metaphysics of *that*. The most sardonic critics of Christianity have had a better sense for the ironies of this story than its assertorical theologians have: consider Nietzsche, or Pontius Pilate. The gospel narrative turns everything topsy-turvy. It does not provide us a public ideology with which to do argumentative battle against the leading contenders in the game of world-definition. It ironically inverts any worldly wisdom. Lord-in-his-kingdom? Sure, look at his purple robe and his royal crown. It is the soldiers who pay him mock-homage, like a gang of boys torturing a cornered animal, who ironically fulfill the gospel vision of divine kingship. There may be an "urgent engagement with actuality" here, but it yields no definition of actuality with which to replace some other enjoying public consensus. This story casually adopts the conventional framework of signification in order to invert and negate it. If I were a German theologian I might say that the Gospel is a word of judgment against all public ideologies, all metaphysical assertions, all the kingdoms of this world. But let us just say that the Gospel is one ironical story, an irony, in particular, against the triumphalistic temptations of the Christian religion and its assertorical theologians. If there is a joke in this divine comedy, the joke is on them.

For when a particular interpretation of our world achieves wide currency, beyond the narrow circle of thinkers who have earned the right to their views, it is always relevant to ask in whose interest such a notion has gained currency. Not only in metaphysics: In whose interest, for instance, are all those literary and theological deconstructionists deconstructing with such ant-like zeal? Popular programs of construction and deconstruction are almost always employed in the service of one or another of this world's principalities and powers. Christian metaphysicians and moralists have contributed generously to this legitimizing program in the great ages of Christendom, and there are theologians politically both left and right who still seem to hanker after those good old days when their fathers in the faith could consider themselves the quasi-official ideologists of great nations, yea, of Western Civilization—and tomorrow the world!

III. An Aesthetic Coherence

In considering that the time is mercifully past for this sort of foolishness (not to be confused with what Paul called the foolishness of the cross), I do not mean that the Gospel offers nothing in the way of a Christian life in the world. To the world-definers and their patrons it presents itself as nothing but ironical inversion, and yet it does have a content expressed in an imaginative form integral to it. Shorn of triumphalism and metaphysical pretension, of what Luther called *theologia gloriae*, Christianity does in fact hang together nicely. It does not need to be inflated into a system comprehending "all transactions with actuality," nor does it require diagrammatic elucidation in order to be coherent. The gospel story and Jesus' own stories and sayings are mutually illuminating enough to form the basis of a *theologia crucis* that retains all the earthiness and paradox that Luther invested in that term. The kingdom of God evoked in the parables, for instance, has the same topsy-turvy irony with respect to worldly kingdoms as Jesus' own kingship has in the passion story, though told with a comic edge that gives the inversion a gentler tone. The comportment appropriate to that kingdom, furthermore, is entirely consonant with the character of that oddest of rulers, and equally at odds with the conditions of other kinds of citizenship. The sacramental heart of Christian worship unites the worshipper in one life, sacrificed and regained, with Christ crucified.

This common life creates what Hauerwas aptly calls "a community of character," and in this outward-looking community the Christian life takes on a characteristic modesty and good humor, at once realistic about the violence of the human condition and hopeful about the human prospect.

I am almost embarrassed to offer such an obvious description of Christianity. It certainly does not render rigorous theological work superfluous—perhaps not even diagrammatic elucidation! But I think my sketch at least suggests the sort of coherence Christianity has, a coherence that I am willing to bear the onus of calling aesthetic. It does not prove that the Gospel's claims about Jesus Christ are historical facts or metaphysical disclosures beyond the wit of heathen philosophy, but the life described does avow these claims in the appropriate way, by being of a piece with them. The same story that unites the life and death of the story-teller with the stories he told also incorporates the common life of those who hear and tell it after him. One could correctly call such a unity of life and belief moral if morality were not conventionally so bound to the application of general principles. Risking another sort of misunderstanding, I think it is more precise to call it aesthetic: a paradoxical story is brought to bear on the imaginative formation of experience. That is the process I tried to describe in the essay to which Professor Hartt responded. Such an aesthetic unity of life and belief, in which women and men have actually lived and for which some of them have died, comprises a logical circle which cannot be segmented into fact-assertive and expressive aspects, truth and symbolism, without doing violence to the imaginative coherence it comprehends.

In quoting from my essay in Part II (p. 282), Hartt correctly infers that I do not think the incarnation is confined to the thirty-odd years of "phasic" time from the birth to the death of Jesus. Resurrection does odd things to phasic time. The life of the resurrected is not a mere extension of phasic time, but a mode of availability to which phasic time is irrelevant. I think it does imply that the Logos is made flesh, his flesh, wherever his story "is told, sung, sacramentally celebrated," or modelled in play-dough. He materializes. If this communication of presence is metaphoric, it is not a mere manner of speaking; it is the integrative movement of one thing into another, a metamorphosis. I agree with Professor Hartt (p. 290) that "the engagement with God is always on the time-frontier," that it is action "running into the future," but it is precisely on that frontier that the metaphoric communication transpires. (Cf. pp. 174-79 of my essay "Unfinished Figure: On Theology and Imagination"; see p. 279 n. 1 of this volume for source information.) It is not clear why "metaphoric imagination . . . cannot, and does not, move the will" (p. 290), unless imagination is understood to be a mere mental act, and metaphor to be a figure of speech. I am told that moving vans in Greece have METAPHOROS printed on their sides. Metaphor transports things from one place to another. Why should this mover of familiar household goods to a strange locale not move the will? Indeed, it may be a better term than "will" for the momentum in which our otherwise dissipated psychic and physical powers are integrated for action on the time-frontier. Take Polycarp or another second-century martyr, who certainly liquidated his holdings and signed on for the duration: if you attributed this startling move to his will-power, the evidence is that he would have protested that he had been moved by Christ himself to be united with him in his crucifixion and resurrection. Now there's a metaphor! And the martyr would have been right.

IV. Pity and Personal Agency

I want to complete this little *Auseinandersetzung* by splitting an exegetical hair with Professor Hartt. Unless, he says in Part II (p. 283), "the New Testament faith is ontologically true: what it says about God, and about human existence and its good and its destiny, is the case," then, he concludes, quoting Paul, "'we are of all men the most to be pitied.'" Actually Paul says that of Christ's resurrection, but that is not the hair I want to split. Let that crux of the story, the crux-surpassed, stand for the whole, as it has earlier in this discussion. So why are we Christians to be pitied if Christ is not raised?

Surely not simply because we will be caught believing something that is not the case. Perhaps Professor Hartt can imagine nothing more pitiable than that. I concede that it would be embarrassing. I spent some of the least pitiable years of my life believing in Santa Claus, and still am not entirely grateful to the mocking second-grader who disabused me. Still, I yielded to superior experience of the world, then as now convinced that one should accept unpalatable truths even if the world turns a little grayer. Hartt usefully distinguishes between belief in the Santa-legend and belief in Christ's gospel, but only to insist that in the latter case we are "of all men most to be pitied" if the story is untrue. Agreed, but not merely in the sense that we shall be found guilty of adding our pennyworth to the great weight of the world's nonsense. Two verses earlier (I Cor 15:17) Paul says, "If Christ has not been raised, your faith is futile and you are still in your sins." But "sins" here are not merely my ill-doings, nor faith a falsifiable belief-system. If Christ be not raised, he is just a corpse and I am just the personal agent I was and am, apart from him. He lives not, neither at God's right hand, nor in the church (which Paul insists is his risen body [I Cor 12]), nor in

Paul himself: "it is no longer I who live, but Christ who lives in me" (Gal 2:20), nor in any other believer ("if any one is in Christ he is a new creation; the old has passed away" [II Cor 5:17]). The Christ who lives has transcended the thirty-odd years of phasic time that ended on a Roman cross, and just to that extent has delivered me from my otherwise total confinement in that frail personal agency that Hartt so highly prizes, with its vulnerable belief-systems. That is why we are so pitiable if Christ does not live: we are still merely ourselves, still in our sins, still cut off from the divine life that created us.

Suspending exegesis for the moment, I want to observe that the status of the personal agent, for which "I" employ this tall thin pronoun, raises the issue on which Professor Hartt and I appear to be most fundamentally divided, though Hartt joins this issue so indirectly that it is easy to miss its importance. For Hartt the self-identity of the personal agent, both human and divine, seems unproblematic. His argument proceeds from its assumed metaphysical standing. That is why he is so incredulous at my suggestion (quoted in Part I) that imaginative activity precedes, in fact forms, personal identity, instead of merely being an expressive faculty of a personal consciousness already formed. Whatever the merits of my explanation, I do want to insist that personal identity is something that needs explaining. Not only is it problematic theoretically: it is in another sense problematic from the point of view of the New Testament. In the latter sense it seems to be precisely what "I" need to be delivered from. That is why I find Hartt's metaphysical commitment to the personal agent in phasic time so at odds with the Christian vision he so eloquently expresses in the closing pages of his reply. Not only is the contemporaneous presence of Christ unintelligible on that basis, but so is the closely related typological interpretation of Scripture discussed in my essay. And that, finally, is why Hartt's own account of typology (Part III) is so unscriptural. The juxtaposition of Christ and Adam, for instance, in that same Pauline chapter to which we have been referring—"For as in Adam all die, so also in Christ shall all be made alive" (I Cor 15:22)—cannot remotely be accommodated to Hartt's formulation, that "the first Adam is" (sober pun forgiven) "an adumbration, in some essential aspects, of Jesus Christ" (p. 285). In Paul's typological usage these two figures have far outgrown the status of two individuals in phasic time, of whom the language of adumbration might be adequate. They have become two living destinies contending on our own time-frontier.

Now I do not want to claim canonical status for my theory of imagination, developed, so far as I can tell, independently of my theological commitments. But it did occur to me that a serviceable theory of imagination might offer some guidance in recovering the force of the

301

traditional typological hermeneutic that I suspect *is* integral to the Gospel. I appreciate the attention of my mentor to this venture, and I acknowledge that he has, as always, succeeded in raising some acute critical questions about it.

But apropos of being pitiable, I suspect that Paul himself voiced what for the New Testament was the most pitiable human predicament when in another famous passage (Rom 7:24) he cried out: Wretched man that I am! Who will deliver me from this body of . . . personal agency, from this tall, thin, all-too-phallic pronoun?

Why the Truth Demands Truthfulness: An Imperious Engagement with Hartt

Stanley Hauerwas

You know you are in trouble when your former teacher criticizes you for trying to develop ideas you thought you had stolen from him. You are in even greater trouble when the criticisms raise issues you are not sure you understand, much less know how to answer. I keep thinking I should have gone to all his lectures. I fear I only heard the ones about story and missed all the meaty stuff about reality—or is it the reality of stuff? For Hartt is determined to make me deal head-on with metaphysical issues, or as he puts it, an imperious engagement with actuality (p. 289), which I have, admittedly, often given, at best, a sidelong glance. That I have done so has partly been because I think others are more skilled to deal with such matters, but also because for theological purposes I think the metaphysical issues are more appropriately dealt with indirectly.

For the contention that such a view is not entirely without precedent in Christian tradition I appeal to that ultimate authority that hovers over all engaged in this exchange—namely, John Wesley. In *A Plain Account of Genuine Christianity*, Wesley says, "If, then, it were possible (which I conceive it is not) to shake the traditional evidence of Christianity, still he that has the internal evidence (and every true believer

Stanley Hauerwas, "Why the Truth Demands Truthfulness: An Imperious Engagement with Hartt," *Journal of the American Academy of Religion*, LII, 1 (March 1984): 141-147.

hath the witness of evidence in himself) would stand firm and unshaken. Still, he could say to those who were striking at the external evidence, 'Beat on the sack of Anaxagoras,' but you can no more hurt *my* evidence of Christianity than the tyrant could hurt the spirit of that wise man. I have sometimes been almost inclined to believe that the wisdom of God has, in most later ages clogged and encumbered for this very end, that men (of reflection especially) might not altogether rest there, but be constrained to look into themselves also and attend to the light shining in their hearts."[1]

For many, I am sure I could have not picked a less happy "authority." To appeal to Wesley on such matters only confirms the suspicion that a pietistic presumption underlies all the talk about story and narrative that avoids questions of truth and falsity. For example, Wesley notes that "traditional evidence is of an extremely complicated nature, necessarily including so many and so various considerations that only men of strong and clear understanding can be sensible of its full force."[2] Some of us, it seems, are trying to avoid the work necessary to develop such a "strong and clear understanding" by falling back on the "internal" evidence we identify with a story that enables us to make coherent sense out of our lives. Such a story may demand that our lives be truthful, but that demand is not sufficient to sustain whether the story is in fact true. The story may have verisimilitude in a manner like Faulkner's "The Bear," but verisimilitude is not sufficient for a story such as we find in the Gospels which require "foundational metaphysical beliefs" because of their "reality-intending" character.[3]

That the Gospels have such a character or that they involve "foundational metaphysical beliefs," I have never sought to deny or avoid. Rather, my concern has been to insist, along the lines suggested by Wesley, that the kind of truth entailed by the Gospels, the kind of demands placed on reality, cannot be separated from the way in which the story of God we claim as revealed in Jesus' life, death, and resurrection forces a repositioning of the self vis-à-vis reality. In a certain respect my claim is stronger than Wesley's, as he gives the impression that you can know the evidence for Christian convictions separate from or prior to the internal evidence. On the contrary, I have tried to maintain that it is impossible to distinguish between "external" and "internal" evidence as the character of Christian belief requires the transformation of the self

1. John Wesley, *A Plain Account of Genuine Christianity*, in *John Wesley*, ed. Albert Outler (New York: Oxford University Press, 1964), p. 192.

2. Ibid., p. 192.

3. Julian Hartt, *Theological Method and Imagination* (New York: Seabury Press, 1977), p. 245.

in order rightly to see the actuality of our world without illusion or self-deception.

In that respect I think I am in fundamental agreement with Hartt when he criticizes those theologians who feel that "the Christian being" is "either a story or it is nothing that can speak to contemporary sensibility." He continues: "This is a counsel of despair. The New Testament faith is not just a story. It is also a strenuous effort to show how the import of the story must be made out: not only understood but, above all, appropriated. That requires theological work. Moreover, both as story and as theology, the Christian faith has now, and has always had, to compete with other stories and other theologies. So I think it is a fundamental and far-reaching mistake to suppose that telling the story is the whole thing. What one makes of the world and of one's own existence on the strength of the story: that is the pay-off. That is what real and decisive case-making is."[4]

I could not agree more as long as Hartt does not mean to imply or suggest that the "pay-off" can therefore be abstracted from the story and made an independent criterion of truth; or, put more exactly, as long as the "pay-off" does not become an independent criterion separate from the concrete story of Jesus of Nazareth. As Hartt rightly notes, Christians claim that story to be the "decisive and ultimate clue to the nature — the being and disposition — of God." A heady claim that certainly seems to be about reality — a reality, furthermore, that is hardly our invention or at our disposal.

Yet central to the ontological claims of that story is that we are captives to sin and, in fact, sinners. We are not just asked to look on ourselves as if we were sinners, as if this is a game or role we play some of the time. On the contrary, to face the character of our sinfulness is to engage actuality in its most imperious form. If in fact the world and ourselves do not answer to that description, which admittedly requires further depiction, then the story Christians tell can at best be regarded as a harmless fiction. But because the story takes out that kind of ontological draft, it is impossible to separate its metaphysical claims from the demands the story places on our lives. The "internal" evidence requires that the "external" have a certain character, the truth of the story requires that we be truthful if we are to see rightly the way the world is.

That the truth demands truthfulness for our ability to acknowledge it rightly is not in contradiction to the primary thrust of Hartt's concern or criticisms. The distinction he draws between expressive and fact-assertive cognitivity may seem to invite a separation between truth and truthfulness; but I do not believe that that is his primary intent, as

4. Ibid., p. 254.

what he means by "fact-assertive" is broad indeed. Rather, I take that distinction to denote the difference between Faulkner's *Absalom, Absalom!*, which demands only verisimilitude, and "fact-oriented history," such as Gibbon, which cannot and should not avoid challenge by the "facts." But Hartt refuses to press even that distinction too hard as he notes that the latter must also tell a story and the former is often drenched in what he calls "historicality."[5]

Moreover, I think he is right to suggest that it is a mistake, in the interest of protecting the gospel accounts from the criteria of "fact-oriented" history, to assimilate the story told about Jesus to verisimilitude. In that respect, many of us who have tried to illumine the kind of truth-claims made by the Gospel by exposing its narrative form may have employed the latter category in a far too crude manner. For as Goldberg and Tilley have argued,[6] the context and form of a narrative make all the difference for assessing the kind of truth-claims that are relevant to that story.[7] Hartt is right to insist that the kind of story we find in the Gospels requires that certain facts be true — that Jesus did call disciples, did get to Jerusalem, was tried, and that his body was missing from his tomb.[8] Moreover, it means that the shape given to Jesus' life through the gospel narratives should correspond to the shape of his life as God's anointed. There can be no attempt to avoid the historicity of the Gospel even if the latter questions cannot but involve judgments very much like those that are involved in verisimilitude. For the construing of a life entails attributing a "shape" to that life that at once determines which "facts" will count without excluding the possibility that other "facts" will make us reconsider how that life is to be understood as well assessed.[9] On such matters, though we may use a

---

5. Ibid., pp. 226-248.

6. Michael Goldberg, *Theology and Narrative: A Critical Introduction* (Nashville: Abingdon Press, 1981), pp. 194-240; Terrence Tilley, "Moments of Truth: Standards of Truth for a Narrative Theology," *Papers in Philosophical Theology of the 1982 Meeting of the AAR.*

7. Tilley argues that the proper mode of assessing stories in a religious context as true or false is to recognize that "true" and "false" are appraisals. Thus a "story can be measured by the extent that it *re-presents* our world (or part of it) in a revealing way; is *coherent* by being consistent with the other facts we recognize, referring and attributing accurately; *shows* a person ways to overcome self-deception; *shows* a person how to be honest in shared moral life; and enables a person to be constant (stubborn) in seeking what is true," "Moments of Truth," p. 3.

8. The resurrection, of course, is not a "fact" such as these, but fundamentally a theological claim, which must be, however, coherent with Jesus' life. The resurrection is not a historical claim so much as it is a history-making claim.

9. Hartt suggests that "a good story enables us to identify . . . real characters interacting with other real characters in situations recognizably mundane no matter how heavily charged with importance they may be. To identify with such a character in such

different set of conceptual reminders, I do not think there is any difference between Hartt and, at least, my intentions. If there is a difference, I suspect it involves Hartt's further claims about ontological presuppositions of the story told in the Gospels. For he is quite right to note that the presuppositions of that story are much more comprehensive than those assessable to a historian working within naturalistic assumptions. The picture drawn by the New Testament about the world is cosmic rather than provincial and anthropocentric. It is a tale about the mortal combat between good and evil—that beyond us lie powers and principalities in the face of which we are powerless without God's intervention. Moreover, Hartt is right that such presumptions cannot be reduced to myths whose import is anthropological without decisively and mistakenly compromising the necessary historicality of the Gospels.[10]

There can be no question that the "New Testament faith is built on the assumption that certain propositions about God are so true that no case has to be made for them"[11] and that the Gospel involves ontological-cognitional claims of a world imposed rather than humanly created. What I have doubts about, however, is whether those ontological claims can be so isolated that they can be metaphysically construed separately from the story.[12] When that is done I fear we have distorted the character of the kind of claims entailed by the Gospel, as the form of that story simply is that of a concrete man in a certain time and place who carried the destiny of God's dealing with his creation. The story of the Gospel is not just necessary for learning how to construe life and the world in the light of such metaphysical beliefs, but the story is necessary for understanding the nature and form of those beliefs. That such is the case does not mean that the Gospel is, therefore, immune from challenge by "actuality" but rather indicates that large claims are involved since the Gospel promises to tell us everything we need to know about the world necessary for our salvation. (There is, of course, much worth knowing for which the Gospel claims no special privilege.)

---

a situation does not mean that we empathize with him or otherwise put ourselves in that situation; though we may come to do both. What is first of all at stake in identification is recognition of real individuality whether or not it is admirable. Thereafter may come acknowledgment of the actual powers which move those individuals. . . . So a story may be truthful, that is authentic, whether or not it is factually accurate," *Theological Method and Imagination*, p. 237. The story of Jesus' life is, of course, extraordinary as it combines ordinary facts with claims of cosmic significance.

10. Hartt, *Theological Method and Imagination*, p. 239.

11. Ibid., p. 241.

12. I am not suggesting that Hartt thinks this either, but if he does not, then we must ask him to spell out further the kind of metaphysical issues he thinks we may be avoiding.

Stanley Hauerwas

To defend these claims involves more metaphysical sense and skills than I possess; so I will simply state my beliefs baldly. What bothers me about Hartt's questions about the limits of "aesthetic truthfulness" (a category I am not sure I want to accept) as a "reliable bridge to actuality," is the assumption that there is something called "metaphysics" that promises a more reliable mode of transportation.[13] I simply do not believe, and I am unclear if Hartt believes, that there is any mode of analysis called metaphysics with its own peculiar subject called being, actuality, and so on. I do not doubt for a minute that the Gospel entails claims that may properly be called "metaphysical," but I do not believe they are known or best displayed by a clearly defined activity called "metaphysics." Nor is it my intention to insist that narrative is capable of making or should be construed so broadly to make irrelevant all "transactions with actuality." Rather, the emphasis on narrative is but the means to note the kind of actuality we believe has grasped us in Jesus of Nazareth.

I certainly do not wish that Christian theology would, nor do I think that it can or should, free itself from classical metaphysical concerns. Rather, I understand my refusal to engage in metaphysics qua metaphysics to be a classical metaphysical position. For I not only think Hartt is right not to ask me to distinguish between cognitional and moral truth; I think it is essential not to draw that distinction. Questions of truth, as Plato, I think, rightly maintained, cannot be separated from questions of the good and the beautiful. The trick, of course, is to know how they are to be distinguished without being separated.[14] I would be the first to admit that I may have got the distinction and the relation wrong, but it should at least be clear that my emphasis on the narrative character of Christian convictions has not been an attempt to avoid truth-claims but to understand better how claims about God entail fundamental assumptions about the narrability of the world and our lives.[15] If that is not a sufficient metaphysical claim to satisfy Hartt, I am afraid I do not know what such a claim would look like.

13. More fundamentally, I wonder about his very way of putting the matter, since to suggest we need a "bridge" between aesthetic truthfulness and actuality seems to imply that he has some privileged mode to actuality that has not been demonstrated.

14. For a much fuller defense of the view I am here asserting, see Hilary Putnam, *Reason, Truth, and History* (Cambridge: Cambridge University Press, 1981).

15. By "narrability" I mean that the world must be a contingent reality that requires a narrative display. If the world existed by necessity, no such narrative would be required, for the world would be open to theoretical explanation. The metaphysical trick, from a Christian point of view, is to show simultaneously how "what is" cannot be other and yet why "what is" is contingent and finite. Finally, "narrability" does not entail that Christians must provide a "superhistory" that encompasses all other subhistories, but rather it requires that no account of the world is final, short of the second coming.

But "about God" is what I take Hartt's central concern to be — for "metaphysics" is but the means he uses to remind us that the import of the story is that our existence has a purpose whose "trajectory lies absolutely in the life of God." And here lies the strong claim that he suspects may be a bullet which some of us may wrongly hesitate to bite, since it entails that the "vectorial structure of an historical situation is such that God is its ground, its providence, and its end." That at least means that God is an agent in a manner that we are not. Only God is an agent capable of self and societal unity, we are at best "vectorial structures."

While I am not sure what I think about Hartt's claim that God's being is not teleologically organized, but displayed teleologically, I think he is right about agency. We are creatures whose ability to be agents is dependent on our willingness to acknowledge that our lives are such only as they are formed by "the proper service of God." Or as I have tried to put it more recently, we are capable of agency, of having character, only to the extent that we are given the means to locate our lives within God's ongoing story.[16] God, at least the God we believe is revealed through Israel and Jesus, is an agent in a manner we cannot be, since our agency, our ability to display the "vectorial structures" teleologically, is dependent on God's willingness to redeem.

Hartt is, therefore, surely right that when the world-action imperatives of the Gospel are engaged, that is, when they are taken seriously as claims about salvation, their ontological seriousness cannot be denied. Yet I do not understand why that entails the further claim that the "fit of the metaphor" cannot be determined by appeal to tradition-narrative. For it is not clear that Hartt is either historically or theologically correct that the "actuality-determination displayed in Jesus" goes beyond the received tradition. Certainly, Jesus is a challenge to some aspects of the tradition, but the cause he represented was in a decisive way congruent with God's purposes from the beginning. What is new is that now that cause has become present and actual in this man's life, death, and resurrection, making possible the reality of God's kingdom for all people.

There is a sense, of course, that this represents a salvation beyond that offered by tradition, for the tradition (or narrative) does not, or at least cannot pretend to, save. God does that. But it is quite another matter to claim that the salvation offered is in discontinuity with all that has gone before. There is discontinuity, to be sure, but it is the discontinuity with our sinful selves, not with tradition per se. Tradition, with

16. Stanley Hauerwas, *The Peaceable Kingdom: A Primer in Christian Ethics* (Notre Dame: University of Notre Dame Press, 1983), chapter 3.

its inextricably social presuppositions, remains necessary for the power "actuality" has to save us from our delusions of grandeur.

There the matter must rest. I confess I wish I had been able to locate more precisely the exact disagreements between myself and Hartt, for I am not one to delight in easy reconciliation, believing as I do that disagreements are more helpful than agreements. I have done little more than to restate my intentions in the hopes of making clear that I do not intend to exclude by the emphasis on narrative the kind of concerns Hartt represents. However, I am acutely aware that I have not been able to do even that as clearly as I would like. I hope at least part of my unclarity is due to the hardness of the issues Hartt raises and that at least I have responded in a manner that might encourage others to take up his challenge in more helpful ways.

Reply to Crites and Hauerwas

Julian Hartt

Stephen Crites and Stanley Hauerwas have richly honored me by taking my comments on their views with such seriousness. It is gratifying though not at all surprising that neither of them looks for cheap victories nor pursues implausible reconciliations of important disagreements. I thank them for these attitudinal benefactions as well as for their instructive comments on my views. Would that my besetting modesty allowed me to accept Crites's unilateral nomination of me for associate membership in the Royal German Theological Union!

It appears that the main points at issue are these: (I) What sort of distinction is to be drawn between fact-assertive (assertoric) and expressive modes of cognitivity (understood: for Christian faith and theology)? (II) What about metaphysics? (III) Truth v. Truthfulness. (The understanding cited in I applies to II and III.)

I

First off I must make two confessions. The first is an apology for even a single use of "assertoric"; it is not found in my American dictionaries but is lifted from Kant's first *Critique*—of course in English translation.

Julian Hartt, "Reply to Crites and Hauerwas," *Journal of the American Academy of Religion*, LII, 1 (March 1984): 149-156.

Julian Hartt

The second confession is that I tended to lump fact-assertions with truth-claims, thus making matters much too easy for Crites: it inspired him right off to accuse me of category confusions (*sic!*), thus at one stroke riling me and the issue; and it gave him an excuse ready at hand for not telling us whether the theologian (not Miss Jones, nor anyone else, on the Creed or at prayer) is supposed to evacuate altogether the fact-assertive mode.

Now I suggest that the nub of the conflict over (I) can be fairly discerned in this sentence from Crites's reply: "But that God raised him from the dead is not a factual statement at all" (p. 295). Does this mean that he rejects any distinction between factuality-criteria employed by modern theologians and those accepted in the New Testament church? Is he really proposing that the r-claim (r for resurrection) cannot be a factuality-claim for the New Testament church because it cannot be so credited by theologians decisively instructed by modern historiographi-cal principles and by positivistic conceptions of empirical verification? In religious concerns and more generally this would be an odd busi-ness indeed; a bit like saying that nobody ever *really* claimed the world is flat because we know it isn't. But only a bit like that. The sticking-point is Crites's appeal to the "empirical" as applied to evidence: it rules out any appeal to the witness of the New Testament save in so far as it makes a coherent and otherwise meaningful conjunction with one's own story and/or with the traditions of a Christian community; and it rules out any strong truth-claims for divine agency. Thus on the latter point he says: "So elusive is divine agency, from any empirical standpoint, that it is always subject to doubt" (p. 295). In sum then the r-claim is invalidated as a truth-claim on two counts. One, there is no empirical evidence available for impartial (= metaphysically and religiously neu-tral) assay. Two, the r-claim invokes a metaphysical causality to account for a putatively historical event, thus violating modern philosophical legislation requiring the immunization of historical explanation against metaphysics *überhaupt*.

As to the first count, it must be conceded that the r-claim is about/for an event in the standard time-space world; thus so far an event like the death of Socrates and the assassination of Julius Caesar. But only so far. Thereafter two great vexations materialize, as noted. The New Testament, alike in story and proclamation, embraces unreserved-ly a divine causality. The other vexation is that no one in the New Tes-tament claims to have witnessed the process, so to speak, but only the effect-aspects of the event; whereas many senators must have observed the process in Caesar's case; and the death of Socrates had several wit-nesses, if you can believe Plato. But the r-claim is not that the process had any (mortal) witnesses but that Jesus Christ became again a living presence self-identified. True, we do not have the testimony of a lot of the senators, and Plato's testimony when weighed in our juristic scales emerges as hearsay, pure though hardly simply.

Granted, then, that the only part of the r-claim for which evidentiary support is submitted in the New Testament bears on the effect-aspect of the event. Can we fairly map the conclusions appropriate to the testing of the evidence? I think this is worth a try.

(a) Whatever its diversities the import of the evidence is clear; but it does not in fact support the claim, whether or not it might work for a different claim, e.g., that the antecedent piety of the disciples disposed them to believe in the resurrection, including the resurrection of Messiah. (Parenthetical question: Who knows that much, if anything, about the antecedent piety of the testifying disciples?)

(b) The evidence is equivocal: it appears to contain contradictory elements, e.g., Jesus appeared first in Galilee; no, in Jerusalem. So again the essential claim is unsubstantiated; it fails because the evidence fails.

(c) The claim is such that it calls for privileged testimony and admits no other. Hence only the putative self-identified beneficiaries of the event are allowed to testify as to its meaning and truth. So the decisive truth-conditions, if not all of them, are intramural, so to speak. This in turn strongly suggests that appeal to privileged testimony, so understood, violates the philosophical assumptions of modernity. Of these hardly any is more precious than the conviction that for the great purposes engaging the mind with the real world the generalities of experience count for far more than the singularities; so that scientific testing presupposes that the generalities are in fact uniform throughout the cosmos.

It can hardly be doubted that in the New Testament the primary witnesses are beneficiaries of the event to which they testify. But I do not think that this is a sufficient reason for invalidating their testimony, unless we assume that their consciousness of having been so graced—in that sense certainly privileged—inspired them to bear false witness, i.e., the event in which they claim to have participated did not in fact occur or it was something different from what they claimed. As we all know the main exegetical-hermeneutical lines have gone off in other directions, notably to the effect that whatever the singularities of their experiences, presumptively forever beyond all recall or reconstruction save imaginational ventures, the New Testament writers had no choice but to express them in the dominant images and concepts of their religious history and environment. And these dominations and prepossessions are not compatible with the perceptual-interpretative grid of our mental world.

That historical-empirical conclusion is logically different from a verdict of false returned against the r-claim. I am not sure that either Crites or Hauerwas finds that distinction useful. Nor is it clear that either of them would unequivocally endorse any of the conclusions (a, b, c) sketched above. In any case I now leave that aspect of issue (I) to consider another one, viz., that I exaggerated or otherwise misconstrued the stake theologians ought to invest in the fact-assertive mode of cognitivity, at least as this bears upon historical events. To this I reply that I do indeed hold that the issue bears on what theologians do or ought to do relative to New Testament truth-claims and to reports of experience and to prevailing winds of philosophical doctrine.

One way of getting into these matters is to take note of Crites's proposal about truth-claiming and believing. His view is that believing x (= a proposition) is the same as holding x to be true; presumably on the grounds that hardly anyone would believe (here = profess?) x if he/she knew, or felt for that matter, that x was not true (functionally = false). I doubt that this view can be easily or convincingly squared with his views about the imaginational-celebrational dimension of faith-in-community. Caught up in the power of that expressive mode, is one likely to ask whether the great clauses of the Creed conform to, faithfully represent, either real history ("Come now, not really 'on the third day'!") or ontological-cosmological actualities ("Come off it: 'Maker of heaven and earth'!")? Now I do not propose that theologians and other professional second-guessers are the only religious folk who get consciously and deliberately into the business of truth-claiming. It strikes me as being the case that theologians characteristically work in adversarial situations in which in fact the essential x's are challenged both within and without the church. For instance, some of the members of the church in Corinth deny that there is such a thing as the resurrection; there is the belief, yes, but it is false and they will have none of it.

In other words a theologian's work inevitably carries him into contested territory where the *story* isn't contested, it is the truth of the proclamation that is denied. Especially that core element of the proclamation: God, his purpose and power, can be wholly trusted and must be purely obeyed, because through him Jesus Christ rose from the dead and became again transcendently a living presence as the Lord in the actual world.

Well, then, when (not if) the proclamation's truth is challenged, what is the theologian to do? I proposed that he or she should venture an ontological transcription of the truth-claim of the New Testament proclamation. I do not suppose that reading "ontological" for "metaphysical" will make the pill easier to swallow or thereafter appreciably lessen the shock to a digestive system inured to skepticism. I am constrained nonetheless to prescribe it, because the claims as well as the stories of the New Testament reverberate with ontological elements. The God of biblical attestation is the agent of all agents. Jesus Christ alone of all beings participating in finitude personally exercises that power; according to *John* this includes the power of "the resurrection and the life." Why then should there be any demurrers from Hauerwas or Crites on the proposition that all things and all events are faithfully understood in relation to God so understood? Do they find something exceptionable in the piety of George Hubert when he prays,

> Teach me, my God and King,
> In all things Thee to see,
> And what I do in anything,
> To do it as for Thee.

Or are they concerned lest a supernaturalist metaphysics might find illicit inspiration from such expressions and from the overwhelmingly actualistic ontological faith of the Bible?

II

Well, then, what about metaphysics? Crites won't have it, neat at least; though he is not reluctant to make strong ontological claims about the actual presence of God in the celebrational enactment of the Story. Hauerwas confesses that he is intimidated by metaphysics whenever he finds himself giving it a sidelong glance, which apparently is not too often. For both of them the cool, dry conceptual abstractions of metaphysical thought cannot make any viable or pertinent connection with the blood, sweat, guts, and tears of historical-existential narrative. Indeed Hauerwas reports a *frisson* regularly induced by a confrontation with the category of Being. For his part, Crites wants no part of thinking which gives high priority to personal identity. I wonder whether *Thou* might seem less dubious ontologically, better grounded empirically, and, God save the mark! less phallic than the *I*?

Should we make another effort to palliate the metaphysical shock by noting that the ontological thing is sometimes done with such notions as Care, Guilt, Fate, and Destiny? It may betray hardness of heart but I think not, largely because I do not find Heidegger's splendidly imaginative destruction of metaphysics credible.

Just in passing I should say that Crites's rejection of the very possibility of a *Christian* metaphysics is a little short-winded. Leibniz, for example, thought he had one. Crites must know where it failed, that is, failed to be Christian. Or does he mean that since metaphysics as such is a failure (not that I think he has been out there rustling the dead horses of logical positivism), a Christian theological venture in that direction is pretty much like sending arguably good money after demonstrably bad? In more sober language, does Crites think that an ironclad case has been made out for metaphysical skepticism; or that indulgence in metaphysical thinking disfigures, or at any rate, distorts Christian theological thinking? I suspect that the latter possibility is closer to the mark.

I turn now to a specific issue in this area, personal identity. In my comments, I said more about personal *agency* than about personal *identity*. It is not very clear to me what Crites's problem is with agency; perhaps he has confused it with the identity question. Does he have trouble making out whether he is a person? Or does he find it difficult to accept the person he is able to make out? Or is his plaint more lightly burdened with existential pathos, concerned, rather, with the absence of a satisfactory *theory* about personal identity? In any case dubiety about self-identity ought not to infect the agency factor. No doubt there are situations in which one cannot make out clearly whether one is an agent or a patient, active or inert, actual or possible. But when one is in fact acting, propounding a theory of the imagination or putting a Herr-less professor in his unenviable place, is there a reasonable doubt about who is doing it? I think not.

Whatever one makes of the Mighty Acts of God as a doctrine of revelation, Scripture is full of agency-actualistic ontology. There real beings are actors, in that prime sense agents. Not much attention is given there to nonhuman agents; those who do appear often have personal characteristics, such as angels, Satan, demons. Granted, we ought not to conclude that Personalism is the sole legitimate construal of biblical faith in the metaphysical mode. But the protagonists of that view do not err in contending that if the Bible is true, then persons, wherever found, are irreducibly real. Exclusively real is another question.

III

We come now and at last to the third main issue, the relationship of truth and truthfulness to each other and to the action-imperatives of biblical faith. So put, the matter discourages high confidence in dialectical measures, such as asking whether Hauerwas and Crites hold their respective proposals to be "true," or at least truer than mine.

It appears to me that there are two sub-issues that demand attention. (1) What about extra-narrational criteria for ascertaining or demonstrating the truth of the narrative? The question comes up because of my contention that an ontological bridge is theologically indispensable. (2) Have Crites and Hauerwas drawn a clear and cogent distinction between coherence as an aesthetic criterion and as a logical criterion?

(1) It is clear that neither Hauerwas nor Crites wants anything so far removed from narrational modes as metaphysics to have any voice in the truth- assessment of narratives for which a revelational magnitude is claimed. Incidentally, I did not propose to employ a metaphysical system to mediate or translate such narratives into non-narrative reality. The issue, thus, is not System. It is, rather, whether the ontological elements engaged in the truth-claims of Christian faith require systematic development by theologians. So "systematic" argues comprehensiveness and coherence as valid and pertinent criteria. Comprehensiveness does not entail the omnivorousness charged against the great Systems of the nineteenth century. Here it means that the categorial spread must not cheat by denying integral reality to whatever in experience has an intuitive claim to it.

Be that as it may, the main action should move upon coherence. What I propose to do now is to address the question whether either mode of coherence (aesthetic, logical) carries us into the action-modality identified in Christian faith as obedience to God's sovereign will. I shall assume we agree that the prime action-modality is to live under the rule (reign) of the love of Christ as befits those who are beneficiaries of his resurrection.

In the logical mode the business of coherence is propositional implication. Persons of Hegelian inclinations may wish to broaden implication beyond either syllogistic linearity or linearity of any other sort. I have no objection to that since "hanging together" is surely richer for logical purposes and others than "can be shown to be derived deductively from. . . ." But the pressing concern here is to preserve the element of noncontradiction as the core component of coherence in the logical mode.

We should hardly doubt that the way a story hangs together is different from the self-consistency of a propositional display. The difference is certainly not absolute—but is it clear? We expect the author of a novel to say and imply consistent things about a given character. Otherwise we should have to say that that character is "unrealized" or, even worse, that the author could not make up her or his mind what to make of that character, leaving it a congeries of conflicting qualities looking in vain for a unifying center. And in a narrative history of the Civil War we would not put up with the author's saying that Lee's bullheadedness about a frontal attack on the Federal center that fateful third day at Gettysburg both was and was not the main reason he lost the battle. The historian can cop an easy plea by saying that Lee's obsession was one causal factor among many. But what tipped the causal

317

nexus one way rather than any other, giving it the shape of the decision that at the least cost the Confederates a bloody victory?

Crites's splendid limning of the Gospel as irony, apropos here
of the criterion of coherence construed as consistency, deserves more
attention than I can give it here. It is largely true, I agree, that neither
commonsensical nor philosophical-logical views of coherence grasp the
intent of the Gospel. If St. Paul has grasped that, then to be possessed
by the mind of Christ is indeed to experience great reversals, upend-
ings, transvaluations: the "natural" is thrashed within an inch of its life
and beyond. But this does not mean that historical and ontological continuity disappears, dies an ultimate death. Quite to the contrary.
Moreover the ironical (= mind-jarring) cast of the power of God
manifested in weakness; of the glorification of the no-account; of the
overturning of the kingdoms of this world and the ultimate irreversible
submission of cosmic dominations and principalities; so far as the mind
of Christ is in us nothing but these radical transformations and novel
transfigurations makes sense, conveys the truth about the human being,
about the course of history, about the fate of nations and of nature as
well, and, above all, manifests the perfect will of God.

I hope this is an appropriate place to express appreciation for
Hauerwas's concern for truth-modalities that are richer existentially
than perceptual correspondences and formal coherences. I agree that
we need to think again about the Platonic conception of an ontological truth, a tradition largely recessive and impotent in modern thought
but once very powerful, as in medieval Exemplarism. And I propose
to use his concern for the moral dimension, truth as truthfulness, trust-
worthiness, veracity, to move to the pragmatical understood as concern for the modes of action and qualities of the agent accepted as
Christianly imperative.

Hence, as I read the New Testament I encounter the claim that
what God did/does in the life, death, and resurrection of Jesus Christ
is the spiritually-existentially potentializing truth available to all who
will accept it. Accordingly the agape-love command prescribes the
"trajectory" binding upon the follower of Jesus Christ, the beneficiary
of his resurrection. It is God who ordains it; it cannot, then, fail to be
the truth of existence, indwelling and absolute. It does not need extensive documentation that failure occurs on the humanward side of
this being-in-truth. The authentic recognition of this besetting actuality requires, in St. Paul's terms, deeds "worthy of . . . repentance"
(Acts 26:20; RSV).

IV

In the end the question is not whether it is possible to unite narrative history with an ontological schematism, and with such a miraculous instrument overcome the intellectual doubts and the moral profligacy of a pagan world. Nor is it the question whether an ontological schematism can somehow emerge as the *real* meaning of Story and Proclamation. I suggest that the main question in these exchanges is something like this: Is not the existential project of Christian life and character like what William James proposed in thinking of verification as making-true? He did not say, making-it-up; the will to believe was not to be confused with the will to make-believe. I think he was talking about how in the decisive engagements with the powers of being we are summoned to actualize a truth-candidate.

Perhaps the allusion to James's views is misleading or just plain wrong. I confess it has in my ears the ring of truth (a report, not a claim). In any case I hope we agree that the proper intentionality of Christian faith and life is to become in truth what God intends.

The Promising God:
The Gospel as Narrated Promise

Ronald Thiemann

My rather formal defense of the intelligibility of belief in God's prevenience[1] must now be supplemented by a more detailed account of the biblical basis for the belief. In this essay I will attempt to show that the biblical narrative does provide an individuating description of God as prevenient God of promise. "Narrated promise" not only provides a coherent and thus intelligible basis for asserting God's prevenience, it is also a notion deeply embedded in the biblical tradition and thus satisfies the criterion of "Christian aptness." I argued previously that the category of narrative is useful for theology because it integrates a central literary genre in Scripture with an organizing theological image. But narrative has the further significance of providing the language by which we specify personal identity. A theology which seeks an individuating identification of God is a theology naturally attracted to narrative.

In order to answer questions which inquire after a person's identity, e.g., "Who is Jane? What is she like?" we relate a story which iden-

1. Ronald Thiemann, "God's Prevenience: The Logic of Promise and Agency," in his *Revelation and Theology: The Gospel as Narrated Promise* (Notre Dame: University of Notre Dame Press, 1985), pp. 92-111.

Ronald Thiemann, "The Promising God: The Gospel as Narrated Promise," in his *Revelation and Theology: The Gospel as Narrated Promise* (Notre Dame: University of Notre Dame Press, 1985), pp. 112-140.

tifies a pattern of behavior as "characteristically hers" and which allows us to attribute to her certain traits of character. Narrative identification thus entails the description of *patterns of behavior* which because of their persistence over time we identify as *characteristic*. These characteristic patterns then warrant the *ascription of character traits* to a persisting subject or self. Narrative identification thereby accounts both for the variety and change of behavior patterns and for the persistence of a subject throughout such changes. If an intelligible narrative account, inclusive of those diverse patterns, can be given, then we can speak of Jane or of God as a persisting identifiable personal subject.[2]

The following narrative accounts will focus on a single New Testament book, the Gospel of Matthew. Ideally a narrative description of God's identity would range over a wider variety of biblical narratives to show how they cumulatively render God as a distinctive personal

---

2. Hans Frei, "Theological Reflections on the Gospel's Accounts of Jesus' Death and Resurrection," *The Christian Scholar* 49, 4 (Winter 1966): 263-306 and *The Identity of Jesus Christ* (Philadelphia: Fortress Press, 1974), has pioneered this use of intention-action models in theology. But Frei insists on the necessity of a dual mode of analysis which employs both an intention-action and a self-manifestation model of selfhood. The latter form of analysis is necessary, Frei argues, to indicate the ultimacy, elusiveness, and persistence (see "Theological Reflections," pp. 280-283 and *Identity*, pp. 94-96) of "the ascriptive center or focus of intentional activity," i.e., "that to which both states of consciousness and physical characteristics are ascribed" ("Theological Reflections," p. 280). He also argues that the latter model allows the description of "the unbroken continuity of identity through its changes" (Frei, *Identity*, p. 44) in a way not possible with the intention-action model.

Though I am indebted to Frei's ground-breaking work, I find his argument for the necessity of the self-manifestation model unconvincing. (Frei himself expresses some reservations about this model in the Preface to *Identity*, p. x.) The intention-action model, employed in the service of a story-bound identification, appears to account for all the elements which the self-manifestation model is designed to elucidate. Alasdair MacIntyre seems to me exactly right when he says, "Personal identity is just that identity presupposed by the unity of the character which the unity of a narrative requires. Without such unity there would not be subjects of whom stories could be told." *After Virtue* (Notre Dame: University of Notre Dame Press, 1981), p. 203. The "ascriptive center" is simply that one to whom traits of character are applied when patterns of behavior are deemed to be sufficiently *persistent* as to be characteristic. If we are seeking formal tools of personal identification, the intention-action model seems to allow talk of the "ascriptive center" and thus of the self's persistence and ultimacy. Whether a self is also elusive can only be determined by its narrative-particular description. In order to account for the self's elusiveness we do not need to reflect on "the fact that one's own acts *now* cannot become objects of knowledge to oneself until they have receded into the past" (Frei, *Identity*, p. 95). However interesting such speculation might be it seems necessary neither for the task of personal identification nor for the broader task of theology.

Finally my claim of inclusiveness for the intention-action model must be judged by the model's usefulness in defining the identity of God and Jesus Christ as depicted in the biblical narrative.

agent.[3] An account of such breadth would, of course, require book-length treatment and is clearly beyond the limits of this project. What my more modest approach sacrifices in scope, it should regain in precision. Theologians have often been criticized for imposing upon Scripture grand interpretive schemes which ignore or violate the structures of biblical texts. Theological interpretation of narrative, if it is to avoid that danger, must be characterized by close textual analysis guided by clear textual warrants. Such analysis requires in turn a limitation of the material to be discussed.

I will undertake a literary and theological analysis of the book of Matthew which seeks a uniquely identifying description of God. I will treat the Gospel as a consciously constructed narrative in which the author uses various literary devices for theological purposes. Relying upon the literary structures Matthew employs and the formal philosophical tools of identity description I will describe Matthew's narrative depiction of Jesus and the implications of that depiction for the identification of God. Such an analysis is congenial to the Gospel, because the theological goal of the book of Matthew is to identify Jesus of Nazareth as Emmanuel, the Son of God,[4] the one who enacts God's intention to save his people from sin through death and resurrection. God is thereby identified as the one whose promises are fulfilled in the mission of the Son of God and who enacts his intention to save in raising Jesus from the dead.

I. The Identity of Jesus Christ

> Now when Jesus came into the district of Caesarea Philippi, he asked his disciples, "Who do men say that the Son of man is?" And they said, "Some say John the Baptist, others say Elijah, and others Jeremiah or one of the prophets." He said to them, "But who do you say that I am?" Simon Peter replied, "You are the Christ, the Son of the living God." (Matthew 16:13-16)

3. For a provisional attempt to do this for Old Testament narratives, see Dale Patrick, *The Rendering of God in the Old Testament* (Philadelphia: Fortress Press, 1981).

4. I agree with Jack Dean Kingsbury that "Son of God" is the key title in the Gospel of Matthew. See especially, *Matthew: Structure, Christology, Kingdom* (Philadelphia: Fortress Press, 1975), pp. 40-83. I will attempt to defend that claim by emphasizing the literary structures which provide the *narrative continuity* within Matthew's Gospel. As a historical critic Kingsbury focuses on the more discreet form-critical units in order to demonstrate the pre-eminence of the title "Son of God." I am not so much interested in defending the pre-eminence of the title as in showing its relation to Matthew's narrative identification of Jesus Christ.

This pericope, long recognized as a turning point in the Gospel of Matthew, poses the question which Matthew's narrative depiction of Jesus seeks to answer. The writer of the Gospel skillfully develops three patterns of identifying discourse which cumulatively display Jesus' personal identity. These narrative patterns, which correspond to the three major sections of Matthew's Gospel, begin with the most general and stylized depictions of Jesus and progress toward greater specificity until Jesus' identity as a particular individual who uniquely fulfills the role of Son of God becomes clear in the crucifixion and resurrection sequence. Jesus is related first to the people of Israel and Israel's God, then to the coming Kingdom of God, and finally to those events of death and resurrection which bestow his unsubstitutable identity. Throughout this narrative progression Jesus' relation to God is subtly but unmistakably indicated.

Matthew deftly controls two types of individuating descriptions. The title "Son of God" specifies Jesus' *formal* identity. The first section of the Gospel (1:1–4:16) establishes the crucial connection between that title and Jesus' unique God-given mission of saving "his people from their sins" (1:21). Through Matthew's careful narrative construction a general title applicable to Israel's kings becomes a specific messianic title applicable only to the one God has chosen for the mission of salvation, i.e., to "the Christ, the Son of the living God." The Son of God is the one who uniquely enacts his Father's intention to save.

The subsequent sections of the Gospel provide the narrative identifications which specify Jesus' *individual personal* identity. In the second section of the Gospel (4:18–20:34) Matthew stresses the ambiguity which characterizes Jesus' personal identity, particularly his identity as Son of God. The narrative operates on two levels, which correspond to the disjunctive reactions of Jesus' hearers to his healing and teaching ministry. On the one hand, Matthew surveys the responses of the Jewish leaders, the crowds, and the disciples, all of whom are either confused about his identity or misidentify him as "teacher," "the carpenter's son," "the blasphemer," etc. On the other hand, Matthew recounts the confession of those who see through the ambiguity to recognize Jesus as the Son of God, e.g., the Gadarene demoniacs, the Roman centurion, and, more importantly, the disciples. Because in this section Matthew portrays Jesus as an agent enacting his own intentions, the relation of his actions to *God's* intentions—and thus his role as Son of God—becomes obscured. Nonetheless, Matthew emphasizes, Jesus remains recognizable as the Son of God by those who have faith.

The final section of the Gospel (21:1–28:20) completes Jesus' personal identification and decisively connects it to the initial formal individuating identification. In the passion narrative Jesus is most sharp-

Ronald Thiemann

ly individuated as a personal agent. Precisely as Jesus acts and suffers in his passion and crucifixion he is also most clearly identified as the unique son of God who obediently enacts the intentions of his Father. In an artful literary and theological conclusion Matthew shows the unity between the intentions of God and Jesus as manifested in the events of the crucifixion and resurrection. In obediently submitting to his crucifixion Jesus of Nazareth shows himself most clearly to be God's Son, an identification which is confirmed and completed in the resurrection. At the Gospel's ending, the careful reader will have discovered the identity not only of the Son of God but also of the one he calls "Abba, Father."

A. 1:1–4:16

In the first four chapters of the Gospel Jesus is identified solely by his relation to the people of Israel and Israel's God. Matthew's descriptions of Jesus function not to individuate him as a particular person but to specify his unique role as Son of God. Matthew avoids all techniques of verisimilitude[5] when describing Jesus in order to focus attention solely upon his mission and the formal identity which God bestows on him through that mission. Jesus is initially identified through his genealogy, which designates him as "the son of David, the son of Abraham" (1:1), thereby linking him to the two great covenantal promises of Israel, the promise of a nation and the promise of eternal Kingship. The inclusion of Tamar, the seductress of her father-in-law, Judah (Gen. 38); Rahab, the prostitute of Jericho (Josh. 2); Ruth, the Moabite; and Bathsheba, the partner in David's adultery (2 Sam. 11) may foreshadow Jesus' mission to sinners and outcasts,[6] but the major function of the genealogy is to show that Jesus is the inheritor of God's promises to Israel.

The nativity stories which follow the genealogy do include realistic elements, but none of them contributes to the personal identification of Jesus. The story of Joseph's dream functions to link Jesus' divine origin with his mission of salvation. Joseph is told that the child which Mary carries "is conceived in her of the Holy Spirit" (1:20) and that his name should be called "Jesus, for he will save his people from their sins"

5. For a discussion of realism or verisimilitude in narrative prose see Robert Scholes and Robert Kellogg, *The Nature of Narrative* (New York: Oxford University Press, 1966), esp. pp. 82-159 and J. P. Stern, *On Realism* (London: Routledge & Kegan Paul, 1973).

6. Most commentators deny this connection, because, they argue, "no moral stigma was attached to these women in Jewish tradition." Francis Wright Beare, *The Gospel According to Matthew* (New York: Harper & Row, 1981), p. 65. Nonetheless, Matthew's inclusion of them is striking, and their role as aliens and outcasts is more plausible given the importance of that literary and theological motif throughout the Gospel.

324

(1:21). All this is accomplished, Matthew informs his reader, to fulfill Isaiah's prophecy concerning the one whose "name shall be called 'Emmanuel' (which means God with us)" (1:23). Matthew moves so swiftly here that the reader may miss the full significance of this complex pattern of identification. Indeed its *full* significance cannot be appreciated without the subsequent narrative development. Matthew anticipates the assignment of the title "Son of God" to Jesus by connecting his divine origin, his name, his role as fulfiller of prophecy, and his mission. As the one conceived by God's spirit, this Jesus, born of Mary, inherits and fulfills the great covenantal promises of Israel by being the one designated to save his people from sin. Consequently he is called "Emmanuel," a name which anticipates his formal designation as Son of God. Thus the name "Jesus" is associated with a rich and complex pattern of identification. Yet these designations remain general and formal. We are told nothing of Jesus' particular identity, not even the conditions of his birth.

This distant perspective on Jesus is maintained in the first lengthy narrative which describes the arrival of "wise men from the East" (2:1). While the story contains elements of verisimilitude, particularly in its description of Herod's frantic efforts to ascertain the location of the child, they in no way contribute to the reader's grasp of Jesus' personal identity. He is merely "the child" whom the magi worship. Indeed, this marvelously crafted story, with its bitter conclusion of the slaughter of the innocents, functions primarily to occasion the flight to Egypt so that Jesus might be further identified with the people of Israel. As God in his great saving act brought Israel out of Egypt, so now he calls out the son of Abraham and David, who is for the first time associated with the implied designation "Son of God." "Out of Egypt have I called my son" (2:15). If we were to ask at this point in the narrative "Who is Jesus?" we could only answer with the formal designations Matthew has provided us. The narrative is constructed in such a way as to focus solely on Jesus' formal identity.

That emphasis is particularly apparent in Matthew's construction of the pivotal baptism and temptation scenes. These stories describe the first actions Jesus undertakes as an independent agent and provide an opportunity for a personal individuating description of Jesus. Though Matthew describes John in vivid detail (3:4-11), he offers no such description of Jesus' behavior or character. He simply states that Jesus appears at the Jordan to be baptized in order "to fulfil all righteousness" (3:15).[7] By recounting Jesus' baptism with such spare narrative prose

---

7. On Matthew's use of the term *dikaiosyne* see Gerhard Barth, "Matthew's Understanding of the Law," *Tradition and Interpretation in Matthew* (Philadelphia: Westminster Press, 1963), pp. 138-139.

Ronald Thiemann

Matthew continues to identify him solely in terms of the formal designations he bears. Jesus—the representative of Israel, conceived by God's spirit, and assigned a mission of salvation—undertakes in his first narrated act to associate himself with those in need of repentance. By focusing so single-mindedly on Jesus' formal identity Matthew is able to weave those various designations into a single individuating identification, Son of God. That title specifies both the unique relation to God and the unique mission of the title-bearer. The Son of God is the one who enacts God's intention to save by virtue of his identification with sinners. In the act of baptism Jesus shows his willingness to undertake the mission implied by that title. Jesus' identity as Son of God, a designation implied in the angel's message to Joseph, is made explicit both by Jesus' act and by God's declaration, "This is my beloved Son, with whom I am well pleased" (3:17). That title, which is so prominent in these early chapters, will appear only four times (8:29, 14:33, 16:16, 17:5) in the large middle section of the Gospel, but will re-emerge as the predominant title in the passion narrative. Jesus' sonship is for Matthew associated with his saving mission on behalf of God's sinful people. With his acceptance of that mission, the Son of God's first step toward Jerusalem is taken here in the waters of the Jordan.

Matthew will begin, in the next section of the Gospel, to describe Jesus as a particular individual, an agent who enacts his own intentions. That description will inevitably obscure the relation of Jesus' actions to God's intentions. Thus in this first section Matthew establishes Jesus' unique formal identity as Son of God. By rigorously refusing to individuate his description of Jesus, Matthew guides his readers to connect the name Jesus with the title Son of God. As he moves toward a more personal identification, however, Matthew needs a category which will allow him to maintain the link between Jesus' emerging intentional actions and God's intentions. Thus in the final stories of this initial section Matthew begins to depict Jesus as the *obedient* Son of God, i.e., the one who purposefully enacts his own intentions in conformity with the intentions of the Father.

The importance of Jesus' obedient sonship is stressed in the story which concludes the first section of Matthew's Gospel, the account of Jesus' temptation. Stylized elements once again dominate the Matthean narrative. Jesus is led by the Spirit into the wilderness to be tempted by Satan, who identifies him as Son of God and seeks to have him deny his sonship. Three times the tempter requests an action of Jesus which will demonstrate that the Messianic age has dawned. In each case Jesus' refusal takes the stylized form of a quotation from Hebrew scripture. The final temptation is set on "a very high mountain" (4:8) where Satan displays the glory of the kingdoms of the world. "All these I will give

you. . . ." Jesus rejects Satan's offer and banishes him from his presence
with a quote from Deuteronomy concerning the true worship of God.

This story is best understood if it is seen as foreshadowing the
concluding scene of the Gospel where Jesus, once again on a mountain,
receives the worship of the disciples (28:17) and announces "all authority in heaven and on earth has been given to me" (28:18). Jesus' ultimate authority is granted in the aftermath of his death and resurrection. Matthew shows in this earlier story that the obedient Son of God
cannot accept such authority prematurely. The true exercise of sonship,
Matthew asserts, consists in obedience to God's will and the fulfillment
of righteousness by the identification with sinners. To accept that mission is, as the subsequent narrative will show, to follow a path to the
cross.

Matthew has in this initial section skillfully constructed the
framework with which the Gospel is to be read. By avoiding the techniques of verisimilitude in his description of Jesus, Matthew focuses attention not upon the individual identity of Jesus of Nazareth but on the
unique saving mission of the Son of God. Jesus is the inheritor and fulfiller of Israel's promises, the designated savior of a sinful people, the
obedient servant who is baptized as an act of identification with those
in need of repentance, and who by virtue of acceptance of his God-be-
stowed mission is Emmanuel, Son of God, who enacts the intentions of
his Father. Having clearly defined Jesus' mission and thereby designated
Jesus' formal identity, Matthew moves in the subsequent chapters to
provide a narrative-based specification of his personal identity.

B. 4:18–20:34

This middle section of the Gospel is a collection of sayings, miracle
stories, and parables and does not exhibit the tight structure of the
first and last sections. Matthew, nonetheless, provides narrative unity
by focusing on the question of Jesus' authority. Jesus' identity is defined in these chapters primarily by his authoritative teaching and
healing ministry, but since Jesus now begins to act as an agent in his
own right, the source and nature of his authority are not readily apparent to his hearers. Matthew surveys the reactions of the Jewish
leaders, the crowds, and the disciples to Jesus' ministry and constructs
a narrative which constantly moves on two levels, stressing both the
ambiguity of Jesus' identity and the continuing possibility of recognizing him as Son of God. That explicit title virtually disappears from
this section as Jesus' identity must be discovered in his words and actions. While the crowds and Jewish leaders represent those who either
remain confused or reject Jesus as Son of God, the disciples repre-

sent those who move from confusion to confession, from "little faith" to true faith.

From the outset of this section Jesus is depicted as an agent enacting his own intentions. "From that time Jesus began to preach saying 'Repent for the kingdom of heaven is at hand'" (4:17). But even as Jesus begins to emerge as a particular individual, his message is characterized by a crucial ambiguity. "From that time" refers to the arrest of John the Baptist, and Matthew attributes to Jesus the identical message which John had proclaimed. Indeed, many take him to be John *redivivus* (14:2, 16:14). Jesus often speaks in his own right ("But I say unto you"), but at other times he speaks on behalf of an obscure eschatological figure ("Son of Man"). He acts with authority and manifests the signs of the kingdom, but regularly attributes healing to the faith of the recipient. His teaching often takes the form of parables which create confusion in his hearers, "because seeing they do not see, and hearing they do not hear, nor do they understand" (13:13). By stressing the ambiguity which surrounds Jesus' person and message, Matthew is able to demonstrate the essential role faith plays in recognizing Jesus as Son of God. To confess Jesus as Son of God in face of the ambiguity which surrounds him is, Matthew argues, to commit oneself to a life of faith and discipleship.

Throughout the first section of the Gospel Jesus is portrayed as a solitary figure, the representative Son of God who speaks in formulaic quotations from Hebrew scripture. As he begins the exercise of his public ministry, however, Jesus speaks in the first-person singular. (First-person locutions occur twenty-three times between 4:19 and 7:29). In addition he calls to himself disciples who will share his mission with him (4:18-22). These disciples do not seek out Jesus and present themselves for instruction in the usual rabbinic fashion. Rather Jesus takes the initiative and creates disciples for his kingdom. "And he said to them, 'Follow me, and I will make you fishers of men.' *Immediately* they left their nets and followed him. . . . *Immediately* they left the boat and their father, and followed him" (4:19-20, 22 [my emphasis]).[8] These brief call narratives give us our first glimpse of Jesus' authority. Matthew's stress on "immediately" emphasizes the powerful effect of Jesus' call, but the brevity of his account maintains a sense of ambiguity about the nature and source of his authority.

The theme of Jesus' ambiguous authority also dominates Matthew's description of his teaching. Jesus is portrayed as the reinterpreter and transformer of the Israelite tradition of which he is the heir. Though

---

8. In contrast to the willingness of James and John to leave their father is the unnamed "disciple" who wants to delay his discipleship so that he might bury his father (8:21-22).

he radically reinterprets the law, apparently by his own authority ("but I say unto you . . . truly, I say to you . . . yet I tell you"), he insists that he remains in continuity with the previous tradition, "Think not that I have come to abolish the law and the prophets; I have come not to abolish them but to fulfil them" (5:17). While maintaining the authority of the law, Jesus exercises his own authority by radicalizing its demands. "You have heard that it was said to the men of old, 'You shall not kill'. . . . But I say to you that every one who is angry with his brother shall be liable to judgment" (5:21, 22). The whole of chapter five is dominated by the formula "you have heard it said. . . . But I say unto you." Despite his evident authority, Jesus' identity remains cloaked in ambiguity. Who is able to interpret the law by his own authority? Does Jesus speak on his own behalf or on behalf of another? When he speaks of God, he refers to him as "the Father" or "our Father" but only once as "my Father" (7:21). The reaction of the crowds exhibits both their wonder and their uncertainty in response to his message. "The crowds were astonished at his teaching, for he taught them as one who had authority" (7:28). Jesus is recognizable to the crowds as a teacher with authority, but his authority is not recognized as the God-given power of the Son of God. Even his disciples do not confess him as Son of God, for when they experience his authority in the stilling of the storm, they ask, "What sort of man is this, that even winds and sea obey him?" (8:27). The answer is delivered in the very next story when the Gadarene demoniacs ironically provide the identification which the disciples cannot give (8:29).

Matthew brings his discussion of Jesus' authority to a climax in the masterfully formed story of the healing of the paralytic (9:1-8). The theme of Jesus' ambiguous authority is given its most powerful expression in a story which, like the entire middle section of the Gospel, operates on two distinct levels. A paralytic is brought to Jesus for healing. "And when Jesus saw their faith he said to the paralytic, 'Take heart, my son; your sins are forgiven'" (9:2). The scribes observing the scene recognize this as an act of blasphemy, for Jesus had taken to himself the divine prerogative to forgive sin. Jesus' reply apparently clarifies the nature of his authority.

> But Jesus, knowing their thoughts, said, "Why do you think evil in your hearts? For which is easier, to say, 'Your sins are forgiven,' or to say, 'Rise and walk'? But that you may know that the Son of man has authority on earth to forgive sins"—he then said to the paralytic—"Rise, take up your bed and go home." And he rose and went home. (9:4-7)

The meaning of Jesus' reply depends on one's answer to Jesus' rhetorical question. If the answer is "your sins are forgiven," then Jesus has presented a straightforward *a fortiori* argument. "It is easier to forgive sins than to heal paralytics. If I can heal this paralytic, then surely I have the power to forgive sins." Matthew certainly intends his readers to grasp this level of Jesus' answer, for it is a direct reply to the scribes' accusation. It is, however, also an argument which the scribes (i.e., those without faith) can understand. In addition it produces the kind of "sign" which Jesus adamantly refuses to provide in the subsequent narrative (16:1-4). How would the logic of the argument proceed if one answered the rhetorical question in the opposite fashion? Matthew's readers know on the basis of the first section of the Gospel that the power to forgive sins is granted to a single human being, the Son of God. Since forgiving sins is a unique action which can be performed only by the Son of God, it becomes the far more difficult action. Thus for Matthew's readers (i.e., those with faith) the logic of Jesus' argument runs in the opposite direction. The healing of the paralytic pales in significance when compared to the forgiving of sins, but that truth can be grasped only by those who in faith recognize Jesus as Son of God. Jesus has thus only apparently provided a "sign" to his accusers. In fact this ironic reply only confirms their faithlessness. Jesus' unique authority is that which he has received from the Father and which he exercises in forgiveness on behalf of his sinful people. But the true nature and source of his authority cannot be known by those who refuse to confess him as Son of God. Matthew concludes this artfully constructed story by attributing to the crowd a middling reaction. While they recognize the God-given authority in Jesus' healing, they do not yet recognize Jesus as Son of God. "When the crowds saw it, they were afraid, and they glorified God, who had given such authority to men" (9:8).

While Jesus' authority is manifested in his reinterpretation of the law, and in his power over disease, the most radical expression of his authority is manifested in his claim to be able to forgive sins. At this crucial point in the narrative Jesus affirms publicly, though ironically, the essential character of his mission on behalf of sinners. Jesus' identification with sinners is reiterated in the verses immediately following this pericope. The special relationship between Jesus and the outcasts of Israelite society is signified by his call to discipleship of Matthew the tax collector (9:9) and his table fellowship with "tax collectors and sinners" (9:10). Again the defenders of the Israelite tradition are appalled at this defiling violation of the law. But Jesus' response is an unequivocal pronouncement of the gracious character of his mission. "Those who are well have no need of a physician, but those who are sick. Go and learn what this means, 'I desire mercy, and not sacrifice.' For I came not to call the righteous, but sinners" (9:12-13). Jesus once again appeals to the Israelite tradition against its contemporary interpreters. His reinterpretation of the law, his power over demons and disease, his association with sinners and forgiveness of their sins derives from the gracious and merciful God who has bestowed this mission upon him. His divine authority is a merciful authority to receive where the law would reject, to love where the law would demand, to forgive where the law would condemn. Jesus' transformation of the law brings to the center of God's relation with sinners mercy, forgiveness, and love. This becomes clear in Jesus' response to the Pharisees' inquiry about the great commandment in the law (22:36). Jesus answers by quoting from the Israelite tradition, first from the *Shema* (cf. Deut. 6:4f.) and then from Leviticus 19:18. "You shall love the Lord your God with all your heart, and with all your soul, and with all your mind. . . . You shall love your neighbor as yourself. On these two commandments depend all the law and the prophets" (22:37-40). Jesus' gracious authority reiterates the very heart of the Jewish faith, thus establishing his continuity with that tradition. But by summarizing the whole of the law and the prophets under these great commandments, he also reinterprets the tradition. For this authority allows the doing of good on the Sabbath (12:1-13) in apparent opposition to the law. Such reinterpretation can only lead to conflict with the defenders of the Israelite tradition. Following the miracle of healing on the Sabbath, Matthew writes, "But the Pharisees went out and took counsel against him, how to destroy him" (12:14).

Following the crucial discussion of authority, Matthew focuses attention on the disciples and their transformation from confusion to true faith. Jesus shares with them his mission and authority (10:1) and begins to instruct them in the "secrets of the kingdom" (13:11). Matthew's description of Jesus becomes increasingly clear as he explicitly assigns him traits of character based on his narrative descriptions. Four times he characterizes Jesus as compassionate (9:36, 14:14, 15:32, 20:34) when confronted by the needs of those in the crowds. He portrays Jesus as speaking openly to his Father in prayer and explicitly defining his divine sonship. "All things have been delivered to me by my Father; and no one knows the Son except the Father, and no one knows the Father except the Son and any one to whom the Son chooses to reveal him" (11:27). Precisely as the disciples are instructed in the secrets of the Kingdom and the identity of its proclaimer, those who refuse to see or hear take "offense at him" (13:57) because he is merely "the carpenter's son" (13:55).

Matthew constructs his narrative in such a way that his readers are gradually led to identify the distant figure of the early chapters, the stylized Son of God, with the concrete person, Jesus of Nazareth. While for some the identification of a particular personal agent, the carpenter's son, with the Son of God is both offensive and blasphemous, Matthew's cumulative narrative depiction argues precisely for that identification. His case is surely not self-evident, for then the response of offense would be logically impossible, but, Matthew argues, it is nonetheless true. To affirm that this particular man is Son of God requires an act of faith and discipleship. Jesus' disciples have been throughout these chapters as confused as the crowds about Jesus' identity. Twice he calls them "men of little faith" (8:26, 14:31) when they express fear during storms on the sea. But on the second occasion, after Jesus has walked on the water and rescued Peter from drowning, they exclaim, "Truly you are the Son of God" (14:33). Such recognition is possible only by those who possess faith, and with that confession the disciples have made the initial movement of faith.

The disciples' confession on the sea anticipates Peter's great confession in chapter 16. Matthew builds toward that confession by interweaving themes from the Gospel's middle portion. Chapter 16 opens with the Pharisees and Sadducees demanding "a sign from heaven." Though Jesus had apparently provided such a sign earlier (9:1-8), he now refuses, saying that they are unable to "interpret the signs of the times" (16:3). Jesus thereupon warns the disciples about "the leaven of the Pharisees and Sadducees," (16:6) which leads to a misunderstanding concerning bread, emphasizing the disciples' inability to perceive. Once again Jesus calls them "men of little faith," a reference which recalls the stories of storm-stilling and the disciples' recent confession of faith. In collecting this disparate material Matthew has reintroduced the problem of the ambiguity surrounding Jesus' identity. The Jewish leaders refuse to recognize who Jesus is, and the disciples, despite their confession, seem once again confused.

In this context of ambiguity, rejection, and confusion Jesus poses the crucial question of his identity, using the obscure eschatological title he used in controversy concerning forgiveness. "Who do *men* say that the *Son of Man* is?" (my emphasis). But he asks the disciples, "Who do you say that *I* am?" and Peter makes explicit the identification between Jesus of Nazareth and Son of God which has been implied by the dramatic actions of the preceding chapters. With this "blessed" confession, revealed by the Father, the second major portion of the Gospel reaches its climax. Matthew thus assures his readers that though ambiguity surrounds the person of Jesus, the Father does reveal his true identity to those who follow him.

But Matthew introduces one crucial modification into his depiction of discipleship. Peter's confession indicates his apparent grasp of the identity and mission of Jesus. But when Jesus begins to share with his disciples the final secret of the Kingdom, which until this time he alone had borne, Peter cannot bear the full implications of Jesus' sonship.

> From that time Jesus began to show his disciples that he must go to Jerusalem and suffer many things from the elders and chief priests and scribes, and be killed, and on the third day be raised. And Peter took him and began to rebuke him, saying, "God forbid, Lord! This shall never happen to you."(16:21-22)

The previous bold confessor objects to any such fate for his Son of God. Jesus' response makes a striking connection with the satanic temptations with which his mission was inaugurated. "Get behind me, Satan! You are a hindrance to me; for you are not on the side of God, but of men" (16:23). If the mission for which he was born, the salvation of sinners, is to be accomplished, the Son of God *must* suffer and die. Anything less is a false notion of sonship which must be rejected. The validity of Jesus' suffering exercise of his sonship is once again confirmed by God in the transfiguration scene in chapter 17, as he repeats the words with which he had inaugurated Jesus' ministry. "This is my beloved Son, with whom I am well pleased" (17:5).

Matthew's message to his reader is clear. Faith entails discipleship. The correlative action asked of those who would follow the Son of God is that they prepare to share in his destiny. "If any man would come after me, let him deny himself and take up his cross and follow me" (16:24). With this climactic revelation of the true nature of Jesus' sonship and the correlative quality of Christian discipleship, Matthew has set the stage for the final and decisive portion of his Gospel narrative. By the end of this second section Jesus has become an individuated agent, and he has been identified as the suffering Son of God. Nonetheless, he has not yet begun to enact that suffering sonship fully. At the end of the Gospel's first section the title Son of God was linked to the bare name of Jesus. By the end of this section that title is linked to an identifiable person, Jesus of Nazareth—the carpenter's son, the compassionate healer and proclaimer of the Kingdom, the one who associates with sinners and tax collectors. And yet the key aspect of sonship—suffering and death on behalf of a sinful people—is present only by anticipation. The events surrounding Peter's confession set a mood of expectation as Jesus begins his trek to Jerusalem (20:17) to fulfill his mission of salvation.

C. 21:1–28:20

The major motifs of Matthew's Gospel reach their culmination in the passion, crucifixion, and resurrection sequence, as Jesus' identity as Son of God is confirmed in a remarkably constructed realistic narrative. Jesus' unsubstitutable personal identity is constituted by these final events, and the reader recognizes that precisely in his individuated personal identity Jesus is Son of God. Thus Matthew's two types of identifications merge in a definitive specification of the identity of Jesus Christ.

Throughout the Matthean narrative we have witnessed a gradual development of the theme in which Jesus is first identified as heir of the Israelite tradition and then increasingly as its radical transformer. Whereas in the earlier stages of the story Jesus' identity is bestowed by the Israelite tradition, in the final portion the tradition is fully transformed so that the true nature of God's covenant can be seen only in light of Jesus' identity. A continuity between old and new remains, but it is a continuity established in Jesus Christ.

Throughout chapters 17 to 20 Matthew portrays Jesus as advancing inexorably toward Jerusalem and his final destiny. As he enters the city of Israel's king and messianic expectation, he is acclaimed with "hosannas" by "the crowds that went before him and that followed him" (21:9). These crowds, gathered from outside the holy city, recognize him as "son of David" who "comes in the name of the Lord." But Matthew carefully indicates that with the exception of the children (a common symbol of the Kingdom) no one in Jerusalem recognizes the identity of this Messiah. "And when he entered Jerusalem, all the city was stirred, saying, 'Who is this?'" (21:10). The expected heirs of the Israelite tradition, the inhabitants of Jerusalem, are for the most part blind to the one who has come as the Son of God.[9] Matthew thus depicts Jesus from this point on in the narrative as the unyielding judge of Jerusalem and the elders of contemporary Judaism. Immediately upon entering the city he drives out the buyers and sellers in the temple, dramatically signifying the advent of the Messianic age,[10] thereby purifying and reclaiming the temple for the transformed Israelite tradition. This process of transforming the temple is symbolically concluded by the tearing of the "curtain of the temple" upon Jesus' death (27:51). Much of the remaining material of chapters 21 to 25 consists of the denunciation and condemnation of the contemporary representatives of the ancient tradition for their lack of repentance and faith.[11]

9. In contrast to the metaphorical blindness of the inhabitants of Jerusalem, Matthew depicts the two physically blind men of Jericho as recognizing Jesus as "Son of David" (20:31), whereupon their sight is restored.

10. See Zechariah 14:21. "And there shall no longer be a trader in the house of the Lord of hosts on that day."

11. Contemporary interpreters must exercise extreme care in interpreting these passages, for they have been the source for much Christian anti-Judaism. See Charlotte Klein, *Anti-Judaism in Christian Theology* (Philadelphia: Fortress Press, 1977). Matthew's Gospel is written at a time when Christianity was an emergent Jewish sect, contending

But what is the nature of this radically transformed Messiah which should make Jerusalem so blind to his identity? Matthew leaves little doubt that the lowliness and humility of the Messiah-king occasions his rejection. His entrance into Jerusalem is linked with a prophecy from Zechariah 9:9. "Tell the daughter of Zion, Behold, your king is coming to you, humble, and mounted on an ass, and on a colt, the foal of an ass" (Matthew 21:5). The king in whom the tradition of Israel finds its culmination is one whose majesty is manifested in humility. The refusal of Jerusalem to accept this lowly Messiah leads to its ultimate rejection and the bestowal of the Kingdom upon those whom Matthew calls "sinners." "Truly, I say unto you, the tax collectors and the harlots go into the kingdom of God before you" (21:31). Thus Jesus' lowliness applies not primarily to his personal style or demeanor but to his identification with those sinners and outcasts for whose sake he humbly and obediently goes to his death. His lowliness is a function of the service he renders in giving "his life as a ransom for many" (20:28).

The identification of Jesus with sinners is made on two other crucial occasions in this concluding section. Jesus' passion is inaugurated in the home of an outcast, Simon the leper, through his anointing by an unnamed woman. Though the disciples object to this waste of oil, Jesus accepts her act as preparation for burial (26:12). Moreover, she received a word of highest praise. "Truly, I say to you, wherever this gospel is preached in the whole world, what she has done will be told in memory of her" (26:13).[12] Although this is a difficult passage to interpret, one possible explanation is that this anonymous woman, one of the least in the Kingdom, becomes the greatest because through her act she draws attention not to herself but to her Lord. She is the epitome of Jesus' charge to his disciples, "Whoever would be great among you must be your servant, and whoever would be first among you must be your slave" (20:26-27).

Following this act of inauguration Jesus celebrates the Passover meal with his disciples, and once again identifies himself and his mission with sinners. The institution of the meal of the New Kingdom takes

---

with other elements in Judaism as rival claimants to the authentic Jewish tradition. The polemic within Matthew cannot be transferred to a situation in which Christianity has become a clearly distinct and numerically dominant religious tradition. For two studies of the problem of the anti-Judaism in Matthew see Lloyd Gaston, "The Messiah of Israel as Teacher of the Gentiles: The Setting of Matthew's Christology," *Interpreting the Gospels*, ed. James Luther Mays (Philadelphia: Fortress Press, 1981), and George W. E. Nickelsburg, "Good News/Bad News: The Messiah and God's Fractured Community," *Currents in Theology and Mission* 4, 6 (December 1977): 324-332.

12. For a recent interpretation of this story, see Elizabeth Schussler Fiorenza, *In Memory of Her* (New York: Crossroads, 1983).

place in the context of the Jewish Passover feast. As he passes the cup of wine to his disciples, Jesus says, "This is my blood of the covenant, which is poured out for many for the forgiveness of sins" (26:28). A continuity remains between God's covenant and the Kingdom inaugurated by Jesus Christ, but the point of continuity is established in the person of Jesus Christ and in his forgiving mission on behalf of sinners.

Throughout my discussion of the identity of Jesus Christ I have emphasized the importance of the title Son of God as the most appropriate designation of the one who enacts this saving mission on behalf of sinners. Significantly that title reappears in the final scenes of the passion narrative. The definitive identification of Jesus as the obedient son of his Father, going to his death on behalf of sinners, is offered in these closing scenes of Matthew's Gospel.

The prayer in Gethsemane portrays for one of the few times in the Gospel the interior life of Jesus and serves as an important source of the claim that he is the obedient Son of God. Jesus, who began his mission as a solitary figure, now faces his final destiny in an even more painful solitude. He asks that three of those disciples with whom he shared his mission and authority share with him the burden of these final hours. His agonized prayer shows that Jesus must face one final temptation to his sonship before his mission is completed. He pleads with his Father that this mission be accomplished some other way than through his death. "My Father, if it be possible, let this cup pass from me; nevertheless, not as I will, but as thou wilt" (26:39). Matthew depicts Jesus as offering his prayer three times,[13] and each time the obedient Son of God becomes more accepting of the necessity of his own death. "My Father, if this cannot pass unless I drink it, thy will be done" (26:42). Finally at the completion of his solitary striving with God, Jesus recognizes that "it must be so" (26:54). In that moment when Jesus affirms for the final time his obedient sonship, he once again becomes a solitary figure. Those disciples who sleep during his agonized prayer forsake him and flee when his captors arrive. The Son of God faces his final destiny alone.

The identity of Jesus Christ as Son of God is fully enacted and established in the crucifixion and resurrection. The trial and crucifixion scenes are dominated by questions and claims about the identity of Jesus of Nazareth. After Jesus is silent in face of the charge of the false witnesses that he would destroy the Temple, Caiaphas, the high priest, demands in words strikingly similar to Peter's confession that Jesus identify himself. "I adjure you by the living God, tell us if you are the Christ, the Son of God" (26:63). Jesus' reply is a simple, "You have said so." Thus the symbol of those elements of the Jewish tradition which reject

13. Is there an echo here of the three temptations of Satan in 4:1-11?

Jesus unwittingly confesses the true identity of the suffering Son of God. So too the inhabitants of Jerusalem who stand at the foot of the cross taunt Jesus in words which ironically acknowledge his true identity. "If you are the Son of God, come down from the cross. . . . He trusts in God; let God deliver him now, if he desires him; for he said, 'I am the Son of God'" (27:40, 43). Even in their blindness those who most clearly reject Jesus make confession to him. Though they do not recognize what they have said, they acknowledge that the true Son of God must be a crucified Messiah. Nowhere is that truth more evident than in the climactic moment of the entire narrative, when Jesus cries again to his Father, "My God, my God, why hast thou forsaken me?" (27:46). Jesus' identification with sinners, his obedience to his mission, is so complete that he suffers their fate: God-forsakenness. As he yields up his spirit the ultimate identification is made by one who stands outside the people of Israel, a Roman centurion, who articulates the theme of the entire Gospel of Matthew. "Truly this was the Son of God" (27:54).

Though in his crucifixion Jesus has been unmistakably identified, the narrative does not end at Jesus' death. Though his death was necessary, it is not the last event in the divine drama. The claim of the Matthean narrative that Jesus of Nazareth is "the Christ, the Son of the living God" remains unconfirmed despite Jesus' obedient enactment of that claim in his ministry and crucifixion. As long as Jesus remained in the grave one could only assert that he willingly died for the sake of his own principles, that he died in accord with his claim about himself. The absolute powerlessness of Jesus at this point in the narrative is the culmination of the development we have witnessed in this final section. The one who was conceived through the power of God's spirit, who enacted his divine authority in his ministry, has in this final stage willingly given up the exercise of that authority (see especially 26:53-54). Beginning with his entrance into Jerusalem and especially following the prayer in Gethsemane, Jesus becomes a passive subject whose destiny is determined by others. Clearly Jesus chooses this passive stance as an act of obedience to his Father, but the possibility that this is a hollow tragic act is raised by his God-forsaken cry on the cross. If Jesus is to be more than a tragic figure victimized by his enemies, then God must act decisively in the fact of his son's powerlessness. The message of the angel at the open tomb announces that God has indeed acted on behalf of his obedient son. "He is not here; for he has risen, as he said" (28:6). God himself completes Jesus' mission by raising him from the dead, thereby vindicating Jesus' claim and confirming his status as Son of God. With the resurrection, Jesus' mission of salvation for sinners is completed and his identity fully enacted. Thus he receives with unmistakable finality the divine authority due him. "All authority in heaven and earth has been given to me" (28:18). The one who was designated Emmanuel at his birth, who enacted that identity through a humble identification with sinners, triumphantly affirms that he is the very presence of God in the concluding words of the Gospel. "And lo, I am with you always, to the close of the age" (28:20).

In this concluding integral narrative Matthew brings together his personal and formal individuating identifications. Jesus of Nazareth, who suffered and was crucified, is by virtue of his resurrection unmistakably identified as Son of God. Jesus is most clearly individuated in his passion and death. Matthew's depiction is vividly realistic and the elements of verisimilitude function to define Jesus' identity. Ironically, Jesus' character becomes most sharply articulated when he no longer controls his own action. His purposive and obedient exercise of mission bring him to Jerusalem, where external circumstances determine his destiny. The Jewish leaders plot against him; one of his disciples betrays him; the Romans execute him. He exercises control over his behavior until the moment in Gethsemane when he submits to his Father's will. The events which then overtake him become the vehicle of the enactment of God's intention to save his people. In order for those sinners with whom Jesus identified himself to be saved, Jesus had to offer his life as a "ransom." Jesus' intentional action once again gives way to the primacy of the Father's intention. But Jesus does not retreat into a stylized representative figure, but is most unmistakably himself in his passion and crucifixion. By maintaining the realism of his depiction, Matthew brings his narrative to its appropriate conclusion. The Son of God who enacts his Father's intentions is this very man Jesus of Nazareth who endures the mockings, the beatings, the crucifixion, and God-forsakenness and so does the Father's will. The unmistakable coincidence of the formal and personal identifications is established in the resurrection, as God alone acts to raise the crucified Jesus from the dead. Jesus, having accomplished his mission, receives his authority and sends his followers out to baptize in the name of the Father who sent him, the spirit who conceived him, and the Son who, having accomplished their salvation, will be with them to the close of the age.

II. God's Identity as Prevenient God of Promise

A. God, the Father of Jesus Christ

Just as the title *Son of God* serves as Matthew's central identifying term for Jesus, so the term *Father* is his most prevalent designation for God. In contrast to one prominent tendency in the Old Testament narratives,

Matthew does not often portray God as a character acting directly within the Gospel stories. Only twice is God explicitly portrayed as an actor, and in each case he is limited to a single speech. "This is my beloved Son, with whom I am well pleased" (3:17) and "This is my beloved Son, with whom I am well pleased; listen to him" (17:5). Matthew's strict limitation of God's direct participation in the narrative action has a double purpose. On the one hand, it focuses attention on the actions of Jesus, who as God's Son is cumulatively identified as the one who acts on behalf of God. To know what God intends, Matthew argues, one must refer to the actions of Jesus narrated in the Gospel. On the other hand, when God does appear in the narrative the dramatic effect of his speech is enormously heightened. God first speaks following Jesus' baptism. God's declaration functions as a definitive identification of Jesus and as the authorization of his mission. God thus identifies himself with this particular man and his mission on behalf of sinners. God's second speech occurs in the aftermath of Peter's confession and immediately following Jesus' revelation that both his sonship and true discipleship entail suffering and death. In the context of the transfiguration, where Jesus is identified both with the Sinaitic covenant (Moses) and with Israel's messianic expectation (Elijah), God again declares his unity with the person and mission of his Son and urges the disciples (and by implication Matthew's readers) to heed him.[14]

The term *Father*, as Matthew uses it, specifies God's unity with the person and mission of Jesus. While Father and Son remain distinct persons (one important consequence of Matthew's direct portrayal of God's speech), God's will or intention is rightly expressed in the actions of Jesus. God's definitive identification and authorization of Jesus and his mission warrant the conclusion that Jesus' obedient actions enact not only his own intentions but also God's. Matthew explicates that unity of intention and action through a careful manipulation of Jesus' speech concerning the Father. Prior to Jesus' sharing of authority with the twelve disciples (10:1), he refers to God almost exclusively as "your Father" (fifteen times). Only once does he call God "our Father" (6:9) or "my Father" (7:21). Following the commissioning of the twelve, however, virtually every reference to God identifies him as "my Father" (eighteen times, eleven of which occur after Peter's confession). Other references to "(the) Father" (11:26, 24:36, 28:19), "his Father" (16:27) or "their Father" (13:43) in every case imply a primary identification of God as the Father of Jesus. Many of these passages cast Jesus in the role

---

14. The final "Hear him" comes from Deut. 18:15. For a more complete account of the Old Testament imagery in this passage, see R. H. Gundry, *The Uses of the Old Testament in St. Matthew's Gospel*, Nov-TSup, 18 (Leiden: Brill, 1976), pp. 36-37.

of judge who clearly acts as the agent of his father's will. But those passages which are most central to the narrative action of the Gospel are Jesus' two prayers to the Father (11:25-30 and 26:36-46).

These two prayers, when interpreted together, specify the relation of Father and Son as one of self-differentiated unity. The first prayer emphasizes the unity shared by Father and Son. "All things have been delivered to me by my Father; and no one knows the Son except the Father, and no one knows the Father except the Son and any one to whom the Son chooses to reveal him" (11:27). Father and Son are differentiated in that the Father is the one who delivers all things (including "all authority" 28:18) to the Son. And yet that differentiation is set in the context of a unity of mutual identification. The Father alone knows the Son, and those who in faith come to identify Jesus as the Father's Son do so by the Father's gracious revelation (16:17). The Son in turn has exclusive knowledge of the Father, and those who learn to identify God as Father do so only through the Son's revelation. Father and Son are thus reciprocally identifiable both to themselves and to those with whom they graciously share their identities.[15] Jesus then proceeds to specify his own identity and that of the Father whose "gracious will" (11:26) he enacts.

> Come to me, all who labor and are heavy laden, and I will give you rest. Take my yoke upon you, and learn from me; for I am gentle and lowly in heart, and you will find rest for your souls. For my yoke is easy, and my burden is light. (11:28-30)

The prayer at Gethsemane completes this complex pattern of relation by stressing the differentiation within the paternal and filial unity. Jesus enacts the Father's will as the obedient Son. That obedience, born of Jesus' intention to act in accord with the Father's will, is most severely tested in the hours before the passion. Thus Jesus pleads that "this cup pass from me," while still submitting to his gracious Father: "nevertheless, not as I will, but as thou wilt." His second prayer indicates Jesus' recognition that the Father's intention must be enacted by his death and that his own intention must conform to the Father's. "My Father, if this cannot pass unless I drink it, thy will be done." For all their unity Son and Father remain distinct persons with distinguishable intentions. Completion of the Father's intention to save his people from their sins requires the conformation of Jesus' intention to that will. Though unified in mutual identification through mutual action, the identity of neither Father nor Son is absorbed in the other. Theirs remains a relation of true mutuality.

These two prayers make explicit the pattern of relation manifest

15. This emphasis is captured in the traditional distinction between the immanent and economic trinity.

in the narrative action of the Gospel. God is depicted in the first section of the Gospel as Yahweh, God of Israel, who conceives a son of the virgin Mary in order to enact his intention to "save his people from their sins." He calls his son "out of Egypt" to inaugurate his saving mission through submission to baptism. Having authorized Jesus' mission by declaring him to be his "beloved son," the Father fades into the narrative background in the middle section of the Gospel. Jesus now takes center stage, as he first ambiguously and then with increasing clarity enacts his identity as the Father's Son. As the readers recognize that Jesus of Nazareth is Son of God, so they also recognize that in Jesus they may know God as Father (5:9, 45). At the crucial turning point of the narrative, as Jesus prepares to go to Jerusalem, the Father reiterates his unity with his beloved Son. In the culminating section of the Gospel, God is identified by this complex relation of unity and distinction. The differentiation of Father and Son is stressed by the fact that Jesus undergoes the events of passion and crucifixion as a solitary individual. The God who appeared at the Jordan and on the mount of transfiguration is conspicuously absent as Jesus suffers and is crucified. Though Jesus implores the Father at Gethsemane, there is no dramatic narrative answer. The disciples continue to sleep as Jesus' betrayer approaches, and the sense of Jesus' isolation is heightened. God's absence from the narrative is most profound when Jesus cries out not "my Father" but "my God, my God, why have you forsaken me?"

If the narrative had ended with the words "And Jesus cried again with a loud voice and yielded up his spirit" (27:50), then Matthew's story would have been as Albert Schweitzer described it.

> There is silence all around. The Baptist appears, and cries: "Repent, for the Kingdom of Heaven is at hand." Soon after that comes Jesus, and in the knowledge that He is the coming Son of Man lays hold of the wheel of the world to set it moving on that last revolution which is to bring all ordinary history to a close. It refuses to turn, and He throws Himself upon it. Then it does turn; and crushes Him. Instead of bringing in the eschatological conditions, He has destroyed them. The wheel turns onward, and the mangled body of the one immeasurably great Man, who was strong enough to think of Himself as the spiritual ruler of mankind and to bend history to His purpose, is hanging upon it still. That is His victory and His reign.[16]

But the narrative continues and describes the descent of an angel whose message defines Matthew's story as "gospel." "He is not here; for he

---

16. Albert Schweitzer, *The Quest of the Historical Jesus* (New York: Macmillan, 1961), pp. 370-371.

has risen, as he said" (28:6). That message casts the reader back to Caesarea Philippi where Jesus concludes his passion prediction with the words "and on the third day be raised" (egerthēnai). The aorist passive verb points to the one who, though apparently absent from the narrative, has acted to raise his Son from death and to grant him his ultimate authority (28:18). By that act the Father not only completes his intention to save but also unmistakably binds himself in differentiated union with his Son. In the resurrection Jesus is definitively identified as Son of God, and God is definitively identified as his Father. Just as the formal identification "Son of God" is given its personal content in the narrated events of crucifixion and resurrection, so also God's identity as Father is specified by those same events. To call God "Father" is to identify him as the one who raised Jesus from the dead.

B. God as Yahweh, the God of Gospel and Promise

The word promise (epangelia) never appears in the Gospel of Matthew. Yet the notion of promise hovers like an enormous parenthesis surrounding the entire narrative. More than any other evangelist Matthew depicts Jesus as enacting the will of the Father by fulfilling prophecy. Fifteen times Matthew explicitly designates a narrative occurrence as fulfilling a prophecy of Hebrew scripture. Such references are especially prominent in the Gospel's first section, where Matthew painstakingly identifies Jesus as the inheritor of Israel's tradition. The stylized use of the fulfillment motif (e.g., "all this took place to fulfil what the Lord had spoken by the prophet") occurs infrequently within the realistic passion narrative, but Matthew's more subtle use of quotations from and allusions to Hebrew scripture is striking.[17] There are at least twenty such instances in chapters 26 and 27 alone.

Matthew achieves a number of purposes by employing the prophecy-fulfillment motif. First, he associates Jesus, Son of God, with the Israelite heritage, thus identifying him as Son of Abraham and David, i.e., as inheritor of the two great covenantal promises. Second, he establishes Jesus' continuity with his tradition precisely as he depicts him as its transformer. Jesus and not the contemporary Jewish leadership is the true interpreter and fulfiller of the law and prophets. Third, and for our purposes most importantly, Matthew uses the prophecy-fulfillment motif to specify further the identity of the God Jesus calls Father. Jesus' Father is Yahweh, the God of Abraham, Isaac, and Jacob, the God whose

---

17. The most thorough study of Matthew's use of Old Testament quotations and allusions is Hubert Frankenmoelle, Jahwebund und Kirche Christi, NTAbh 10 (Münster: Aschendorff, 1974).

promises the prophets declared and Jesus now fulfills. The God of Israel is the Father of Jesus Christ. Thus to call God "Father" is, Matthew argues, to identify him as Yahweh, the one who raised Jesus from the dead.

There is one final way in which God can be identified on the basis of Matthew's Gospel. Jesus' death and resurrection, which provide the final identification of both Father and Son, also accomplish the salvation of sinners. Because Jesus successfully completed his mission, the disciples' confession "You are the Christ, the Son of the living God," has been confirmed. Matthew constructs his narrative in such a way that his readers are led to identify with the disciples in their transition from confusion to faith. The narrative thus functions not only as a description of past events but as an invitation to the reader to share in the disciples' confession of faith. That is to say, the narrative serves as both report and proclamation. If Jesus is Son of God, then he has accomplished the salvation of all sinners who in faith confess his name and undertake the life of discipleship. Matthew's narrative is thus "gospel," the proclamation of the good news concerning Jesus Christ.

The word *gospel (euangelion)* appears only four times in Matthew. The first two times it appears in the formulaic sentence "And he [Jesus] went about . . . teaching in their synagogues and preaching the gospel of the kingdom and healing every disease and every infirmity among the people" (4:23, 9:35). This phrase first occurs at the outset of Jesus' own ministry in chapter 4 and is repeated in chapter 9 immediately prior to the commissioning of the twelve. Matthew does not use the word *gospel* again until chapter 24 when, shortly before the passion narrative, Jesus warns of the signs which will accompany "the close of the age" *(synteleias tou aiōnos)* (24:3). "And this gospel of the kingdom will be preached throughout the whole world, as a testimony to all nations *(pasin tois ethnesin)*; and then the end will come" (24:14). The word *gospel* appears for the final time in the enigmatic story which introduces the passion account, Jesus' anointing with oil by an unnamed woman. After indicating that she has anointed him for burial, Jesus says, "Truly, I say to you, wherever this gospel is preached in the whole world, what she has done will be told in memory of her" (26:13). These broadly separated uses of the word *gospel* capture the progression inherent in Matthew's narrative. The "good news" is originally that authoritative message which Jesus preached and enacted in his teaching and healing ministry. Then it is that message which the disciples proclaim when they are given "authority . . . to heal every disease and every infirmity" (10:1). Gradually the scope of the good news widens to include "the whole world" and "every nation." Finally the content of the gospel itself shifts subtly but importantly at the point of the passion narrative.

Ronald Thiemann

Jesus refers simply to "this gospel" which "when preached to the whole world" will serve as a memorial to this unnamed woman. That memorial is accomplished when the gospel becomes *this narrative* concerning Jesus of Nazareth, the Son of God. When the narrative which identifies Jesus as Son of God is proclaimed as gospel to all nations, this woman, whose act inaugurates Jesus' passion, will be forever remembered. The "gospel" within Matthew's narrative shifts from the message Jesus proclaimed to the message proclaimed about Jesus. That important shift is culminated when, in the final verses of the Gospel, the resurrected Jesus again shares his authority with his disciples, sends them to make disciples "of all nations" *(panta ta ethnē;* 28:19, cf. 24:14) and to baptize them "in the name of the Father, and of the Son, and of the Holy Spirit," and finally promises to be with them until "the close of the age" *(synteleias tou aiōnos;* 28:20, cf. 24:3). As they now baptize in his name, so when they proclaim the "gospel" they proclaim his story. Matthew's story appropriately ends with Jesus' *promise,* for this narrative, seen from the perspective of its own ending, functions for its readers as gospel, i.e., as the *narrated promise* of Jesus of Nazareth, Son of God.

C. God's Prevenience

The Gospel of Matthew provides the requisite individuating description of God. God is identified as Yahweh, the God of promise, the Father of Jesus Christ, who by raising Jesus from the dead accomplished his intention to save his sinful people. *A God so described cannot be other than prevenient.* In part that conclusion follows from the way this description of God fulfills the conditions of authentic promising.[18] As God of promise Yahweh is the one who specified his intention to save through his prophets, who designated Jesus' death and resurrection as the acts whereby he would enact his intention, who in his declared unity with Jesus identified himself as Father and undertook the obligation implied in his promise, and who, when he raised Jesus from the dead, uniquely fulfilled the conditions of his own promise. God as identified in Matthew's narrative is alone the gracious initiator, actor, and fulfiller of his own promises. The central act in this complex intentional action is the raising of Jesus from the dead, for in that deed both Father and Son are definitively identified, and God's promise is fulfilled. Yahweh, who called forth creation from the void and formed Adam from the dust of the ground, now raises his Son from death in a second uniquely creative act. The God who raised Jesus from the dead is necessarily prevenient.

18. See Thiemann, *Revelation and Theology,* chapter 5, pp. 108-111.

Matthew's narrative portrayal of God demonstrates that God's prevenience is a necessary implication of his identity as God of promise. Theology would be well advised to follow the logic of Matthew's identifying description by locating its justificatory account of God's prevenience neither in the *prolegomena* to theology nor in a separate doctrine of "God's Word" but within its account of God's identity. *The doctrine of revelation ought to be a subtheme within the doctrine of God.* When the justification of God's prevenience is internally related to God's identity, then the significance of God's *triune* identity begins to emerge. Precisely as God is described in his intertrinitarian relations his essential graciousness becomes evident. To designate God as triune is to assert that his utter graciousness, i.e., his prevenience, is a necessary implication of his identity. I am going to argue, by way of conclusion, that Matthew's narrative description of God and the belief in prevenience it implies receive their most precise theological redescription in certain trinitarian categories. I cannot in this brief space articulate a full doctrine of the trinity,[19] but I do want to indicate how Matthew's identifying description of God has a characteristically trinitarian character which theology ought to enhance and develop.

The concluding verses of Matthew provide the trinitarian baptismal formula which becomes the basis for the triune shape of Christian liturgy. Matthew certainly does not develop a complete account of the identities of Father, Son, and Spirit, nor of their unified interrelation. His depiction of the Spirit is particularly lean. The Spirit is one who conceives Jesus and leads him into the wilderness following his baptism. The Spirit is further present in the form of a dove as God declares Jesus to be his Son. Other than these two events, the Spirit is absent from the narrative flow of the Gospel. Yet these stories, when bolstered by Jesus' references to the Spirit, allow the construction of a minimal identity. The Spirit is described as being "of God" (3:16; 12:18, 28) or "of your Father" (10:20). The Spirit, moreover, is the one who will empower the disciples to speak in the persecutions of the end-time (10:20). These few references show the Spirit to be the means of God's relation to his Son and the source of power for the disciples' witness.

When this spare description is added to the much richer depiction of Father and Son one can see the emergence of an incipient conception of God as triune. The mysterious relation of three to one is surely present. The Father is clearly identified with Yahweh, and both Jesus and the Spirit are said to be "of God." When Jesus is granted final authority his disciples worship him, an indication of his equality with

---

19. An excellent discussion of the doctrine of the Trinity is Robert Jenson, *The Triune Identity* (Philadelphia: Fortress Press, 1982).

God. In the baptismal formula all three persons are assigned equal status, implying a coequal relation as God. But whether Matthew actually teaches a doctrine of three in one is neither particularly important nor interesting. That the elements for the subsequent development of the doctrine are present is unquestionable.

Much more important for our purposes is the way Matthew conceives God in a relation of differentiated unity. Both the distinctions and the unity in the relation among Father, Son, and Spirit are narrative-based. Each person is given a particular name and an unsubstitutable role in the narrative action. The Father promises, enacts his intention to save, and fulfills his promise by raising Jesus from the dead. The Son is conceived, receives a mission of salvation, and obediently accomplishes that mission through crucifixion. The Spirit conceives Jesus, confirms his Sonship, and empowers the disciples' witness. Despite their irreducible particular identities, all three "persons" are mutually and necessarily related. In declaring Jesus to be his Son, the Father ties both his identity and action to the Son. Jesus is obedient Son only in relation to the Father who designated his mission. The Spirit establishes the relation between Father and Son in the act of conception. Though distinguishably identifiable, the identities of all three persons are mutually and necessarily related. They live in a self-differentiated unity.

One final element of Matthew's narrative identification deserves mention. The Father and Spirit (most particularly the Father) are hidden but active during the crucial events of crucifixion and resurrection.[20] Jesus alone is present, and yet he is powerless and unable to act. The power which is exercised in the resurrection is that of the Father, who is never depicted in these concluding events. The theme of God's hidden but active power has a long history in biblical narrative[21] and suggests the complex patterns theologians must devise if their redescription of God is to be grounded in such a narrative depiction. God must be conceived in such a way that both his hiddenness and presence in human history are accounted for. That pattern cannot simply be correlated with the pattern of Father and Son, for though the Son does enact the Father's intentions, the very fact that we can identify those intentions as the *Father's* curbs any attempt to conceive of the Father as eternally hidden. The distinction between hiddenness and presence must

20. Hans Frei, *Identity*, makes this point particularly well. "In his passion and death the initiative of Jesus disappears more and more into that of God; but in the resurrection, where the initiative of God is finally and decisively climaxed and he alone is and can be active, the sole identity to mark the presence of that activity is Jesus. God remains hidden, and even reference to him is almost altogether lacking. Jesus of Nazareth, he and none other, marks the presence and action of God" (p. 121).

21. See Thiemann, *Revelation and Theology*, chapter 4, pp. 88-90.

rather cut across the entire conception of God as Father, Son, and Spirit. That is, of course, what the Cappadocian fathers attempted to do in devising the distinction between the "immanent" and "economic" trinity.[22] That distinction guards both the hiddenness and the presence of God's identity, because it asserts that the self-differentiated unity we observe in God's narrative relations is a reiteration of God's inner but hidden identity. The narrative description of God is reliable, because it shows us God's "immanent" identity though an "economic" depiction. God's hiddenness is not some elusive self lurking behind or beyond the narrative depiction. God's hiddenness is simply a quality of God which the shape of the narrative itself indicates. God is the perfection of agency, the one whose activity is not limited by anything beyond the reach of his intentional control.[23] That is to say, God is a self-constituting agent who exercises sovereign control over his own identity. If he should intend that his identity be shared with that which is external to him, that sharing is grounded solely in his sovereign intention.[24] Or to put the matter differently: if we come to know God's identity, we do so by grace alone.

A triune conception of God's identity, grounded in a biblical narrative description, is a natural and appropriate vehicle for the expression of God's gracious prevenience. The promising God deigns to share his identity with us and thereby established a relation with our human concepts and categories, enabling them to be the vehicle of his communication. But that relation is established in such a way that God's prior gracious initiative is necessarily implied. If it is this God—Father, Son and Spirit—whom we are able to identify, then that identification has been enabled by his gracious action. God, conceived as triune, is a God necessarily prevenient.

22. See Jenson, *The Triune Identity*, pp. 103-159.
23. This formulation of the perfection of God's agency is from Thomas Tracy, *God, Action, and Embodiment* (Grand Rapids: Eerdmans, 1983), p. 244.
24. Matthew makes this point with Jesus' prayer in 11:27.

God, Action, and Narrative: Which Narrative? Which Action? Which God?

Michael Goldberg

I

Over the past decade, one theme has reverberated increasingly throughout certain theological circles: our ability to know God and his actions depends on our capacity to know how to identify him as an agent whose characteristic patterns of behavior find display within the context of some narrative.[1] Indeed, that motif underscoring the significance of a narrative framework for our talk about God and his activity resounds in two recent books with noteworthy clarity and vibrance. While Thomas Tracy's *God, Action, and Embodiment*[2] offers a powerful piece of philosophical theology exploring the relations among narrative, identity, and divine agency, Ronald Thiemann's *Revelation and Theology*[3] provides a provocative ex-

---

1. Compare, e.g., Stanley Hauerwas, Richard Bondi, and David B. Burrell, *Truthfulness and Tragedy* (Notre Dame: University of Notre Dame Press, 1977); Johann Baptist Metz, *Faith in History and Society* (New York: Seabury Press, 1980); George Stroup, *The Promise of Narrative Theology* (Atlanta: John Knox Press, 1981); George Lindbeck, *The Nature of Doctrine* (Philadelphia: Westminster Press, 1984).
2. Thomas F. Tracy, *God, Action, and Embodiment* (Grand Rapids: Eerdmans, 1984).
3. Ronald F. Thiemann, *Revelation and Theology: The Gospel as Narrated Promise* (Notre Dame: University of Notre Dame Press, 1985).

Michael Goldberg, "God, Action, and Narrative: *Which* Narrative? *Which* Action? *Which* God?" *Journal of Religion*, 68, 1 (January 1988): 39-56.

ample of doctrinal theology analyzing the gospel as a distinctive kind of divine speech-act, namely, the "narrated promise" of God. At a basic level, each work—and perhaps Thiemann's even more than Tracy's—seeks to address an audience skeptical of the conceptual coherency of a biblically rooted theism; accordingly, to the extent that these "narrative theologies" put such doubts to rest, Christian theists would seem to have ample cause for celebration.

Yet even if a narrative theology such as Thiemann's should succeed in meeting the challenges of Christianity's "cultured despisers," breaking out the hats and horns might be premature, for another set of interrogators awaits with questions that might prove the special undoing of an expressly *Christian* narrative theology. Importantly, these questioners, like Christianity itself, take their cue from a tradition bespeaking both a theism and a narrative. And who are these interlocutors? Jews.

What Jews have asked of Christians for the past two millennia is nothing if not narrative dependent: what justification do Christians have for identifying the deity whose salvific activity is depicted in the gospel story with the One whose saving acts are portrayed in Israel's prior story? That question raises the issue of coherency anew, for it calls on a Christian narrative theology to produce the specific story-grounded warrants—for example, the continuities of story line, theme, and characterization—that show that in the storied life, death, and resurrection of Jesus Christ the character ultimately to be acknowledged *as* "God" coheres with the character *of* God previously manifested through certain characteristic actions performed on Israel's behalf, *particularly* those actions paradigmatically recounted in Israel's "master story" of the Exodus.[4] Accordingly, any justifiable talk about such matters as God, action, and narrative must adequately address *the relevant particulars: Which narrative? Which action? Which God?*

II

At the outset of *God, Action, and Embodiment,* Tracy makes mention of the fact that often, when we are interested in someone's identity as a *distinctive individual,* that is, when we want to get to know that person

---

4. See Michael Goldberg, *Jews and Christians, Getting our Stories Straight: The Exodus and the Passion-Resurrection* (Nashville: Abingdon Press, 1985), pp. 13-15. By "master story," I mean the kind of core, foundational narrative that, in providing a community with its paradigmatic "model of understanding the world and . . . guide for acting in it" (p. 13), simultaneously gives rise to that community's most elementary, and often most distinctive, convictions about reality.

Michael Goldberg

at a level deeper—and more revealing—than "name, rank, and serial number," we may well ask the question, "What's he like?" In response, we are frequently told something about what the person has done; more specifically, we are told "a story the point of which can be expressed by saying that the actions narrated in the story display the person's characteristic energy or ambition or wisdom or avarice or the like. The characterizing term directs attention to particular features of the story, suggesting that it be viewed in a certain light. The story, in turn, fills out the detail of the characterization, giving it concreteness."[5]

Thus, these distinctive patterns of action, when narrated in sufficient detail, enable us to attribute certain *character traits* to the person, and on the basis of such attribution, "we are," Tracy comments, "entitled to expect behavior characterizable by that term in the person's future."[6] Following Gilbert Ryle, Tracy views character traits as kinds of "dispositional properties" describing an enduring propensity of a person, *an agent*, to behave in specific ways in particular situations over a broad span of time.[7] Significantly, a set of story-bound[8] character traits provides us with a means not only of individuating an agent and his behavior but also of *evaluating* them. In sum, a narrated identification yields both a character within a story-context and *that character's character* besides.[9]

Furthermore, as Tracy makes abundantly clear, the logic inherent in the concept of a character trait requires "that any behavior [it is] used to appraise be *intentional* action and any individual [it is] used to characterize be an *agent*."[10] That is, our predicating character traits of a person depends on our being able to say of the behavior being characterized that it has been undertaken *on* purpose or *for* some purpose and that it has been regulated in accord with that purpose, as, for instance, by the person's having followed some rule or norm articulating what counts as correct performance.[11] And what has all this finally to do with our characterization of God and his actions? Writes Tracy: "If we are to say that God is loving or just, we must be prepared to point to actions in which his love and justice are displayed. Love and justice will be at-

5. Tracy, *God, Action, and Embodiment*, p. 3.

6. Ibid., p. 7. Naturally, we are entitled to look as well into the person's past for further indications of such behavior.

7. Ibid.; see Gilbert Ryle, *The Concept of Mind* (New York: Barnes & Noble, 1949).

8. For Tracy's notion of "story-bound" (as opposed to "story-relative") identification, see *God, Action, and Embodiment*, pp. 79, 167-168 n. 16.

9. Compare also James W. McClendon, Jr., *Biography as Theology* (Nashville: Abingdon Press, 1974), chap. 1.

10. Tracy, *God, Action, and Embodiment*, p. 4.

11. Ibid., pp. 22, 40.

tributes of God only if these terms are appropriate appraisals of his actions. The meaning of these attributes will be tied logically to the account that we give of what God has done and is doing. The particular way in which God is loving or just will appear in the story we tell about God's activity in relation to his creation."[12] Consequently, no matter what claims we would make about God's acts, both our reference to those acts and our characterization of them will crucially depend on our being able to tell a story that ties events together in an intelligible pattern that is itself tied to the purposive activity of God.[13]

Hence, on the basis of such a story-bound identification linking God to some uniquely characteristic set of possibilities and relations, Tracy claims we can form a logically individuating description of both God and his actions,[14] and he therefore suggests that God might be most distinctively characterized as that "logically singular instance of intentional agency" or, more simply stated, as "the perfection of agency."[15] As perfection of agency, God will be radically self-creative (i.e., intending all that he is), all powerful (i.e., facing only those limitations that are either necessary or self-imposed), and fully unified as a self.[16] Importantly for our purposes, this last divine character trait means, according to Tracy, that God's activity will display the fullest possible integration and coherence such as no phase of his actions in the past will ever be abandoned in the present or future but will instead be continually affirmed and advanced in each new act. In Tracy's words, "there will [thus] be no inconstancy in God's action—*none of the disillusioned reassessments and sudden reversals* that may punctuate the life of a human agent."[17]

III

"No inconstancy in God's action"—that idea might well serve as the motto for the Christian narrative theology proposed by Thiemann[18] since, in his view, God's hallmark character trait is the constancy expressed through his promise keeping. Thus, says Thiemann, "God is

12. Ibid., pp. 19-20.

13. Ibid., cf. p. 78.

14. Ibid., see pp. 74-77. Tracy's point of departure here is P. F. Strawson's *Individuals: An Essay in Descriptive Metaphysics* (Garden City, N.Y.: Doubleday/Anchor Books, 1963).

15. Tracy, *God, Action, and Embodiment*, pp. 76, 126.

16. Ibid., p. 126.

17. Ibid., p. 136; italics mine.

18. A theology that is explicitly indebted to Tracy's account of divine agency; cf. Thiemann, *Revelation and Theology*, pp. 107-108.

Michael Goldberg

identified primarily as the *God of promise* whose promises receive *narrative enactment and fulfillment* in the history of Israel, and the life, death, and resurrection of Jesus."[19] Especially in the face of various "foundationalist"[20] and "functionalist"[21] theologies—which Thiemann believes empty Christianity's historic claims concerning God of their distinctive content—narrative becomes an indispensable conceptual category for reasserting the specificity of God's identity since "1) it provides a coherent theological alternative to those theologies focused on the primacy of philosophical anthropology; 2) it provides a way of construing the canon as a whole which integrates scripture's first-order language and theology's second-order redescription; 3) it focuses attention on the centrality of God's agency within biblical narrative and Christian community."[22]

Of special concern to Thiemann are traditional Christian doctrines of revelation and God's prevenience, and he looks to narrative to supply the means for locating those doctrines within a Christian "conviction set" and, moreover, for explicating their logic in the process.[23] Indeed, Thiemann argues that only within the kind of narrative framework found in the "logically odd category of 'gospel'" can Christian convictions exhibit any intelligibility or justification at all.[24] Drawing on the work of J. L. Austin, he contends that the gospel narratives, when rehearsed in a certain circumstance — generally one of Christian worship — and by a certain person—typically a minister of the gospel—function as several distinct, albeit intimately related, speech-acts: report, proclamation, and, above all, promise. By reporting the reconciliation effected in the past by God's action in Jesus Christ, the story told through the gospel simultaneously proclaims the good news of the availability of that gift of God's reconciliation in the present and ultimately prom-

19. Thiemann, *Revelation and Theology*, p. 100.

20. By "foundationalism," Thiemann means the view holding that "knowledge is grounded in a set of non-inferential, self-evident beliefs which, because their intelligibility is not constituted by a relationship with other beliefs, can serve as the source of intelligibility for all beliefs in a conceptual framework. These non-inferential beliefs function as the givens or foundations of a linguistic system because the mode of their justification is direct and immediate" (*Revelation and Theology*, p. 158 n. 20).

21. By "functionalism," Thiemann means a "neo-Wittgensteinian option, represented by David Kelsey and Charles Wood," which seeks to ground the authority of theological claims *solely* within the context of the usage to which they are put within a particular community; cf. Thiemann, ibid., pp. 56-63.

22. Ibid., p. 84.

23. Ibid., pp. 70-71. Thiemann borrows the notion of "conviction set" from James W. McClendon, Jr., and James M. Smith, *Understanding Religious Convictions* (Notre Dame: University of Notre Dame Press, 1975).

24. Thiemann, *Revelation and Theology*, p. 81; cf. also, e.g., pp. 72, 75-77, 154.

ises the final triumph of that God's reconciling activity in the future.[25] For the gospel's hearers, the appropriate "uptake"—the appropriate reaction to the prior action of the divine agent narratively revealed—thus becomes crystal clear; both the gospel's speech-acts (report, proclamation, *and* promise) and the gospel's speakers (minister *and* God) ought to be considered *trustworthy*, hence meriting a response of faith.

As a concrete case in point of his more formal claims, Thiemann undertakes a "literary and theological analysis" of the Gospel of Matthew,[26] stating that such an analysis is "congenial" to Matthew since the book's goal is "to identify Jesus of Nazareth as Emmanuel, the Son of God, the one who enacts God's intention to save his people from sin through death and resurrection"(p. 322). Against the backdrop of the narrative, the dynamic of the gospel is to give an increasingly specific identity description of Jesus, thereby revealing his acts to be the enactments of God's intentions for Israel and the world. Or as Thiemann puts it: "those who learn to identify God as Father do so only through the Son's revelation. Father and Son are thus reciprocally identifiable both to themselves and to those with whom they graciously share their identities" (p. 340).

Hence, in the initial four chapters of the Matthean account, Jesus is portrayed in rather general terms that are intended, not so much as a material description of him as an individual person, but as a formal assignation to him of a unique role—the Son of God, the quintessential inheritor of the saving promises made to Israel by Israel's God[27] (p. 324). The middle section of the Gospel (4:18–20:34) then serves to lead its hearers (or readers) to "gradually . . . identify the distant figure of the early chapters, the stylized Son of God, with the concrete person, Jesus of Nazareth"(p. 331). Such identification, however, is by no means easy because, from the beginning of this section, Jesus is pictured as an agent whose actions are ambiguous in their meaning. Little wonder, then, that Jesus' acts are often misunderstood, as, for instance, when the scribes in Matthew 9:3 accuse Jesus of blasphemy for healing a paralytic by forgiving his sins; they wrongly believe that Jesus *has arrogated to himself* the prerogative of God. Hence, only those who can recognize Jesus as the Son of God can acknowledge the truth of what it is he does (p. 330).

Part of what makes both recognition and acknowledgment so difficult is that the Son of God's saving mission seems more and more to

25. Ibid., pp. 81-82; see also p. 135.

26. See his essay, "The Promising God," pp. 320-347 in this volume.

27. C.f., e.g., Matt. 1:1 characterizing Jesus as "the son of David, the son of Abraham."

Michael Goldberg

entail suffering by Israel's messiah. That leitmotif reaches its clearest articulation in the Gospel's concluding section (21:1–28:20) relating the passion and resurrection. As Thiemann insightfully notes, Jesus' true character is ironically—but crucially — revealed most sharply when, given over to death on the cross, he no longer possesses the capacity to act for himself; it is exactly in the face of Jesus' own powerlessness that God's power is most definitely manifested when, through the resurrection, "the unmistakable coincidence of the formal and personal identifications is established . . . , as God alone acts to raise the crucified Jesus from the dead" (p. 338).

Thus, says Thiemann, "the decisive Christian belief is that God is identifiable in Jesus Christ,"[28] and the only way of justifying that conviction is through a theology that begins with attention to the narrative that gives rise to it. In that narrative, "the promise of Christ" bears a threefold meaning: the future act to which God has originally committed himself (in Israel's previous story), the fulfiller of that original commitment, *and* the agent of God's new commitment.[29] Hence the Gospel, properly understood, is quite literally a "narrated promise" that its hearer is invited to recognize as "God's personal promising address," thereby evoking "a correlative response of faith and discipleship."[30]

IV

Why is it then that Jews have for over two thousand years failed to make such a response? What is it in the gospel's narrated promise that they have failed to recognize? All along, Thiemann has rested his case on a methodological approach described as a "holistic form of justification" that seeks to ground Christian claims by locating them within a coherent pattern of relationships displayed by a Christian conviction set.[31] He readily admits that "holistic justification works most simply when the two parties engaged in discussion share a set of common background beliefs but dispute the propriety of holding a particular dependent belief. . . . In the process of rational persuasion one party might seek to show the other that [the latter's] defense of [some specific belief] is inconsistent with the background beliefs they hold in common. Whether or not that approach is successful, the disputants share a fairly stable

28. Thiemann, *Revelation and Theology*, p. 188 n. 10.
29. Ibid.; cf. e.g., p. 104.
30. Ibid., p. 145.
31. Ibid., pp. 72-78.

core of background beliefs as the basis for their discussion."[32] Clearly, according to both Christianity's traditional confession and Thiemann's own theological account, Christians do in fact claim to share with Jews just such a common core of background beliefs, and, hence, if Thiemann's views on the potential usefulness of holistic justification are to prove even minimally convincing, the disputed belief between Jews and Christians that "God is identifiable in Jesus Christ" would seem an appropriate test case. But here, of course, a narrative-based test would seem most appropriate of all, for it is the background context of a common narrative—that is, God's saving acts on Israel's behalf—that engenders whatever common background beliefs Jews and Christians may share. Failing to engage in that kind of narrative exploration, a Christian narrative theology such as Thiemann's cannot but look unfounded.

In fact, in its virtual disregard of Judaism, Thiemann's narrative theology does take on that look. One is hard-pressed to find any indication that Thiemann has tried to understand Israel, its story, or Judaism on their own terms. His only understanding of such matters seems to have come from Matthew's perspective—which may be already to beg the question.[33] To be sure, part of Matthew's project is to show how the story of the Christ unfolds from the Jews' own story—especially from their story of the Exodus[34]—and, therefore, Matthew attempts to forge

32. Ibid., p. 76.

33. Ironically, only when Matthew's perspective seems to Thiemann to be expressly a polemic against Jews and Judaism does he feel the need to comment on the possible inadequacy of a Matthean vantage point: "Contemporary interpreters must exercise extreme care in interpreting these passages, for they have been the source for much Christian anti-Judaism" (ibid., p. 184 n. 10). Yet without further work at trying to understand how Jews might have understood Israel's story, Thiemann "continues a dangerous tradition of Christian imperialism toward other religions" that he himself (rightly) castigates (ibid., p. 187 n. 9). Indeed, among contemporary Christian theologians and particularly among so-called narrative theologians, Paul van Buren stands virtually alone as one who has gone to significant lengths to come to grips with Jewish self-understanding and its implications for Christianity. See his *Discerning the Way* (New York: Seabury Press, 1980) and *A Christian Theology of the People Israel* (New York: Seabury Press, 1983); these two books are part of a projected four-volume "theology of the Jewish-Christian reality" (van Buren's subtitle for each volume). At any rate, unless an account such as Thiemann's more explicitly and consistently evidences a certain historical-critical detachment in its reading of biblical narrative, it will lend credence to what may well be the most damning indictment of narrative theology, namely, that such theology is at bottom only a sophisticated fundamentalism, and thus a sophistic fideism, to boot.

34. Hence, the Matthean narrative is consciously replete with Exodus-linked allusions and parallels, such as, e.g. a tyrant bent on infanticide to thwart the divine will (cf. Matt. 2:1-8, 16, and Exod. 1:8-12, 15-22), flight to a foreign land to escape death at the tyrant's hands (cf. Matt. 2:13-14, and Exod. 2:15), safe return following the tyrant's death (cf. Matt. 2:19-21, and Exod. 4:19-20), the beginnings of a new community formed at a meal preceding a great saving act (cf. Matt. 26:26-29, and Exod. 12:21-28).

a strong bond of continuity between the two narratives through an emphatic characterization of God as one whose hallmark character trait is his constancy in keeping his past promises.

Yet despite Matthew's best efforts at establishing a narrative-based continuity between his rendition of God's steadfastness and the one given by Exodus, an essential discontinuity may nevertheless remain, especially if the two stories differ markedly—and perhaps even incommensurately—in their respective depictions of *what* it is God promises and, moreover, *how* God then acts to keep faith with what he promises. That narrative-dependent difference may consequently be at the heart of many of the differences between Jews and Christians.

Unfortunately Thiemann, whose articulation of Israel's prior saga seems so thoroughly *and uncritically* dependent on Matthew's telling of it, seems never even to have imagined that the two narratives may hold out fundamentally differing visions of *the particular nature* and *the specific enactment* of the divine promise. Thus, he says, for instance, "Jesus is initially identified through his genealogy, which designates him as 'the son of David, the son of Abraham' (1:1), thereby linking him to the two great covenantal promises of Israel, the promise of a nation and the promise of eternal Kingship. . . . [The] major function of the genealogy is to show that Jesus is the inheritor of God's promises to Israel"(p. 324). Elsewhere, he similarly writes: "[Matthew] associates Jesus, Son of God, with the Israelite heritage, thus identifying him as Son of Abraham and David, i.e., as inheritor of the two great covenantal promises" (p. 342). However, while it is certainly the case that the Abrahamic and Davidic covenants are part of "the Israelite heritage," it is undeniably the case as well that to identify them as "*the* two great covenantal promises" is to commit an egregious error, for in the heritage of the people Israel, there is a *third* great covenantal promise besides, that is, the one associated with Israel's becoming a *people*[35] in the first place: Sinai.[36] Sinai is both literarily and theologically the high point of Israel's story of the Exodus from Egypt. In a sense, it can even be considered the turning point in Israel's larger epic, for whether in regard to God's promise to Abraham that his progeny shall form a blessing-bearing, landed nation or to David that his heirs shall constitute an eternal dynasty to rule that nation-state, before Israel's story line winds it way to the place where those pledges can be fulfilled, it first makes an absolutely crucial stop

---

35. That is, as distinct from an extended kin-group, or from a social class (i.e., *'abiru*), or from what Exodus 12:38 dubs "a mixed multitude." For a further elaboration of this point, see E. A. Speiser's classic article "'People' and 'Nation' of Israel," *Journal of Biblical Literature* 79 (1960): 157-163.

36. Compare Exodus 19–20, esp. 19:1-6.

at Sinai. For that very reason, Israel's subsequent *corporate* destiny, as well as the future fate of *individual* Davidic kings, are both worked out against the backdrop of the covenant at Sinai; breaches of that covenant can (and do) entail the dispersion of Abraham's descendants from the land and the removal of various Davids from the throne.

But strikingly, Matthew's opening genealogical identification of Jesus omits any reference or allusion to the Sinai covenant, and therefore Thiemann, too, presumably skips over it. In the process, a major guiding theme in Israel's story has been simply excised from Christ's story, at best to be relegated to the status of an *Old Testament.*[37] Such a move is surely possible; Christian tradition has historically made it, and Matthew theologically implies it.[38] Even so, one may still want to question the justifiability of that move *literally*, that is, from the standpoint of literary coherence and unity vis-à-vis story line, theme, and characterization. For as even Thiemann himself explicitly reminds us, despite certain discordances plainly evident in both good stories and among the Bible's own stories, "theologians . . . should, nonetheless, continue to seek the configural narrative unity of the biblical witness."[39] Unless Christian theologians—Thiemann included—can do that, they may be forced to say that their canon includes within it the chronicles of an alien religion[40] and thus commit the old Marcion heresy all over again— only this time under the banner of "narrative theology."

Being at the vertex of Israel's story, the Sinai covenant bears the imprint of a distinctive "narrative shape"; shaped by the story that precedes it, it shapes in turn the story proceeding from it. Whereas the promises made by God to both Abraham and David can be characterized as being examples of a *unilateral "covenant of grant,"* the divine promise made at Sinai is characteristic of a *bilateral "treaty."*[41] For this latter kind of covenant to be fulfilled, the parties to the pact must all faithfully fulfill its mutually binding stipulations. By contrast, as the very concept of

37. As Jon Levenson notes in his extremely penetrating study, *Sinai and Zion* (Minneapolis: Winston Press, 1985), while some Christians never tire of claiming that, in the biblical period, the Sinai covenant was superseded by the Davidic, the fact remains that although "the Davidic covenant never displaced the Sinaitic in the Hebrew Bible, it did, in a sense, in the New Testament" (p. 216).

38. Compare, e.g., Matthew 5:17-20; 23:1-12; 28:16-20.

39. Thiemann, *Revelation and Theology*, p. 86.

40. Compare Levenson, *Sinai and Zion*, pp. 216-217, and A. H. J. Gunneweg, *Understanding the Old Testament* (Philadelphia: Westminster Press, 1978), esp. pp. 142-172.

41. Compare M. Weinfeld, "The Covenant of Grant in the Old Testament and in the Ancient Near East," *Journal of the American Oriental Society* 90 (1970), and Levenson, *Sinai and Zion*, pp. 100-101. More specifically, the pact at Sinai between God and Israel formally manifests, as biblical critics have long recognized, many of the same characteristics of a Hittite suzerainty treaty.

"grant" implies, for the former sort of covenant to be realized, *no act of mutuality is required; only the party that is the grant's initiator* is under obligation to keep faith. Thus, insofar as the divine promises to Abraham and David reflect covenants of grant, their full enactment—their fulfillment—depends *solely on God's constancy* to his commitments—and consequently *not* on any corresponding human steadfastness. As a result, whether for the Abrahamic covenant or the Davidic, the working out of such a grant-type promise lies, in Jon Levenson's words, "beyond the vicissitudes of history, since they cease to be critical. This covenant fixes attention to that which is constant beneath—or perhaps I should say, above—the flux of history. . . . And since the focus is upon the constancy of God rather than the changeability of man, it brings to light what is secure and inviolable."[42] Levenson states that, in comparison, "the Sinaitic texts tend to emphasize the precariousness of life and the consequent need for a continuously reinvigorated obedience."[43]

Indeed, much of the drama inherent in the Exodus narrative results from the uncertainty of having the enactment of God's oft-repeated promises of deliverance await some reciprocal human act. Thus, for instance, God's capstone saving act in Egypt—the tenth plague—*requires* some complementary action on Israel's part for her salvation to be accomplished. For although the Lord may "go through . . . Egypt and strike down every first-born in the land . . . , both man and beast" (Exod. 12:12), unless the Israelites take some action on their own—that is, properly marking their doorposts (Exod. 12:21-27)—not one Israelite will be saved. Salvation is a *joint enterprise* between the divine and the human, with each side's taking an active role in bringing the project to fruition.

That theme reaches the apex of its articulation at the story's apex —Sinai—where the divine promise held out to human beings (to be, e.g., a "treasured people," "a kingdom of priests," "a holy nation") is accompanied by a stipulation entailing a correlative human commitment: "Now, therefore, if you will obey . . . and keep My covenant. . . ." (Exod. 19:5). From the vantage point of Sinai, standing at the center of the Exodus narrative, whatever salvation is wrought by God is never worked by him alone but always *in conjunction with* and *on conditions of* some mutual action by human beings. The Sinaitic covenant is therefore emblematic of what Brian Wicker has called a "story-shaped world."[44]

---

42. Levenson, *Sinai and Zion*, p. 101.

43. Ibid.

44. Brian Wicker, *The Story-Shaped World* (Notre Dame: University of Notre Dame Press, 1975); for further instances of mutual divine-human interaction in Exodus, cf. e.g., 2:23-25; 3:1-4; 14:10-15.

Of course, the covenants embedded in Matthew's narrative also give voice to a world shaped by narrative; the shape, however, is one far different from that of Exodus and Sinai. For the divine action depicted in Matthew unfolds according to the dynamic of the covenants of grant alluded to in Jesus' genealogy: whatever saving action occurs happens *solely* through God's initiative and, moreover, through *God's activity alone.*

Indeed, throughout the course of the Matthean narrative, humankind is consistently pictured as being wholly unable to lend any hand at all to the work of its salvation. The Jews, the Romans, even Jesus' own disciples, all fail to respond appropriately to God's call; instead, they all lend a hand in pushing Jesus one step closer to the cross, thereby pushing away their best chance—the world's best chance—for being saved. Consequently, as Thiemann has rightly pointed out, it is precisely in Jesus' suffering on the cross—that is, in the Son's *passive* acceptance of what happens to him so as to be fully obedient to the Father's will—that the *agony of God* becomes most vividly apparent. Or, as Hans Frei has perceptively commented, "In his passion and death the initiative of Jesus disappears more and more into that of God."[45] Accordingly, at the story's climax—the resurrection—things manage to work out after all not because of any human doings but, as Thiemann correctly sees, only because of God's doings, when Jesus is revived solely by the powerful actions of God alone. Thus, whereas the Sinai "covenant-treaty" may bespeak a precarious open-endedness to human life and history, the new covenant of which the Gospel speaks (cf. Matt. 26:26-29), reflecting the logic of the covenants of grant from which it takes its cue, transcends historical vicissitudes. Human salvation need never be put in doubt, not because of what human beings might do or fail to do, but because of what *God has already done,* God acting absolutely *unilaterally,* God acting *completely graciously.*[46] However, Matthew's narrative does more than reveal a pattern of divine activity unlike that exhibited in the events leading up to Sinai; the Gospel discloses a concrete sign of that activity that is radically different, too. To quote Frei again: "In the resurrection, where the initiative of God is finally and decisively climaxed and he alone is and can be active, the sole identity to mark the presence of that activity is Jesus. . . . *Jesus of Nazareth, he and none other, marks the presence of the action of God.*"[47] But while in Matthew's

45. Hans Frei, *The Identity of Jesus Christ* (Philadelphia: Fortress Press, 1975), p. 121.
46. Compare John Howard Yoder's *The Politics of Jesus* (Grand Rapids: Eerdmans, 1972); Yoder comments that as a result of God's historically decisive action in Christ, the Christian church is not called on to "attack the powers; this Christ has already done." Instead, "the church concentrates upon not being seduced by [the powers]. By her existence she demonstrates that their rebellion *has been vanquished*" (p. 153; emphasis added).
47. Frei, *The Identity of Jesus Christ*, p. 121; emphasis added.

narrative this one person Jesus is the most distinctive sign of God's presence, in the Exodus narrative it is, by contrast, the *whole people Israel* that serves that function. Prior to the advent of the so-called plagues, God is depicted as summing up for Moses their purpose, indeed the raison d'etre behind the Exodus: "I will harden Pharaoh's heart that I may multiply my signs and portents in the land of Egypt. When Pharaoh will not listen to you, I will lay my hand upon Egypt and bring out my ranks, my people, the Israelites from the land of Egypt by great acts of judgment. *Then the Egyptians will know that I am the Lord when I stretch out my hand over Egypt and bring out the Israelites from their midst*" (Exod. 7:3-5). That theme is significantly deepened during the fourth plague. The three preceding plagues have struck Egyptian and Israelite alike. The fourth plague, however, adds a novel wrinkle; it shall not fall on Israel as it does on Egypt. As God instructs Moses to announce to Egypt: "Let My people go that they may serve Me. For if you do not let My people go, I will let loose swarms of insects against you. . . . *But on that day I will set apart the region of Goshen, where My people dwell, so that no swarms of insects shall be there, that you may know that I the Lord am in the midst of the land. And I will make a distinction between My people and your people. Tomorrow this sign shall come to pass*" (Exod. 8:20-23).[48] From the vantage point of the Exodus story, *the community of Israel* is itself to be God's most vivid, distinctive sign to the world of his saving activity in the world. The people Israel's ongoing presence, not only in surviving Egypt but in outliving its subsequent tormentors, will provide the best *physical evidence* of God's living presence still active in the midst of humankind.

Hence, given the gospel story's characterization of the saving activity of the character it points to as "God," a characterization differing so markedly from that found in Israel's earlier saga, identifying this Matthean "God" as being *one and the same character* referred to in Exodus may prove much tougher than Thiemann has assumed. At many crucial junctures in Matthew's story line, the character of the work and person of Jesus Christ appears to be strikingly *out of character* for the One, who by dint of certain characteristic redeeming acts attributed to him in the going out from Egypt, originally became acknowledged as Israel's God and Lord. In the end, Matthew's narrative may cast God's action in such an uncharacteristic light that the contention that "God is identifiable in Jesus Christ" might lie open to serious dispute. Indeed, in light of the story of the Exodus, God might well be *unrecognizable* in Jesus Christ.

---

48. Compare also Exodus 9:1-5, where the theme of Israel as God's sign is enunciated again.

V

What are the implications of the foregoing analysis for Thiemann's broader theological proposal? Are Christians, to use Thiemann's phrase, "warranted in believing God's promises to be true"?[49] In partial answer to that question, Thiemann makes the important observation that

> the justifiability of one's trust in the truthfulness of a promise is never fully confirmed (or disconfirmed) until the promiser actually fulfills (or fails to fulfill) his/her promise. Until the time of fulfillment the promisee must justify trust on the basis of a judgment concerning the character of the promiser. It is justifiable to trust a promiser if his/her behavior on balance warrants that trust. Thus investigation into [the] warranted assertability [of Christian claims] must examine the identity of the promiser, the nature and context of the promises, and the demands made of those who await their fulfillment. It is only in the context of that relationship that Christian claims to truth can be justified.[50]

Yet as a result of an examination of Israel's core story of the Exodus, the justification of "Christian claims to truth" would appear to be extremely problematic, precisely because that selfsame story-based examination casts radical doubt not only on "the identity of the promiser," but also as importantly on "the *nature* . . . of the promises, and the *demands* made of those who await their fulfillment." In the end, the *character* of the promiser in whom one is asked to put one's trust is thrown into the most radical doubt of all.

What exactly is the nature of the promise that Jesus is meant to fulfill? Thiemann, following Matthew, repeatedly designates Jesus as the one who is "to save his people from their sins."[51] But surely the salvation spoken of in Exodus—and in countless other episodes in Israel's story—is not a deliverance from the people Israel's sin but from *the sin of other peoples' oppression of Israel.* Thus, Exodus 6:6-7 pictures God as identifying himself to Moses—and to Israel—by saying: "I am the Lord [literally: 'YHVH']. I will free you from the burdens of the Egyptians and deliver you from their bondage. I will redeem you with an outstretched arm and through extraordinary chastisements. And I will take you to be My people and I will be your God. And you shall know that I, the Lord [YHVH], am your God who freed you from the burdens of the Egyptians."[52] Even later,

---

49. Theimann, *Revelation and Theology*, p. 94.
50. Ibid.
51. Matthew 1:21; cf., e.g., pp. 322, 324-327, 336 in this volume; Thiemann, *Revelation and Theology*, p. 150.
52. And, of course, see as well God's self-identification in Exodus 3, particularly in verses 6-10.

when, for example, during the Babylonian captivity, Israel's oppression is thought to have been brought about by Israel's own sins through her transgressing the Sinai covenant, we nevertheless find prophetic visions of salvation, such as Isaiah 52:1-10, which is not only filled with Exodus-related images of deliverance but which also envisages the sins committed by Israel's captors *against* Israel — *and thus against Israel's God* — as being those iniquities that truly trigger the Lord's saving action. Hence, the fact that Jews should not see Jesus as the messianic bearer of God's promised salvation should come as no surprise, for whatever salvation Jesus may have to offer is indiscernible as having anything to do with the specific nature, the particular rationale, of the divine salvation previously promised in Israel's epic. As Maimonides states the issue: "Thus Jesus the Nazarene, who imagined himself to be the Messiah . . .—how could there have been a greater failure than he? For all the prophets said that the Messiah would redeem Israel and save them, and ingather their exiles, and strengthen [observance of] the commandments. But *this one* caused Israel to be destroyed by the sword, for their remnant to be scattered and humiliated, for the Torah to be abandoned, while leading most of the world astray to worship a god other than the Lord."[53]

Now one might hypothetically say at this point that in the face of such problems as Israel's inability to be faithful to the stipulations of the "old" covenant, thereby making its promise unable to be fulfilled, God issued a "new" covenant whose promise could be realized through the utterly faithful medium of Jesus Christ. Additionally, to support this idea of a divine readjustment to new circumstances, one might, invoking Tracy, go on to argue that God, as "the perfection of agency," possesses the capacity to readapt his activity "with a peculiar thoroughness, [being] capable of stunning revision in the pattern of his life."[54] Nevertheless, one ought perhaps to stop here and take note of some other points that Tracy raises. For as he quite rightly indicates, to be an "agent"—whether human *or* divine—is, logically speaking, to be a unified, enduring individual, and, therefore, "a series of discontinuous actions cannot constitute the life of an agent."[55] Consequently,

> the more radical this reorganization of activity becomes, the more profound the problems will be for describing this agent as an individual who endures through time. At some point, depending upon the par-

<hr>

53. *Mishneh Torah,* Hilchot Melachim 11:4. Interestingly, Maimonides, like Matthew, makes explicit reference to prophetic assurances about the fulfillment of God's promises. Obviously, however, once again, the specific nature of those promises is the very thing at issue.

54. Tracy, *God, Action, and Embodiment,* p. 131.

55. Ibid.

ticular features of the case, we will no longer be able to refer to *an* agent. . . . We will [likely] say that the language of agency has broken down into incoherence, so that we cannot speak of an agent at all in this case. This might happen, for example, if we were to claim that a particular agent could utterly disregard his own past actions, so that each new phase of his activity would be initiated without reference to those that preceded it.[56]

In other words, if the change in an agent's characteristic activity is sweeping enough, our giving a coherent characterization of that agent may become well-nigh impossible. At the very least, a thoroughgoing readjustment of our assessment of that agent's character—and particularly if the activity constitutes so thoroughgoing a readjustment of an agent's prior promises as to signify the agent's renouncing them.

Importantly, the story-grounded question put by Jews to Christians is *not* whether God, "the perfection of agency," *could* perform the activity attributed to Jesus Christ and thereby thoroughly change the nature of his promise—along with the demands on those awaiting its fulfillment, as Paul, for instance, suggests in Galatians 3. Rather, the narrative-framed issue Jews pose to Christians asks more fundamentally—and crucially—whether God, "the covenantally faithful one," *would* do such a thing. For an affirmative answer might seriously negate the characterization of this God as being scrupulously true and faithful to his word. If indeed the conditions for salvation have become fixed by that Sinai covenant made between God and the people of Israel, then not only have human beings become bound by that compact's terms, but the Lord himself has become likewise pledged to follow its provisos. Thus, in this arrangement binding God and humankind as *co-partners in salvation,* each side has become obligated to fulfill its own part of the pact, and obviously the failure to do so counts as a significant covenantal breach. But conversely, and of no less import, each side, divine as well as human, has become similarly obliged not to overstep itself by attempting to play the other's role—thereby resulting in an equally dire breach of faith between them. In Jewish eyes, were God to have acted in the way ascribed him by Matthew's story, he would, through his very actions, have radically undermined—even reneged on—the terms of the agreement. For in attempting to effect salvation in the very person of Jesus of Nazareth, God would have in essence been playing both parts — his own and that of humanity—consequently usurping the role previously accorded, for better or worse, to humankind alone. As Jean Soler has

56. Ibid., p. 132.

insightfully noted alluding to the idea of Jesus' being "very God and very man": "It [is] very understandable that the [Jews] did not accept the divine nature of Jesus. . . . A God become man was bound to offend their logic more than anything else."[57]

Hence, from a Jewish viewpoint informed by the Exodus story —as well as by a large part of Israel's later story—had God acted in the way attributed to him by the gospel, he would have in the process revealed the character of both himself and his promises as being far from trustworthy, indeed, as being inconstant and untrue.[58] And let us be clear: a characterization of God as inconstant, untrue, and finally unfaithful to his promises causes as many difficulties for Christians as it does for Jews. Peter Geach, for one, has realized that and has therefore pointedly remarked that although lying and promise-breaking are "logically possible feats" for God, nevertheless, "Christian faith . . . collapses unless we are assured that God cannot lie and cannot break his promises."[59] Obviously collapsed as well would be the very ground a Thiemann seeks for justifying Christian trust and the truth of Christian claims.

And one more thing would be on the brink of toppling, too: any justifiable talk of God as "the perfection of agency." We remember that one characteristic Tracy gives of such an agent is that "all of [his] activity . . . will display the closest integration and coherence."[60] And yet, suppose one asserts that, due to certain obstacles presented by human frailty, infidelity, and sin, God has found it necessary to "go back to the drawing board" to revise comprehensively his previous "plan of salvation," that is, to alter decisively both the content and the dynamic of his prior saving promise. It will likely prove no small task to maintain our characterization of God as that perfection of agency who manifests, in Tracy's aforesaid words, "no inconstancy in . . . action—none of the disillusioned reassessments and sudden reversals that may punctuate the life of a human agent."[61]

The difficulties of that task notwithstanding, Christians from Matthew to Thiemann have clearly been attempting to carry it out for quite some time. They have tried to show continuity and coherence between Jesus' story and Israel's by appealing to certain general notions such as

---

57. Jean Soler, "The Dietary Prohibitions of the Hebrews," *New York Review of Books* (June 14, 1979): 30.

58. See Goldberg, *Jews and Christians*, pp. 216-217 in particular, but cf. as well pp. 213-224.

59. Peter Geach, *Providence and Evil* (New York: Cambridge University Press, 1977), p. 15.

60. Tracy, *God, Action, and Embodiment*, p. 136.

61. Ibid.

"covenant" and "promise" that are common to both narratives. In the last analysis, however, that kind of project may be every bit as unjustified as attempting to show that because a German and an American play something each calls "football," both must have the same sport in mind. What obviously would be required to clear up the confusion would be a closer inspection of the particular contexts delineating what counts as "playing football" for each one. Through our investigation of those contexts, not only will we learn that the activities that characterize scoring (and thus ultimately *winning*) in American football are of a different sort than those found in German football, but we will also discover something more fundamentally significant: that what we have in fact are two separate games with distinctly different characters. Consequently, even though the American and the German may both speak of "football," what is actually being meant by each and, moreover, what is actually being referred to by each is his own distinctive pastime, which in several important ways is quite unlike the sport played on the other side of the Atlantic.

In conclusion, if a *Christian* narrative theology, whether Thiemann's or anybody else's, is to have any hope of proving warranted at all, then the task of justification must reflect continual attention to the particular narrative contexts in which such a theology has both its source and ground.[62] Unless Christians at least *attempt* to show such constant attentiveness not only to Jesus' story *but to Israel's also,* then in their talk about God's action, trying to identify some act as being characteristically "divine" will be perhaps the least perplexing uncertainty confronting them. For even more disturbingly, they will encounter abiding doubts whether in uttering the name "God," they mean and refer to the same deity revealed as that central character in Israel's story—a story claimed, after all, to be their story, too.

---

62. See Michael Goldberg, *Theology and Narrative: A Critical Introduction* (Nashville: Abingdon Press, 1982), chap. 6.

Contributors

David Burrell, Theodore Hesburgh Professor of Humanities, University of Notre Dame.

Stephen Crites, Professor of Religion, Wesleyan University.

David F. Ford, Lecturer in Theology, Birmingham University.

Hans Frei, Professor of Religious Studies, Yale University, until his death in 1988.

Michael Goldberg, Consultant on Professional Ethics to the Georgia Supreme Court and the State Bar of Georgia, Atlanta, Georgia.

Julian Hartt, Professor Emeritus of Religious Studies, University of Virginia.

Stanley Hauerwas, Professor of Theological Ethics, The Divinity School, Duke University.

L. Gregory Jones, Assistant Professor of Theology, Loyola College in Maryland.

Nicholas Lash, Norris-Hulse Professor of Divinity, Cambridge University.

Alasdair MacIntyre, Professor of Philosophy, University of Notre Dame.

Johann Baptist Metz, Professor of Fundamental Theology, University of Münster.

H. Richard Niebuhr, Professor of Theology and Christian Ethics, The Divinity School, Yale University (1931-1962).

Martha Nussbaum, Professor of Classics and Philosophy, Brown University.

Michael Root, Professor at The Institute for Ecumenical Research, Strasbourg, France.

Ronald Thiemann, Dean of the Divinity School, Harvard University.